Managing Welfare Reform in New York City

Managing Welfare Reform in New York City

Edited by E. S. Savas

ROWMAN & LITTLEFIELD PUBLISHERS, INC.
Lanham • Boulder • New York • Toronto • Oxford

ROWMAN & LITTLEFIELD PUBLISHERS, INC.

Published in the United States of America
by Rowman & Littlefield Publishers, Inc.
A wholly owned subsidiary of The Rowman & Littlefield Publishing Group, Inc.
4501 Forbes Boulevard, Suite 200, Lanham, Maryland 20706
www.rowmanlittlefield.com

PO Box 317
Oxford
OX2 9RU, UK

British Library Cataloguing in Publication Information Available

Library of Congress Cataloging-in-Publication Data

Managing welfare reform in New York City / edited by E.S. Savas.
   p. cm.
   Includes bibliographical references and index.
   ISBN 0-7425-4927-5 (cloth : alk. paper)—ISBN 0-7425-4928-3 (pbk. : alk.
paper) 1. Public welfare—New York (State)—New York. 2. Public welfare
administration—New York (State)—New York. 3. Welfare recipients—
Employment—New York (State)—New York. 4. New York (N.Y.)—Social
policy. I. Savas, Emanuel S.
HV99.N59N52 2005
361.6'8'097471—dc22   2005014241

Printed in the United States of America

∞ ™ The paper used in this publication meets the minimum requirements of
American National Standard for Information Sciences—Permanence of Paper for
Printed Library Materials, ANSI/NISO Z39.48-1992.

*To my wife, my children, and
my grandchildren, with love*

Contents

Figures

Tables

Abbreviations

ACCIS	Automated Child Care Information System
AFDC	Aid to Families with Dependent Children
AFIS	Automated Finger Imaging System
AJOS	Administrator/Job Opportunity Specialist
CASAC	Certified Alcoholism and Substance Abuse Counselor/Counseling
DAS	Division of AIDS Services
DASIS	Division of AIDS Services and Income Support
DVL	Domestic Violence Liaison
EAEP	Employability Assessment and Employment Plan
ESP	Employment Services Placement
EVR	Eligibility Verification and Review
FAO	Functional Assessment Outcome
FAP	Family Assistance Program
FIA	Family Independence Administration
FSP	Food Stamp Program
FTR	Failure to Report
FTC	Failure to Comply
HASA	HIV/AIDS Services Administration
HHS	Health and Human Services
HRA	Human Resources Administration
ISAR	Income Support Application Rejection
ITA	Individual Training Account
JTPA	Job Training Partnership Act
MA	Medical Assistance
NYCWAY	New York City Work, Accountability, and You
OASAS	(New York State) Office of Alcoholism and Substance Abuse Services

OCSE	Office of Child Support Enforcement
OTDA	Office of Temporary Disability Assistance
POISED	Perfect Opportunity for Individual Skills and Educational Development (services for pregnant participants)
PRIDE	Personal Roads for Individual Development and Employment
REOP	A case reopened (or in process of reopening) after earlier closure
SACAP	Substance Abuse Central Assessment Program
SACC	Substance Abuse Core Coordinator
SAP	Skills Assessment and Placement
SI	Single Issue
SN	Special Needs
SNA	Safety Net Assistance
SSI	Supplemental Security Income
TANF	Temporary Assistance for Needy Families
VESID	(New York State Office of) Vocational and Educational Services for Individuals with Disabilities
WIA	Workforce Investment Act
WMS	Welfare Management System
WRA	(New York State) Welfare Reform Act

Acknowledgments

Without Mayor Rudolph W. Giuliani's determined leadership in reforming New York City's welfare system, this book could not even be contemplated. Jason A. Turner, the Commissioner of Social Services and Administrator of the Human Resources Administration (HRA), was the principal figure carrying out the mayor's policy, and he recognized the importance of documenting how the program was successfully carried out despite the city's unpromising climate for welfare reform. Moreover, he continued to provide critical advice about this book long after he left city government, in addition to writing the closing chapter. He deserves not only my gratitude, but also the thanks of all who will benefit from learning how welfare reform was done in New York. I'm very grateful to HRA for supporting this undertaking, which was carried out via a cooperative agreement with the City University of New York. It has been a privilege to work with the talented group of authors and scholars represented here, and I appreciate their indulgence with respect to my editing their work. I thank Antigoni Papadimitriou for her outstanding administrative assistance.

I am particularly indebted to Dr. Swati Desai, Executive Deputy Commissioner of HRA's Office of Program Reporting, Analysis, and Accountability; the depth of her knowledge and that of her colleagues—and the breadth of her patience—were of invaluable assistance to the contributors and to me as she helped us assemble and understand much-needed information for this book during the last few months of the Giuliani Administration. Finally, Commissioner Jason Turner and I would like to thank the Achelis and Bodman foundation for its support for work leading to this publication.

Material in chapter 5 from *The Crime Fighter* by Jack Maple, copyright © 1999 by Jack Maple, is used by permission of Doubleday, a division of Random House, Inc.

I

OVERVIEW

1

Introduction to Welfare Reform under Mayor Giuliani

E. S. Savas

"New York City should enroll as many welfare applicants as possible and make it easy for needy people to apply. This would be good for the city's economy because it would bring a great deal of federal money into the city; it is really an economic development program." Although not a direct quotation, this was the policy recommendation of Mitchell I. Ginsberg, commissioner of Welfare and administrator of the Human Resources Administration (HRA), to Mayor John V. Lindsay in the late 1960s. (Commissioner Ginsberg had been a dean at the School of Social Work of Columbia University.) The recommendation (from "Come and Get it" Ginsberg, as he was dubbed) was given orally at a cabinet meeting in the Blue Room in City Hall; as First Deputy City Administrator, I was present at the meeting.

Mayor Lindsay adopted this policy, and a vigorous program was activated throughout the poorer areas of the city. Idealistic believers in the Great Society, community development groups, and antipoverty activists fanned out to encourage individuals to sign up for welfare. A simple, one-page self-declaration of need sufficed as an application. Eligibility checking was perfunctory and occurred much later, if at all. Not surprisingly, the number of welfare cases soon doubled.

It took almost thirty years for the full scale of the human disaster to be recognized in New York and elsewhere. Broken families, single-parent "families," and "intergenerational welfare dependency" grew as teenage pregnancy and illegitimate births mushroomed. Generations came—and went—quickly as alarming numbers of fatherless youths dropped out of school, became addicts, and engaged in bloody but brief criminal careers. Public housing projects and other buildings were vandalized, neighborhoods became danger zones, and slums proliferated. Rightly or wrongly, much of the blame gradually came to be leveled at "welfare." Anecdotes and perceptions about "welfare queens" fueled taxpayers' increasing resentment. Hard-working, low-income, tax-paying families envisioned government-subsidized indolence and promiscuity and seethed with anger and frustration.

THE CHANGING CLIMATE

It was in this environment in 1993 that Rudolph W. Giuliani was elected mayor of New York, the first Republican since John Lindsay was elected in 1965. As a mayoral candidate, Rudolph Giuliani learned about America Works. This is a private company that enters into performance-based contracts with local governments to place welfare recipients in jobs; it receives the bulk of its money if—and only if—the former welfare recipient stays at the job for at least six months. Giuliani said, "The liberal world was incensed about the fact that America Works would 'make a profit from welfare.' The company was tying its profit to getting people a job, though, and the concept appealed to me immediately."[1]

Mayor Giuliani had strong, moral beliefs—based on his upbringing—about the relation of man and society. He said,

> I believe that the social contract is reciprocal. For every right there is an obliga-
> tion, for every privilege there's a duty. Traditional welfare—a check arrives with
> virtually no obligation—deprives people of that relationship. Either they don't
> have a sense of the relationship between privilege and duty and you haven't
> helped put it there, or they had it and you helped them lose it. The recipients
> don't feel connected to society, and the taxpayers fund a system that they feel
> finances a permanent underclass. . . . It's patronizing and even cruel to hand
> over money without hoping for anything in return, as though the able-bodied
> recipients were somehow beneath the expectations that every other member of
> society embraces. We believed that if the city was going to help the welfare
> recipient, then it had a right to ask for something in return. This was the genesis
> of the city's workfare program. . . . I wanted to know if there was anything
> under federal law that prohibited me from requiring welfare recipients to do
> public works, as they had in Roosevelt's Public Works Administration. We've
> got a lot of work that needs to be done in the city. There were plenty of people
> getting welfare checks. Could we get them to do that work? . . . Nobody had
> ever done anything like this in New York, and nowhere in the country had any-
> thing like it been tried on the scale I planned.[2]

Mayor Giuliani learned that it was, in fact, perfectly legal to require wel-fare recipients to work and so he promptly started a workfare program a year into his administration. Recognizing that more than a million New Yorkers were on welfare and that the city could not possibly find private-sector jobs for everyone, he started workfare gradually, without announcing a major program and bold targets. Only when the city knew how to do it, and systems were in place to identify people who needed jobs and to find jobs for them, would the city consistently issue statistics.[3]

At the same time, nationally, pressure grew to change what was widely perceived as a broken system. The opportunity came in 1994, when Republicans won a majority of the House of Representatives for the first time in decades, and Congressman Newt Gingrich became Speaker of the House. He led a total overhaul of the welfare system, one that President Clinton, a Democrat, endorsed after proclaiming "the end of welfare as we know it." The result was passage of the Personal Responsibility and Work Opportunity Reconciliation Act (PRWORA) of 1996. PRWORA replaced the Aid to Families with Dependent Children program (AFDC) with the Temporary Assistance to Needy Families program (TANF). This was followed in New York State a year later by the Welfare Reform Act (WRA), which gave local governments in the state flexibility and resources to carry out their own welfare reform initiatives.

These historic acts ended the right to cash assistance and introduced work requirements and lifetime limits on public assistance benefits for individuals. Critical goals of the legislation were to make public assistance (under New York's Family Assistance and Safety Net Assistance programs) temporary—conforming to TANF—and to help needy individuals and families move from economic dependence on welfare toward economic self-sufficiency.

Before the passage of WRA in 1997, the major income support programs in New York State were Aid to Families with Dependent Children (AFDC), General Assistance or Home Relief (HR), the state's AFDC waiver demonstration project (operating in 14 counties), Supplemental Security Income (SSI), the state's Earned Income Tax Credit, and food stamps. At the time of PRWORA, New York State had one of the largest public assistance caseloads (enrolled in AFDC or Home Relief) in the nation and was also one of the most generous in terms of benefits. For example, in 1995, New York had the second-highest AFDC caseload in the nation (on average 456,900 families per month). New York State's Home Relief program was the largest in the nation relative to need, and the number of recipients served each month was the highest in the nation. Annual Home Relief expenditures, divided evenly between the state and local county governments, totaled $1.1 billion in 1995, the most spent for any General Assistance program in the country.[4]

After passage of WRA, former AFDC recipients came under the new Family Assistance (FA) program for a lifetime maximum of five years. The Safety Net Assistance (SNA) program replaced the Home Relief program. Under SNA, single adults and childless couples (formerly covered under the

Home Relief program) receive cash assistance for two years, after which benefits are to be provided in the form of noncash payments for housing and utilities. Individuals losing Family Assistance eligibility after five years of coverage may continue to receive noncash SNA benefits indefinitely if eligible. The welfare reform legislation strongly emphasized work, requiring able-bodied welfare recipients to work for their benefits. The legislation also gave local governments flexibility to structure their programs to meet local needs and to provide the types of assistance FA and SNA participants needed to make the transition from dependency to unsubsidized work and self-sufficiency.[5]

MAYOR GIULIANI'S INITIATIVE

Mayor Giuliani quickly embraced the goals of national welfare reform and exploited the new policy environment created by the dramatic changes in welfare law. The welfare caseload in the city peaked during his first year in office, 1994, and declined in a steep and steady pattern thereafter (see chapter 2), as he aggressively expanded his workfare program.

> The welfare reform initiative . . . looks . . . like [a] win-win [situation]. Recipients got the money they needed and the dignity that comes from work, taxpayers felt their funds weren't being thrown into the East River, and everyone in the city got cleaner parks and other services. Not everyone saw it that way. The people who make their living representing the "best interests" of those on welfare—what I've taken to calling the "compassion industry"—didn't like the plan. Nor did the politicians who thought that appearing sensitive to the downtrodden meant keeping them permanently dependent. If I had waited until everyone was on board it never would have happened.[6]

He proceeded to implement the country's most ambitious scheme to find work for welfare recipients. In his first major initiative during his first term, he expanded the Work Experience Program, a work-for-welfare requirement that had long languished for lack of attention, into a major force for caseload reduction. During his second term, Mayor Giuliani sought to institutionalize work as the central activity of those who were in need of temporary assistance. He recruited Jason A. Turner from Wisconsin and appointed him administrator of the Human Resources Administration and commissioner of the Department of Social Services. Turner had directed Governor Tommy Thompson's "Wisconsin Works" Project (W-2), a work-based alternative to replace the contentional welfare program.

Turner shared the mayor's zeal for reform, as well as the mayor's philosophical commitment to a work-based program. He had enunciated the following philosophical principles for Wisconsin:

- For those who can work, only work should pay.
- We should assume everybody is able to work, or if not, is at least capable of making a contribution to society through work activity within their capabilities.
- Families are society's way of nurturing and protecting children, and all policies must be judged in light of how well these policies strengthen the responsibility of parents to care for their children, rather than whether they facilitate any state role. Both parents, whether or not living with their children, are assumed equally responsible for their care.
- The benchmark for determining the new system's fairness is by comparison with low-income families who work for a living, not by comparison with those receiving various government benefit packages whether inside or outside the Aid to Families with Dependent Children (AFDC) system.
- The culture of entitlement has undermined the status that used to be attached to work and self-sufficiency. The system rewards of Wisconsin Works (W-2) are designed to reinforce *appropriate* behavior.
- Individuals are part of various communities of people and places. We should pay attention to how communities affect families and how they can support individual efforts to achieve self-sufficiency.
- The new system should provide only as much service as an eligible individual asks for, rather than with any and all available services. Many individuals will do better with just a light touch.
- We should abandon our assumptions about government's traditional role in managing programs and look to private alternatives using markets and performance mechanisms to best achieve our objectives.[7]

"[Commissioner Turner] oversaw some of the most successful welfare-to-work initiatives in the history of urban America," said Giuliani, "we were about halfway to our goal when Jason Turner came in. He spearheaded the transformation from welfare agency to employment agency, creating twenty-seven job centers throughout the city. It was a brilliant and successful metamorphosis, but it was also enormously controversial in liberal circles in New York."[8] Turner stressed that work is a requirement for benefits, just as it is for wages. Liberals attacked Turner on every possible occasion but Giuliani supported him without hesitation, recognizing that the motive for the onslaught was to cripple or kill welfare reform.

HRA'S STRATEGY

The city promulgated its comprehensive strategy in a document labeled "Ladders to Success," which presents an all-encompassing approach for its public assistance, welfare-to-work, and support programs. The ladder analogy represented the four steps that participants take to move up to their

highest possible level of self-reliance: (1) The first rung of the ladder is helping participants find alternatives to dependence; the program begins with an
in-depth interview that helps people identify resources that will help them
escape the welfare trap. (2) The second rung is labor force attachment; those
applying for public assistance must participate in structured job searches
while their applications are being processed. (3) Third is the simulated workweek. Participants are expected to devote full time to developing the skills
and attitudes needed for economic independence. (4) The top rung is work;
every public assistance recipient who is capable of working is required to
work, preferably in unsubsidized employment. In some cases, participants
work in subsidized jobs or community service. The entire program represented by the ladder is flexible and adaptable.[9]

In an altogether too-rare example of a visionary strategy for a government
agency at the time, HRA articulated a clear mission and set forth its new
organizational goals and values:

HRA Mission

- Make work central in the lives of every able-bodied New Yorker now
  receiving public assistance.
- Ensure that those needy individuals who meet eligibility requirements
  are provided food, shelter, temporary financial assistance, medical care,
  counseling, and other essential services.

HRA Goals

- Defeat dependency
- Strengthen individuals and families
- Change unproductive behaviors
- Improve public safety
- Reduce taxpayer cost
- Promote community responsibility
- Provide a safety net, where necessary

HRA Values

- Deliver program services with professionalism, accountability, and
  integrity
- Reward excellence
- Encourage innovation and risk-taking
- Treat others fairly and with respect
- Manage public resources responsibly
- Promote a professional workforce

- Instill a "winning team" orientation that overcomes obstacles in pursuit of this mission.[10]

IMPLEMENTING HRA'S STRATEGY

Many organizations generate well-meaning and well-written strategy documents that, alas, never see the light of day; they founder on the shoals of implementation. This was not the case at HRA. An encrusted and tradition-bound organization that had long since adopted—and been mired in—an unquestioned faith in the culture of welfare dependency was turned around. With Commissioner Turner as ringmaster, the elephant executed a dazzling pirouette.

The organizational culture was transformed to serve the new strategy, as Levine describes in chapter 3. The former Income Support Centers became Job Centers, whose goals were to act quickly and effectively to

- Promote the well-being of individuals and families through work
- Help individuals find jobs
- Provide a one-stop community based approach for all services, including jobs, food stamps, Medicaid, child care, transportation, and child support
- Provide work-based activities for all able-bodied participants
- Promote professionalism, accountability, and integrity with employees and participants
- Provide emergency and temporary financial assistance while supporting the participant's efforts to find a job.

Effective new procedures were established to verify the eligibility of applicants for public assistance; Clark discusses the process and its results in chapter 4. Sophisticated computer-based systems were developed to enable employees to spend more time with participants—helping them understand and meet their work obligations—and less on internal record processing. HRA systems were integrated with New York State systems. JobStat was a critical management tool that monitored the performance of the Job Centers with respect to the job status of public assistance (PA) applicants and recipients; it was modeled after the police department's heralded CompStat system, which gained widespread admiration and emulation for its role in enabling the police to drive down crime in New York. Sherwood reviews the powerful JobStat system in chapter 5.

The ultimate aim of the entire program was to "engage" everyone in the PA population. Besharov and Germanis discuss this concept and the results in chapter 6. "Work First" became the operating principle for PA applicants. Active job search and participation in job readiness programs were automatic and mandatory during the 30-day application period. Case management was consolidated, so that eligibility for assistance and help in moving to a work regimen were unified. Case managers helped applicants plan for work; motivated, educated, coordinated, monitored, and evaluated their progress; and adjusted the plan with the applicant as necessary. Financial planners, employment planners, skills trainers, and job-search advisors worked with PA applicants and PA recipients. Links with businesses were established for job placement purposes. Those who could not get unsubsidized employment were given assignments in the Work Experience Program (WEP) working in public agencies. Indeed, the New York City Department of Parks and Recreation was the largest workfare employer in the United States, employing 20,000 people in the course of a year.[11] Clark gives a detailed report on WEP in chapter 7. In addition to WEP, contractors—like the above-mentioned America Works—were hired through performance-based contracts to place PA applicants and recipients in private sector jobs. (See chapter 8 by Barnow and Trutko.)

Cash assistance and emergency assistance were available in certain circumstances for those individuals who could not readily enter the world of work. Financial aid was paid by Electronic Benefit Transfer, allowing PA recipients to use the equivalent of credit cards; this national program was much more efficient than past mechanisms.

In keeping with the principle that almost everyone could work, special programs were created for special populations. These include people with physical or medical limitations, victims of domestic violence, drug and alcohol abusers, AIDS patients, and pregnant women. Satel reviews the programs for these groups in chapter 9.

Although HRA is not the primary agency for dealing with the homeless, it dealt with some of their special problems; its program is summarized by Main in chapter 10. HRA created a panoply of programs to divert various populations from homelessness.

Overall, the design and administration of HRA's system of public assistance underwent a profound transformation. The Rube Goldberg–type drawings in figures 1.1a and 1.1b depict the ultimate result: a directed flow of applicants and beneficiaries in a smooth-flowing pipeline, with management of the system, and of system performance, through JobStat.

CHANGE IN PUBLIC ASSISTANCE CASES

The dramatic annual reduction in the caseload, ranging mostly from 30,000 to 80,000 cases a year, is evident, beginning immediately after Mayor Giuliani's first year as his program kicked in. Table 1.1 summarizes the change in the number of public assistance cases over the twenty-year period, 1985–2004, which encompasses Mayor Giuliani's eight years in office, 1993–2001. The number of cases started climbing in 1988, peaked at 562,943 in 1994, and

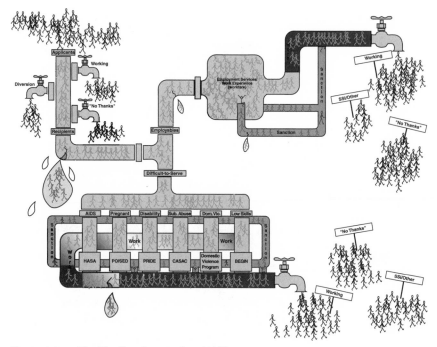

Figure 1.1a.   The Pipeline Approach to Welfare

declined to 220,211 at the time of Mayor Giuliani's departure at the end of 2001 (a 61 percent reduction) and to 205,141 (a 64 percent reduction) at the end of Mayor Michael R. Bloomberg's first year. Because many cases involve children, the number of persons on public assistance, including children, is much greater than the number of cases; in June 2004 it was 437,500,[12] a reduction of 62 percent from the 1995 figure of 1,160,000.

POST-GIULIANI: MAYOR BLOOMBERG CONTINUES THE POLICY

The downward trend in the number of welfare cases continued after Mayor Giuliani's term ended on December 31, 2001, despite the significant economic contraction in New York City that started in early 2001 and the terrorist attack of 9/11 later that year. It slowed down, however, to a drop of 15,000 cases in 2002 compared to a drop of 34,000 cases in 2000. By 2003 the overall caseload turned up for the first time since 1994, rising by 8,000 to 213,000 cases in December 2003 and to 219,000 cases by June 2004, as shown in table 1.1.[13]

Mayor Bloomberg basically continued and even improved upon the Giuli-

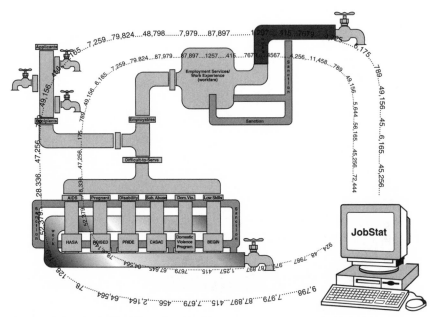

Figure 1.1b.   The Welfare Pipeline: People, Activities, and Information

Source: Created by Project Match for the panel "Are Radical Management Reforms More Necessary to Employment and Case Declines than Policy Changes? The New York City Experience." APPAM fall research conference. November 2002, Dallas, Texas. Copyright [c] 2002, by Project Match—Families in Transition Association.

ani Administration's welfare reform initiative. "We will not go back to the way things were; we will not allow our city to recede to the culture of dependency." He endorsed the key aspects of welfare reform: that welfare should be temporary, that fraud would not be tolerated, and that every able-bodied recipient must participate in workfare as a condition of receiving benefits. He said, "We continue to believe that the best way to develop employment skills is through work experience." The city should be "innovative and relentless" in moving people from welfare to work. "The best social program is a job," he said, echoing President Reagan's statement, and he explicitly rejected the idea that education and training programs for those on public assistance are a substitute for work.[14]

At the same time, he began looking ahead at the next phase of welfare reform: preventing new people from joining the welfare rolls and keeping those who got off from going back on. He emphasized support services such as child care to keep people off, and he pressed for more flexibility in using federal welfare funds on programs directed toward young people at risk of becoming welfare recipients; he considered education to be the key. Although the mayor favored an expanded definition of welfare reform and

Table 1.1.   Change in Number of Public Assistance Cases in New York City, 1985–2004

Year ending December	Total Number of Public Assistance Cases (Family and Safety Net)	12-Month Change
1985	394,411	
1986	379,200	(15,211)
1987	350,579	(28,621)
1988	351,387	808
1989	369,765	18,378
1990	413,611	43,846
1991	469,946	56,335
1992	511,872	41,926
1993	540,248	28,376
1994	562,943	22,695
1995	482,663	(80,280)
1996	430,357	(52,306)
1997	379,896	(50,461)
1998	323,716	(56,180)
1999	286,199	(37,517)
2000	252,011	(34,188)
2001	220,211	(31,800)
2002	205,141	(15,070)
2003	213,164	8,023
Jun 2004	218,591	

Source: Adapted from New York City Independent Budget Office, "Despite Recession, Welfare Reform and Labor Market Changes Limit Public Assistance Growth," *Fiscal Brief*, August 2004.

didn't believe in measuring success only by the reduction in caseloads, it was clear that he did not want to see a rise in the rolls.[15]

Mayor Bloomberg continued the successful practice of paying job-placement contractors for their performance, that is, making payment contingent not only on placing recipients but also on their staying on the job for a specified period. Nevertheless, he did not renew the contract with the largest contractor, who did a poor job, while continuing to renew contracts with many of the others.[16] Another emphasis has been to move many of the sickest recipients off the city's rolls either onto the federal program, Supplemental Security Income, or into work programs commensurate with their abilities.[17]

Early in his administration, Mayor Bloomberg made it a top priority to challenge and change the court rulings that had hamstrung the city's homeless policy since 1981, and he succeeded. The Appellate Division of the Supreme Court of New York ruled that there is no "boundless and unprecedented entitlement" to shelter; the city does not have to "provide shelter to everyone upon demand without determining financial need, without conditions and without a time limit." It can require clients to cooperate in rehabilitation programs and in looking for other housing. The court continued, "Contrary to plaintiffs' contention, there is nothing in the decree that provides or even suggests that the [city] undertook to provide shelter unconditionally, indefinitely or regardless of need."[18] Moreover, the city could suspend from its homeless shelters men who refuse to cooperate in assessing their needs or are too disruptive. The city could establish reasonable standards to ensure that homeless individuals take steps to achieve self-sufficiency. This obvious and common-sense position has to be considered an extraordinary policy breakthrough in New York City. Mayor Bloomberg went further in 2004 and extended the same principles to housing assistance for the homeless that were applied to cash assistance for welfare recipients, namely, time limits and personal responsibility.[19]

RESULTS OF WELFARE REFORM

Welfare reform worked well according to many measures. June O'Neill and Sanders Korenman in chapter 11 present their careful analysis showing that the proportion of single mothers on welfare declined sharply in New York City after 1996 while at the same time the proportion who worked climbed impressively, and by about the same amount. The decline in welfare participation rate was much larger in New York than in other cities.

Moreover, the average annual income of single mothers in New York, counting those with zero income, increased by close to $5,000 annually, including both earnings and income from the Earned Income Tax Credit (EITC). This more than compensated for the loss in reported welfare benefits between 1993–1994 and 1999–2000, which came to about $1,700 annually, averaged over all single mothers, including those with zero welfare income. In summary, single mothers, the dominant category of public assistance cases, saw their incomes rise by more than 20 percent. And the longer they worked the better off they were economically, as their skills improved, their seniority with the same employer grew, and their wages rose. Poverty rates dropped 50 percent for women who worked and stayed off welfare for four years. "Welfare reform succeeded because it made going to work more attractive than going on welfare," said O'Neill.[20] Kaushal and Kaestner also found that welfare reform induced unmarried women to move from welfare to work and improved their financial status.[21]

Welfare reform had another important effect: a nationwide decline in child poverty, contributing significantly to the record 27 percent drop from the peak in child poverty in 1993 to the lowest level since the mid-1970s in 2001. The reduction was particularly pronounced among black and Hispanic children; it declined by almost one-third, far exceeding historical trends. Among such children living in single-mother households, an increase in mothers' employment and earnings—no doubt driven by the demands of welfare reform—accounted for almost 40 percent of the decline. The improvement in economic well-being of children cannot be accounted for by normal fluctuations in the economy.[22]

Other researchers looked at the reasons why welfare reform worked nationally. Not surprisingly, management practices and the structuring of agency responsibilities are important. When public managers redirect their staffs to focus on the new goals of welfare reform, give clear signals about what is expected, and provide resources and incentives to change the old way of administering the welfare business, staffs will realign their priorities.[23] Commissioner Turner did just this, as Levine explains in chapter 3. Other researchers also found strong evidence that administrative action to move clients into work, coupled with administrative commitments, can provide important links between policy goals and policy outcomes.[24] Larry Mead supports this last point: "grant levels, work and child support requirements, and sanctions are important explainers of change, along with some demographic terms and unemployment. These policies in turn are tied to states' political opinion, political culture, and institutional capacity. Moralistic states seem the most capable of transforming welfare in the manner the public wants."[25] Mayor Giuliani's basic belief in the value of work made New York a "moralistic city" in this respect. Not all parties praise welfare reform in New York, however. A committee of lawyers points to violations of the rights of the poor and cites reports by advocacy groups that claim an increased use of emergency food aid and increased homelessness.[26]

Commissioner Jason Turner concludes this volume in chapter 12 as he looks back and reflects on his experiences running the seminal welfare reform program under Mayor Giuliani. It is a riveting account of the trials and tribulations of a change agent in this hothouse environment, a description that should become a classic in the public administration literature.

THE INFLUENCE OF AMERICAN WELFARE REFORM IN EUROPE

The successful reforms in New York and elsewhere in America have met with keen interest abroad. As Europeans contemplate the unsustainability of their welfare states, they have begun to reconsider their policies on welfare, unemployment insurance, labor laws, and pensions. While the traditional left decries the "Americanization" of their social policies, elected officials in several countries are advancing American-style social policies. Former Commissioner Turner has been actively advising governments and change agents in Europe and elsewhere. At a conference on welfare reform in Budapest in late 2004, under the theme "Work First Europe," European officials described their actions and acknowledged the successes of American reforms. Post-socialist countries, the former Soviet satellites, fearing that adopting the Western European model would lead to similar serious problems down the road, are looking with relief at the alterative American model. One of the states in the Federal Republic of Germany, Hesse, adopted "Wisconsin Works" (designed by Turner) following the visit of its governor to Wisconsin. (A major difference between W-2 and New York's program is that in the former vendors were paid based on their success in reducing the caseload, with a portion of the resulting savings going to the vendor; this is a much more powerful incentive than New York's, where successful vendors were paid a fee for performance. Also, W-2 imposes "full family sanction" rather than "partial sanction" for those who fail to show up to work; see chapter 4. Hesse embraced the more potent program.) Welfare reform in the United States, as exemplified in Wisconsin and New York, is poised to influence welfare policy throughout the industrialized world.

NOTES

1. Rudolph W. Giuliani, *Leadership* (New York: Miramax Books, 2002), 162.
2. Giuliani, *Leadership*, 162.
3. Giuliani, *Leadership*, 163.
4. Burt S. Barnow and John Trutko, unpublished, untitled manuscript, 2003.
5. Barnow and Trutko, 2003.
6. Giuliani, *Leadership*, 163.
7. Jason Turner, *Wisconsin Works: Four Chapters from the Conceptual Plan*, State of Wisconsin, April 1995.
8. Giuliani, *Leadership*, 235.
9. Human Resources Administration, City of New York, *Ladders to Success: Innovations in City Government*, June 2000.
10. *Ladders to Success*, 4.
11. Keith Kerman, Chief of Operations, New York City Department of Parks and Recreation, statement to the author, November 9, 2004.
12. New York City Mayor's Management Report, Fiscal 2004, 40.
13. New York City Independent Budget Office, "Despite Recession, Welfare Reform and Labor Market Changes Limit Public Assistance Growth," *Fiscal Brief*, August 2004.
14. Tony Coles, "Welfare: Mike Hangs Tough," *New York Post*, May 16, 2002, 33.
15. Coles, "Welfare: Mike Hangs Tough."
16. Michael Cooper, "Disputed Pacts for Welfare Will Just Die," *New York Times*, October 4, 2002, B1.
17. Jennifer Steinhauer, "Bloomberg Aims to Move Many Infirm Welfare Recipients into Work Force," *New York Times*, May 10, 2003.

18. Thomas J. Main, "Common Sense on Homeless," *New York Post,* June 11, 2003.

19. George T. McDonald, "Mike's Tough Love: Doing Right by the Homeless," *New York Post,* November 13, 2004, 19.

20. June O'Neill, "Welfare Reform Works," *New York Post,* April 14, 2003, 29.

21. Neeraj Kaushal and Robert Kaestner, "From Welfare to Work: Has Welfare Reform Worked?" *Journal of Policy Analysis and Management* 20, no. 4 (2001): 699–719.

22. June O'Neill and Sanders Korenman, *Child Poverty and Welfare Reform: Stay the Course* (New York: Manhattan Institute, 2004).

23. Norma M. Riccucci, Marcia K. Meyers, Irene Lurie, and Jun Seop Han, "The Implementation of Welfare Reform Policy: The Role of Public Managers in Front-Line Practices," *Pubic Administration Review* 64, no. 4 (July/August 2004): 438–48.

24. Jo Ann G. Ewalt and Edward T. Jennings, Jr., "Administration, Governance, and Policy Tools in Welfare Policy Implementation," *Public Administration Review* 64, no. 4 (July/August 2004): 449–62.

25. Lawrence W. Mead, "Welfare Caseload Change: An Alternative Approach," *Policy Studies Journal* 31, no. 2 (2003): 163–85.

26. Committee on Social Welfare Law, "Welfare Reform in New York City: The Measure of Success," *Record of the Association of the Bar of the City of New York* 56, no. 3 (Summer 2001): 322–57.

2

Overview of Welfare Reform[1]

Demetra Smith Nightingale

Federal welfare reform legislation enacted with the Personal Responsibility and Work Opportunity Reconciliation Act (PRWORA) in 1996 increased the emphasis on work and work requirements and imposed lifetime limits on the receipt of welfare benefits. While PRWORA gave state governments the discretion to redefine their welfare programs, New York City, like many other jurisdictions, had already been reforming welfare for over a decade, since the late 1980s. When Mayor Rudolph Giuliani was elected in 1993, welfare reform was one of his high-priority issues. The policies of Mayor Giuliani and the Human Resources Administration (HRA) became a rallying point for proponents of strong work requirements and mandatory workfare, as well as the subject of highly charged criticism and lawsuits by opponents, including advocates for the poor and community activists.

The New York State Welfare Reform Act (WRA) of 1997, passed in conjunction with PRWORA, gave New York City additional flexibility to develop goals for welfare reform. The WRA, while ensuring that New York State met the requirements of PRWORA, also established provisions for welfare reform programs unique to the state. In particular, the WRA renamed and revised the cash assistance programs in New York. The Family Assistance (FA) program replaced Aid to Families with Dependent Children (AFDC). While many provisions of FA remained the same as AFDC (e.g., benefit levels of $577 for a family of three), the law incorporated other provisions of PRWORA into the FA program, including stronger work requirements and the 60-month federal time limit. Other FA provisions developed by HRA to implement welfare reform are

18

unique to New York City, such as requiring that applicants for welfare actively search for a job during the 30-day period when eligibility is determined.

The WRA also established the Safety Net Assistance program (SNA) to replace the Home Relief program (often called General Assistance in other states), which provides cash assistance and services to those not eligible for FA (mainly single individuals and childless couples, but also families who have exhausted their benefits under TANF/FA). Receipt of SNA cash benefits is limited to two years, after which individuals in need may continue to receive noncash benefits and services such as food stamps and housing assistance.

INTRODUCTION

In the early to mid-1990s, New York City's primary work component for welfare recipients who were able-bodied and employable was workfare, through the Work Experience Program (WEP). Welfare recipients were required to work a certain number of hours in public or nonprofit WEP assignments as a condition of receiving their grant, but not for regular wages. New York City's WEP became the largest workfare initiative in the nation, with nearly 35,000 individuals in public and nonprofit assignments at its peak in 1999.

By 2001, the focus of New York City's work-welfare policies had shifted dramatically. WEP was still the primary work component, and employment continued to be the ultimate objective. The basic WEP design, however—which was developed to require individuals to work off their cash grants at the minimum wage for up to 35 hours a week—gradually evolved into a more complex system of WEP and other options. That system allowed work-mandatory recipients to participate in three days a week of work experience or workfare plus two days of some other activity, including education, training, treatment interventions, or other services.

The experiences, evolution, and lessons learned in New York City are highly relevant to national policy as well as to the continuing refinement of city policies. First, New York City represents the largest urban welfare caseload in the nation. As shown in figure 2.1, from its peak in 1994 to 2002 New York City's welfare population dropped by over 60 percent, similar to the decline nationally and in most other jurisdictions. Still, over 400,000 individuals were receiving welfare in the city[2] in 2002 at a *monthly* cost of over $100 million. Thus, the sheer size of this caseload—FA in New York City represented one out of every 13 TANF cases in the nation in 2001[3]—makes an examination of the work policies in New York City particularly important for national policy considerations.

Adult Recipients

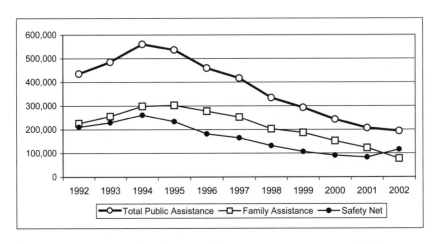

All Recipients (Adults and Children)

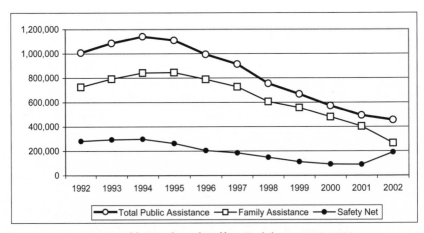

Figure 2.1. Average Monthly Number of Welfare Recipients, 1992–2002

Source: 1994–2002: HRA Fact Sheets, http://www.nyc.gov/html/hra/html/hrafacts.html.
1992–1993: Sorted PA eligibility files. 2002 values are an average of January through March only.

Note: The SNA caseload increase after 2001 reflects the fact that FA cases were beginning to reach the federal time limit and converting to SNA-non-cash.

In addition, the experiences in New York City in the 1990s as it attempted to revamp the entire welfare system—organizationally and philosophically—offer important lessons about the feasibility and limits of (1) implementing large-scale work experience/workfare programs; (2) restructuring and modernizing a large, entrenched bureaucracy; and (3) adapting service programs to changing policy and economic conditions and caseload characteristics.

This chapter summarizes New York City's initiatives to move public assistance recipients from welfare to work during the Giuliani Administration between 1994 and 2001.[4] The study is based on qualitative and quantitative information from multiple sources. Structured, confidential interviews were conducted with selected officials, administrators, and line staff at all levels, in all agencies, and with service contractors. (The terms "contractors" and "vendors" are used interchangeably.) In addition, HRA data were analyzed for the city as a whole and for each region, all local Job Centers, all vendors, and all special work programs. Finally, key HRA reports and policy manuals and the annual Mayor's Management Reports were reviewed, as well as reports published by non-HRA organizations, researchers, and agencies. Together, these sources provided a rich supply of information about the programs and policies.

Despite the volume of information and data collected and analyzed, there are some important limitations to this study. First, under Commissioner Jason A. Turner, HRA developed a new data and performance tracking management system that became operational in 1999, and it was not always possible to compare earlier and later data. Second, while the research team visited dozens of offices and programs and interviewed nearly 100 administrators, staff, and community advocates, it was not possible to interview individual welfare recipients, and their perspective may differ from that of program and agency staff. Similarly, although local office operations and service delivery were observed, it is not possible to attest to the detailed nature of agency and client interactions or the intensity or quality of services delivered. Finally, key policy changes, especially those instituted in the late 1990s, are described, but many of the policy changes made earlier, beginning in 1993, could not be addressed in detail. In addition, implementation of some recent policy changes could not be observed. The overall analysis, however, explains how HRA approached welfare reform and how it operated at the end of 2001. The next section discusses the administrative policies and systems that created the infrastructure for welfare reform. The section after that addresses the work requirements, work activities, and principal work programs, and in turn is followed by a section on work programs that serve special populations, particularly those previously not subject to work requirements. The final section summarizes the overall implementation of the city's work programs in the 1990s and discusses implications for national and local policies and programs.

ADMINISTRATIVE CONTROL

An important part of New York City's welfare reform involved extensive administrative actions to centralize policies, program guidelines, and information systems, and to increase accountability of welfare offices and service contractors. The effort included a major reorganization of HRA to focus on the goals of employment and enforcement of strict work requirements and the creation of sophisticated information systems to track clients and monitor program performance.

Restructuring the Organization

Major changes were made to further the new philosophical approach to welfare, "work first." The change in HRA's organizational culture is discussed in detail in chapter 3.

Structural Change

HRA was reorganized in the late 1990s at both the administrative level and at the service delivery level, specifically to increase the emphasis on employment. Six regional director positions were created to oversee six regional welfare offices—one for each of New York City's five boroughs, and one to oversee services delivered citywide to clients with special needs, such as substance abuse or a mild disability. While regional directors are permitted some discretion in tailoring services to meet the needs of clients within their jurisdictions, HRA relied on this centralized structure as a way of communicating its changing mission to all HRA staff, reinforcing the priority placed on employment, and ensuring that the new policies were followed.

To emphasize employment unequivocally, welfare offices were converted gradually to Job Centers. (In the prior administration, they had already been renamed Income Support and BEGIN [Begin Employment Gain Independence Now] Employment Centers.) The conversion began in March 1998, was halted by court injunction for two years, and was completed by May 2001.[5] Individuals apply for public assistance benefits at Job Centers and must participate in activities and services designed to move them into work prior to being approved for cash benefits. Staff in the Job Centers both determine eligibility for benefits and provide access to employment and training services, generally through vendors located on site.

Staff Reorganization

In addition to converting local offices into Job Centers, HRA converted front-line welfare workers into Job Opportunity Specialists (JOS). It integrated the duties of the eligibility and employment staff in the Job Centers into the new JOS position. That is, JOS workers are responsible for intake as well as employment-focused case management, with smaller caseloads than had been the case for line staff under the prior system. Conversion to the JOS position began in Spring 2001, and most conversions were completed by the end of the year.

Employees had the choice of converting to the JOS classification or retaining their old classification. The majority agreed to the JOS conversion, although there was some lingering concern related to job security since the new classification had not yet been incorporated into the collective bargaining union contract. In some offices, workers who opted not to convert to JOS faced involuntary transfer to other Job Centers.

Line staff seemed to agree with the general shift in policy and programs toward employment. But the shifts in job responsibilities represented by the JOS conversion and the increased use of contractors for employment assistance, described below, may actually have diminished the role of HRA workers in assisting clients to find employment. For example, many of the JOS workers in the past had been responsible for providing employment assistance, beginning with the Work Incentive Program in the early 1980s and continuing through the BEGIN program into the early 1990s. Several former BEGIN workers expressed frustration that their new JOS assignments involve less counseling of clients and more routine case processing. Some JOS workers who had previously been responsible for intake and eligibility determination explained that they had been excited about becoming JOS workers because they thought they would be actively involved in providing employment services, and were disappointed that their primarily role in this area is to make sure clients know they have to work and then refer them elsewhere for services. JOS workers in several offices noted that they have limited access to computers and to employment-oriented data files and other resources that could help them provide employment assistance to clients.

Expanded Program Responsibility

At about the same time that HRA was restructuring its offices, its administrative responsibilities in the area of employment also expanded beyond those directly related to TANF. In early 1999, the mayor transferred authority for about $80 million a year in federal adult training and employment programs funded under the Workforce Investment Act (WIA, formerly the Job Training Partnership Act, JTPA) from the City Department of Employment to HRA. (Youth programs and funds were not transferred.) HRA was also designated by the governor to administer the federal Welfare-to-Work (WtW) grant funds available to the city through a resource allocation formula established by Congress (about $45 million in each of two fiscal years, 1998 and 1999). In addition, HRA applied for and received directly a federal competitive WtW grant of $2.9 million from the U.S. Department of Labor in 1999 to be used over five years. HRA also administered the federal food stamps employment and training program. Thus, HRA directly controlled virtually all funds that could be used to provide employment services to welfare recipients.

Contracting for Services

The above changes were accompanied by a shift in the way employment services (especially those funded through the various HRA funding sources) are provided to public-assistance recipients and other disadvantaged persons: mainly by contracting out employment services specifically funded by the TANF block grant and consolidating other contracts with employment service providers.

Previously HRA (and the Department of Employment before 1999) had contracted with 80 to 100 vendors to deliver employment services to economically disadvantaged adults using JTPA funds, and to welfare recipients through the HRA special-needs programs. Some providers had multiple contracts. Like several other jurisdictions around the country, the Giuliani Administration encouraged agencies to expand the use of contractors, with competitive sourcing and performance standards but it also wanted to streamline the system. Therefore HRA designed a single solicitation using several funding streams, which resulted in 15 "super" service-provider contracts for TANF, SNA, food stamps, and WIA-adult programs. Each of the 15 primary contractors (which included both private for-profit companies and nonprofit organizations) was required to have several subcontractors (most of which are nonprofit, community-based organizations). Many of the prime contractors and subcontractors had in the past received their own direct contracts from the Department of Employment.[6]

The contractors assess welfare applicants and recipients referred by Job Center staff and provide job search and placement assistance and some limited training and other pre-employment support services intended to lead quickly to employment. In general, participants referred to Skills Assessment and Placement (SAP) and Employment Services Placement (ESP) contractors are placed in work experience program (WEP) assignments (also called workfare), often concurrently with participation in other job-search or work-related activities. For those individuals not in full-time WEP, ESP contractors continue to provide job readiness, search, and placement activities for two days a week, while individuals work in WEP assignments the other three days to meet the 35 hours of mandated work participation. The "three-plus-two" model largely replaced "basic" WEP where individuals worked five days a week. (Work-related activities and sequencing are described in the next section.)

Prior to welfare reform, HRA had contracted for services primarily on a cost reimbursement basis, but now, in addition to the superstructure for contracting, HRA instituted performance-based contracting with all SAP and ESP vendors. Contracts are awarded on a fixed-price basis that includes significant built-in performance incentives for the contractor. Payments to contractors are contingent upon meeting performance criteria, especially job placement and job retention. (See chapter 8 for details on this topic.)

Improving Information Exchange

HRA placed a high priority on information flow and upgrading information technology in order to communicate policy changes to line staff, to monitor Job Center and vendor performance, and to track participants through the system.

Top-Down Information

In order to implement fundamental welfare reform, the philosophical shifts and broad policies had to be understood by line staff and translated into day-to-day service delivery. They were aggressively disseminated through agency-wide meetings, town hall sessions, and monthly training sessions that conveyed how policies and program directives fit together. HRA established regular weekly meetings with Job Center directors to review center-specific statistical performance reports from JobStat data (see below), on caseload management, employment-related activities, sanctions, and fair hearings. In addition, frequent and numerous directives on policies and procedures were e-mailed to administrators at Job Centers across the city.

HRA line staff generally endorsed the new policies. The strength of that endorsement was dampened to some extent because some staff worried that resources were not adequate to provide the long-term services they feel clients need to achieve lasting economic independence. Concern was also voiced about the effects of the economic downturn in late 2001 on newly employed, low-wage, low-skilled workers, and HRA's ability to sustain needed supports over time.

Bottom-Up Information: Tracking Clients and Job Assignments

New York State manages all the eligibility and payment transactions in the state through its Welfare Management System (WMS). HRA has a complementary system, the New York City Work, Accountability, and You (NYCWAY) system, implemented in 1999, for tracking its clients. Different from WMS, it provides a capability of assigning individuals to ESP and SAP vendors and tracking the work participation status of individual public-assistance recipients. The two systems, WMS and NYCWAY, function together; when a public-assistance case is opened, a record is automatically created in both systems.

HRA, SAP, and ESP staff record client activities and status directly into the NYCWAY system. Clients' attendance in workfare and other activities are tracked, and their progress is monitored. Through an interactive link to other state and local labor data bases with market information, staff in some SAP and ESP vendor locations also receive immediate access to lists of job openings. While this was observed in some locations, not all workers were aware of or able to access labor market information at the time of our visits.

Bottom-Up Information: Increasing Accountability

The NYCWAY data system is linked to several other reporting systems, permitting HRA and vendors to track performance of Job Centers and vendors, to track individuals, to assess performance of service providers, and to verify payment claims and process invoices.

JobStat (from "Job Statistics") is a powerful data system that provides HRA with performance data to monitor each Job Center's performance across a set of standardized measures. Monthly JobStat reports highlight the performance of each Job Center. HRA senior administrators meet with managers from two or more Job Centers weekly on a rotating basis and use these reports to evaluate the strengths and weaknesses of each. HRA also introduced CenterStat, a system that tracks performance of individual workers within a Job Center, thus refining even further the accountability for performance. (See chapter 5 for more on JobStat.) In a similar manner, Vendor-Stat enables HRA, as well as each ESP and SAP prime contractor, to monitor vendor performance across a set of agreed-upon performance indicators. VendorStat reports are generated monthly for each site location of every vendor in the city, and the performance indicators are calculated for each site, for the vendor as a whole, and for all vendors in the system. HRA administrators hold weekly meetings with vendor representatives to review Vendor-

Stat reports; these meetings are often coupled with the JobStat meetings of the same Centers. (See chapter 9 for more on VendorStat.)

Adopting Work-Oriented Goals and Policies

As HRA developed more sophisticated performance measurement systems for vendors and Job Centers, it also set goals for a range of outcomes from case closures and client recidivism to administrative errors and "wins" at court hearings. It promoted two goals in particular—"full engagement" and job placement—as its major priorities in welfare reform.

Full Engagement and Sanctions

The first step in mandating a strict work requirement involved identifying and locating every adult recipient in the caseload and assessing his or her status with regard to employability. The new data and client tracking systems allowed HRA to call each recipient in for assessment and assignment, which included determining the precise status of everyone receiving assistance benefits (e.g., whether they are working or have medical problems).

HRA reached this goal—termed "full engagement"—in December 1999. Full engagement represented a major step toward work implementation. As a matter of practice, however, full engagement does not mean that all public assistance recipients are working. Instead, full engagement means that all recipients are accounted for, that is, they are undergoing assignment or assessment, engaged in employment or work activities, sanctioned for noncompliance, or appropriately classified as exempt from work activity. In other words, full engagement is a milestone of administration, not participation. This is no small feat, for 100 percent engagement means that every public assistance (PA) recipient is accounted for in one of these categories. Figures 2.2 and 2.3 show engagement levels of adult cases (cases with at least one adult present) over time, in absolute numbers and as a percent of all adult cases, respectively. Several trends are evident. First, the proportion of adult cases required to participate in a work activity ("engageable") rose sharply as work requirements were broadened to include previously work-exempt populations (populations which are discussed below). Second, the proportion of engageable adult cases accounted for ("engaged or in process") also rose sharply, reaching 100 percent (full engagement) at the end of 1999. Third, the number of adult PA cases actually engaged in employment or work activities (the lowest line on the charts) remained relatively constant over the entire period, but increased proportionately with the decline in the overall caseload.

Participation in employment and work activities might be increasingly dif-

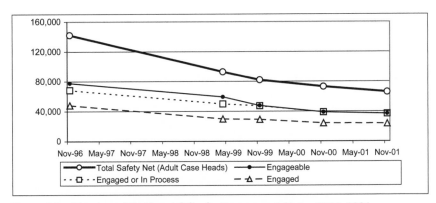

Figure 2.2.   Number of Welfare Adults, by Engagement Status 1994–2001

Combined Public Assistance Population (FA plus SNA)

Source: PA Eligibility File, HRA Engagement Reports. Snapshots from selected weekly reports.

ficult for some individuals remaining on the caseload, particularly in SNA; this includes single individuals and childless couples, who tend to have barriers to employment and poor employment histories, and former FA recipients who have been transferred to SNA after reaching their time limits for benefits without becoming self-sufficient. While the proportion of adult cases actually engaged continued to rise for the FA caseload, the pattern was virtually unchanged for the SNA caseload. Full engagement involves a strictly enforced sanction policy—all noncompliant recipients must be "engaged" in the sanctioning process, which includes fair hearings and conciliation. If adults on welfare fail to comply with work requirements, they

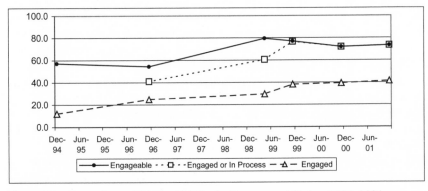

Figure 2.3.   Percentage of Welfare Adults, by Engagement Status, 1994–2001

Combined Public Assistance Adults (FA plus SNA) Family Assistance Adults

Source: PA Eligibility File, HRA Engagement Reports. Snapshots from selected weekly reports.

lose (only) their portion of their household's grant (i.e., in New York there is no "full family" sanction). For example, a family of three will lose one-third of its payment. Sanctions for individuals in families who have a first offense remain in effect until the individual complies; for the second offense, the sanction is in effect at least 90 days or until compliance, and for the third offense the sanction is for at least 180 days or until compliance. As of late November 2001, 15,000 FA cases were under sanction and another 15,000 were in the sanctioning process. While the sanction rate (percentage of adult cases under sanction or in the sanction process) for SNA remained at approximately 10 percent between 1996 and 2001, the sanction rate for FA adult cases remained at approximately 30 percent for the past several years.[7]

Recipients can contest the sanction by requesting a "fair hearing." The number of such hearings rose through the decade, although a larger percentage of these requests in 2001 (53 percent) did not actually lead to fair hearings compared to prior years.[8] HRA attributes the decline in the number of fair hearings to new mediation policies in 2001 that resolved appeals before a fair hearing, meaning the client withdrew the request. (See chapter 6 for more on full engagement.)

Job Placement

The other HRA priority is to encourage welfare applicants and recipients to work rather than receive welfare. To measure progress toward that objective, HRA tracked the number of individuals each year who begin employment. New York City had been setting job placement goals for public assistance recipients since at least 1995, but after the achievement of full engagement these goals became more publicized and more ambitious. After approximately 67,000 work-ready cash assistance and food stamp recipients entered employment during 1999, HRA set a goal of 100,000 recipients in jobs in 2000 and 150,000 in 2001. Each year's total goal was divided into subgoals for each Job Center.

Just as HRA's definition of "engagement" includes more than just those who are actually working, the definition of "job placement" includes more than just those welfare recipients who are placed in jobs. In 2000, 132,000 job placements were documented, and in 2001, there were 135,000. The job placement number is based on all public assistance beneficiaries, including those on food stamps who are not receiving FA or SNA, and the placement number includes (1) individuals placed during the FA or SNA application process who are diverted from the rolls altogether; and (2) individuals who started a job and received any welfare assistance during the same year, who are identified by Job Center or vendor staff through regular reporting procedures (self-reported or placement by staff into a job), or who are identified through quarterly employer reports filed with the state for unemployment insurance purposes. (HRA refers to these as "employer-reported" placements.) Two other qualifications apply to the job placement measure. First, an individual is counted as employed only once in any given year. Second, job placements are counted only if they raise an individual's earnings to at least $100 a week.

Thus, for citywide purposes, there is a total employment goal in terms of the number of clients applying for or receiving benefits who go to work— not a job placement *rate* in terms of a percentage of clients or recipients in any one program who enter employment.

Of the 135,000 job placements in 2000, about half (68,000) were documented by vendors or by Job Center staff using clients' self-reported employment or records of direct job placement through a contractor. Another 16 percent (21,000) were self-reported nonpublic assistance, food-stamp recipients, and the rest—34 percent (46,000)—were employer-reported placements. Of the contractor-reported and Job Center–reported placements, about 11,000 (or about 16 percent of the 2001 placements) occurred while the individual was in an ESP or SAP vendor program (split fairly evenly between the two). The SAP component is intended not only to provide assessment and job-search assistance, but also to divert, if possible, the applicant from needing public assistance in the first place. Of the approximately 38,000 applicants referred to SAP in 2001, about 15 percent obtained employment; and approximately 20 percent of those applicants who entered a job did not open a public assistance case.[9] Of the approximately 42,000 individuals referred to ESP vendors in 2001, about 13 percent entered employment. (See chapter 8 for more on job placement.)

Summary: Administrative Control

The conversion of welfare offices to Job Centers, beginning in 1998, reinforced the goal of reducing the welfare caseload and the goal of requiring or encouraging employment of those considered employable. Citywide client tracking through the NYCWAY management information system made monitoring the stated goals possible—both those goals set for HRA and its contractors and those mandated for individuals applying for or receiving welfare. The infusion of new top management, changes in policy and client processing, the centralized management information system, and central control of work assignments helped the city achieve its goals.

WORK ACTIVITIES

A primary goal of welfare reform in New York City in the 1990s, was "to make work central in the lives of every able-bodied New Yorker now receiving public assistance."[10] HRA embraced a "work-first" philosophy, which emphasizes moving welfare recipients into work or work-related activities as quickly as possible. Thus, HRA's welfare reform approach is based on strong work requirements, immediate job search during the application process, and cash assistance as a temporary measure. Every applicant and recipient of cash assistance, whether in FA or SNA, is expected to engage in activities organized around work. Indeed, applicants for public assistance sign a Statement of Mutual Expectations that says, "If I am applying for cash assistance, I understand that cash assistance is temporary and that I am committed to the goal of self reliance. I am responsible for participating in activities to reach this goal and, if it is determined that I am employable, to look for and accept work."

The basic goals and structure of welfare reform under Mayor Giuliani are described in HRA's 2000 report, *Ladders to Success: Innovations in City Government*. As noted in chapter 1, the report delineates four rungs on the "ladder" leading from welfare dependency to economic self-sufficiency: (1) *assisting participants to find alternatives to dependence*, that is, identifying individual circumstances and alternative resources to welfare receipt; (2) *labor force attachment* through structured job search while applicants are awaiting approval for cash benefits; (3) the *simulated workweek*, in which recipients are engaged full-time in work plus other activities to start "developing the skills and attitudes that lead to economic independence . . . to address the problems that led to long-term dependence"; and (4) *work* in full-time unsubsidized employment, subsidized employment, or a community service job. The program is to be flexible and adaptable, permitting the creation of a customized package of activities and services that facilitate the transition to work and self-reliance. At the same time, though, the system continued to emphasize intensive verification of information for eligibility determination, up-front job search for applicants, and mandatory work assignments for recipients.

The principal employment activities begin at the point of application and are intended to attach the individual quickly to the labor force and lead to termination of cash benefits.[11] Another set of activities, discussed in a later section, is available for smaller numbers of special populations, such as recipients with medical limitations or those who are already working and require skill-upgrading services. For most of the caseload, including most in special programs, the emphasis is on three components: (1) Skills Assessment and Placement (SAP), provided during eligibility determination; (2) Employment Services Placement (ESP); and (3) Work Experience Program (WEP) assignments, which are made once individuals are receiving benefits, and generally in combination with each other.

Application for Welfare

The welfare service delivery process in effect in New York City at the end of 2001 was intended to sort out those truly in need of assistance and to divert others into jobs or other alternatives to cash assistance through the use of up-front job search and an intensive eligibility verification process. Figure 2.4 shows the flow of applicants at a Job Center. An individual applies for welfare benefits at a local Job Center in the zip code of his or her residence. A receptionist logs identifying information into the state's Welfare Manage-

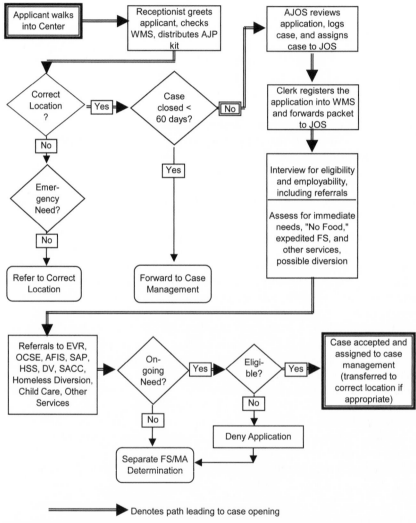

Figure 2.4.   Job Center Flow Chart for Public Assistance Applicants

Source: New York Human Resources Agency. "AJOS" is Administrative Job Opportunity Specialist; "JOS" is Job Opportunity Specialist

ment System (WMS) to determine the applicant's welfare history and check emergency needs (e.g., food, utilities cut off, imminent eviction) and then schedules an interview, often the same day, with an HRA worker who identifies specific needs and potential barriers to self-sufficiency. The worker also explains public assistance eligibility requirements including participant responsibilities, self-sufficiency goals, work requirements, payment levels, time limits, and types of emergency assistance available that might allow the individual to avoid FA/SNA assistance altogether.

First-time applicants and reapplicants (i.e., applicants whose cases have been closed for more than 30 days) are required to appear for another in-person interview, generally held within three to four days, at a special Eligibility Verification Review (EVR) unit, located in 2001 in Brooklyn. EVR, initiated in 1994, involves an in-depth eligibility examination, fingerprinting, and a home visit. Applicants who fail to comply—either do not report to the EVR unit or refuse to cooperate with the home visit—are automatically denied public assistance benefits. (See chapter 4 for a fuller discussion of EVR.)

Eligibility is determined within 30 days for FA cases and 45 days for SNA cases from the date a signed application is submitted. At any point during the application process or once on the rolls, individuals with particular problems or needs may be referred for specialized services, for example, medical services, substance abuse treatment, child care, or domestic violence assistance.

Individuals who claim medical or mental health problems are referred to a special contractor, Health Services Systems, for further assessment to determine employability or to refer for treatment or other types of assistance (e.g., Supplemental Security Income [SSI] or Social Security Disability Income [SSDI]). Individuals demonstrating substance abuse can be referred to a Credentialed Alcoholism and Substance Abuse Counselor (CASAC) for full assessment and/or referral to inpatient or outpatient treatment.[12] (See chapter 9 for a discussion of employment programs for substance abusers.)

Financial benefit amounts are calculated automatically by WMS based on the applicant data. For example, in July 2001, most families (i.e., "case units") of three were eligible for assistance if their earned income was less than $667 per month. Benefits are paid to accepted applicants, and rejected applicants can appeal. The typical new recipient with no other income receives the basic grant, the maximum shelter allowance, and the maximum food stamp benefit consistent with the cash grant, as shown in table 2.1. Payment is made by Electronic Benefit Transfer using one card, with separate accounts for cash assistance and food stamps.

Employment Services

Individuals are required to participate in employment search through SAP while their application for cash assistance is being processed. Once an application is approved, the client enters the process depicted in figure 2.5.

Table 2.1.   Public Assistance Benefits, New York City, July 2001

	Number of Persons in Case Unit			
	1	2	3	4
Maximum Public Assistance Grant*	$352	$469	$577	$688
Maximum Food Stamps given maximum PA Grant**	$100	$166	$233	$284
Maximum combined Public Assistance and Food Stamps	$452	$635	$810	$972

*Includes state maximum shelter allowance with heat. Grants for three-quarters of NYC public assistance households are calculated on this basis.

**Assumes maximum Food Stamps Program excess shelter cost deduction based on average shelter allowance granted in benefit payments calculations in September 2000 (the latest available), but no other deductions.

Source: Michael Wiseman, "The Public Assistance Process," unpublished manuscript. Calculated from data in New York City Human Resources Administration, *HRA Facts*, July 2001.

Overview of SAP Services

Every new welfare applicant, unless otherwise diverted to a special program, must go through the skills assessment and placement process with an SAP vendor while his or her application for benefits is being considered—that is, prior to receiving benefits. SAP services last from four to six weeks or until a client is approved for TANF benefits. The services are aimed at quickly assessing individual needs and interests, providing job readiness skills, and attempting to attach applicants to jobs as quickly as possible to avoid the need for welfare receipt at all. Each SAP provider is assigned to serve specific Job Centers, and each Job Center is served by just one SAP vendor. Most SAP providers locate some staff at Job Centers for intake and initial assessment. While service details vary by vendor, SAP activities generally include a group orientation and assessment session, testing (including the Test of Adult Basic Education), development of an individual service strategy, workshops on work preparedness and job search skills, and initiation of self-directed job search. SAP vendors (like ESP vendors) may also offer to a small number of participants, directly or by referral, very short occupational courses (from one day to three weeks, depending on the curriculum and the vendor) for certification in security, customer service, computer, and in work as a home health aide. SAP vendors may also refer applicants to classes in English as a Second Language or for GED (General Education Diploma) preparation or to BEGIN for more remedial services (called BEGIN Managed Programs). (See chapter 8 for more on SAP and ESP contracts.)

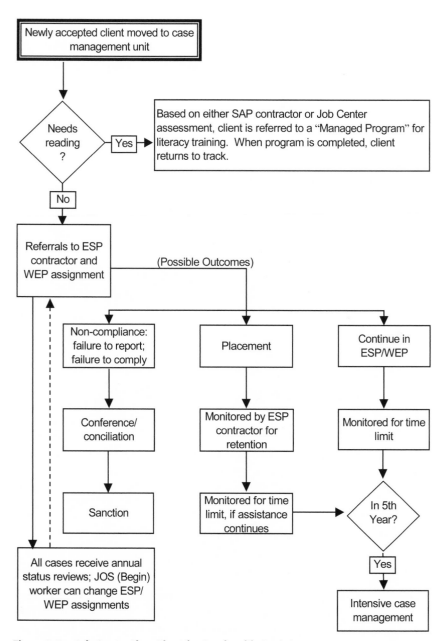

Figure 2.5. Job Center Flow Chart for Employable Recipients

Overview of ESP Services

Once applicants become active recipients, most are reassigned to Employment Services Placement (ESP) vendors. Job Center staff assign new recipients to ESP contractors based on an automated computerized assignment system (randomly, but generally in the borough where they live).[13] In addition to new cases, ESP contractors receive some ongoing FA and SNA recipients who are reassigned from other ESP contractors. Each ESP contractor also provides services under its contract with HRA to nonpublic assistance food stamp recipients and to some individuals who receive no public assistance but have low income and qualify for services under WIA.

FA and SNA recipients are assigned to an ESP provider for up to six months, at which time their status is reassessed by HRA, and a decision is made to keep the individual with the ESP provider or move the individual to another ESP provider or special program. In reality, according to several ESP staff, within about three months, most individuals assigned to an ESP provider are reportedly either placed into jobs or the case is returned to a Job Center for sanctioning (e.g., for failure to report for services or to comply with work requirements) or for reassignment to another vendor or special HRA program.

The mix of services varies by vendor, though in all cases there is a clear emphasis on rapid work attachment and relatively few individuals are engaged in job training activities (typically very short-term training). If an individual has not yet been placed into a job after an initial period of about two weeks, he or she receives a WEP assignment, again handled through an automated computerized assignment process. The WEP assignment typically is for three days a week. The remaining two days a week the individual is to report to the ESP provider for job readiness, search, and placement activities. Some ESP programs also offer various other preemployment services including some limited occupational preparation. This blended approach—three days of WEP and two days of ESP activity, often referred to as "three-plus-two"—is designed so that recipients are engaged in ongoing activities essentially full time (i.e., 30 to 35 hours a week).

SAP and ESP Activity Levels

Job Centers began to refer FA and SNA participants to SAP and ESP vendors in Fiscal Year (FY) 2000 (July 1999–June 2000). The number of individuals citywide enrolled with SAP vendors increased from 8,137 in FY 2000 to 37,331 in FY 2001; the number of individuals enrolled with ESP vendors similarly increased from 11,470 in FY 2000 to 44,530 in FY 2001.[14]

About one-quarter to one-third of the individuals referred to either an SAP or ESP vendor do not show up. Of those who do appear, about one-third are placed into jobs.[15] It was not possible in this study to determine how many of the individuals who did not show up entered employment instead or turned to other sources of non-HRA assistance. About 3,000 welfare recipients a month in 2001 were similarly referred to ESP vendors. Of the recipients referred to an ESP vendor in 2000 and 2001, about 26 percent did not appear or return. And 29 percent of those seen by ESP programs were placed in jobs.

Work Experience

Some form of workfare has existed for many years in New York City for single adults and childless couples on public assistance (the former Home Relief population). Known in the early 1990s as the Public Works Program (PWP), workfare was expanded to include AFDC recipients as part of the early welfare reform efforts of the Giuliani Administration, and the name was changed to Work Experience Program (WEP).

Overview of WEP[16]

Although the policy initially was to place every able-bodied individual receiving cash assistance into a WEP assignment, WEP itself has gone through several iterations in the course of implementing welfare reform, with increasing attention to various strategies, including adopting the "three plus two" model, placing more emphasis on moving individuals out of WEP and into unsubsidized employment, and strictly enforcing work requirements.

For example, over time more attention was paid to recipients approaching their federal time limit on cash benefits, which required modifying some WEP features. In the summer of 2001, HRA surveyed WEP participants to obtain information about participants' goals so that worksite supervisors could more actively help individuals make the transition to regular jobs. Some WEP supervisors explained that they became more diligent about reminding participants that these jobs were not permanent and that they needed to try to find permanent unsubsidized employment.

WEP program administrators also noted that, compared to prior years, there was more emphasis in 2001 in making WEP more responsive to participant needs. For example, the Parks Department adjusted the work hours for WEP assignments (changed from 7:00 am–3:30 pm to 9:00 am–5:30 pm) to accommodate women with children and tried to assign participants close to their homes or their children's schools. HRA also granted four weeks of excused absence from workfare if child care was not available, and up to two days without a doctor's note for illness or to care for a sick child.

The effect of these and other modifications, as well as the overall decline in welfare caseloads, is evident in the WEP activity trends over time. Participation in basic WEP declined substantially because more participants are in part-time WEP assignments. About three-quarters of the WEP participants in 2001, both FA and SNA, were in the combined "three-plus-two" WEP model, spending three days a week in WEP and engaging in other activities two days a week, including job search, training, substance abuse treatment, or education, rather than in basic WEP for five days a week.[17] Figure 2.6 shows that overall WEP activity has declined since 1999 and that basic WEP as a share of all WEP declined sharply. "Basic" WEP (that is, five days a week of workfare with no accompanying job search, education, or training) was no longer the dominant work activity for either the SNA or FA cases in work activities in New York City as of the end of 2001. In the last week of November 1999, 39 percent of all adult public assistance cases engaged in an activity were in WEP; by the last week of November in 2001, about 25 percent of these adults were in WEP. Similarly, in the last week of November 1999, there were over 27,000 adult public assistance cases involved in basic WEP assignments, representing about one in three engaged adult cases. As of the last week of November 2001, the number of adult cases participating in basic WEP was just over 2,000, representing about 3 percent of engaged adult cases.

Nature of WEP Assignments

The number of hours of work experience per week a welfare recipient can participate in WEP is limited by the federal Fair Labor Standards Act to the combined value of a family's public assistance and food stamp benefits,

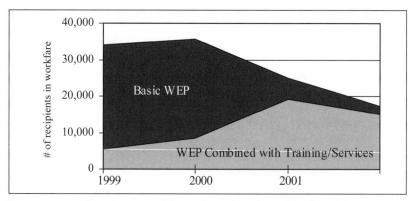

Figure 2.6.   Number of WEP Participants in Basic and Combined Models, 1999–2001
Based on snapshot counts.

divided by the minimum wage. Engagement in other HRA-authorized activities, such as job search, basic education or GED preparation, and job training, are required of participants to supplement WEP hours to meet the 35-hour simulated workweek requirement. The most typical arrangement currently, as noted above, is for the workweek to consist of three days (20 hours) of work—either regular employment or, characteristically, a WEP assignment—and two days (15 hours) of other activities, such as job preparedness and job search, provided by an ESP vendor, which are deemed necessary to achieve independence. Guidelines for the maximum duration of WEP assignments vary across WEP sites—typically ranging from six months to one year (though worksite staff also report that the limitation is not consistently monitored or enforced).

WEP assignments are principally in city agencies, but many are in private nonprofit agencies. The Department of Parks and Recreation was the largest user of WEP workers in 2001 and was typical in terms of types of jobs. The assignments were primarily in three main areas—clerical, custodial/maintenance, and human services (such as work at day care and senior centers). WEP slots represent an important portion of the workforce of several of the city's agencies, and a Parks administrator indicated that participants in WEP have accounted for up to about 20 percent of that agency's maintenance staff. Although WEP workers were distinguishable by their uniforms, WEP participants worked side-by-side with regular Parks Department maintenance staff; therefore it is not surprising that some WEP workers reportedly resented the fact that they did not receive regular pay or fringe benefits. On the other hand, supervisors reported that many WEP workers, especially those with limited work experience, were quite comfortable in their assignments and not anxious to seek regular employment. (See chapter 7 for more on this issue.)

From the beginning, WEP has always been administered centrally by HRA. Rosters of WEP slots and WEP assignees are issued biweekly to agencies and organizations hosting WEP workers. Agencies, vendors, and worksite supervisors have no control over when assignments are made or who is assigned to a particular worksite, or when a participant may be transferred from one site to another.[18] All of these decisions are made automatically through the NYCWAY data system.

Worksite sponsors report attendance biweekly to HRA, but worksite supervisors have some discretion in mediating compliance with attendance and work requirements. If a participant does not work all the scheduled hours for which he or she is not excused, the individual is to be dropped from the WEP assignment and a conciliation notice issued by HRA (the first step in the sanctioning process). Individuals assigned to WEP are expected to continue to seek paid employment and are granted excused absence from work assignments for hours involved in job interviews (but such interviews must be documented).

A major policy shift occurred in 2001, as HRA began planning for the first cohort of recipients who would be reaching their federal time limit. Instead of traditional WEP assignments, several thousand individuals were offered paid short-term employment, to encourage the transition to work through temporary paid assignments. For example, the Wage Subsidy or Temporary Work Program used a private company, Temp Force, to place individuals into one-year clerical, custodial, and other temporary jobs (offering no fringe benefits) in city agencies and private businesses. Participants work four days a week and spend the fifth in job search activities. Between March 2001 and October 2001, the program had served 3,500 participants.

Summary: Work Activities

A key focus of welfare reform in New York City in the 1990s was its strong emphasis on work-first principles to move welfare applicants and participants as quickly as possible into unsubsidized jobs. HRA contracted with SAP and ESP vendors to provide a range of employment-related and support services to either divert applicants from receiving welfare in the first place or to direct FA and SNA recipients as quickly as possible toward self-sustaining employment. In particular, there was a significant shift away from basic WEP workfare and toward mixing work experience with a range of other activities, especially work readiness and job placement activities.

REACHING SPECIAL POPULATIONS

HRA broadened its welfare-to-work initiatives in 1999 to include recipients with special needs, many of whom had previously been exempt from work and were difficult to serve. This policy reflected the underlying philosophy of welfare reform that "barring permanent or severe disability, every adult is capable of some kind of work."[19] If an individual faces a barrier to immediate employment, he or she should still be engaged in structured work activities with special assistance.

Several programs were developed for specific populations. Some programs operate in conjunction with HRA's ESP and WEP programs, and some operate separately with funding from other sources. Some of the programs have been operating for over a decade, while others are more recent. All, however, maintain the same HRA work-centered policies while blending work with education, special services, or treatment. Due in part to these initiatives, the proportion of adult FA and SNA recipients subject to mandatory work requirements rose from about half of all recipients in 1996 to about 80 percent in 1999 (and nearly 90 percent for FA alone).

A special HRA Resource Development (RD) office receives funding from city, state, and federal agencies to design and implement initiatives to serve some special populations, such as students in college. As part of the administrative reorganization discussed earlier, offices serving specialized populations were brought under HRA's regional management and included within the goal-oriented and work-focused administrative structure. Services were centralized, administratively and operationally, at a Special Needs Job Center in lower Manhattan (though some Job Centers are dedicated for particular populations, such as immigrants and residentially treated substance abusers). Recipients with special needs are instructed by letter to report to the Special Needs Job Center, or are referred to the center by workers at other Job Centers. Figure 2.7 charts the process.

The effectiveness of these various programs in terms of employment outcomes is not yet known. At the time of the fieldwork, several had been recently developed, and none had been formally evaluated. Over 70,000 individuals in 2001 were expected to receive services through these programs, which, as described below, range from assessment (such as for substance abuse) to referral back to the regular employment programs to referral to more specialized services and treatment. Each of the special population programs is described in the following sections and summarized in table 2.2. Services for other special populations with which HRA works are provided through designated Job Centers (e.g., homeless, veterans, victims of domestic violence, SSI recipients, and senior citizens).

Recipients with Medical Limitations or Disabilities

The PRIDE (Personal Roads to Individual Development and Employment) program, which began in July 1999, provides case management, education, work experience, and employment to individuals who formerly were exempt from work requirements due to physical limitations or medical conditions. Employment services available to this population used to be limited to the WEP Medical Limitations program, which has had enrollees since at least 1994. At the beginning of FY 2000, the PRIDE program began offering education and training along with work experience—although PRIDE did not become a mandatory program until March 2001. The State Office of Vocational and Educational Services for Individuals with Disabilities (VESID) provides case management and contracts with five vendors (Brooklyn Bureau of Community Service [BBCS], National Center for Disability Services [NCDS], Goodwill, FEGS, and Fedcap Rehabilitation Services),

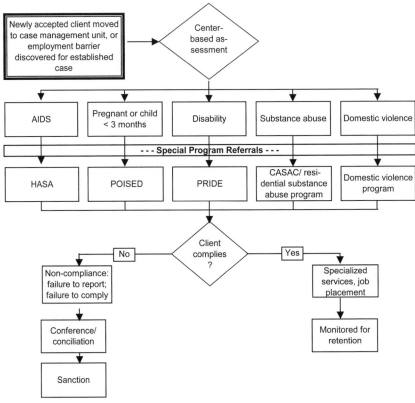

Figure 2.7. Flow Chart for Difficult-to-Serve Public Assistance Recipients

Key:
CASAC   Certified Alcoholism and Substance Abuse Counseling
HASA   HIV/AIDS Services Administration
POISED   Services for pregnant participants
PRIDE   Services for persons with mental or physical disabilities

Source: New York City Human Resources Administration

separate from the SAP and ESP contracts, to provide PRIDE participants with such services as secondary assessments, work activities (including educational and office skills instruction), and job placement.

Letters were sent by HRA to recipients who had been classified as work exempt because of medical conditions, requiring that they go to a Job Center to be assessed for employability. A client who alleged an inability to work was required to produce documentation from a doctor. Since 2001, PRIDE is a mandatory program and medical assessments have been contracted out to Health Services Systems, Inc., which conducts a five-day assessment. Depending on the result, a client may (1) be exempted from work activities

Table 2.2.   Programs Serving Special Populations

Special Population	Program	Approximate Number of Participants		
		Fiscal Year 2000	*Fiscal Year 2001*	*First 4 Mos., Fiscal Year 2002*
Medical Condition/ Disability	PRIDE			
	Received Case Management	13,478	12,060	3,698
	Referred to Work Activity Provider	8,769	7,985	3,071
Pregnant/ New Mother	POISED			
	Enrollments	941	1,796	470
	Job Placements	—	386	186
Substance Abuse Problem	SASC, RTSC			
	Total Assessed	27,327	36,549	12,086
	Intensive (Treatment Only)	9,485	16,593	5,734
	(%)	(35%)	(45%)	(47%)
	Non-Intensive (Treatment + WEP)	13,163	15,176	3,000
	(%)	(48%)	(42%)	(25%)
	No Treatment Needed	3,804	4,108	3,324
	(%)	(14%)	(11%)	(28%)
Student, Two-Year College	CUNY WEP			
	Enrollments	—	1,154	—
	Job Placements	—	160	—
College-Level Work Study	COPE			
	Average Monthly Enrollment	—	400–500	—
Already Employed	CUNY In-VEST			
	Total Participation	269	222	119
	Found Better Jobs	99	63	8
	(%)	(37%)	(28%)	(7%)
	Closed PA Cases	—	42	15
	(%)		(19%)	(13%)
Under Sanction/ Risk of Sanction	Charitable Choice Initiative			
	Total Assessed	—	4,000–5,000	—
	Sanctions Lifted	—	900	—
Caretaker, Asthmatic Child	The Asthma Project	—	(starting in 2002)	—
Limited English/ Basic Skills	BEGIN-Managed Programs			
	Total Participation	—	11,699	—

Source: "Human Resources Administration," Mayor's Management Reports.

entirely; (2) begin a 30- to 90-day "wellness program" designed to get a medical condition under control and under the supervision of the client's doctor; (3) be determined employable with limitations and assigned to PRIDE; or (4) be determined employable without limitations and assigned to WEP. According to HRA staff, since the inception of PRIDE, approximately 40 percent of clients undergoing this assessment have been found employable with limitations and presumably without the program would have been considered unemployable.

If a client is deemed employable with limitations, a PRIDE caseworker conducts a short interview, about 45 minutes, to determine education and employment background and child-care needs. Clients are then assigned to a vendor based on their residential zip code. The vendor conducts a second assessment, which must be completed within 60 days. This assessment includes reading level, education, and medical history. A state VESID counselor is on-site at each vendor, and clients are given special WEP assignments—developed by PRIDE vendors and separate from the citywide pool—to Work-Based Education (WBE) for GED or other educational activities, or more commonly to Work, Employment, and Training (WET). Vendors are encouraged to make WEP assignments within 10 days. PRIDE WEP follows the same three-day work/two-day training structure as other WEP assignments, and assignments are designed to last for not more than six months in order to encourage job placement. Clients not placed in jobs may be assigned to an additional six months in PRIDE WEP.

The program was not fully operational until well into 2000, and in 2001 nearly 20,000 were served. According to HRA staff, this population has substantial employment difficulties and only about 10 percent have been placed.

Pregnant Recipients and New Mothers

The POISED (Perfect Opportunity for Individual Skills and Educational Development) program started in FY 2000 to serve public assistance recipients who are pregnant or new mothers. In the first year, enrollment was lower than expected due to the difficulty in identifying and enrolling pregnant recipients, but it grew in FY 2001 when the program expanded to include mothers with children up to three years old.

Pregnant women participate in POISED-1, which combines classroom instruction and job preparation; mothers of young children participate in POISED-2, which requires three days a week of WEP and two days of job search. In January 2002, HRA implemented POISED-At-Home, which provides health, academic, computer, and parenting training to women who are exempt from work activities due to high-risk or advanced pregnancy or children under thirteen weeks of age. Work activities, when required for POISED, tend to be office assignments rather than more physically demanding work (e.g., at the Parks Department). Despite the small size of POISED, it represents a philosophical change from the mid-1990s, when pregnant women and mothers of young children had been exempt from work.

Recipients Requiring Substance Abuse Treatment

Services and programs for substance abusers are coordinated through the Substance Abuse Tracking and Reporting System (STARS). The Substance Abuse Service Center (SASC) provides substance abuse treatment concurrently with employment activities, while the Residential Treatment Service Center (RTSC) manages residential treatment programs.

When a recipient is identified as having a substance abuse problem—either during the application process or later (e.g., by a WEP supervisor)—he or she is referred to a Credentialed Alcohol and Substance Abuse Counselor (CASAC) for further assessment. Similar to the medical assessments conducted for PRIDE, the CASAC assessment finds the recipient's case either "intensive," leading to full-time (presumably in-patient) treatment for at least 90 days; "non-intensive," in which less than 15 hours of treatment a week (presumably out-patient) is required and the client is referred to WEP for assignment; or "no treatment needed," where the individual is deemed not to require any special service, meaning he or she is expected to comply with the work requirements. In 2000, the SASC assessment concluded that 11 percent of individuals did not require any special services (that number increased to 14 percent in 2001). The rest received either intensive or nonintensive services (with a higher percentage receiving intensive services in 2001).

Thus, unlike earlier years when substance users were required to participate in basic WEP assignments, under this new initiative, nonintensive clients were offered a greater variety of activities to combine with WEP, including treatment as well as job-search assistance and training.

Recipients in School

Several initiatives were designed for welfare recipients who were enrolled in certain kinds of education programs. The reasoning is that many students in the general public work and go to school at the same time, and therefore fairness dictates that a welfare recipient should not be excused from working while attending school.

City University of New York Work Experience Program (CUNY WEP)

CUNY WEP was created in October 2000 to accommodate FA recipients matriculating in two-year college programs. State welfare law allows work-study and internship programs to qualify as primary work activities for public assistance recipients subject to work requirements, and these programs are not subject to the 12-month training limit. New York State law, however, does not permit enrollment in nonvocational training, such as a liberal arts curriculum, whether in a two-year or a four-year degree program. In New York City, prior to the expansion of workfare to FA recipients in 1996, welfare recipients who were full-time students were exempt from work requirements.[20] When workfare became mandatory, several schools reported that many students were dropping out of college. To allow those enrolled in degree programs to complete their education, HRA and CUNY developed a separate WEP program for welfare recipients subject to work requirements who are enrolled in school.

The CUNY WEP program places students in WEP assignments for the necessary number of hours each week to meet the 35-hour requirement. CUNY WEP operates at 17 colleges (on-site at four community colleges) and in collaboration with many nonprofit organizations. Approximately 300 individuals are on the CUNY WEP roster at any one time. The Jewish Community Council of Greater Coney Island assesses client interests, develops and places individuals in appropriate WEP assignments, and monitors and reports attendance (and hours) to HRA. Assignments are reportedly made near home or school to accommodate the schedules of students who are also caring for children. The program also attempts to create assignments that reflect the student's educational concentration. Thus, an individual majoring in nursing might be assigned to a senior care or rehabilitation facility, or someone majoring in education might be assigned to an after-school, tutoring, or day-care program. Further, assignments at nonprofits require a minimum of three consecutive hours, which is deliberately intended to enable sufficient time for meaningful, productive work. Although CUNY WEP participants are expected to be completing degree programs, and the program does not routinely track employment outcomes, of the 1,154 CUNY WEP enrollments in 2001, 30 were hired into regular jobs at their WEP assignment, and 130 found other full-time employment.

College Opportunity to Prepare for Employment (COPE)

COPE is a work-study option at the college level. Students who are enrolled in vocational training at the time of their application to welfare and have received less than 12 months of job training are permitted to continue in their programs full-time while receiving public assistance. For those students who have reached the 12-month training limit, COPE provides internships, job-search, and job-placement activities that count as the first 30 hours of work activity. CUNY is the contractor for COPE, and COPE is available to students at the 17 CUNY campuses, 10 of which have COPE offices on the campus.

COPE developed procedures that enable the university to monitor attendance in class, work-study assignments, and internships to ensure that enrolled TANF recipients maintain 35 hours of school plus work activity. The COPE office also provides case management, information about and referral to support services, help to navigate the HRA system, help in identifying and negotiating internships, assistance in securing financial aid, and help in keeping up with academics and remaining in school. CUNY has job development staff for job placement and retention. Between 400 and 500 CUNY students participate in COPE each month. Reimbursement to CUNY is tied to placement and retention in jobs, with payment milestones for placement into nonsubsidized employment, verification of 30-day job retention, verification of 90-day job retention, and a bonus for jobs that provide an annual salary of at least $25,000 and/or documented health benefits.

Individual Vocational Education and Skills Training (CUNY-InVest)

InVest—a collaboration of CUNY, the New York State Department of Labor, the Higher Education Services Corporation, and the Human Resources Administration—is an initiative designed to help upgrade skills and obtain higher wages for those TANF recipients who are already employed at least 20 hours a week, but who are still receiving public assistance. The InVest program provides short-term (up to one year) vocational training at CUNY colleges (for example, training to become nurses' aides, medical billing clerks, or administrative assistants). Under the program, training costs and instructional materials are paid for, and participants may receive case management, child-care referral assistance, and help with job placement. As shown in table 2.2, the number of participants in InVest is small, and individuals are either referred to the program by Job Center staff or hear about the program and enroll on their own.

Recipients Under Sanction or at Risk of Sanction

The Charitable Choice initiative was developed to attempt mediation with clients in sanction status, presumably to avoid legal appeals and fair-hearing procedures. It was started as a pilot project with total funding of $6.3 million. HRA contracted with faith-based organizations to work with FA families who have been sanctioned or are at risk of being sanctioned. Contractors assess the reasons for participants' noncompliance and provide support and case management necessary to cure the sanctions, enroll participants in job-readiness training, and place them in jobs. In 2002, the project was a collaboration of HRA, the State University of New York Research Foundation, and four consortia of faith-based and nonprofit organizations that cover the five boroughs.

HRA provides names, phone numbers, and addresses of those who have been sanctioned, and the contracted organizations send letters to them and follow-up with interviews. One of the four organizations contracted under this initiative is faith-based (the Mission of Mercy in Brooklyn), and each of the other prime contractors has several subcontractors, many of which are faith-based. Each Job Center has a liaison with one of the contracted organizations. Sanctioned clients are scheduled for interviews with a vendor at a Job Center. During the interview, the staff person from the faith-based organization tries to determine the reason that an individual is still in sanction and identify what the individual needs to do to have the sanction lifted.

Recipients Needed at Home

The Asthma Project, begun in late 2001, is a work initiative targeting TANF participants who are the heads of households caring for an asthmatic child. The project is operated by CUNY Hunter College Center for Occupational and Environmental Hazards (COEH) under an HRA contract. The project involves outreach to FA recipients who are currently unengaged due to home-care responsibilities for school-age children who suffer from asthma. The program begins with an assessment and development of an individualized action plan, which identifies the services needed by the family to facilitate engagement in training and employment. Program staff provide case management and help locate appropriate and convenient services, such as specialized child care or schools for asthmatic children. The program also provides a job-readiness workshop for the parent. The contract is performance-based, with maximum payment per participant of $2,000, based on completion of three milestones: completion of assessment, provision of case management, and engagement as job-ready.

Recipients with Limited English or Basic Skills

BEGIN (Begin Employment Gain Independence Now) Managed Programs started in 1989 under the AFDC program as a pilot partnership between the city's Board of Education, HRA, and CUNY to serve clients with language and/or reading barriers to employment. When welfare reform policies went into effect in 1994, BEGIN was gradually replaced by new work components (currently SAP, ESP, and WEP) and former BEGIN offices or units were merged into the restructured Job Centers. BEGIN Managed Programs have continued, however, and provide a range of services, including comprehensive case management, educational instruction, and job-readiness services, designed to serve TANF parents (or those who were previously on TANF and have incomes below 200 percent of the poverty level) who require more intensive employment preparation due to limited English language or low basic skills. Eighty percent of those served have limited English language skills and/or a reading level below sixth grade. BEGIN Managed Programs have also expanded beyond language and literacy skills to include basic education, occupational/vocational training, and work experience. Some contractors operate learning labs at Job Centers. Programs generally follow the HRA model of 35 hours per week (three days in a work-based activity such as WEP and two days in a classroom activity such as ESL instruction). Contractors, including CUNY and community-based organizations, provide services. Training offered through BEGIN Managed Programs is longer than that available through WEP to accommodate the limited language skills of participants.

Participants are referred to BEGIN Managed Programs by HRA Job Center staff, HRA workers outstationed at SAP vendors, or sometimes by ESP vendors. According to the program director, enrollment in BEGIN Managed Programs declined during the period when HRA emphasis was on implementing the SAP and ESP contracts and services, but referrals to BEGIN started to increase again in 2001, when 11,699 participants were served.

Summary: Reaching Special Populations

Special programs have become a more substantial portion of the overall HRA work policy since late 1999. In part this is due to caseload declines that meant a higher proportion of the work-mandatory recipients remaining on the rolls had special needs or serious barriers to work. The shift to special programs also reflects a desire on the part of HRA administrators to expand the underlying work-centered focus of welfare reform to a broader group of recipients, especially those receiving FA. In addition, more emphasis has been placed on attempting to work with those in the sanction and conciliation process, presumably to avoid having to proceed to formal fair hearings. The special population programs are funded using a combination of TANF, WtW, WIA, and special state funds.

The special programs are designed to combine the strong work requirements of welfare reform with the recognition that some specific groups are likely to require substantial services and special interventions if they are to become employable. The same "three-plus-two" model is used in nearly all the programs—three days of work or WEP plus two days of some other service or intervention. Discussions with HRA staff, Job Center staff, vendor staff, and community representatives show general support for special programs. Their main concerns are the distance some individuals had to travel to the Special Needs Job Center in lower Manhattan, where many of the programs are housed, and the difficulty some contractors had reconciling the work requirement procedures and sanctioning process with their mainstream activities such as education or substance-abuse treatment. Employment and compliance with the work requirements are HRA's top priorities in these programs, just as they are in the HRA Job Centers and the regular SAP and ESP programs.

SUMMARY

Welfare reform became a major policy priority in New York City in the 1990s. During Mayor Rudolph Giuliani's administration (1994–2001) the city's welfare system was redefined around work and organizationally restructured. The scope and scale of change in New York City's welfare policies in the 1990s were dramatic and wide-ranging. Without question the city's welfare reform became work-centered, with a strong emphasis on ensuring that all able-bodied adults are subject to work requirements, that sanctions are imposed promptly on those who do not comply, and that those who are not employed in the regular labor market are assigned to WEP jobs. The specific features of the work programs, particularly WEP, changed considerably over the Giuliani period, reflecting both a decline in welfare caseloads and changing priorities based on operational experience. By 2002, the work requirements were implemented through a network of programs that placed recipients in a mix of work experience plus some education, training, treatment, or other services, rather than full-time workfare as in earlier years. Also, over time, many special work-centered initiatives and programs were established to target individuals with particular needs and employment barriers.

The Early Giuliani Years

During the eight years of the Giuliani Administration, the types of work activities acceptable to meet the work requirements changed. From 1994 to mid-1999, the work policies in welfare reform were characterized mainly by the following:

- *A strong emphasis on work requirements and imposition of sanctions* for recipients who did not meet those requirements. In December 1994, fewer than 60 percent of cases with an adult were subject to mandatory work requirements (i.e., "engageable"), but by April 1999, 79 percent were. Over the same period, there was also increased emphasis on sanctioning individuals for noncompliance. The percentage of adult cases in some phase of the sanctioning process (but not yet sanctioned) went from about 8 percent in November 1996 to about 14 percent in April 1999.
- *Mandatory workfare jobs.* The emphasis on workfare increased in the 1990s. Able-bodied adults receiving Home Relief in New York City (the predecessor program to SNA) have long been expected to work in unpaid jobs; and in 1996 workfare was extended to parents of dependent children receiving FA. Individual recipients not employed in the regular labor market were required to report to WEP jobs, mainly in public agencies. By early 1999, over 30,000 persons in a given week were in "basic" WEP workfare jobs—that is, traditional unpaid workfare assignments.

The Later Giuliani Years

Beginning in 1999, the city's work-centered welfare reform was characterized by the following:

(1) *Continued emphasis on work requirements and sanctioning.* Most adults on welfare continued to be subject to work requirements, and "universal engagement" became a top management priority. About 73 percent of cases with an adult on welfare in the city in the last week of November 2001 faced mandatory work requirements (i.e., were "engageable") and 13 percent of adult cases were in the process of being sanctioned; another 9 percent had actual sanctions in effect.

(2) *A shift in WEP, allowing and supporting more education and training rather than just basic workfare.* In the last week of November 2000, about 25,000 persons were in WEP assignments, but only about 25 percent of those were in basic WEP. The other 75 percent were in WEP assignments that combined work experience with some other activity such as job-readiness services, short-term training, or education— usually three days a week of work experience or workfare (21 hours) plus two days of some other activity (14 hours). This is often referred to as the "three-plus-two" model for full-time activity, defined as 35

hours a week. In comparison, in the first week of April 1999, nearly 90 percent of WEP assignments had been of the basic workfare type.

(3) *Special work experience and other work-oriented programs and initiatives for certain populations, including those with more serious barriers to work.* Special programs serve persons with substance abuse problems, physical or mental health limitations, limited English ability or reading skills, persons in the sanction process, welfare recipients in college, pregnant mothers, and mothers of newborns. In fiscal year 2001, about 70,000 individuals were involved at some point with one or more special programs, and many were also required to participate in a workfare component. Each special program includes some services designed specifically for individuals with certain needs or situations.

Accomplishments and Concerns

One major administrative accomplishment was the creation of a new, computer-based management information system. This allowed HRA to continuously review and access improved information about the entire caseload and identify the status of each client, not just in terms of benefits and payments, but also the degree of engagement: employability, work requirements, entry into employment, employment services, attendance at activities, and progress toward time limits.

As in any major systemic change, especially in a jurisdiction as large as New York City, there were different perspectives on what the changes actually were and how successful they are. Understanding the various issues and perspectives is important because together they represent the reality of the system in the city.

HRA central office administrators were generally pleased with the progress made toward implementing strong work requirements, modernizing the management information systems, restructuring local offices into Job Centers, and streamlining the vendor contracting system. Throughout the HRA bureaucracy, there was general agreement with the basic principles of work-centered welfare policies. Vendors and providers—many of which were community- and faith-based organizations—understood HRA's work-focused policies, were committed to HRA's contract performance criteria, and welcomed the opportunity for work as contractors or subcontractors.

There were concerns about the work-centered policies, however. Some advocates and community groups worried that the strict procedures and work requirements as well as the sometimes complicated logistical arrangements involved in traveling between offices, and often between boroughs, hindered some eligible individuals from receiving benefits and services. Job

Center staff generally agreed with the work focus of welfare reform, but several were concerned about the effects on participants and were frustrated in their jobs. Some Job Opportunity Specialists, for example, felt that they were primarily processing paperwork, imposing work requirements, referring clients elsewhere, and initiating automated sanctions, rather than providing employment or related services directly (because much of the employment casework had been transferred to outside vendors).

A common concern expressed throughout the system in 2002 was that the strict work-focused welfare reform objectives had been much easier to accomplish a year earlier. For example, as more adults on welfare were mandated to meet work requirements, the individual programs had to serve more clients who had substantial barriers to employment. And the economy in 2002 was not as strong as in the late 1990s, so individuals reportedly were having more difficulty finding regular jobs. Some vendor staff and a few Job Center staff indicated they were less comfortable than they had been a year earlier with having to impose strict requirements and sanctions.

Lessons Learned

Both the accomplishments and the concerns offer lessons regarding the implementation of work-centered welfare reform, with implications for national welfare policy and for other states and jurisdictions proceeding with their own reforms.

Emphasizing both work requirements and skills development need not be incompatible. New York City administrators, while maintaining a clear priority on strong work requirements, also recognized the need for initiatives that improved work skills and employability or alleviated barriers to employment, exemplified in the "three-plus-two" strategy. This was accomplished by (1) decreasing the emphasis on basic workfare and increasing the emphasis on complementary employment services, (2) contracting with specialty vendors for targeted interventions with special needs populations, and (3) simultaneously continuing to restructure and improve basic welfare procedures in HRA offices.

Flexibility is critical for reaching locally defined objectives and priorities. The welfare reforms begun in New York City in 1994 were modified in 1999 and again in 2002. Once the initial welfare caseload decline had leveled off, leaving a greater fraction of recipients with barriers to full employment, administrators revamped their programmatic approaches to allow a broader range of activities than just regular employment or basic WEP assignments to "count" toward fulfilling the work requirement. Federal and state policies under PRWORA and TANF allowed enough flexibility for HRA to adjust its welfare programs within the framework of very strong work-focused, core policies. The city used that flexibility to implement a highly decentralized network of special programs operated by a range of organizations, including community-based nonprofit entities, faith-based organizations, and public higher education institutions, allowing each to focus on its particular area of expertise.

Management and performance measurement systems are central to achieving goals. Like many jurisdictions in the 1990s, the welfare data and management information systems in New York City were outdated and inadequate for monitoring progress toward welfare reform goals and for managing a complex system of contractors. HRA made technological development a high priority in order to track whether the agency, its local offices, and its vendors were making satisfactory progress. While the system is still being perfected, it allows HRA administrators to communicate a consistent set of goals and priorities based on employment and to institutionalize the use of the data for ongoing management.

Welfare reform in New York City continues to be a work in progress, evolving and adapting to the needs of clients, changing economic conditions, results of performance measurement, and improvements in management information systems. And while the work emphasis has remained strong, the array of services and the definition of "work activity" have expanded so that even if the strong work focus were to be modified, the administrative reporting and management systems could be used to help reach redefined goals. While there may be philosophical disagreements with the strict work requirements implemented during the Giuliani Administration, the management systems and program networks established during that period represent a basic foundation that can be refined and improved to build upon the experiences of the past decade and to meet the challenges of a changing population and a changing economy, as well as changing political priorities.

NOTES

1. This chapter is a condensed summary of, and draws heavily from, a comprehensive Urban Institute report prepared with funding from the New York Community Trust and the New York City Human Resources Administration. See Demetra Smith Nightingale, Nancy Pindus, Fredrica D. Kramer, John Trutko, Kelly Mikelson, and Michael Egner, *Work and Welfare in New York City During the Giuliani Administration: Status and Future Directions* (Washington, D.C.: Urban Institute, May 2002). Opinions expressed are those of the author and do not represent positions of NYCT, HRA, the Urban Institute, its funders, or its trustees.

2. As of March 2002. This figure includes 118,000 former Family Assistance Recipients who, after reaching their five-year TANF limit, were transferred to the Safety Net Assistance Non-Cash Program. Source: Human Resources Administration, www.nyc.gov/html/hra/pdf/facts0302.pdf.

3. The average monthly TANF caseload nationally in FY 2001 was 2.12 million, and the average monthly NYC Family Assistance caseload in that year was approximately 161,000. Sources: U.S. Department of Health and Human Services, www.acf .dhhs.gov/news/stats/familiesL.htm; New York City Human Resources Administration, www.nyc.gov/html/hra/html/hrafacts.html.

4. Nightingale et al., *Work and Welfare in New York City.*

5. The conversion process was interrupted in January 1999 by a federal court order ruling that it illegally deterred applicants and denied benefits, contrary to federal law governing the Food Stamp Program. Conversions resumed after a two-year hiatus and modification in eligibility procedures to conform to federal requirements for food stamps.

6. Several also had their own competitive WtW grants directly from the U.S. Department of Labor. This study did not closely examine the interaction of these separate non-HRA funded WtW grants programs with the HRA-funded programs and activities, although some reference is made as appropriate in subsequent sections of this chapter.

7. PA Eligibility File, Engagement Reports. Figures are snapshots from selected weekly reports.

8. 2001 Mayor's Management Report.

9. As discussed in the next section, about one-quarter of applicants referred to SAP do not show up, and therefore probably are not approved for welfare and do not result in open cases.

10. City of New York, Human Resources Administration, *Ladders to Success: Innovations in City Government* (2000).

11. We did not, however, fully examine the entire intake, application, and eligibility determination procedures.

12. Services for participants who are deemed unable to work due to the severity of their substance abuse or other problems are discussed below.

13. Individuals with other barriers to employment are assigned to other units within HRA and to other contractors. See the next section for additional details on programs targeted on the special needs of participants.

14. Preliminary data for the first four months of FY 2002 (when annualized) indicate that ESP and SAP participation levels are slightly above those recorded for FY 2001 (about a 15 percent increase in SAP and a 25 percent increase in ESP participation over participation levels recorded in FY 2001).

15. It is possible some reapplied later, complied with SAP requirements, and subsequently received welfare, but that information is not reported separately.

16. For a detailed discussion of the Work Experience Program, see chapter 7.

17. This is a snapshot figure indicating whether or not a WEP participant was in the combined WEP model at a specific date; more than three-quarters of WEP participants were probably in the combined model at some point during their WEP assignment.

18. Parks Department staff, for example, noted that although they operated two job assistance programs as an ESP vendor, their own WEP participants frequently could not take advantage of these opportunities because they had already been assigned to other ESP vendors.

19. City of New York, Human Resources Administration, *Ladders to Success.*

20. In 1995, for example, there were reportedly 28,000 CUNY students on public assistance; in 2001, there were about 7,000.

II

ELEMENTS OF WELFARE REFORM

3

Changing the Organizational Culture

Arthur L. Levine

Under the leadership of Jason A. Turner, commissioner of the New York City Human Resources Administration (HRA) from February 1998 to December 31, 2001, HRA was transformed. The agency, which previously was concerned almost exclusively with determining the initial and continuing eligibility of welfare recipients and dispensing cash benefits, with few effective programs for helping clients to become self-sufficient, became a new HRA in which helping clients find employment became the overriding mission. By December 31, 2001, the number of people on welfare in New York City had been reduced to 467,000, less than half of the peak in March 1995 of 1,160,000. In contrast to previous years, in 2001 every HRA client, except those who were exempt, were engaged in employment or in an activity defined as work related. This record of accomplishment was directly related to organizational changes in HRA and particularly changes in organizational culture.

INTRODUCTION

Between 1994 and 2001, the New York City Human Resources Administration (HRA) experienced significant changes. The impetus for these changes came from two main sources. First, the election in 1993 of Rudolph Giuliani as mayor brought a new philosophy of government to the city. The focus of welfare policy and administration shifted from providing cash benefits to developing programs that would help clients find work, thereby moving them to self-sufficiency and reducing the welfare rolls. Also, accountability for performance and effective administration was emphasized.

The first two commissioners of HRA under former Mayor Giuliani began the process of change. This process was greatly accelerated with the appointment of Jason A. Turner as commissioner in 1998. Turner had been instrumental in developing model programs in Wisconsin that placed welfare recipients in jobs rather than prolonging their dependency on benefits. Under Turner's leadership, HRA became a vastly different organization in terms of policy, management, and culture.

The second impetus was the passage in 1996 of the federal welfare reform act, known officially as the Personal Responsibility and Work Opportunity Reconciliation Act. This act required the states to adopt welfare-to-work programs and set limits on the amount of time recipients could continue to receive welfare benefits.

Today HRA is a profoundly different organization than it was in the 1980s and early 1990s. Changes have taken place in the mission and goals of the agency and in management, communication, information systems, facilities, and organizational structure, processes, and culture. Perhaps the most difficult of these changes was the change in organizational culture. Because culture is so crucial to the ways that organizations operate and implement policy, the main focus of this report deals with culture change. The other organizational changes have been major contributors to the change in culture and will be discussed in this context.

Research Questions

Several questions arise concerning organizational change in HRA. How were these changes accomplished? How could a culture that had been engrained in the New York City welfare agency for decades be changed in only a few years? How was resistance to change overcome? What management approaches contributed to these changes? Can the many changes, and particularly the change in culture, survive new political, economic, and budgetary environments and become institutionalized? If so, how could this be done? Are the changes in HRA applicable to other welfare agencies?

The chapter addresses these questions; it does not evaluate the welfare reform movement or welfare reform policy. It deals with the application of public administration and management to effect change in HRA and its culture.

ORGANIZATIONAL CULTURE

Organizational culture may be defined as the beliefs, values, norms, attitudes, practices, and customs of an organization. Languages and symbols are important elements of culture. Cultures are often expressed as assumptions—beliefs that define the way things are done.[1]

The Culture of Welfare Agencies

Studies indicate that the primary focus of welfare agencies in the United States had long centered on providing cash benefits to clients, with employment programs taking second place.[2] In order to shift the culture of welfare agencies toward the values of employment and self-sufficiency, it would be necessary to change the dominant ethos from eligibility and compliance to one in which clients and welfare workers are engaged in the common tasks of finding work and arranging child care and other support services needed to help clients keep their jobs. It was argued that to accomplish this, there would have to be a major change in culture, given the many years in which the earlier culture had been ingrained.[3]

Culture in HRA prior to Welfare Reform

The culture in HRA prior to the early 1990s was similar to that of other welfare agencies in the United States. It was believed that the best way to serve clients was to provide cash and other benefits. If a client could get a job and move off welfare, this was all to the good. But it was generally believed that, by and large, welfare recipients had little chance of finding jobs due to their lack of skills and motivation. It was also believed that long-term education and training programs would prepare recipients for finding whatever few jobs might be available. The emphasis, however, was not on developing specific and targeted programs for job search or for matching training to the job market. While job-search programs existed, they were not integrated into the process for managing cases, and there were few strong incentives for job-search programs to place welfare clients in jobs. Both workers and clients at HRA grew accustomed to a system in which cash benefits were dispensed for long periods of time—with no expectation that clients were likely to leave welfare.

The Present Culture in HRA

Today the culture of HRA has changed significantly. The agency is committed to helping clients become self-sufficient. Active job-search programs, training, and support services are geared to helping clients find and retain jobs. HRA officials now believe that clients can and will become self-sufficient and that proactive administration can help achieve this objective.[4] According to interviews with officials and workers at HRA Job Centers, frontline workers generally share this belief. This view is shaped, of course, by time limits on welfare and requirements that clients must participate in work-related activities, such as job search or training, in order to receive benefits. Interviews at Job Centers indicate that clients also have come to realize that they are expected to participate in work-related activities.

How Was the Culture Change Accomplished?

Several factors contributed to the change in HRA culture. These included both external factors and internal management changes.

Changes in Laws

In addition to the 1996 welfare reform act, the enactment of the Temporary Assistance for Needy Families block grant legislation, also in 1996, and the New York State Welfare Reform Act of 1997 established a new framework for the policies and administration of HRA. These laws ended the entitlement for cash assistance, established time limits for receipt of cash assistance, gave New York State increased discretion in providing benefits and setting program rules, and gave local governments increased flexibility in designing welfare-to-work programs. The enactment of these laws sent a clear message to welfare agencies and their staffs that requiring work for all clients able to work was the clear policy of the federal and state governments and that this policy was supported by the public.

Role of Mayor Giuliani

The mayor was known as a strong advocate of the welfare-to-work concept. Even before the 1996 Welfare Reform Act, the mayor pushed for policies and programs designed to provide effective job-related training and job-search assistance to welfare recipients. He gave strong and unwavering support to HRA initiatives designed to implement these objectives.

Role of the Early Commissioners

Three HRA commissioners served under Mayor Giuliani. The first two, Marva Livingston-Hammons (January 1994–February 1997) and Lillian Barrios-Paoli (February 1997–December 1997), laid the building blocks for change in HRA. Commissioner Hammons spearheaded a new and improved eligibility-review process. Commissioner Barrios-Paoli initiated a process to make sure that every HRA client who was not exempt was engaged in work or work-related activity.

Role of Commissioner Turner

Mayor Giuliani's third appointee was Jason A. Turner. During his tenure (February 1998–December 2001), Commissioner Turner initiated major changes that transformed HRA. Almost immediately after he was appointed, Turner stressed that the overriding mission of HRA is to achieve self-sufficiency for clients. He established clear and practical goals to further that mission and took several important steps to help ensure that the goals would be reached.

Turner understood that without the support of top people in the agency, it would be very difficult, if not impossible, for him to achieve his goals. After working with, interviewing, and reviewing the performance of 13 top HRA managers, he decided to retain four, while informing the other nine that they would not have positions in his administration. Turner judged that the managers who were not retained, while competent, would not be committed to his initiatives. Most of these people found jobs in other New York City agencies. Turner believed that the four managers he retained would be very supportive and would have strong incentives to work with him, since they were selected to play key roles.

In addition, Turner brought into the agency several people who had worked with him in Wisconsin. They were placed in both top and mid-level positions. The two most prominent of these new managers were Mark Hoover, who was appointed first deputy commissioner, and Andrew Bush, appointed executive deputy administrator for policy and programs. In Turner's view, the personnel changes made in the first few months of his tenure were critical to achieving the new mission and goals of the agency.[5]

Turner also improved communication within the agency to make sure that all agency employees were aware of its mission and goals, restructured HRA to make it more flexible and responsive, initiated incentives for employees whose performance contributed to meeting agency objectives, and set up a system to monitor and track performance using advanced information technology. He gave attention to the facilities used by clients, HRA officials, and frontline workers and made sure that improvements were made to job-search and job-related training programs.

Outside observers as well as HRA officials agree that Turner's leadership was a major factor in effecting organizational change.[6] Nina Bernstein stated in *The New York Times*, "To an extraordinary degree, Mr. Turner, the welfare commissioner, has succeeded in reorganizing a notoriously unmanageable bureaucracy around his work-first philosophy. City and state welfare officials point to recent studies finding that overall, the economic circumstances of poor New Yorkers improved substantially in the later 1990s, while the welfare rolls sank."[7] By December 31, 2001, the number of people on welfare in New York City had been reduced to 467,000, less than half the March 1995 peak of 1,160,000.

Heather MacDonald wrote in the *New York Post* in February 2002, "Jason Turner accomplished this bureaucratic rebirth through charisma backed up by tough accountability measures. His passionate belief in work inspired HRA staff, but he followed up that passion with strict performance demands. Taking his cue from the NYPD's revolutionary crime-tracking system called CompStat, Turner held welfare officials accountable for finding welfare recipients jobs."[8] The HRA adaptation of CompStat is called JobStat, which is discussed below.[9]

Change Agents

In addition to the commissioner, several HRA officials acted as internal change agents to spur innovation and implementation. These included Mark Hoover, the first deputy commissioner; Patricia Smith, the executive deputy commissioner; Seth Diamond, deputy commissioner; Amy Peterson, project director for employment programs; and Dr. Swati Desai, acting executive deputy administrator. These officials worked closely with top and mid-level officials to ensure that changes were understood and implemented. Andrew Bush, who was HRA's executive deputy administrator for policy and program analysis before he left the agency in mid-2001 for a position in the Bush Administration (no relation), also played a vital role in developing and analyzing programs.

These officials worked as a team to reshape programs and processes. They had a strong sense of commitment to the new mission and goals, and they agreed that outcome-based management—rooted on accurate, timely, and reliable performance data—was the key to their implementation. To that end, the officials created an innovative information system that formed the basis for JobStat. They also held weekly meetings to review progress and obstacles and to explore new ideas. These meetings were marked by a spirit of cooperation and a freewheeling give-and-take and were not given over to second-guessing or finger-pointing. The work of the team was an important factor in progress toward HRA goals, according to team members.[10] This team approach to management was clearly demonstrated during meetings I had with these officials. The close working relationships they developed among themselves and with the commissioner resulted in a coordinated and integrated approach to problem solving and helped to ensure that new initiatives would take into account their impact on related programs.[11] Regional managers and center directors who took particularly active roles in promoting new initiatives and programs also acted as change agents.

Mission and Goals

The new HRA mission needed to have clear and practical goals for which officials and frontline workers could strive. Starting in 1999, HRA established yearly goals as a way of setting priorities and focusing the efforts of programs and administrative processes. The goal in 1999 was full engagement of all HRA clients. This meant that every client who was not exempt due to physical or mental disability or specific family duties (such as the need to take care of an aging, ill parent) had to be in a work or work-related program, including training or education, or under review. This initial goal of engagement laid the basis for achieving other goals.

Mastering the challenge of full engagement was extremely important. In 1999, an average of 33,000 clients were not engaged—that is, they were not participating in work-related programs or otherwise having their situations addressed. To complicate matters, as clients became engaged, others became "unengaged." That HRA was able to reduce unengaged cases to zero was a major accomplishment. This was done by active management and through the JobStat process, discussed below.[12] The effort toward full engagement gave managers and center directors an in-depth knowledge of caseload dynamics. Virtually every action taken by the agency with respect to a client had to be understood and tracked. Managers and center directors had to learn to monitor and analyze their caseloads and to develop and track indicators of caseload management.

The goal for 2000 was that 100,000 clients would be placed in jobs (this goal was exceeded by 33,000). The goal for 2001 was 150,000 jobs. Despite the recession and the adverse economic impact of the September 11 attack on New York, which cost the city as whole 132,400 jobs in 2001,[13] HRA was able to place 131,000 clients in jobs in 2001. Active management and JobStat were the keys to meeting the new agency challenges.

The annual goals compelled officials at the HRA headquarters, regional managers, and center directors to consider whether programs and activities were contributing to or hampering goal achievement and encouraged them to take actions to further goal achievement. For frontline workers, the goals provided a context for relating daily work to agency objectives. The goals also laid the basis for constructive competition among regions and centers for improving performance.

Vendors for Job Search

To help find jobs for clients, HRA contracts with several vendors who assess clients, perform job searches, and provide training and placement. These vendors have been successful in helping clients get jobs, which gives confidence to frontline workers that goals can be achieved and provides job satisfaction. Vendor contracts are performance based—vendors are paid only for actual job placements and job retention, rather than for performing specific tasks. This provides vendors with an incentive to conduct assessments carefully and to relate training to the job market. (Vendors are paid for training by vouchers issued to clients by HRA.)[14] Recently, the centers have become more active in developing their own job-finding programs. Center-sponsored job fairs have been a good source for leads to jobs.

MANAGEMENT

Studies have shown that the direction of organizational change, and particularly culture change, can be supported by internal changes in management, communication, and organizational structure.[15]

Accountability and Performance

The most important managerial innovation made by Commissioner Turner and his management team was the emphasis on managing for accountability and performance. This approach represented a major departure from earlier years, when management focused on determining initial and continuing eligibility of clients and processing applications. In contrast, management under Turner focused on achieving specific objectives that placed clients on a path to self-sufficiency: full engagement, jobs, and other work-related activity. Emphasis was also placed on important intermediate objectives such as timely handling of cases and reducing errors. Managers, supervisors, and frontline workers were held accountable for their actions and were evaluated on their performance in specific tasks that were needed to achieve objectives. Monitoring and evaluating performance through Job-Stat and other tracking and reporting mechanisms were used to ensure accurate and timely documentation of progress. In short, a web of managerial approaches was put in place to help ensure that goals would be met. Top managers, supervisors, and frontline workers were clearly shown that their actions in support of achieving these objectives would be constantly reviewed. In this way, the culture of the agency began to change from a passive view of administration that relied on routine procedures to a proactive mindset that stressed accomplishments that helped clients find jobs and become self-sufficient.[16]

Unified Case Management

Under the unified case management concept, one frontline worker is able to provide several different services for a client: screening for eligibility, social-service counseling, and job placement with the help of vendors. This has been accomplished by establishing a new position, Job Opportunity Specialist (JOS), which combines the duties of two previous positions: Eligibility Specialist and Employment Specialist. The JOS is empowered to deal with all facets of a case while at the same time having a comprehensive view of the regulations and services available.

Several frontline workers told me that although the JOS position requires more work compared to their old jobs as eligibility or employment specialists, the work is more satisfying and the ability to help clients is greater. Unified case management also prevents the client from telling one story to the eligibility specialist and a different one to the employment specialist. For the client, there is an advantage in having to deal with just one case manager rather than the several frontline workers required in the past.

The importance of unified case management and JOS for effecting culture change cannot be overemphasized. In interviews, job opportunity specialists told me that their new duties give them a broader perspective on the needs of clients: They see the client as a person, rather than a number, for the first time.

Communication

Commissioner Turner recognized that simply announcing a new mission and setting goals was not enough, and that he had to be personally involved. He held a series of meetings at Town Hall, a large auditorium in midtown Manhattan, in which he discussed the new mission of self-sufficiency and encouraged both HRA officials and frontline workers to work toward the new goals for the agency. Every HRA employee attended one of these meetings. Turner also made regular visits to HRA centers, including unannounced visits, in order to observe firsthand the work and problems. When problems were discovered, he took action to help the centers solve them. Both HRA officials and outside observers of welfare administration in New York City told me that this personal involvement by the commissioner was unprecedented. They said that the commissioner's actions were a major reason why organizational change was achieved.[17]

There were several other initiatives as well. HRA officials instituted regular meetings at headquarters with regional managers and center directors. At the center level, the center director meets regularly with top staff members, and there are periodic meetings with all employees. The meetings are not merely to disseminate general information or to give pep talks—they deal with substantive issues and are used to air and solve problems. JobStat meetings, discussed below, provide a great deal of two-way communication between headquarters and the centers, and CenterStat meetings (also discussed below) facilitate communication between the center director and center staff. Other measures to ensure good communication include frequent e-mail and telephone conferences between headquarters and the centers and among centers.[18]

Changes in Organization Structure

Three changes have contributed to the change in culture, combining eligibility and employment, regionalization, and decentralization.

Combining Eligibility and Employment

First, the HRA eligibility and employment functions were combined organizationally and within the centers. Previously, these had been two distinct functions in different parts of the agency. Communication was poor. There were long delays between the time a case was opened and when that case was referred to the employment service. Further delays followed as the employment service learned about a client and set up a job search. It was not uncommon for a year to pass between the time a case was opened and the first job search took place. The separation and delays seemed to justify the attitudes, prevalent in the organizational culture of the 1980s and early 1990s, that finding jobs for clients was not practical and that cash was the only feasible way to help clients. The importance of combining the eligibility and employment functions to the change in culture is indicated in a study of welfare offices in four states. In those offices in which eligibility and employment services were separate, workers saw little or no change in their day-to-day duties, causing them to doubt whether real change in the mission and goals of the agency was taking place. "Increasingly, workers tended to liken the possible success of welfare reform to the fact that their own jobs have changed very little since welfare reform."[19]

Establishing the JOS position in HRA, which combines the eligibility specialist and employment specialist duties in one position, brings this structural change directly to the frontline worker level.

Regionalization

The second structural change was regionalization, so that each center in a specific borough reported to a regional manager. This change provided management with a better understanding of the problems of a specific region, the demographic composition of each borough, and the ethnic backgrounds of the clients living there. It also facilitated communication among centers in a region.

Decentralization

A third major structural change was the decentralization of authority to the regional and center levels. Regional managers have more discretion in developing programs and directing center activities than previously. In contrast to earlier years, center directors are responsible for employment programs, which helps them integrate various center operations to further employment goals. They also have greater discretion in directing day-to-day operations. These structural changes supported the change in culture by giving managers greater flexibility in affecting day-to-day tasks geared toward furthering self-sufficiency.

Tracking and Analyzing Performance

It is necessary to have reliable and accurate tracking mechanisms in order to monitor and evaluate agency programs and actions effectively.

JobStat

Gathering data and tracking task performance is done very well by JobStat. Line managers are able to examine and judge their performance regularly based on indicators showing their center's success in promoting employment and self-sufficiency. In regularly scheduled meetings, center directors describe and defend their performance before a panel of senior HRA managers, including the commissioner, his top staff, and the appropriate regional manager. The meetings are built around compilations of various performance indicators—the JobStat report—and are in essence statistically oriented reviews of Job Center performance. While the JobStat process is vital for tracking performance, it has a greater value in educating managers and center directors in how to improve their management and analytical skills and in demonstrating how effectiveness and accountability can be increased.

A study of JobStat notes that the performance indicators used in JobStat are valuable tools for teaching and learning because they point to bottlenecks or trouble spots and to units that have management problems. Therefore, in order to perform well in the JobStat environment, line supervisors and managers of direct service units must become analysts. The JobStat process also gives officials and center directors a broad view of the operations and problems of the agency as a whole—to which they had not been exposed in their previous experience (see chapter 5). Center directors are not necessarily put on the spot for numbers that do not reach goals. They are expected, rather, to understand and explain shortfalls and develop plans to deal with them.[20]

HRA officials, center directors, and frontline workers, as well as outside observers, credit JobStat with providing both managers and employees with an excellent method for gauging progress toward goals, identifying problems before they get out of hand, pinpointing the source of errors, and providing valuable information on how to correct errors.[21] Using JobStat provides managers and frontline workers with confidence that they can be more effective in helping clients move to self-sufficiency, thereby supporting the new culture in the agency. JobStat helps center directors understand, analyze, and explain their operations.[22] The JobStat process fosters accountability and increases the managerial and technical capabilities of both headquarters officials and center directors.

When data and performance indicators are displayed and analyzed, the relationship among various actions becomes evident. For example, when a center fails to meet standards for timeliness, error rates, application processing, or incidence of complaints or fair hearings, the impact of such shortfalls on goal achievement becomes clear. Thus, officials, regional managers, and center directors and supervisors see that the way they manage these matters is key to meeting employment goals. This affects the perception of managers and frontline workers as to what tasks are most important, and in turn influences the values, practices, and beliefs of managers and workers, thus helping to modify organizational culture.

CenterStat

To complement JobStat at the center level, the agency utilizes CenterStat, in which job-center performance data are disaggregated to the level of groups or units of frontline workers and to individual workers. Regular meetings are held by the center director and top staff with supervisors to go over these data. Statistics such as timeliness and error rates are used to evaluate performance. The source of shortfalls, including the performance of groups and individual workers, can be identified and tracked. In addition, the process points to unusually good work by groups or individual workers, providing a basis for special recognition. CenterStat also helps to evaluate groups and individuals to determine the need for reconfiguration or training. In interviews, center directors stressed that CenterStat has been a major help to them in managing center operations.[23]

CenterStat is still relatively new, and some centers are grappling with how best to implement it. Some supervisors are not yet accustomed to reporting on and analyzing group or unit performance and the measures used to evaluate performance. As this approach becomes more familiar and supervisors and frontline workers understand it better, CenterStat could become the basis for systems thinking by center directors, supervisors, and frontline workers. This would enable them to relate unit and individual actions to agency-wide initiatives and goals. If this happens, the change in culture would penetrate deeply into the working level.[24]

VendorStat

Similar in format to JobStat meetings, VendorStat meetings are a way of reviewing the progress and problems of vendors based on statistical performance indicators. Immediately following the weekly JobStat meeting, in the same room, one or two vendors defend their performance before the same senior staff and the directors of the job centers they are serving. The meetings are very helpful to HRA officials in reviewing the performance of vendors who assess clients' capabilities for employment, provide job-related training, and help clients find jobs. Based on VendorStat data and the discussions and analysis that are stimulated by the data, informed determinations can be made by HRA officials and center directors as to how to manage the placement and training programs and whether to retain or terminate specific vendors.

Incentives and Awards

To motivate employees, HRA developed awards and incentives for outstanding performance by centers, groups, and individuals. Initially, these were symbolic rather than providing significant monetary benefits. They included gift certificates at Staples stores and other similar awards. Nevertheless, they did provide recognition to centers and workers who did unusually good work. Merit pay was subsequently awarded to job opportunity specialists. The award is substantial—10 percent of the annual salary. In the first round of these awards, 25 percent of all job opportunity specialists received merit pay. Centers also take pride in establishing good performance records as indicated by JobStat.

Technology and Facilities

The improvement in technology and physical facilities available to frontline workers and clients was a major plus in helping to change HRA culture. The agency renovated several centers so that the work environment is clean and comfortable, and lighting, heating, and air conditioning meet high standards. Each frontline worker has a computer on his or her desk in many centers, and the information system facilitates more accurate work. Streamlining of information flow and communications has been aided by the "paperless office" initiative. Replacing paper records with an organized database of case histories has enabled faster location of case records and reduced multiple return trips by clients due to misplaced or lost records.

The impact of modern, attractive facilities and advanced technology was clear in the contrast between two centers I visited. One, in Brooklyn, was newly renovated and had the latest in computer technology, with a computer on the desk of each frontline worker. Another, in the Bronx, operated in a very old, run-down building—a shabby and depressing work environment. Computers dated back to the 1980s and frequently were not operational. Most workers did not have computers on their desks. At the Brooklyn center, frontline workers I interviewed were happy with working conditions and had positive attitudes toward their work and toward their new JOS responsibilities. At the Bronx center, workers complained strongly about working conditions. While some I interviewed were satisfied with their jobs, many were unhappy and frustrated, and some felt that the JOS duties put too much of a strain on them compared to their previous work under their old titles. At both centers, caseloads were high (more than 100 per frontline worker), but complaints about caseloads were much more pronounced at the Bronx center.

Similarly, HRA headquarters moved from an aged building on a drab street into the upper floors of a modern office building in the booming financial district of downtown New York. Sleek, new office furnishings replaced the dreary décor of khaki-colored, surplus-World-War-II filing cabinets and the like. The effect on employee pride, morale, and performance was electric.

Symbols and Terminology

Important clues to the nature of an organization's culture are the symbols and terminology used in agency activities. Such terms as "welfare office" and "income maintenance" connote a reliance on benefits. Commissioner Turner wanted to emphasize jobs and self-sufficiency. One way to do so was to change HRA symbols and terminology to make them consistent with these goals. Therefore Income Support Centers became Job Centers and caseworkers were renamed Employment Specialists to emphasize the focus on helping clients prepare for and find jobs. The new title of Job Opportunity Specialist also has symbolic meaning; it implies that opportunities for employment exist and that jobs will be sought and filled through HRA programs.

Attention to the Needs of HRA Employees

Culture change has been facilitated by careful attention to the needs of HRA employees at all levels, from top officials to frontline workers.

Upgrading of facilities and technology (discussed above) and providing training for new job challenges are major factors in enhancing job satisfaction, according to top officials, center directors, and frontline workers. Job opportunity specialists were concerned about the lack of a salary increase following their conversion to the JOS title and the need for more training for their new responsibilities. These issues are discussed below.

Attention to the Needs of Clients

HRA was concerned with the needs of clients for job-related training and job placement. Clients I interviewed were impressed by the services related to training and job search. HRA also sought to make visits to centers less confusing and complex for clients by setting up information stations where clients can be directed to the appropriate frontline worker. Center staff I observed were responsive to telephone inquires from clients.

The improvement of the past few years in serving clients is directly related to the emphasis by HRA on becoming more responsive to clients and providing timely services. Two of the most important performance indicators in JobStat—timeliness and errors—deal with these. Among the benefits of Job-Stat and the new proactive managerial culture is the ability to track accurately the responses of centers, groups, and individual workers. This makes it easier to assure that problems are addressed and that such issues as child care or access to food stamps or Medicaid are handled promptly. When complaints about lack of response or timeliness are made, the JobStat process can be used to pinpoint the reasons for the deficiencies and correct them.

OBSTACLES TO CHANGE

Several obstacles were encountered in the process of changing the culture. To a large extent these were overcome through management initiatives.

Resistance by Frontline Workers

Some frontline workers were skeptical that programs to implement the changes that were initiated would, in fact, be carried out. During 2000 and 2001, HRA took several steps to dispel this skepticism and overcome resistance to change. These include an effort to clearly explain the benefits of the JOS position so that full and comprehensive service can be given to clients. In addition, incentives and awards, including merit-pay bonuses for job opportunity specialists, helped workers realize that the changes offer advantages in the form of increased compensation and opportunities for career development.

Another source of continuing skepticism is the idea that the changes initiated by HRA would not outlast the administration of a new mayor and commissioner. However, the fact that programs and processes designed to implement the culture change are well in place dispelled much of this concern.

A significant obstacle to implementing the change in culture was the reluctance of some frontline workers to convert to the JOS position. Some workers feared that they could lose seniority after conversion to the new title, despite assurances by HRA that seniority is protected. Another concern among frontline workers is that union-based benefits may be reduced or lost. Three unions are involved: Local 1549 of District Council 37, AFL-CIO, represents eligibility specialists and clerical workers; Local 371, also a part of DC 37, represents employment specialists; and Local 1189 of the Communications Workers of America represents supervisors of frontline workers. One of these unions, or perhaps a different union not presently representing HRA workers, will be chosen by job opportunity specialists to represent them in a forthcoming election. Some workers worry that the newly elected union will not offer the benefits, such as health insurance or education assistance, that they currently receive as members of their present unions, or that such benefits will be reduced.

Resistance by Unions

The position of the unions on JOS varies. Local 1549 opposed conversion. It contends that workers in the new position will experience conflicts of interest since they will be screening for eligibility and providing services.[25] (HRA officials say they have not encountered such a conflict with job opportunity specialists and do not believe this will be a problem.) Local 1189 also opposed conversion, while Local 371 did not oppose conversion to JOS and has at times appeared to favor it.

Union opposition prompted some members of the unions that opposed JOS to be even more hesitant about conversion. The situation is complicated by the fact that at present there is no salary increase for workers who convert to the JOS position—they continue to earn the same salaries they received as eligibility or employment specialists. Salary changes will be part of a new contract for job opportunity specialists that will be negotiated by the union that is elected to represent them.

In order to help compensate job opportunity specialists, HRA instituted merit pay for those in the JOS position who have performed especially well. The merit pay award is 10 percent of the annual salary. Only job opportunity specialists are eligible for merit pay, which will be awarded twice each year. The first round of merit pay was awarded to 25 percent of all job opportunity specialists. This action drew a strong reaction from all three unions. They filed a lawsuit accusing HRA of unfair labor practices.

Despite the concerns of some workers, conversions to JOS proceeded steadily. As of September 2003, 77 percent of workers eligible for JOS had converted to the new title.[26] Many considered conversion advantageous because they expected salary increases once a new union was chosen and saw the work as more challenging and satisfying and perhaps a stepping-stone for career advancement. Merit pay is a further inducement. In addition, conversion was perhaps spurred by the realization that workers who did not convert might be transferred to other locations.

Role of Center Director

Although the factors discussed above are important in the decision of workers to convert to JOS, interviews with HRA officials indicate that the center director is the key to the conversion rate at a center. In centers in which the director is enthusiastic about the new JOS position and meets with workers to explain the advantages of the new title, conversion rates range from 70 to 80 percent of eligible workers. In centers where the director has not taken such action, the rates are considerably lower, from 30 to 50 percent.

Resistance by Vendors

Accountability and performance requirements are central features of new HRA contracts with vendors who assess, train, and find jobs for clients. Under these contracts, vendors are paid only for successful job placement and job retention, rather than for activities leading to placement. This is in contrast to the line-item contracts used in previous years, in which vendors were paid for conducting job-placement activities regardless of their success. Vendors were hesitant to agree to these arrangements, since several months could elapse between the time the vendor begins efforts to find a job for a client and when actual placement is made. During that period, the vendor would have to spend money on payroll and other costs without receiving any fee. HRA addressed this problem by providing advances to vendors to help them meet ongoing expenses. HRA also pointed out to vendors that under performance-based contracts, vendors would have a great deal of independence and discretion in how they conducted work. Under line-item contracts, HRA had to approve the hours of work as well as other items. Under performance-based contracts, the vendor is free to administer services as it thinks is best. Results, not process, are measured. This permits the vendor to be more flexible and potentially more creative, efficient, and effective. Vendors ultimately came to terms with performance-based contract requirements.[27]

Security in the Centers

A concern indirectly related to effecting culture change is the physical security of frontline workers. In interviews, nearly all frontline workers told me that they feared that they might be hurt in violent outbreaks that occur periodically at centers, especially during evening and night overtime hours. Workers told of threats by clients who said that the workers would "be pulverized" once they left the center building. These workers said that security was not adequate. They would like to see New York City police assigned to the centers. They complain that the private security guards, while doing their jobs, are not permitted to arrest or detain violent clients and are not armed. In a violent situation, the guards are instructed to call 911. As an alternative to having police, workers would like to have government guards who are "peace officers" and are armed. HRA officials told me that they had requested police assignments but that they could not be obtained. HRA is working on having peace officers assigned to centers. When workers do not feel safe in their place of employment, their feelings of insecurity may affect their attitude toward the change in culture. Some may be tempted to leave HRA for this reason.

SUSTAINING THE CHANGE

Generally, organizations go through four stages to achieve change. First, leadership decides that change is needed to move the organization in a new direction. Second, the organization announces that change is coming, and new goals, programs, and procedures are developed to implement the change. Third, the new programs and procedures are incorporated into the work and routines of the organization. Top and middle-level officials and frontline workers perform tasks and routines that incorporate and help implement the change. Finally, the change is institutionalized through widespread acceptance at all levels of the organization. The values, assumptions, beliefs, attitudes, and practices of officials and employees at all levels are supportive of the change.

The change in culture at HRA clearly advanced through the first three stages. Interviews indicate that officials and frontline workers accepted the mission and goals of HRA, although there are some workers who are resistant, as discussed above. Most clients, as well, understand that work or work-related activity is required to receive benefits, unless they are disabled.

It appears, however, that culture change has not been fully institutionalized at HRA. Studies of organizational culture have shown that reaching this final stage generally takes many years.[28] Major efforts to change the culture at HRA began only in 1998 with the arrival of Commissioner Turner. In this short time, substantial change in the culture took place. But interviews and observations indicate that some officials, frontline workers, and clients still believe that conditions could change, leading to a reversal of the trends of those four years. Nevertheless, the chances that the changes will become institutionalized are good, as long as the preconditions for sustaining the culture change are met.

Preconditions for Sustaining Culture Change

For organizational change to be long lasting at HRA, it must be institu- tionalized. Cultures that are institutionalized can withstand temporary set- backs in terms of budget, support from the top echelons of government, the legislature, or the press. The adverse economic impact resulting from the September 11 attack, including significant budget deficits for New York City and a bleaker outlook for employment in the city, have only added to the challenges that HRA must face. For HRA, it is important that the main pil- lars of the present culture remain intact.

Support of the Mayor

Continued strong support from Mayor Bloomberg for continuing the policy and administrative initiatives that help clients move to self-sufficiency is imperative for the culture change to last.

Strong Leadership from the New Commissioner

The key to effecting culture change in HRA was the leadership of Com- missioner Turner. His constant efforts to get across the new mission and goals of the agency and to continuously and forcefully communicate with officials and frontline workers, combined with the changes made in the structure and processes of the agency, have been essential to realizing the change in culture. The chances for institutionalizing the culture change of the previous administration will be much greater if Commissioner Verna Eggleston continues and strengthens the initiatives of Commissioner Turner. The public statements of both Mayor Bloomberg and the commissioner indicate that they will retain those initiatives. An early sign that this will be the case is the decision to continue the policy of not accepting a federal waiver from food-stamp rules. The waiver would allow jobless adults with- out children to receive food stamps beyond the current limit of three months in a three-year period without the requirement to engage in work-related activity for 20 hours per week. The waiver is available to communities with high unemployment. In a written statement, Eggleston said, "We can do more for our clients by declining the waiver and by identifying each individual's capacity and tailoring assistance to move them to the maximum level of self-sufficiency."[29]

Attention to the Needs of Frontline Workers

The change in culture cannot survive if frontline workers become disenchanted or even hostile to the mission and goals of the agency. The JOS position is seen by frontline workers as an excellent concept that helps them serve clients more effectively and gives them a broader view of the services available. They welcome the chance to engage in intensive case management. Workers are concerned, however, that caseloads are too high to permit them to give the time and attention needed for intensive case management. They also feel strongly that the new responsibilities and additional work involved in the JOS position call for a significant raise over their present salaries as eligibility or employment specialists, as well as additional training to prepare them for their new responsibilities. It is important for HRA to move on these issues to the extent possible consistent with the stringent fiscal condition of the city government.

Good Relations with Unions

Thus far unions have not presented a major obstacle to culture change. Union opposition to the new JOS position caused some workers to hesitate to convert to JOS, but this was not a major impediment to conversion. Unions strongly opposed HRA, however, in several matters, including pay scales, security at the centers, and merit pay for Job Opportunity Specialists.

Unions will be important in sustaining the change in culture, especially since the September 11 attack. Large budget deficits impacted the city. A hiring freeze was put into effect. Cooperation of the unions on a citywide basis was sought by Mayor Bloomberg as a way to hold the line on costs.

Attention to the Needs of Clients

HRA has been very focused on helping clients find jobs and providing job-related training. Clients I interviewed appreciated these efforts; however, they were concerned about other issues. Some complained that workers did not treat them with respect, or "talked down" to them. Others complained about long waits to be seen. At the Bronx center I visited, it was not uncommon for a client to wait from three to eight hours for an initial intake interview. One client I interviewed had been waiting for three hours to see a worker so that he could show proof that he attended college classes as a requirement to keep receiving benefits. Some of these problems may be unavoidable at present, given the new intake process in which the JOS both screens for eligibility and provides other services.

Clients are also concerned about getting timely child care in locations near their homes—a concern also shared by job opportunity specialists whom I interviewed. This issue is complex. Center directors and HRA officials told me that there is no shortage of child care for clients. Available child-care facilities, however, may not be in locations convenient to the homes or work places of clients. HRA is committed to placing children of clients who are working or engaged in a work-related activity in certified child care, but not necessarily in the location preferred by the client. As one HRA official said, "Everyone who works and has young children must put up with some inconvenience, whether they are on welfare or not."

While some of the complaints of clients may be exaggerated, the views of clients have an impact on culture change. Ultimately, the institutionalization of culture change depends on the attitudes of clients as well as HRA officials and workers. Many frontline workers have relatives or friends who are clients. Naturally they are influenced by the views of such clients. It appears that clients for the most part have accepted the reality that they must be engaged in work-related activities to receive benefits and that their goal should be self-sufficiency. Yet there remains the feeling among clients, revealed in interviews, that welfare-to-work may not be a lasting policy and that the enforcement of this policy will be relaxed in the future. A study of welfare offices in four states noted that some clients did not believe that benefits would be cut off when they reached the time limit for welfare assistance.[30] Job opportunity specialists at HRA centers also told me that some clients hold this belief.

To the extent possible, service to clients should be improved. At the same time, clients should be impressed with the fact that failure to engage in work-related activity will result in sanctions and that time limits are real. It is important for clients to understand that even though clients who have hit time limits may be eligible for the New York State Safety Net program, work is a far better alternative. Subsequently HRA took steps to place clients who are nearing time limits into subsidized jobs with private employers or city agencies.

HRA responded to client needs in other significant ways. Through Job-Stat, HRA emphasized that taking timely action on cases and reducing errors are important indicators of performance.

Retention of Structural and Process Changes

It is important to retain the changes in organizational structure and the ways cases are processed, particularly with the JOS approach, because they reinforce the change in culture. The vendor system for assessment, job search, training, and placement should be retained, and reviewed and strengthened periodically, because of the key role that vendors play in finding jobs for clients.

Ongoing Monitoring and Evaluation

Although the changes in HRA have resulted in great progress toward goals, ongoing monitoring and evaluation of programs and activities must be constant and vigorous to ensure that backsliding does not occur.

Staff Training

The changes that have taken place at HRA have been so extensive and dramatic that it will be necessary to reinforce new behaviors and practices with training and to prepare staff for new challenges that will emerge due to the tightening job market and reduced city budgets. In interviews at job centers, supervisors and frontline workers made it clear that they needed more training in new procedures and programs, including working with vendors to place clients in jobs. HRA hired many new job opportunity specialists in 2001. These people need extensive training. Further, JOS duties represent a new approach to serving clients and helping them find employment. HRA is aware of the need for a new emphasis on staff training. The question is, how can this best be accomplished? Are there sufficient officials and managers available to conduct such training without neglecting other duties? Would outsourcing provide trainers with sufficient knowledge and sensitivity? How can training costs be covered within a constrained budget?

CONCLUSION

The changes that took place during the eight years of the Giuliani Administration, and particularly during the tenure of Commissioner Turner, transformed HRA in many ways. These changes have made the agency stronger and more flexible, and therefore much better able to achieve its mission of helping clients become self-sufficient through employment. The change in culture, which is very hard to achieve in any organization, has been dramatic. Support and leadership from the current mayor and the commissioner—and their successors—will be needed to ensure that the changes, and especially the culture change, become institutionalized. Given such leadership, organizational accomplishments thus far provide a solid basis for assuring that the changes last.

Can the HRA Experience Be Applied to Other Jurisdictions?

Although New York City has a very large welfare caseload and is replete with many complex problems, the lessons of the HRA experience in organizational change should be applicable elsewhere. The problems that faced HRA in the early 1990s are still common in welfare administration throughout the United States: lack of emphasis on programs to help clients find and keep work; training that is unrelated to the job market; lack of reliable and timely statistics on performance; poor coordination among the functions of eligibility determination, social services, and employment; unwieldy and inefficient organizational structure; poor communication; and inadequate technology and facilities.

It should be stressed, however, that culture change cannot be accomplished simply by changes in policy or in mission and goals. These are only the first steps. In addition, leadership from chief executives and top agency officials is needed. The changes have to be supported by proactive, outcome-based management for accountability and performance, accompanied by appropriate changes in communication, organizational structure, and technology and facilities. In addition, major upgrades of information systems are needed to monitor and track activities, to improve accountability, and to pinpoint the sources of problems. This in turn requires that managers and supervisors think in systems terms and become analysts of agency actions and obstacles. Managers and supervisors have to be capable of handling these advanced tasks, which necessitates careful selection of those to be placed in key roles. Formal and informal training are also important elements to ensure that personnel understand and are motivated to achieve program goals. Unified case management and tracking systems such as JobStat are vital administrative innovations for implementing the shift toward new directions.

Culture change has to be approached with the understanding that many problems and obstacles have to be addressed at the same time and supported by innovative programs and projects. Even seemingly minor modifications, such as the change in terminology from "income support centers" to "job centers," are needed to reinforce the reality of culture change. Attention to the needs of clients and frontline workers is essential to ensure that the entire organization is involved and accepts the new culture.

It is also important that changes be accomplished within a few years. Time limits imposed by welfare-reform legislation, and the need to demonstrate that the transition from cash benefits to work is feasible before critics declare the new policies to be impractical, make it imperative that real progress be made in a short time frame. An extended timetable is not a political reality.

Welfare reform as implemented in New York City need not be unique to this city. The changes made by HRA can be applied to other jurisdictions as long as there is executive leadership and vigorous management for accountability and performance.

NOTES

1. James E. Swiss, *Public Management Systems: Monitoring and Managing Government Performance* (Englewood Cliffs, N.J.: Prentice Hall, 1991), 316; Grover Starling, *Managing the Public Sector,* 5th ed. (Fort Worth, Tex.: Harcourt Brace College, 1998), 479.

2. Irene Lurie and Norma M. Riccucci, "Changing the 'Culture' of Welfare Offices: From Vision to the Front Lines," *Administration and Society* 34, no. 6 (2003): 655–77.

3. Lurie and Riccucci, "Changing the 'Culture' of Welfare Offices."

4. HRA has been proactive in managing several programs, including its focus on engaging all clients in some welfare to work activity.

5. Jason A. Turner, HRA commissioner (1998–2001), telephone interview, April 25, 2002.

6. Gordon L. Berlin, Manpower Development Research Corporation, telephone interview, September 14, 2001; Gregory Gomez, regional manager, Brooklyn, HRA, interview, September 24, 2001; Irene Lurie, professor, Department of Public Administration and Policy, State University of New York at Albany, telephone interview, November 14, 2001.

7. Nina Bernstein, "As Welfare Comes to an End, So Do Jobs," *New York Times,* December 17, 2001, A1, F3.

8. Heather MacDonald, "Bloomberg's Test," *New York Post,* February 15, 2002, 33.

9. Commissioner Turner introduced several proactive programs. HRA has programs to enroll clients in Medicaid, particularly low-income women during pregnancy and when they enter hospitals to give birth, as well as helping clients over 65 enroll in Medicare.

10. Swati Desai, acting executive deputy administrator, HRA, telephone interview, February 13, 2002; Seth Diamond, deputy commissioner, HRA, telephone interview, February 22, 2002.

11. Heather MacDonald ("Bloomberg's Test," 2002) credits Hoover with finding "creative ways to weave reciprocity and responsibility throughout the city's huge social service empire. As a result the city is in a far better position for weathering the post 9/11 downturn than had the welfare culture been left intact." As deputy commissioner, Hoover oversaw the internal operations of HRA and the interfaces between HRA and other city social services agencies.

12. Andrew S. Bush, Swati Desai, and Joanna Weissman, "New York City's JobStat Program: Managing for Performance in Large Welfare to Work Organizations," presented at the conference "Boosting Effectiveness in Urban Welfare Programs," Washington, D.C., July 19, 2000.

13. Leslie Eaton, "Worst Job Loss in a Decade," *New York Times,* March 6, 2002, B1. In 2002 and the first six months of 2003, additional job placements were reported.

"Despite the weakening economy, HRA helped its customers find a reported 133,645 jobs in calendar year 2002. In the first six months of 2003, HRA customers found an additional 30,242 jobs. Of those who found job, 79 percent were retained for three months and 69 percent were retained for at least six months. From January 2002 to June 3003, the welfare rolls were reduced by 37,613 people." City of New York, HRA "A Time for Examination, A Time for Discovery, A Time for Accomplishment." January 2002–June 2003 Progress Report, 2003, 6.

14. For a discussion of the advantages and disadvantages of vouchers in comparison to contracts for social services, see: E. S. Savas, "Competition and Choice in New York City Social Services," *Public Administration Review* 62 (2002): 82–91.

15. Lurie and Riccucci, "Changing the 'Culture' of Welfare Offices."

16. The link between management strategy and culture change was discussed by Louis V. Gerstner Jr., chairman and CEO of IBM, in an article in the March 10, 2002, *New York Times:* "You cannot talk a culture into changing. You've got to point to fundamental strategic changes in a company you are going to implement and then drive the execution of that strategy. And it is in the execution of that strategy that the culture begins to change." Steve Lohr, "He Loves to Win, At IBM, He Did," *New York Times,* March 10, 2002, Sec. 3, 1, 11.

17. Berlin interview, 2001; Gomez interview, 2001; Lurie interview, 2001.

18. See Starling, *Managing the Public Sector,* 482. He states that to effect culture change a manager should "overcommunicate," that is, provide a constant and pervasive message of the culture change to all employees.

19. Lurie and Riccucci, "Changing the 'Culture' of Welfare Offices," 666. The four states studied were Georgia, New York, Michigan, and Texas. The jurisdictions studied in New York were Albany County and Suffolk County. The study did not include New York City.

20. Bush, Desai, and Weissman, "New York City's 'JobStat' Program."

21. Berlin interview, 2001; Gomez interview, 2001; Angela Johnson, director, Euclid Jobs Center, telephone interview, October 23, 2001; Dianne Rabain, acting director, Fordham Job Center, interview, November 15, 2001; Patricia Smith, executive deputy commissioner, HRA, telephone interview, October 29, 2001.

22. The effectiveness of the JobStat process was apparent during my attendance at a JobStat meeting on August 23, 2001, at HRA headquarters.

23. Johnson interview, 2001; Rabain interview, 2001.

24. Kay E. Sherwood, telephone interview, February 14, 2002.

25. An official of Local 1549 told me that this union is in favor of the mission and goals of HRA to achieve self-sufficiency for clients. The union disagrees on implementation methods, including the new Job Opportunity Specialist (JOS) title. The union believes that job opportunity specialists make many more errors than when they were in their former titles because of the complexity of their new duties and a lack of training. The union believes that HRA has denied eligibility to persons who are eligible by applying unwarranted interpretations of eligibility rules or telling clients to seek other sources of aid before applying for benefits. The union believes HRA culture has changed and that it now embraces a "tough love" approach. Daniel Parsons, assistant to the president, Local 1549, District Council 37, telephone interview, November 13, 2001.

26. Data from Angela Sheehan of the HRA Office of Policy and Program Analysis, September 2003.

27. Amy Peterson, telephone interview, February 22, 2002; Virginia Cruickshank, senior vice president, Federation Employment and Guidance Service (FEGS), telephone interview, February 22, 2002.

28. Swiss, *Public Management Systems,* 317; Starling, *Managing the Public Sector,* 481.

29. Nina Bernstein, "New Clues Emerge on Mayor's Welfare Policy," *New York Times,* November 20, 2002, B3.

30. Lurie and Ricucci, "Changing the 'Culture' of Welfare Offices."

4

Protecting against Welfare Fraud

James Clark

When Mayor Rudy Giuliani assumed office in 1994, the welfare rolls in New York had reached new highs and the morale of the Human Resources Administration (HRA) had reached new lows.[1] One in four New York women and children were welfare recipients and the Safety Net Assistance (SNA) general-assistance program was out of control. With such a high proportion of the population receiving assistance, many New Yorkers questioned the eligibility of all who claimed a need for assistance. Compared to other areas of the country, why on a per-capita basis would New York have twice as many people needing welfare? Were providers who claimed to be providing assistance to recipients scamming the city and not providing the services for which the city was being billed? Were ineligible recipients receiving funds? Were the federal funds and state matching funds for recipients being appropriately distributed? Reforming welfare would be a principal task of the new administration and combating fraud was a key component of that effort.

In September 1993, just prior to the election, mayoral candidate Giuliani said in a speech that New Yorkers possessed a "sense of dread" that came from an acceptance of what Democratic Senator Patrick Moynihan had termed "defining deviancy down." Giuliani invoked the "broken windows" theory, popular among some criminologists, that ignoring minor crime paved the way for more serious crime. Intimidation by panhandlers and squeegee window-washers at traffic lights and an acceptance of minor drug dealers on street corners had to stop, Giuliani said, and he would stop it if he were elected mayor. Mute acceptance of dependency and welfare fraud were part of the problem.[2]

DIMENSIONS OF WELFARE FRAUD

Mayor Giuliani was sure to encounter resistance to any initiative that might be seen as an attack on the integrity or honesty of persons seeking or obtaining welfare assistance.[3] Although many Americans had heard of "welfare Cadillacs" and "welfare queens," based on the author's prior experience most welfare administrators in other states believed that welfare fraud was not widespread. We were to learn that the situation in New York was very different.

On February 2, 1994, in one of his first meetings with the media, the mayor outlined several initiatives that he thought would bring the budget back in line with projected revenues. He wanted to cut 15,000 employees from the city payroll, sell off the city hospitals, and cut a billion dollars from the city budget. Included in his plans was the fingerprinting of welfare recipients. Giuliani had received only 5 percent of the African American vote, and some in that community saw his attack on welfare as a form of retribution for their lack of support, inasmuch as four-fifths of welfare recipients were members of minority groups, primarily African American. City Councilman Enoch Williams, an African American, said, "This document jumps on the back of poor people."[4]

The homeless were omnipresent in New York's streets and subways, and the mayor's initiative to deal with them met stiff opposition from Norman Siegel, director of the New York Civil Liberties Union, and Mary Brosnahan, director of the Coalition for the Homeless. They never missed an opportunity to denounce the mayor and his administrators. The homeless were harassing pedestrians, and most New Yorkers had come to accept them as part of the misery of everyday life in the city; the mayor had not. The squeegee men soon disappeared after 75 of them were arrested. The homeless were rousted out of the subways and alcoves of buildings and were offered shelter. Panhandlers were cited for impeding the flow of traffic or for harassment.[5] Arrests for misdemeanors jumped from 90,000 in the year prior to Mayor Giuliani's election to 220,000 in 1994. Siegel saw the initiatives as criminalizing poverty, but he and the other advocates were marching against the wind. In 1995, at the mayor's urging, the city council passed additional laws to curb panhandling.

Although panhandling and homelessness were not the same as applying for or receiving welfare, they were linked. The mayor was living up to his promises and was bringing a new value system to the city. He called his critics "apostles of dependency" and defenders of the "old way of thinking."[6] He was particularly concerned about the city's unique welfare program for single persons. The Safety Net Assistance (SNA) program cost the city $1.9 billion a year and received no federal matching funds. Although other cities had "general relief" programs, most had eliminated them in the 1980s and

1990s as city and state revenues were stretched thin by growing federal programs that required matching funds. New York's program provided $325 a month to a single, unemployed person.

The mayor asked his staff to justify the existence of SNA and threatened to get rid of it. Richard Schwartz, a key advisor to the mayor, was assigned to investigate the program. Schwartz reported that the chances of fraud in the program were great, and he recommended that every applicant receive a home visit before becoming eligible for assistance. At a press conference the mayor announced the new home visit policy and said that HRA workers would begin visiting the homes of applicants and interviewing their neighbors and landlords.

In January 1995, following the elimination of a similar assistance program in Pennsylvania, the mayor stated that the city was intent on cutting back SNA and limiting assistance to 90 days.[7] He said the new application rules were designed to eliminate the cheaters who were giving honest recipients a bad name. Standing next to Governor George Pataki, the mayor said that the existing system was in effect urging people to "please come and take the money."[8] In a few months the approval of new applications for SNA fell from 65 percent of applicants to 40 percent, and millions of dollars were saved. Pataki and the mayor would work with the legislature over the next two years to try to rid the state of the SNA program, but the Democrat-controlled state assembly blocked their efforts.[9]

Welfare fraud took many forms in New York:

- A person would apply for welfare at different locations using different forms of personal identification, thus creating the impression that there were two different applicants. These heralded cases were often cited in the press and represented thousands of dollars in misspent tax dollars.
- Welfare workers created false cases and had checks for these fictitious persons sent to their own relatives or friends.
- People applying for assistance provided inaccurate information about their financial resources on their applications or failed to report changes in their financial situations. This not-uncommon type of fraud would occur when an applicant was actually working, but claimed not to be, or was earning more income from employment than he or she reported.
- An applicant or recipient received income from a third party and the income was not reported. This most often happened when a "significant other" moved into the household and became a second source of income for the family.
- Recipients and applicants failed to report income from other sources, such as a lottery, a lawsuit, or an inheritance.

Many who worked in welfare agencies, and the public advocates who spoke on their behalf, found the system so niggardly that serious efforts to uncover fraud—or "error" as it was called in social-work rhetoric—were seen as not in keeping with the values of social work. It was "understood" that it was almost impossible to live and support a family on the welfare stipend, and that for many welfare families getting money under the table or by working "off the books" as a day laborer or domestic was an acceptable "part of the game." Seldom was the idea discussed that by ignoring the issue, agency workers were sending clients the message that it was "OK" to cheat, and that the government really didn't expect them to behave differently.

Jason Turner, the architect of Wisconsin's welfare reform program, was recruited by Mayor Giuliani and appointed HRA Administrator and Commissioner of the Department of Social Services. He brought with him Mark Hoover as first deputy commissioner. In an interview with the author, Hoover said that when he first started working for HRA, he learned that the agency considered some welfare fraud acceptable. One advocate remarked in a meeting with Hoover that most people cheated on their income taxes, and what did Hoover expect given the small amount of assistance that recipients received? A May 1997 article in the *Village Voice* told of a woman who had ripped off the system for $1,100 when she failed to report that she had received a grant for $4,725 and a biweekly stipend of $325 and continued to draw welfare for herself and her out-of-wedlock child. The story was written sympathetically in a tone that implicitly endorsed the fraud and faulted the system for asking her to repay the money.[10] This was a striking illustration of Senator J. Patrick Moynihan's observation about "defining deviancy down," where the city's politicians and citizens had become inured to a pattern of deviant behavior, violent crime, and family disintegration, and considered them normal.[11]

Among welfare professionals it was commonly believed that many recipients worked in the underground economy or were self-employed and did not report their incomes. Nationally and in New York "no show" rates for mandatory work programs averaged 50 percent. Many welfare workers believed that the reason for noncompliance was that many recipients were already employed "off the books" and did not have the time to participate in mandatory work programs. They were engaged in fraud, but some recipients, advocates, and welfare workers rationalized it as an appropriate response to an inadequate amount of assistance. People who adopted this line of reasoning believed that welfare recipients would be working if they could and thus by not reporting income the recipients were only doing what was necessary.

In New York, if a person failed to complete a work assignment in the Work Experience Program, the Temporary Assistance for Needy Families (TANF) grant would be reduced by the amount of the grant for the one noncomplying member. This reduction was called "sanctioning," and almost half of all of the "engaged" TANF cases were sanctioned cases.[12] This strongly suggested that many of the welfare families were not complying with the work requirements because they didn't have time: They were already engaged in other activities or in work. They were making a conscious decision to forgo the full amount of the welfare check in return for the acquiescence of the welfare agency, which then looked the other way.

Some recipients worked in "uncovered employment" and did not report their pay. New York had a plethora of entrepreneurial street vendors who sold everything from watches to ties to gray-market videos and music. "Uncovered employment" was the vernacular used by the Department of Labor to refer to employment in which the employer skirts federal tax and payroll obligations. It is "day labor" or labor where there is no deduction for social security or unemployment insurance. People who were self-employed and did not file income tax returns or social security payments were also "off the books." They were "uncovered" in the sense that they were not covered by social security benefits and unemployment insurance.

Commissioner Turner saw part of the battle as changing the culture of HRA to produce more professionalism, accountability, and program integrity for both the staff and the recipients of assistance. He understood that to ignore or comply with fraud was to say to members of minority groups, who represented 80 percent of the city's welfare population, that they were somehow different and should be held to a lower standard than other Americans.

Turner and Hoover would become revolutionaries and start one of the largest public work programs for welfare recipients since the New Deal and the Works Progress Administration. But as their quest redefined the relationship of the city to its welfare recipients, it also set a new standard for accountability among welfare workers and the people receiving welfare. As one HRA staff member told me, "The issue was that we wanted to be responsive to the law and the need of the people we served. It was right for the recipients to be honest and it was right for us to ensure that we were meeting need and not greed!"

Turner recognized that some people were receiving assistance although they were not entitled to it. He wanted to avoid spending the city's limited tax resources on those who were not eligible, and he wanted program accountability. Ensuring that people applying for assistance were really eligible and recapturing monies misspent on those who were not eligible would become cornerstones of HRA policy.

Many states, when given the opportunity in the federal welfare legislation of 1996, had passed legislation that allowed for a "full family sanction"—the reduction of the welfare grant to zero for the whole family of a noncomplying recipient rather than just for the one noncomplying individual in the family. This approach was proving to be an effective tool in gaining compliance or, conversely, in reducing the number of families receiving assistance. States with full family sanction were in many cases experiencing reductions in their TANF caseloads of 60 and 70 percent. If people were not working and they depended on the TANF grant, they could be expected to comply with the work requirements. If they could not comply with the work requirement because they were already employed, it was irresponsible for government to support the dishonesty by providing any grant at all, even a lower amount.

In an interview, Commissioner Turner said that he believed the full family sanction was desirable, but he doubted that the state legislature in New York would support such a provision. A form of the full family sanction was operational in New York, however, in the Home Relief or Safety Net Assistance program. If a SNA recipient didn't show up for work, he or she was removed from the welfare rolls; because there was no other family member, the grant was stopped rather than merely reduced. Some HRA workers believed that although many recipients and applicants were working in the underground economy or worked as street vendors, many might be disabled by addiction or mental disease and as such were eligible for federal assistance through the federal Social Security Act.

ASSURING PROGRAM INTEGRITY

The Giuliani Administration initiated a number of efforts to contain and minimize welfare fraud. The changes resulted in the steepest decline in fraud in the history of the New York welfare system. The Giuliani Administration cut the number of welfare recipients by 60 percent, with the total number of recipients falling from 1.16 million at the peak in 1995 to 467,000 when he left office.[13] The efforts of the fraud and income-verification staff played a large part in paring down the number of recipients.

Verifying Eligibility for Assistance

A 1995 initiative to combat welfare fraud in Westchester County received a great deal of local and national publicity: The county welfare commissioner began face-to-face and in-house investigations of welfare applicants. According to Assistant Deputy Commissioner Peter Jenik, New York City had started a similar pilot program in the early 1990s and was encouraged by Mayor Giuliani to go ahead and implement the Westchester program throughout all the boroughs. The new initiative was called the Eligibility Verification and Review (EVR) system. A home visit to every applicant was unique; very few jurisdictions in the United States required continuous, 100 percent eligibility verification.

It was a method that was to prove particularly effective with the SNA population. As noted earlier, in New York a person without dependents could obtain assistance for himself through SNA. The program was aimed primarily at single men who were out of work and needed shelter, food, and medical care. The population was less stable than the AFDC (Aid for Dependent Children) or TANF population and tended to change addresses and employment frequently; therefore the program had the potential for abuse and fraud. Establishing eligibility through home visits and income verification for everyone would, it was thought, result in significant reductions in the Home Relief or Safety Net population. Indeed, the sanctioning rate for SNA recipients grew from 13.1 percent in the year ending July 1, 1994, to 30.2 percent in the year ending July 1, 1995.[14] According to Assistant Deputy Commission Jenik, 30,000 enrollees in the SNA program failed to appear when called in for interviews and were dropped from the rolls.

Many observers thought that the reason for the declining caseloads was the Work Experience Program (WEP), which required people to work in public service jobs in return for assistance. Others within the agency saw the crackdown on fraud as equally important. Jenik said that most people who left the Safety Net/Home Relief part of welfare since 1998 did so as a result of the EVR initiative. Eric Plasa, a director of EVR, estimated that more than half of the welfare reductions in since 1998 occurred as a result of the Eligibility Verification Review (EVR) unit and the policy changes made by the Giuliani Administration.

When Mayor Giuliani assumed office, the city had only about 200 investigators and support staff to address welfare fraud. Commissioner Turner and First Deputy Commissioner Hoover asked the mayor to expand the Bureau of Fraud Investigation and the Bureau of Eligibility Verification unit and to ensure that they had the necessary tools in terms of personnel and automation. In meetings with the mayor, the discussion turned on the issue of return on investment. EVR administrators could point to millions of dollars gained from a relatively small investment in investigative staff. For example, in the area of pharmaceutical fraud, the staff grew from two investigators per borough to seventeen. As a result of the impressive results, the size of the EVR staff grew from 200 to almost 1,700.

In the beginning the focus was on new SNA applicants. The EVR staff started in one borough and then expanded to the other boroughs. Later they checked the TANF applicants. Finally, in 1998, they widened their search to include all existing recipients; this changing population was checked in two cycles of eligibility verification. Thus there were three home visits for every welfare recipient: once at application and twice more between 1998 and 2000.

Regular visits to all existing clients were curtailed as investigators became more familiar with the characteristics most associated with fraud, and the EVR focused again on high-risk recipients. The computer matches with banks, credit lines, and new hire reports collected by the Labor Department gave clues as to which recipients and applicants were most likely cheating. If someone was reported as a new hire but there was no change in the grant amount, it was likely that the person had gone to work and not reported the change to HRA. This was reason for another home visit or a call to the person to come in for an interview with investigative staff. The new hire list and the unemployment wage file did not always work in uncovering unreported income, however. People who were self-employed, working off the books, or engaged in illegal income-producing activities had to be found through other methods. When an investigator saw that a person had good credit and was charging a good deal of money on his credit card, it was usually a good indication that the recipient had other income resources that were not being reported.

False documentation was another area that required fraud investigation. Eligibility workers were trained by the EVR staff to identify fraudulent documents. For example, birth certificate numbers issued by the state contained within the number a code that indicated the year of birth. An applicant or recipient who provided a birth certificate with a number that did not correspond to the person's birth year raised a red flag for investigators and police. This often happened while the person was still making application. "We did it on the spot," said Assistant Deputy Commissioner Jenik.

Matches were made with banks, credit agencies, the Department of Labor's unemployment wage files, vehicle registrations, and other sources to see if a person who was an applicant or recipient of welfare had assets or earnings that exceeded the eligibility criteria. Although many states and cities had similar systems in place, New York was unique in the emphasis on this function. The information gathered was then used in conjunction with face-to-face and in-house interviews to verify that the person receiving welfare aid was in fact entitled to it. Eligibility verification was done for TANF, food stamps, and Medicaid.

Home visits revealed that some welfare families received rental income by subletting rooms in their apartments. Others claimed to be paying a higher rent than they were actually being charged, making them eligible for a higher welfare grant, according to James Nelkin, director of the Office of Revenue and Investigation. In some cases, two people would claim the same residence and rent on different applications. In checking with the landlord, the rent amount would be correct, but the city was counting it twice because two people were claiming the same expense. In a strange way, the home visits were reminiscent of a bygone era when social workers went to the homes of people needing assistance and counseled them. The EVR visit helped restore some semblance of community values and a degree of probity in a system that accepted and even encouraged fraud through lack of oversight.

Nelkin believes that the system changed because of the administration's emphasis on welfare fraud and because the recipients who had cheated the system were now largely off the rolls: "We are now getting to a population where there is less fraud. They know we check and fingerprint and they self-selected themselves out of the system." He said his office was developing a data warehouse that would integrate information from several agencies and allow historical analysis of people applying for assistance. "A critical element of our success has been the cooperation that was received from other city agencies," said Nelkin. He considered the food stamp regulations prohibiting home visits to be a problem and the unavailability of income-tax information on applicants and recipients still a mountain to be climbed.

Mayor Giuliani was a breath of fresh air for the investigative staff. As a former prosecutor he appreciated the work necessary to make a case and gain a conviction. He also supported the notion that new staff members should have a background and training in law enforcement. Historically, one could become an HRA investigator without such qualifications; this changed under the former-prosecutor-turned-mayor. Under the new rules, job candidates were required to have a degree in law or criminal justice or three years of experience as an investigator in order to be considered for a position with the agency.

Jenik had been a New York City police officer and the head of a fraud unit for a major insurance company. He explained that it was important to have people with the proper education, training, and experience doing fraud and investigative work. He also pointed out that a special relationship with the NYPD, FBI, and Secret Service was necessary because the investigative staff had no arrest authority. "We could throw 20 people into an investigation," said Jenik. Trust between the agencies was facilitated because the personnel involved had similar backgrounds and respected each other.

Front End Detection (FED) badges issued to the investigative staff helped them in their work. This official identification helped when conducting investigations in housing projects or seeking information from landlords or others. The blue shield looked much like a NYPD detective badge, but Jenik said there had been no misuse of the badges by HRA employees. "The staff are aware that flashing the badges improperly can lead to dismissal," he said.

The cooperation between the Office of the State Attorney General and HRA's investigative staff was unusually good. In many jurisdictions, welfare fraud was not considered to be a major crime, and prosecutors were reluctant to use their limited resources for that purpose. In New York, however, people started going to prison for welfare fraud, and sentences of five to fifteen years were not uncommon. Jenik said that sometimes welfare fraud led to convictions in other areas like insurance fraud, narcotics, and various scams.

One HRA initiative resulted in a reduction of $1 million a month in Medicaid expenditures. Medicaid patients were getting prescriptions filled for growth hormones and bodybuilding drugs and then selling the drugs to people who worked out in the city's gyms. Once HRA cracked down on buyers and sellers, the number of prescriptions being written dropped dramatically.

Just before Mayor Giuliani assumed office, the small investigative staff was dismayed when Governor Mario Cuomo replaced the Electronic Benefit Transfer (EBT) card used for food stamps. EVR had developed an identification card that carried the person's photograph. In addition, the system required the person who obtained the food to sign a voucher attesting to the transaction. Federal food stamp officials had complained that it was offensive to require someone to sign and attest to the transaction, and the photo made it difficult for someone to send a family member to the store to get food. But the change from a photo ID card to one without a picture opened the door for criminal activity. The new card and redemption system failed to provide the evidence needed for convictions when someone traded their food stamp allotment for cash or drugs. In the absence of the signature, one needed to have photographs and other evidence to prove that the person using the stamps was an unauthorized user. Today's EBT card still suffers from this lack of accountability; given recent technological advances, the card could now carry an electronic picture and a credit/debit account of benefits.

According to EVR Director Laura McCullen, the new high-priority status given the unit, increased staffing, and improved technology were the primary reasons for its success. "Before Mayor Giuliani, we had little in the way of technology or support. We would have to get in a line to use one of the two vehicles assigned to the unit and even then the car might not be working," said McCullen. She added,

> [Now] we have computers that tie us to all of the resources that we formerly had to obtain manually and through friendships that we had with people that worked in other agencies such as housing, labor, or health. I can get on the computer now, gain access to the health department records, and ensure that the birth certificate in front of me is not a forgery. It is like night and day between this administration and the past in terms of professionalism and concern for the integrity of the program. We have more accountability for staff and customers.

McCullen went on to say that "Mr. Turner cared about how people were dressed and how they treated our customers. It impacted on how everything worked, and on how people related to each other."

Fingerprinting

Fingerprinting is an important element of EVR. As a welfare reform director in Florida and in South Carolina, I heard presentations by vendors of fingerprint imaging machines. These services were expensive and controversial, and administrators needed to ensure that taxpayers would receive a favorable return on their investment. I recall a comment by one vendor that although only one in 3,000 applicants would be found trying to cheat the system, the state would nonetheless save money because the number of people who applied for aid would fall by 3 to 5 percent. That's because some applicants for welfare assistance do not want to be fingerprinted and are willing to forgo their benefits if fingerprinting is required. This suggests that such applicants were wanted for some infraction. Given Mayor Giuliani's determination to reduce crime, this might have been even more important than catching people who were attempting to secure benefits at more than one location or in more than one state.[15]

New York City signed a fingerprint-imaging contract for $13 million, and the mayor's critics questioned the wisdom of the expenditure. A 1997 study suggested that it had not been cost effective in reducing fraud, but this study did not consider the value of reduced applications or the merit of catching wanted felons.[16] In fact, a search of the files of outstanding warrants in New York revealed that many people wanted by the police for other reasons were welfare recipients or applicants. As a result, more than 7,500 welfare recipients were taken into custody in New York, and an additional 1,750 wanted felons were taken into custody when they applied for assistance. Presumably this contributed to the large reduction in crime that occurred under Mayor Giuliani. So successful was the initiative, according to HRA Deputy Commissioner Albert Giove, that the NYPD officer in charge of warrants received a promotion and a larger staff.[17] The Boston Police Department sent buses and carted off two busloads of welfare applicants who had outstanding warrants in Boston and were caught when they showed up to claim welfare benefits in New York. According to Assistant Deputy Commissioner Jenik, much of this occurred when software changes enabled the different computer systems to "talk to each other." Fingerprint imaging would find expanded use with the passage of the 1996 federal welfare reform legislation, which had a clause that made it illegal for people who had outstanding warrants to receive welfare payments.

Third-Party Recovery

Another example of money recovered as the result of a new initiative of the Giuliani Administration involved people who had been injured by a third party and, as a result of the injury, obtained medical care and in some cases cash assistance from taxpayers. Often the person who was liable for the injury was insured. The insurance company, therefore, is a "third party" responsible for reimbursing taxpayers for HRA's expenses on behalf of the welfare recipient who was injured by the insured. It wasn't, however, until the Giuliani Administration that pursuit of the insurance companies became a priority. Liens in the amount of $35.5 million were placed on property and assets of people responsible for causing injury to recipients of TANF and

Medicaid in 2001. This was an innovation that reflected the real-world focus of the mayor and his experience as an attorney and prosecutor. He was upholding the mandate of his election that people should be responsible and that the government had a responsibility to make everyone who dealt with the city accountable.

Eligibility for Supplemental Security Income

First Deputy Commissioner Hoover believed that substantial savings could be realized if the city checked to see if individuals receiving SNA or TANF assistance were misclassified and could be eligible for Supplemental Security Income (SSI). If the cost burden were shifted to the federal government, both the city and the beneficiary would be better off. Social Security provided a higher level of payment to recipients than either the city's Safety Net Assistance program or the federal TANF program.

Applying SSI to the city's 28,000 HIV recipients could also achieve savings for local taxpayers. But the city had to find a way to have HIV-infected people apply for Social Security. The courts had ruled that people infected with HIV could not be subjected to the same eligibility criteria by virtue of local law, therefore they were outside the normal income-verification system. Unfortunately, aid recipients with HIV/AIDS had no incentive to change their benefactor from the state and city to the federal government. The public housing assistance they received was a key factor. Beneficiaries with HIV/AIDS didn't want the complications of dealing with two agencies. Hoover believed that it was in the interests of both New York and the city's HIV-infected population to work cooperatively on this issue. It would remain a challenge into the administration of Mayor Bloomberg and to the Congress as it considered renewal of the 1996 welfare reform legislation in 2003.

Welfare: A Loan, Not a Gift

Welfare payments are not a gift. In most states recipients have an obligation to repay the money if their circumstances change. The death of someone on public assistance should—but in the past did not always—prompt an effort to attach the estate of the deceased. In New York and in most states there are laws to recoup money from the estate of the former recipient. In most states one's home had not been considered an asset for purposes of eligibility, but it became an asset when the recipient died. The welfare application stated that the assistance being provided was recoverable from the estate of the recipient, but few states bothered to pursue the necessary legal actions because few welfare recipients ever had enough income to leave an estate. As welfare eligibility became more relaxed and allowable assets increased, however, it was becoming more likely that some individuals would have estates against which the state could make claims. Mayor Giuliani pursued this repayment, and in 2001 more than $11.6 million was collected from the estates of deceased beneficiaries.

Medicaid and Nursing Homes

Medicaid eligibility for nursing-home assistance represented a special case. Nursing-home care was very expensive and persons of moderate income could not make the payments needed for care of a loved one in the infirmity of old age. In addition, many middle-class people felt that long-term care should be covered by Social Security and were shocked to learn that it was not an included benefit. To pay for such care often would require that the couple spend its retirement savings, thus leaving a spouse in poverty. It also would mean that the couple had to spend the inheritance they had planned to leave to their children or grandchildren. In most states a person who sought to become eligible for Medicaid and nursing-home assistance could not do so unless his spouse was also indigent. Historically, parents often transferred their assets to their children or other family member to become eligible for Medicaid. (They have been called the "synthetic poor.") This allowed the spouse who remained at home to keep assets that were technically in the hands of their children. Congress addressed this issue and made it illegal to transfer resources within three years prior to entering a nursing home. Thus if people had bank accounts with savings or other liquid assets, they would have to "spend down" those assets until they became eligible to have Medicaid assume the nursing-home costs.

In New York, the legislature passed laws that allowed the spouse who had not entered a nursing home to retain up to $84,000. This relatively generous state policy made it worthwhile for the city to devote resources to recoup welfare payments from those with enough assets. Mayor Giuliani therefore expanded the Bureau of Fraud Investigation. People who obtained nursing-home care for their spouses but had more than $84,000 were pursued to an extent unlike that in prior administrations. In 2001 HRA obtained $9.7 million from people whose assets were greater than New York's $84,000 limit and whose spouses were in nursing homes.

The automated linkage with tax and bank information systems allowed the city to recover welfare funds that were obtained fraudulently. Face-to-face interviews and home visits with applicants were intended to thwart those who wanted to obtain welfare funding illegally. For example, some people might claim that they were living in private housing and paying a certain rent, when in fact they would be living in subsidized housing and not paying any rent. When records were checked and it was discovered that the person was not paying rent, they either became ineligible or eligible at a reduced payment level. In 2001, HRA collected $9 million as a result of litigation involving unreported income, concealed assets, and illegally transferred funds.

Medicaid

Medicaid in general and prescription drugs in particular now consume a major part of the Medicaid budget in New York and other states. The cost of prescription medicines to the state and the federal government has become the second most costly item in the Medicaid budget, exceeded only by inpatient hospital services. In one short decade, prescription drugs as a percentage of the Medicaid budget grew from 8 percent of the budget to 17 percent. New York City spent almost $1.5 billion dollars to provide prescription medicines to welfare recipients in 2001.

HRA took several steps to curb the spiraling costs of medical care for the indigent. The Prescription Drug Fraud unit grew from a staff of four investigators in the prior administration to forty. Working with state and federal officials, they identified $3.65 million in fraud and $500,000 in cost-avoidance for total savings of $4.15 million in 2001. This also resulted in 120 arrests and 183 case closings in the first months of the year.

Food Stamps

In 2001, the federal government sued the city for conducting an eligibility check on every applicant for food stamps or recertification. The U.S. Department of Agriculture's Food and Nutrition Service (FNS) argued that only people who were suspected of fraud should be checked. It was frustrating for Commissioner Turner to have a federal agency in Washington block the city's effort to reduce fraud and deny flexibility to state and local welfare administrators. HRA therefore discontinued inspecting people for food-stamp fraud and carried out home visits only on TANF/PA and Home Relief cases. Nevertheless, some people still would not go to the Fraud and Investigation unit to complete their food-stamp applications and thus were not receiving benefits; it appeared that the fear of being found guilty of some type of fraud related to TANF limited enrollment for food stamps.

The FNS for years had emphasized reducing the error rate. Special financial incentives were provided to the states that had the lowest error rates. For example, in 1996 South Carolina received a large check from the regional FNS administrator because its error rate was one of the lowest in the country.

But error-rate reduction is not synonymous with fraud detection or recipient employment. Error rate has two components, client error and administrative error. Error-rate oversight tended to focus on agency error and not on fraud. Administrative error could be a failure to calculate the correct grant amount and therefore paying too much or too little to the recipient. It could also result from not having referred a person to the state employment office. The oversight procedure was a bureaucratic quagmire, however, with volumes of regulations and monitoring that seemed to focus on process more than outcome. When I was appointed director of welfare reform for Florida in 1982, I visited several local application offices and examined some case records. I found copies of forms used to refer persons to the state Job Services offices. The forms had been filled out but remained in the file. I asked why they had filled out the form and not sent it on to Jobs Services and was told that the Department of Labor would not service the food-stamp referrals unless it was compensated financially. Nevertheless, FNS regulations required that applicants be referred, and if the form did not appear in the file when audited by FNS, it would constitute an error. Staff time and paper were being wasted because the regulations required it even though the intended activity couldn't occur! FNS, a federal agency, knew that when it released a report each year to local newspapers and television stations lamenting the high percentage of cases in error, it would embarrass the governor and his welfare commissioner. It was and continues to be a form of intimidation that undermines state–federal relations.

FNS has never focused on fraud by or employment of food-stamp recipients. The suit brought by FNS against New York was in keeping with an organizational culture that valued broad food-stamp coverage and an easy application process over fraud reduction and employment. I raised this point with Deputy Secretary of Agriculture for Food and Nutrition Eric Bost in the spring of 2002. He was formerly the social services director in Texas and he told me that he had a different job now, and it required a different approach. I interpreted his remark to mean that the powerful constituency groups that FNS dealt with, namely farmers, food distributors, grocery stores, and surplus-commodity food vendors, were not keen on limiting the number of recipients or the amount of food being distributed.

Client error represented about half of the state or city errors. Generally they consisted of unreported income or claiming family members that no longer lived in the household. The latter occurred when someone went to work or a family member left the household or died and the change in family circumstances was not reported. The money lost through agency error could not be recaptured because it was not the fault of the client. Client error was recoverable, but in most cases the recovery required by federal regulations would be a few dollars a month for many years. The vast majority of errors involved small amounts of money, less than a thousand dollars, which were seen by administrators as not worth the cost of recovery. Thus most client error was never pursued and clients understood that a little bit of fraud was acceptable.

HRA First Deputy Commissioner Mark Hoover believed that focusing broadly on reducing the error rate was a waste of time because it was determined primarily by the fraud rate. Only by reducing the fraud rate could you reduce the error rate. But the federal government either did not agree with this or agreed only that error could be pursued solely on the basis of other information that indicated that an investigation was warranted. As noted above, FNS interpreted federal law as precluding fraud prevention through blanket reviews. Only evidence of individual fraud could be used to initiate an in-home visit.

Child-Only TANF Cases

A "child-only" TANF case is one in which the recipient is a child abandoned or orphaned by the parents and left with a relative. The income of the caretaker is not counted and the state and city provided assistance on behalf of the child. In most states and cities it usually was assumed that child-only cases were not fraudulent. Caretakers were free to earn money and have their assets excluded from the eligibility limits because it was only the child that received the assistance. Some HRA staff were convinced, however, that some children were put in the care of a grandparent as a way of continuing assistance to people who became ineligible for TANF when their youngest child reached adulthood. Crack cocaine and alcohol were probably equally responsible for the number of children being raised by a grandparent.

In an innovative step, the city started checking the eligibility of child-only TANF cases. According to Albert Giove, deputy commissioner for revenue and investigation, the agency found one unusual case in which a child had $5 million in the bank as the result of a wrongful-death suit. The child's caretakers knew that the child was entitled to the money, but thought it could only be used when the child came of age. They did not understand that the funds could be put toward the cost of raising the child, including his housing and education. The outcome made everyone happy: The lives of the child and his caretakers were improved and the state was reimbursed for funds it had expended.

Public Housing

Public housing represented another area with great potential for fraud and, correspondingly, for productive investigative work by HRA. New York provides housing assistance to the majority of its welfare recipients, dispensing about twice as much aid to TANF cases proportionately as most states did. This is presumably due to the cost of housing in the city. According to Dr. Swati Desai, HRA deputy commissioner for research and planning, almost 70 percent of welfare recipients in New York received housing assistance in 2001. Assistance to such a large number of recipients was costly and required coordination with the New York City Housing Authority to assure that the recipients were entitled to it.

HRA was particularly affected by a court ruling requiring that housing assistance be provided to homeless people with HIV on the day of their request. People soon discovered that they could go in and claim they were homeless and HIV-positive and receive an immediate housing grant. One administrator told me that many Russian immigrants attempted to bilk the system by claiming to be homeless and HIV-positive when they were not. When housing records were checked it was discovered that 31 claimants were not HIV-positive, were not homeless, and in fact listed the same apartment as their residence. When called into the Fraud and Investigation unit, they admitted to the fraud and explained that they needed the money and this was an easy way to obtain it.

Although communication between the housing agency and HRA had been limited, Commissioner Turner saw a window of opportunity. If computer records between the two agencies could be matched, the potential for fraud could be reduced. This had been impossible because the software was incompatible. Changing the software to allow the two agencies to examine each other's records proved to be a significant step in reducing fraud.

State–City Coordination

Divided jurisdictional authority was another problem facing New York City. Much of the authority that the city needed to control waste and fraud rested with the state. Although the state granted the city limited investigative authority and worked with the city, some HRA administrators believed that more could be accomplished if the city had greater flexibility in its efforts to reduce fraud and waste. For example, in the case of Medicaid pharmaceutical fraud, the licensing function rested with the state. Controls that the HRA staff might have imposed on providers and their practices in order to reduce fraud were outside their jurisdiction. Still, with the additional resources provided by the mayor and time-tested approaches that examined such anomalies as spikes in billing or billing by a "mom and pop" pharmacy that was ten times the typical amount, the city was able to initiate investigations and recoup money.

If the city had authority to limit the number of pharmaceutical providers and require that providers be bonded for fraud, it is possible that more savings would accrue to both the city and state. For example, other states have employed a strategy to curb pharmaceutical costs that might be effective in New York. The city would need the discretion to require managed care providers (HMOs for Medicaid recipients) to control the cost of pharmaceuticals and limit the prescribing of brand-name drugs. When Florida limited the number of brand-name drugs prescribed by physicians to three from a list of preferred drugs, the state started saving $5 million a month. The Florida system requires that when the limit on brand-name drugs is reached, other prescriptions either have to be for generic drugs or require a telephone call to authorize deviation from the state policy. If New York were to impose a similar restriction, $50 million could be saved.

As an alternative, because all Medicaid is provided by managed care or health maintenance organizations (HMOs) in New York, the state should consider requiring HMOs to include the cost of pharmaceuticals in the capitated rate. Based on the experiences of other states where the managed-care contract includes the cost of drugs, it seems likely that the HMOs would be able to control the prescribing patterns of physicians better than the current system does. The Medicaid pharmaceutical budget in New York City exceeded $1.5 billion in 2001. Providers might be willing to contract for a lower price, knowing that they could control costs more easily than the state or city can. This would be a win/win/win solution, with patients continuing to get their medications, the city spending less, and HMOs increasing their profits.

Self-Enrollment After 9/11

The response of the city to the terrorist attacks of September 11, 2001, included a self-declaratory enrollment in Medicaid. Those who thought they were eligible could enroll in Medicaid for three months, and the city would check their eligibility later. According to Deputy Commissioner Hoover, 170,000 New Yorkers took advantage of this offer. Based on the current level of estimated average expenditures of $500 per household per month, this could cost the city $25 million dollars. Assistant Deputy Commissioner Jenik told me in late December 2001 that the city was initiating investigations into some of these Medicaid cases and would have most of the new cases reviewed in 2002. It will be interesting to other states and the federal government to know what degree of fraud, if any, occurred as a result of the city's acceptance of self-declarations in this tragic circumstance.

RECOMMENDATIONS

Great strides have been taken, but additional improvements are possible. The following changes should be considered as the city faces budget constraints and falling revenues:

- The city should examine current Medicaid pharmaceutical expenditures and study ways to reduce them. As mentioned above, one way is to amend managed care contracts to incorporate medicines as part of the capitated rate. A second is to seek an amendment in state law to limit the number of brand-name drugs or prescriptions that can be written without prior approval.

- The state should consider amending the current law to reduce the limit of $84,000 in assets that a family is allowed to keep if a family member is placed in a nursing home.

- The state and city should consider a full family sanction as part of their effort to reduce fraud. Under current law it is an option open to the state; however, in New York a person employed "off the books" can continue to receive a reduced TANF grant. The U.S. House of Representatives considered legislation that would require a full family sanction for noncooperating recipients in its 2003 debate on extending the 1996 welfare reform law of 1996.

- The state should consider eliminating the Safety Net Assistance program, which costs the city over $800 million a year. Most other major states and cities have abandoned this program, and Governor Pataki and Mayor Giuliani were probably correct in their initial inclination to eliminate it.

CONCLUSIONS

New York City under Mayor Rudolph Giuliani initiated a level of welfare oversight that was greater than that of any other state or local government in America. Welfare caseloads declined about 60 percent and substantial funds were recouped from those not entitled to welfare. The most significant elements of the new system included a staff increase from 200 to almost 1,700 investigators, home visits to all applicants and existing recipients, and aggressive prosecution of fraud. The new system forged new relationships and a sharing of information with other city departments to detect fraud. A special relationship with law enforcement agencies was created, and that relationship assisted in the capture or arrest of many individuals who were wanted by the police. Perhaps most importantly, there was a change in culture. HRA officials and line staff understood that the mayor supported them and that fraud of any kind at any level would not be tolerated. In May 1999, Vice President Al Gore presented the New York City administration and HRA with Washington's Hammer Medal for eliminating more than 1,000 fraudulent applicants from its disability rolls and saving a total of $15 million. Ironically, the vice president received overwhelming support in his subsequent bid for president from people who condemned Mayor Giuliani's welfare initiatives.[18]

NOTES

1. "NYS Welfare Rolls Continue to Lower: Smallest Population in 30 years," *Times Newsweekly*, September 7, 2000.

2. Andrew Kirtzman, *Rudy Giuliani: Emperor of the City* (New York: Harper-Collins, 2000), 55.

3. J. Browne, "Giuliani's Plan to End Welfare Meets Stiff Opposition," *New York Amsterdam News*, July 30, 1998.

4. Browne, "Giuliani's Plan," 76.

5. Browne, "Giuliani's Plan," 88.

6. Browne, "Giuliani's Plan," 173.

7. Reginald Patrick, "Public Assistance for Childless Adults to Change: Mayor Says the Program will be Gradually Reduced," *Staten Island Advance*, January 4, 1995.

8. Kirtzman, *Rudy Giuliani*, 172.

9. "Welfare Reform: Blocked in Albany," *Daily News*, July 7, 1997.

10. Robert Shulman, "Perpetrating a Fraud," *Village Voice*, May 6, 1997.

11. Kirtzman, *Rudy Giuliani*, 33.

12. New York City Department of Human Resources, "Weekly Engagement Report," August 7, 2001.

13. HRA, OPPA charts of trends in SSI recipients, food stamp recipients, MA enrollees in New York City, March 1995–September 2001, October 17, 2001.

14. Paul Moses, "Thousands Sanctioned Off Welfare," *Queens (New York) Newsday*, May 5, 1996.

15. "State OKs Workfare Drug Testing, Finger Printing," *Staten Island Advance*, June 11, 1997.

16. LynNell Hancock, *Hands to Work: The Story of Three Families Racing the Welfare Clock* (New York: HarperCollins, 2001), 84.

17. Hancock, *Hands To Work*, 83.

18. Hancock, *Hands To Work*, 85.

5

Managing the Welfare System with JobStat

Kay E. Sherwood[1]

When Mayor Rudolph W. Giuliani adopted welfare reform as a major policy thrust of his administration, he created the need for a suitable management information system. In 1998, New York City's Human Resources Administration (HRA) began to develop such a system to support the shift in the agency's mission from providing financial assistance to low-income people to assisting low-income people to become self-sufficient. HRA's information system, called JobStat, was modeled on CompStat, created by the New York City Police Department (NYPD) to provide accurate, timely information about crime in order to increase the department's effectiveness in preventing and reducing it. While policing and providing assistance to people in poverty are not much alike, the challenges of agency performance and staff accountability are, particularly on the scale of New York City's public services.

This chapter describes the system as it was in late 2001, about two and one-half years after JobStat had been up and running in HRA. It was written with managers of other public welfare agencies in mind—to help them consider whether JobStat is suited to their goals and organizations, and to help them anticipate issues in building and maintaining the JobStat approach to performance measurement and accountability. The chapter begins with a description of JobStat and its roots in the NYPD CompStat system. The main discussion takes up practical questions: Can JobStat be a tool for smaller welfare agencies? What are optimal organizational conditions for adopting JobStat? Which performance indicators should be selected? Who should be involved in system design? What has been learned in the New York City environment about data, data sources, and technology that might apply to other welfare agencies? How does JobStat unfold over time? An example of an actual JobStat report is included, as well as an appendix detailing performance indicators adopted for the third year of JobStat operation in New York City.

COMPSTAT INFLUENCES NEW WELFARE MANAGEMENT TEAM

Soon after arriving from Wisconsin in 1998, one of the first acts of newly appointed HRA Commissioner Jason Turner was to take his top managers to view a session of CompStat at NYPD headquarters. Even before Turner's arrival, CompStat had been credited with substantial crime reduction results under Mayor Giuliani and his first two police commissioners, William Bratton and Howard Safir. By 1998, at the beginning of the mayor's second term, major felony crimes in the city were at half their 1993 levels;[2] murder and non-negligent manslaughter declined 66 percent between 1993 and 1999.[3]

As Turner's team took their seats in the back of the cavernous room that was set aside for the regular CompStat sessions, it became apparent that this formal assembly chaired by the deputy police commissioner made the invited precinct commander and his patrol, detective, and narcotics team apprehensive about the questioning to come. Turner was later to use his presence at JobStat meetings, with a deliberate, structured formality similar to this CompStat scene, to convey to HRA field managers the importance and centrality of these reviews to the success of the agency's self-sufficiency mission; this heightened the anxiety attending the sessions, which in turn resulted in increased preparation for the sessions by both central and field office staff.

As the session at Police Plaza unfolded, the deputy police commissioner and headquarters staff relentlessly questioned the precinct commander over an apparent pattern of robberies within his district's main public housing project. Although the precinct commander asserted there were no connections, the headquarters team hammered away, asking about similarities in the robberies' time of day, the mode of operations, and other characteristics. The precinct commander, unable to satisfactorily answer, was left to agree that he would check arrest records, outstanding warrants, juvenile crime records, and other clues to help narrow the possibilities and bring an end to the crime spike.

What impressed Turner most about CompStat was not primarily its use of data, then considered one of the signature characteristics of this crime-fighting system. Rather, it was the fact that a huge government agency had managed to assemble all of the elements of its multifaceted machine in one physical location with the singular purpose of finding solutions to advance its mission of fighting crime. This was contrary to Turner's experience in government, in which it was typical that large agencies lose their ability to focus as day-to-day leadership and energy are exerted by the agency's component subparts (e.g., the welfare eligibility section or the information technology unit). Each of the component parts of a large government organization usually has a function defined narrowly enough to be understood and acted upon by its leaders and employees, although these narrow functions do not necessarily add up to the best advancement of the agency's overall mission. (For this reason Wisconsin's W-2 welfare reform, designed and led by Turner prior to his HRA appointment, had broken up its large Milwaukee operation into smaller manageable parts and privatized the operations.) CompStat showed the HRA team how it might develop a system of management that could transform the agency's actions right down to the worker level to align them with the overall agency mission.[4]

WHAT IS JOBSTAT?

JobStat is a system that encompasses the collection and analysis of information about essential functions and outcomes of welfare reform and the production of performance indicators and their use by welfare agency managers and staff, from the chief agency executive to line supervisors. JobStat is also a tool to educate, focus, and empower welfare agency managers and staff and to hold them accountable for the results of their work. As Andrew Bush, the principal architect of JobStat, described it, "The point is being able to take policy objectives and make them effective on the street. JobStat involves every manager at every level looking at the same indicators of the most important agency operations and outcomes of the agency mission in order to determine current status, trends, and problems and discuss solutions."[5]

The JobStat system has these key elements:

(1) A series of reports, produced on a regular schedule, that display timely, updated performance indicators for each agency unit—called "Job Centers" in New York City—that has responsibility for directly providing services to welfare clients. (In 2001, there were 27 Job Centers and three units managing special cases citywide.)

(2) A regularly scheduled meeting in which Job Center managers discuss their performance indicators with higher-level agency managers, identifying operational problems and solutions and resources they need to improve their performance. At HRA, two of the approximately thirty

Job Center managers reviewed their centers' performance at each
weekly meeting with the commissioner and his top aides.
(3) An automated database that is fed data items from appropriate automated and manual sources, and software programs that generate Job-
Stat performance indicator reports and change them as needed.

These three elements are the bare bones of the JobStat system. Over time,
HRA developed several enhancements, including:

(4) A system of reports and forums for frontline workers, called Center-
Stat, that disaggregates Job Center performance data to groups of
frontline workers and to individual workers; these disaggregated indicators are the basis for regularly scheduled meetings of managers and
staff within Job Centers.
(5) A system of performance indicators for vendors that provide services
to the agency's customers—services that are on the "critical path" for
better performance of the Job Centers. As with the JobStat parent system and CenterStat offspring, VendorStat involves data collection and
analysis, regular production of performance indicators, and regularly
scheduled discussion with agency managers.
(6) A data "warehouse" intended to enable the users of JobStat data, especially users within Job Centers, to produce their own reports without
relying on the central office team of technicians who are responsible
for producing JobStat reports used by agency managers.

JobStat as an effective management tool entails additional—essential—
capacities and resources, including:

(7) A cadre of people who provide technical assistance to the users of the
performance indicator reports, particularly the managers and supervisors of the Job Centers.
(8) A top-level agency team that focuses on goals for overall agency and
Job Center performance, provides the resources necessary to improve
performance, and identifies and implements policy-level solutions to
performance problems of the Job Centers.
(9) A system of incentives for rewarding good performance and addressing poor performance that encompasses compensation, assignments,
staff size, training, material enhancements for Job Centers, recognition, and other valued aspects of work.

Arguably, JobStat also encompasses a tenth element: automated case
tracking systems that enable and require HRA frontline staff to keep up with

what work-related activities are mandated, scheduled, and fulfilled by each adult who receives aid.

The bare-bones JobStat system is a natural one for introducing accountability because it makes Job Center performance transparent. With enhancements, accountability and transparency are extended to the level of frontline worker groups, individual workers, and vendors. The JobStat management tool increases the capacity of Job Center managers and staff to improve their units' performance once it has become transparent.

Jack Maple was the creator of NYPD's CompStat system. His version of how such a system works is, "[A] Comstat meeting is a way of sharing crime data that recognizes why the first step to crime reduction itself—the gathering and analyzing of accurate, timely intelligence—has to be quickened by the heat of accountability."[6] Substitute "welfare and employment data" for "crime data" and "the first step to increasing self-sufficiency" for "the first step to crime reduction itself" and the description fits JobStat.

SITTING IN ON A JOBSTAT SESSION

All of the elements of JobStat outlined above, from data and performance indicators to the use of a top-level team, come together once a week for a JobStat session in a specially designated "Situation Room." Each session is the culmination of one week's work culling and preparing performance data by central office staff, reviewing reports, and preparing questions. The central office efforts are matched or exceeded by the staff of the local Job Centers that are "on" for that week. At the Job Center level, performance indicators are reviewed in comparison with other Job Centers, with the borough and the city, and answers are prepared to the central office questions that can be anticipated.

The Situation Room is a large room on the commissioner's floor of HRA headquarters in lower Manhattan, which has computer connections with HRA's main information system and the ability to display on a wall screen any automated report or file, from citywide caseload trends to activity within an individual case file. A systems technician familiar with all aspects of the system's records projects on the screen data relevant to whatever inquiry or conversation is taking place in the meeting.

Attending the meeting from headquarters are the HRA commissioner or his designee, the head of the agency's policy and research staff,[7] and all the top operations officials. In addition, representatives from central support functions, such as facilities, systems, and equipment, also frequently attend so that any shortcomings in these areas identified in the discussions can be immediately addressed. From the Job Centers (i.e., field staff), the Job Center director and his or her top staff are in attendance. Finally, the private employment and training vendor(s) that provide services to Job Center clients participate when their Job Center contract managers are being reviewed. Usually, about twenty people participate in a JobStat session.

The head of the Office of Policy and Program Analysis chairs the meeting and leads the questioning; responding are the heads of the Job Centers being reviewed. Information on the performance charts for the specific Job Center usually precipitate the initial questions. (See table 5.1, for example, which is an abbreviated version of the weekly JobStat report on the performance of a particular Job Center, and see appendix for definitions of the entries.) These reports track the performance of the Job Center against specific targets, reviewed against trends, other Job Centers in the region, and the city as a whole. The questioning often takes the form of asking the Job Center director and staff to explain "outlier" indicators, either positive or negative ones. For instance, the questioner may ask why a Job Center has had reduced job placements over the most recent period or has been unable to assign many of its new recipients to work activities within the time allotted. This questioning leads to operational discussions, with the Job Centers often identifying problems that both sides then discuss.

After discussions with the Job Center staff, the employment and training vendor usually participates in similar questioning, and often discussions turn to process inefficiencies that need resolution, for example, proper referrals from the Job Center to the vendor or the swift processing of employment information necessary for the vendor to be paid on its performance contract.

JobStat sessions usually end with a list of action items for improvement that headquarters and field office each take away. For the Job Center, the JobStat issues raised form the basis for subsequent CenterStat sessions at the Job Center in which center supervisors participate in reviewing and understanding the results of the JobStat review. The Job Center director plays the role of host, with group supervisors in the role of operations heads. Finally, supervisors themselves may bring back to their groups questions that need addressing and ideas for future improvement.

WHO NEEDS JOBSTAT?

JobStat fits particular welfare agency circumstances: when there is a need to shift from a procedural model of service delivery, in which compliance with procedures and efficiency matter most to performance, to an outcome-oriented model in which judgments are required by line workers and supervisors, and what matters most to performance is deep understanding of overall agency goals and of how different operations affect one another. Specifically, JobStat was created to support a shift from welfare as an eligibility-based system of financial assistance—in which determination of eligibility and accurate calculation of benefits and timeliness were of greatest importance—to a system intended to leverage financial assistance to move the client in the direction of self-sufficiency. This shift entailed, at all levels, knowledge growth, knowledge utilization, organizational structure, staff competencies, and staff values and beliefs.

Who needs JobStat? Public welfare agency executives who seek to transform their organizations into flexible "learning organizations" that can (1) deliver services that require frontline worker and supervisor judgments consistent with overall agency goals; and (2) identify performance problems and solutions at the front line, and initiate communication about these to improve the whole system.

Does the size of a welfare jurisdiction matter? The designers of JobStat noted that size and centralized management have gone together:

> Since traditional welfare programs stressed accurate benefits management and uniform case treatment, larger welfare jurisdictions usually developed highly centralized management and program support structures—characteristics that in the old welfare world offered economies of scale. However, helping people achieve self-sufficiency requires creative and responsive local administration.[8]

Nevertheless, the utility of JobStat is *not* limited to large welfare agencies, according to Andrew Bush, executive deputy administrator of HRA and principal architect of JobStat.[9] JobStat is a tool to manage complexity born of multiple interconnected processes, particularly in organizations with multiple goals. A welfare agency of almost any size could benefit from JobStat because the process of assisting low-income people using public funds is extraordinarily complex. Different rules govern cash assistance, food stamps, medical assistance, work efforts on the part of aid recipients, and child care, but coordinated agency activities are required for each recipient. Further, welfare agencies must manage a dynamic caseload both because the individual circumstances of people receiving assistance are changing, which affects the amount and types of assistance provided, and because the universe of people the agency must keep track of is always changing.

The task of improving self-sufficiency adds to the complexity of managing welfare agencies of all sizes because it requires more local intelligence, local solutions, and local information while keeping track of the global picture of welfare reform. There is no formula for how to achieve the self-sufficiency goal. There are resources and levers that must be managed by direct service workers and their supervisors, using their judgment, within certain bounds. HRA Commissioner Jason Turner said about the task of improving self-sufficiency: "It's a craft." When craft work is at the heart of an agency's operations, the ability to pinpoint where it seems to be more successful and where less successful is crucial to improving overall agency performance. JobStat offers this capability.

Table 5.1. Typical JobStat Report

WAVERLY (13) JOB CENTER

JobStat Report, Index 2.0   **April, 2001**

	A	B	C	D	E	F	G	H	I	J
Director: Jerry Eberts				Cases		6,540				
Since: December, 2000				Engagables:		3,908				
Deputies: Joan Bridges				Active SI		791		%FA	%FA Egbl	%SI
SAP Vendor: Curtis since July 2000						Center		38%	44%	11%
Region Managers: Priscilla Ganoe						Borough		64%	66%	6%
Dpty Rgn Mgrs: J. Philip; P. Howard; H. Anne						Citywide		67%	70%	5%

			Center							
			Actuals			**Performance Relative to Goals**				
		Apr - 01	3Mo. Avg	YTD Avg	2000 Avg	Apr - 01	Rk	3 Mo.	YTD	RK
Index 2.0 Score						**31.5**	**11**	**31.9**	**29.4**	**11**
Employment				INDEX SUBTOTAL:		**10.4**	**21**	**14.1**	**13.3**	**17**
PLACEMENTS			Weekly Average							
1. Closed for Earnings		20.3	22.8	20.6	19	54%	12	70%	58%	12
2. Not Opened for Earnings		2.3	2.3	2.4		3%	11	30%	26%	3
3. Budgets Completed		12.0	14.1	16.5	9	1%	26	10%	21%	23
4. Qual. Reported Placements		31.0	34.8	32.9	27	48%	16	62%	57%	14
RECIDIVISM										
5. Recidivism Rate - 3 Mo.		39.5%	29.6%	28.9%		0%	27	0%	0%	20
6. Still Off PA at 3 Mo.		10	15	18	56	0%	28	16%	23%	18
7. Recidivism Rate - 6 Mo.		37.4%	32.8%	33.6%		0%	14	0%	0%	18
8. Still Off PA at 6 Mo.		21	14	13	56	43%	14	14%	9%	22
Administrative				INDEX SUBTOTAL:		**19.7**	**2**	**17.0**	**15.6**	**4**
TIMELINES										
9. PA Ap Timely Rate	Feb	65.0%	88.3%	91.3%	95.8%	0%	23	0%	0%	11
10. FS Ap Timely Rate	Feb	100%	99.3%	99.5%	99.2%	100%	1	78%	83%	5
11. Overdue FFR		5	8	16	14	24%	3	0%	0%	10

			Center							
			Actuals			**Performance Relative to Goals**				
		Apri - 01	3Mo. Avg	YTD Avg	2000 Avg	Apri - 01	Rk	3 Mo.	YTD	RK
ERROR RATES										
12. WMS 16-Day Err. Avg.		1	1	1	4	92%	10	90%	91%	4
13. WMS Total Error Avg.		124	116	143		60%	12	70%	60%	7
14. FA $ Error Rate (FFY)	Jan	0.0%	3.4%	3.4%	2.3%	14%	7%	14%	14%	7
15. FS $ Error Rate (FFY)	Jan	5.2	7.4%	7.40%	8.8	7%	9	7%	7%	9
PROCESS/FAIR HEARINGS										
16. M A SD-Ref. Rate										
17. Access Spot Viol.		0	0.0	0	0.0	100%	1	100%	100%	1
18. FH Request Rate	Mar	4.0%	3.9%	3.80%	4.0%	25%	12	28%	30%	15
19. MDR Impact Rate	Mar	55.8%	66.1%	64.2%		60%	15	77%	74%	9
20. MDR Client Accept Rate	Mar	47.4%	43.4%	41.4%		46%	7	39%	36%	2
21. FH Withdrawl Rate	Mar	7.4%	6.1%	7.00%		0%	26	0%	0%	25
22. FH Reversal Rate	Mar	11.7%	14.6%	14.7%		89%	4	69%	69%	7
23. FH Win Rate	Mar	80.9%	79.3%	78.4%		44%	7	37%	34%	11
24. PA FH Comply Rate	Mar	99.0%	95.7%	95.1%	89.6%	90%	5	57%	51%	6
25. FS FH Comply Rate	Mar	100.0%	100.0%	96.4%	88.0%	100%	1	100%	64%	13

WAVERLY (13) JOB CENTER

JobStat Report, Index 2.0   *April, 2001*

	K	L	M	N	O	P	Q	R	S	T	U	V
Over 48		**Center**		**Citywide**	**Center Job Goal**			3,769	Pvty Rt:		*13%*	
Months		1140	17%	69,047	35%	*Job Placements Toward Goal*			%Blk:		*14%*	
		Weekly Vender Referrals				In Apr	YTD	Cumulative YTD	%Hisp:		*25%*	
		Apr-Appl	Under	YTD	Center	3%	15%	577	%White:		*5%*	
SAJP		94%	1	74	Borough	3%	16%	3,699	%Other:		*2%*	
ESP			54	39	Citywide	3%	16%	23,864	%Unknown:		*54%*	

	Region				**Citywide**				**Index**			
	Performance Relative to Goals				**Performance Relative to Goals**				**Center Thresholds**		**Center Points**	
	Apr - 01	3 Mo.	YTD	2000	Apr - 01	3Mo.	YTD	2000	Low	Excel.	Apr - 01	Avail
	23.6	**18.3**	**17.1**	**27.1**	**18.7**	**18.0**	**17.5**	**26.1**			**31.5**	**100**
	10.7	11.6	11.9		11.9	13.2	13.6				10.4	45
1.	43%	46%	43%		45%	51%	49%	57%	9.8	29.3	3.8	7
2.	9%	16%	14%		2%	5%	6%		1.9	14.0	0.1	3
3.	14%	19%	26%	45%	18%	22%	30%	52%	11.7	36.7	0.1	5
4.	45%	52%	51%	4%	50%	56%	56%	24%	15.6	47.7	4.8	10
5.	0%	0%	0%		0%	0%	0%		25%	5%	0.0	6
6.	8%	17%	24%	11%	16%	30%	35%	18%	11	36	0.0	6
7.	0%	0%	0%		0%	0%	0%		30%	10%	0.0	4
8.	43%	17%	15%	25%	46%	24%	19%	31%	10	35	1.7	4
	9.7	5.3	4.4		4.2	3.3	2.7				19.7	40
9.	0%	0%	0%	64%	0%	0%	0%	0%	95%	100%	0.0	2
10.	0%	0%	0%	78%	0%	0%	0%	3%	97%	100%	2.0	2
11.	0%	0%	0%	0%	0%	0%	0%	0%	7	0	0.9	4

	Region				**Citywide**				**Index**			
	Performance Relative to Goals				**Performance Relative to Goals**				**Center Thresholds**		**Center Points**	
	Apri - 01	3 Mo.	YTD	2000	Apri - 01	3 Mo.	YTD	2000	Low	Excel.	Apr - 01	**Avail**
12.	86%	0%	0%	54%	0%	0%	0%	0%	12	0	3.7	4
13.	63%	46%	38%		18%	0%	0%		240	48	2.4	4
14.	0%	0%	0%	0%	0%	0%	0%	0%	4%	0%	0.1	1
15.	0%	0%	0%	0%	0%	0%	0%	0%	8%	0%	0.3	4
16.									80%	100%	0.0	2
17.	100%	100%	92%	87%	100%	99%	94%	83%	1	0	1.0	1
18.	22%	24%	26%	15%	10%	15%	19%	6%	5%	1%	0.1	0.5
19.	48%	59%	61%		72%	71%	73%		20%	80%	0.6	1
20.	8%	9%	11%		10%	3%	2%		20%	80%	0.7	1.5
21.	8%	14%	18%		29%	20%	16%		5%	0%	0.0	1
22.	15%	3%	8%		8%	20%	21%		25%	10%	0.9	1
23.	11%	5%	9%		11%	16%	16%		70%	95%	1.3	3
24.	0%	0%	0%	0%	0%	0%	0%	0%	90%	100%	3.6	4
25.	76%	64%	30%	0%	45%	32%	5%	0%	90%	100%	2.0	2

THE ORGANIZATIONAL CONTEXT

JobStat supports the changes needed to reform welfare, but it would be a marginally effective tool for most welfare agencies if nothing else changed. As Peter Senge observed about how structure influences behavior, "When placed in the same system, people, however different, tend to produce similar results."[10] In New York City's public welfare system, organizational changes were needed to create a decentralized structure in which local intelligence, local solutions, and local information could be harnessed to achieve centrally determined goals for increased self-sufficiency of the welfare population. Other welfare agencies interested in developing a JobStat performance monitoring system need to look at their own organizations with the following principles in mind.

Congruent Boundaries of Responsibility and Accountability

In order to establish and enforce accountability effectively, the boundaries of responsibility in a welfare reform agency must encompass the systems and resources needed to produce desired outcomes. In other words, responsibility and authority must be coterminous. In the development of JobStat, VendorStat came about because Job Centers were accountable for the performance of people outside their responsibility, that is, the vendors. VendorStat is a tool that enables Job Center managers to hold vendors accountable to them, making the Job Centers' boundary of responsibility coterminous with its sphere of accountability.

Public welfare agencies have gone back and forth since the 1960s between two organizational models for providing assistance: (1) an integrated model in which financial assistance and other services for clients were managed within the same organizational units, often by the same generic case worker or case manager who was assigned responsibility for assisting individual low-income people with all or most of their needs; and (2) a "separation of services" model in which financial assistance was provided by eligibility and income maintenance specialists apart from and independent of services intended to increase work and self-sufficiency or to address mental health, medical, parenting, child health, or other personal problems. With the introduction of TANF's consequential work and self-sufficiency goals, the separated model has major disadvantages for managing individual cases, particularly because, under TANF, welfare grants are a stronger-than-ever lever for work effort by recipients of aid.

Before 1998, New York City's HRA had a division of financial assistance with local direct service offices responsible for determining the eligibility of applicants for aid within a geographic area and for continuously assuring that the benefits provided to eligible people were consistent with the rules, that is, until the people served were no longer eligible. HRA had a separate division, with separate local offices covering separate geographic areas, responsible for providing employment services and enforcing work require-ments for all applicants and recipients of aid who were determined "employ-able." These two agency divisions were merged at about the same time JobStat was introduced; jurisdictions, or "boundaries of responsibility," were reorganized so that one local office under one office director controlled both the resources and the levers available to increase self-sufficiency among its geographically defined population. Along with this structural change, a significant name change was made: Income Support Centers became Job Centers. Once one local office under one director had both responsibility and the means to affect performance, accountability for results could be pin-pointed.

The equivalent policing solution is "unity of command." In the New Orleans Police Department, where Jack Maple worked after he left the NYPD, the organizational structure problem was one of separate commands and reporting lines, for uniformed patrol, detective, and narcotics divisions. Maple described this situation as typical for police organizations:

> Detectives and Narcotics worked downtown and answered only to themselves. If a district commander had a serious problem with a violent drug crew, he had to petition headquarters for help and then sit and wait until Narcotics got around to it. But Narcotics didn't set priorities the way a district commander would. They tended to judge jobs according to how strong a case they could develop and how many guns and drugs they could throw on a table when their seemingly never-ending investigation was done.
>
> The detectives didn't even have desks in the districts. A district commander might have concerns that a recent homicide could spark a series of retaliation shootings, but if the original homicide wasn't a priority downtown, there was nothing the commander could do to speed the investigation.[11]

The unity of command approach put together teams of detectives, narcot-ics officers, and patrol officers under the command of a borough commander (in New York City) or precinct captain to address a particular local problem. The centralized specialists were given temporary or permanent assignments that were borough- or precinct-based, that is, geographically determined.

Stable Management and Supervision

An effective performance accountability system requires relative stability in the assignments of management and supervisory personnel. If the people responsible for producing results are changed too frequently, they can neither put their mark on the work of their units, nor take credit (or be blamed) for the unit's performance.

The advantages of stability have to be weighed against the need to reward good performance and punish poor performance, which often means promoting people out of their previous responsibilities, moving effective managers to units that need improvement, and moving ineffective managers out of the agency or at least out of key roles.

Stable Goals and Priorities

Relative stability of goals and priorities is also necessary in an effective performance accountability system. Predictability supports incentives for high performance, maximizes learning throughout the agency about what improves performance, and enables executives to gauge the capacities of the managers and units responsible for achieving the goals. Rapidly changing goals can result in rapid changes in operational direction that confuse what is being learned about causes and effects. Rapidly changing goals can also make success look to staff like a moving target, contributing to frustration and a sense that there is no way to succeed, and thus dampening initiative and enthusiasm.

For the first year of JobStat implementation, HRA adopted a single agency goal as the focus of operations and performance reporting and kept the focus of JobStat reports, meetings, technical assistance, and the operations of the Job Centers on that goal until it was achieved. (The goal was to reduce the number of "unengaged" recipients of aid to zero, which is discussed below.) In the second year of JobStat implementation, HRA adopted another goal— 100,000 job placements; with the same concentrated effort, it was achieved and exceeded by the end of the year. At the same time a single agency-wide goal was being worked on, the JobStat system developed and tracked ten major indicators of performance, which measured the efficiency and effectiveness of the processes that affected achievement of the primary goals. (By 2001, 32 indicators were being tracked.)

The principle of stable goals and priorities has to be weighed against the need to respond to new circumstances. In welfare agencies that have historically been crisis oriented—like New York City's HRA—it is difficult to establish effective management of day-to-day operations and sustain a focus on achieving high performance in those operations if managers and staff are diverted to handle other problems. An organizational approach for responding to new circumstances while keeping the whole organization focused on the principal goal is to create special teams and bring in outside resources to develop solutions. Following the NYPD's model for responding to what chiefs learned from CompStat, HRA practiced "rapid deployment" strategies both to manage short-term situations and to create and introduce fixes for long-standing problems.

Structures that Maintain Consistent Focus in Crisis-Driven Environments

Welfare agencies with multiple and divergent goals need to be structured to ensure consistent management focus on performance in each area, particularly to not let the high-profile, crisis-driven programs undermine progress in lower-profile functions.

One reason that some organizations are constantly fighting fires is that fires are constantly erupting, and responding to fires is part of their responsibility. For example, some public agencies responsible for administering TANF are also responsible for protecting children from abuse and neglect, ensuring the safety and quality of publicly subsidized child care, and providing housing and services to the homeless. Child protection responsibilities, in particular, tend to draw top-level managers into crisis management because of the media attention to fatalities resulting from abuse or neglect. In large urban areas, the situations of homeless people can get dangerous and generate headlines overnight as a result of a single incident or the onset of cold weather. Welfare operations, on the other hand, are not usually incident driven or dramatic enough to interest the mass media and, thus, tend to be neglected by welfare agency executives when crises in other areas of responsibility erupt.

HRA shed responsibility for child welfare, child care, and homeless services in the 1990s, which probably enhanced its ability to focus on engaging recipients of cash assistance in work-related activities and moving them toward self-sufficiency. A former HRA Deputy Commissioner for Management Planning David Butler observed, "When HRA did all those other things, it was impossible to keep top-level managers' attention on one area for long."

WHICH PERFORMANCE INDICATORS MATTER?

Performance indicators for welfare reform, and for JobStat specifically, are founded on a conception of the work as case "flow" into and out of the agency's purview. People needing help come to the welfare agency, which then processes them through a series of steps that leads to their becoming self-sufficient and no longer in need of help; that is, they are no longer cases. This is fundamentally different from "servicing a case" in the pre-reform world of income maintenance, which entailed processes to stay on top of changing client circumstances, but not necessarily processes to change those circumstances. Generally, then, good performance in welfare reform means smoothing the flow, reducing the volume of the flow onto welfare, and increasing the rate of flow off welfare.[12]

To enhance performance in these terms, managers of welfare agencies interested in developing a JobStat performance monitoring system should choose

- indicators that reflect important management objectives and strategies,
- indicators of "critical path" activities, and
- indicators of performance in administering financial assistance.

Indicators that Reflect Important Management Objectives and Strategies

HRA executives chose to use "unengaged cases" as their first principal performance indicator in JobStat, with the objective being to "engage" everyone. (The technical definition of "engagement" is complicated, but essentially reflects a combination of efforts by the agency and efforts by applicants and recipients of aid to increase work or take steps toward self-sufficiency.) The decision to focus on this indicator of agency performance was motivated by three factors:

(1) The need to "get a handle on the caseload," that is, to understand who the recipients were in terms of their longevity, their employability status, and their actual work-related capabilities and issues. The agency's multistep process of attempting engagement with everyone was expected, first, to increase work among recipients, but second, to discover what resources would be needed to achieve self-sufficiency goals, such as job-training programs and substance-abuse treatment programs. (Although JobStat did not include major indicators of welfare "diversion," a substantial amount of agency effort went into new and more active upfront procedures for working with applicants to identify alternatives to welfare and then a more stringent Eligibility Verification Review [EVR—see chapter 4] to ensure that those who wished to apply for welfare were truly without resources.)

(2) The desire to make a policy statement that, in exchange for publicly funded benefits, all recipients of aid would be required to work or make other efforts toward self-improvement and self-sufficiency. Only temporary, clearly defined pauses in activity by aid recipients were expected and accepted.

(3) The need to "get a handle on the Job Centers" and to demonstrate to frontline staff and supervisors that it was neither inevitable nor acceptable that people would "fall through the cracks" of the system of obli-

gations. Historically, HRA and other large welfare agencies were known for their tendency to engage aid applicants and recipients once, assess and classify them, and then neglect to track or respond to their changing circumstances with respect to employment.

The process of working through exactly what engagement meant in New York City's welfare system also helped in refining the JobStat management information system, one purpose of which was to enable agency staff and managers to know at all times the status of every applicant and recipient of aid in relation to financial and work-related requirements. Table 5.2 is a citywide "Engagement Report" from JobStat for the week of July 9, 2001. It presents, with explanations, the number of cases and percentage of active cases that are engaged and unengaged in categories according to the situations or activities that define their status as well as cases that are temporarily or indefinitely unengageable.

The bottom line of table 5.2 is zero cases unengaged out of about 223,000 active cases. The JobStat method of accounting for the status of all Family Assistance (TANF) and Safety Net (non-TANF) cases provides an interesting comparison with historical "insider" views of welfare. Although the 2001 data on case engagement is generally in stark contrast to the situation at the end of 1994, when 175,000 of the 544,000 total cases were classified as "temporarily unengageable," the absolute number of cases classified as "indefinitely unengageable" did not drop so remarkably: only from 69,292 in December 1994 to 61,697 in October 2001. In October 2001, these cases constituted almost one-third of the caseload; in an otherwise dramatically reduced caseload, these might be considered the "neediest of the needy," that is, those verifiably lacking alternatives.

The historical comparison comes from the pre-TANF era of welfare, when individuals heading the indefinitely unengageable cases were referred to as "unemployable." At that time, there was a "one-third/one-third/one-third" operating assumption, which was shorthand for estimates that one-third of welfare case heads were permanently unemployable, one-third could work, with some assistance, and one-third had personal problems that made holding a job difficult. Historically, the attention of welfare-to-work programs was focused on the individuals identified as able to work with some assistance. HRA seems to have extended its mandate to work with—that is, to "engage"—the whole two-thirds of the caseload not considered indefinitely unengageable (the "unemployables" of the pre-TANF era).

Welfare agencies that have mastered "engagement" might start by focusing on work-related performance indicators in a JobStat system, such as the amount of work and earnings among aid applicants and recipients, the proportion of the caseload meeting a part- or full-time work standard, the rate of case closings because of higher earnings, the rate of returns to aid among

Table 5.2. Engagement Status of Public Assistance Cases as of July 9, 2001

Case Status	FAP		SNA		Comments
	Number	Percent of Undercare Cases	Number	Percent of Undercare Cases	
Total Active Cases	147,269		75,347		Families and individuals receiving assistance with particular needs (e.g., rent arrears)
Single issue	3,778		6,741		
Total Undercare Cases	143,491	100.0%	68,606	100.0%	Cash assistance
Unengageable	46,380	32.3%	28,743	41.9%	
Indefinite	38,790	27.0%	22,697	33.1%	Case head receives SSI, DASIS, child-only cases, aged case head
Temporary	7,590	5.3%	6,046	8.8%	Temporary incapacity, child < three months, SSI pending, temporary exemption, limitations— pending PRIDE scheduling
Engageable	97,111	67.7%	39,863	58.1%	Percentages here and below refer to all engageable cases
Engaged	54,156	55.8%	25,226	63.3%	
Work	40,534	41.7%	14,793	37.1%	
Employment	27,240	28.1%	2,372	6.0%	
Budgeted	23,913	24.6%	1,227	3.1%	Subject to earnings disregard
Other	3,327	3.4%	1,145	2.9%	
WEP	11,997	12.4%	6,632	16.6%	Typical schedule is for 20 hours per week in WEP job and 15 hours in other activities related to enhancing employability.

Wage Subsidy	1,123	1.2%	4	0.0%	
Other	51	0.1%	458	1.1%	
Substance Abuse Residential Treatment	123	0.1%	5,327	13.4%	
Other Participation	13,622	14.0%	10,433	26.2%	Includes education, training, job search, students over age fifteen, persons in substance abuse treatment (often in combination with training, job search), rehabilitation, and persons exempted because of home obligations.
In Engagement Process	10,937	11.3%	7,298	18.3%	Scheduled for eligibility, contractor assignment appointment, or otherwise under review
In Sanction Process	32,018	33.0%	7,339	18.4%	
Conciliation/Conference/NOI	12,752	13.1%	5,823	14.6%	State law requires HRA to send clients believed noncompliant a "notice of intent" to sanction
Awaiting Conciliation Scheduling	2,397	2.5%	712	1.8%	
Sanction in Effect	15,345	15.8%	199	0.5%	Benefits reduced; virtually all are TANF (Family Assistance) cases
Queued for Fair Hearing	1,524	1.6%	605	1.5%	
Unengaged	0	0.0%	0	0.0%	

Source: New York Human Resources Agency. Family Assistance (TANF) and Safety Net cases are combined.

recipients whose cases were closed for earnings, and the proportion completing agency-prescribed education and job-training activities. Performance indicators of increasing interest to HRA officials at the end of 2001 were measures of the work and earnings of aid recipients nearing the end of their five-year welfare careers under TANF, the proportion whose cases were closed for earnings before reaching the limit, and those who reached the limit with no earnings.

Indicators of "Critical Path" Activities

The federal TANF legislation and state and local TANF options set the parameters for ultimate welfare reform outcomes, such as the proportion of the caseload working at least 30 hours per week, but JobStat-like performance indicators also need to measure the agency processes that are on the critical path to achieving the ultimate outcomes. For example, one of the simplest to understand but most difficult to implement processes in the nation's job-training system for low-income people has been the referral from welfare agencies to job-training programs. Usually a negotiated agreement between a private job-training vendor and a public welfare agency is put in place, the vendor guarantees a certain number of job-training slots to the welfare agency (and, often, hires the staff to register, assess, and instruct the negotiated number of trainees), and very few welfare recipients turn up for training. A JobStat-like system needs to help frontline staff, supervisors, and agency managers monitor this step in a process that is supposed to produce the self-sufficiency outcome.

In addition to this critical-path activity, tracked through VendorStat in New York City, JobStat tracks a number of administrative events in welfare cases that can essentially derail applicants and recipients from a path to self-sufficiency, either because HRA cannot enforce work requirements under TANF rules when these events occur or because the automated systems involved in managing the financial side of welfare and the "engagement" side are designed to accept information about events in unvarying sequences. (See discussion in the next section and appendix.)

Indicators of Performance in Administering Financial Assistance

The agency processes that provide accurate and timely financial assistance interact with and affect processes designed to increase self-sufficiency. Welfare systems that do poorly in administering financial assistance make it difficult to engage aid applicants and recipients in the processes that lead to self-sufficiency. Reflecting the importance of financial assistance administration to HRA's agency goals for employment, in 2001 JobStat's 100-point per-

formance indicator index used to compare Job Centers to each other allocated 45 points to employment indicators, 40 points to administrative
indicators, and 15 points to self-sufficiency progress indicators. (The self-
sufficiency indicators measure various Job Center achievements in minimizing clients' "down time" and maximizing their engagement in processes
expected to lead to self-sufficiency.)

Even though welfare reform puts the spotlight on agencies' success in
moving people toward self-sufficiency, few of the requirements for administering financial assistance were eliminated with the shift from AFDC to
TANF. There is much to monitor for each case, and while management
information systems for financial assistance handle much of the budgeting,
payment, and notification work, workers still must enter the right types of
information accurately and in a timely way and monitor and respond to
changes in case status. Errors and backlogs in the administration of financial
assistance can undermine achievement of employment goals. Errors increase
workload and can snowball into programwide or officewide delays and
backlogs, taking staff attention away from who is not engaged, who needs
additional job training, who has failed to comply with work requirements,
and who should be referred for medical evaluation. Some errors lead to fair
hearings, a process that essentially makes recipients unavailable for participation in work activities. Some errors and backlogs make it impossible for
agency units to claim credit for work that has actually been done or for
achievements that are tracked by performance indicators. (For details, see
appendix.)

When performance indicators for administering financial assistance were
included in JobStat so that the system covered both the employment and aid
functions of the merged Job Centers, center managers realized that efficient
financial assistance operations and high performance on employment indicators go hand in hand. This occurred because, for the first time, the managers
had concrete evidence of both types of performance in an integrated reporting format.

WHO NEEDS TO BE INVOLVED IN DESIGNING AND IMPLEMENTING JOBSTAT?

Organizational behavior wisdom says that the end users of a management
information system should be consulted in the design process. While this
wisdom certainly applies to JobStat, it is useful to consider the following:
(1) Who are all the potential end users and what are their different purposes
and needs, especially in terms of a hierarchy from direct-service staff and
supervisors up to managers of direct-service units, managers of multiple
direct-service units, and top-level agency managers? (2) What are the differ-

ent functional perspectives, talents, and resources needed to create a JobStat system? And, (3) What internal agency staff and external people should be recruited for the work of building and running a JobStat system?

Users of JobStat

With its CenterStat worker-level enhancement and contractor-focused VendorStat, JobStat's user audience includes virtually the whole welfare agency line structure from local Job Centers to regional managers (organized mainly by New York City boroughs) to top-level executives, as well as some support units, such as the fair hearings structure. Whatever organizational structures are relevant for other welfare agencies interested in building a Job-Stat system, each set of users has to play a role in testing and revising JobStat data, reports, and processes; however, not all need to be involved in initial system development. The most important users to involve in the development stage of JobStat are the agency executives with the vision of what is needed to reform welfare and how JobStat can support the reform, people with the functional perspectives described below, and people with frontline experience.

Agency Functions: Operations, Analysis, and Systems

These three agency groups—operations, analysis, and systems—must be involved as a team in the development and implementation of JobStat and, ideally, they should be organized as a task group without other responsibilities, at least for the first few months of development. The Operations group includes managers who know how financial assistance and employment services are delivered, what the problems of performance are, and especially how frontline managers think about their work. (In New York City, "frontline experience" is represented in the Job Center managers because, historically, almost all of these managers have been promoted from within the ranks of direct-service workers. In welfare agencies where this is not the promotion practice, frontline workers should be represented in the JobStat development team's Operations group.) The Analysis group includes people with experience using data from the agency's automated and manual sources and, especially, with detailed knowledge of the origin and meaning of data items and how the data are reported and aggregated. The Systems group includes people who know all of the existing data systems that support operations as well as how to build and integrate into the agency a management information system that has the capabilities and features needed for JobStat. In addition, it is helpful to have general project management staff that provide liaison between the groups and keep development on track.

Internal and External People

People who are not welfare agency employees or even public employees can support the development of a JobStat system in many ways. Private consultants and contractors accomplish much of the information technology work done in public agencies already. Likewise, the technical aspects of JobStat do not necessarily require agency employees. The key roles for agency employees are leadership, decision-making, and expertise and experience with the programs and data of the agency. System design, programming, report development, technical assistance to users, project management, and many other JobStat tasks can be assigned to non-agency staff with the appropriate technical, interpersonal, and organizational skills.

The main advantage of using external people to develop JobStat is flexibility, especially when a contractor has the ability to bring in and move around people as needed. However, if the system is dependent on outsiders and no internal capabilities are built over time, it can be difficult to institutionalize the system, maintain it, and adapt it as policies and programs change.

The role of the existing internal MIS organization deserves close attention and careful management because large public agencies have special problems with systems development. Often, MIS managers in large public agencies, including welfare agencies, do not see either the agency executive or the agency's operations leaders as their "customers." In addition, there are constraints on their ability to solve agency MIS problems, including constraints on resources, hiring talent, and designing agency-specific solutions (as opposed to achieving cross-government efficiencies through centralized, generic systems). The JobStat challenge is to engage the internal MIS staff productively when the temptation is to try to develop a JobStat system independent of the agency MIS group in order to achieve a fast start. Total independence is usually impossible because JobStat requires data from existing welfare agency data systems, and agency MIS groups are usually not enthusiastic about data systems developed and maintained by policy and research people. Thus, welfare agencies planning to develop a JobStat system may need to consider teaming an experienced consultant with the internal MIS leader(s) and creating additional incentives and recognition for internal MIS performance.

DATA, DATA SOURCES, AND TECHNOLOGY: TRADEOFFS AND LESSONS

In the twenty-first-century IT world, HRA's JobStat is relatively unsophisticated. It was built in part on an existing automated, case-management information system originally intended to keep track of the employment activities of non-TANF aid recipients, a system that is not connected to the principal MIS for financial assistance, called the Welfare Management System (WMS), which was designed and is operated by New York State. An important tool provided to help line workers achieve the performance goals that JobStat tracks is simple, paper "work lists" of cases that need attention. Further, the database used to construct performance indicators is separate from the sources of data and is programmed independently to produce indicator reports. In other words, JobStat is a fairly low-tech solution to managing the shift from a minutely specified procedure-based service to the practice of a craft.

One of the reasons that JobStat is not a state-of-the-art system is that its architects wanted something that could be in place within a year. Jack Maple faced even less favorable circumstances in the NYPD and took the advice to work with what was available. He describes the advice:

> Bratton was putting together informal sit-downs for his executive core with some of the top corporate executives in America. . . . [W]e had a kind of meeting of the minds with Jack Welch of GE. Welch had come in talking a language we could hardly comprehend—secretaries who were buying boats with the pro-ceeds from their incentive packages, research and development budgets running into the millions—but when I pointed out that we were attempting to turn around an organization that literally had to go begging just to buy the acetate sheets we needed to put our original maps on an overhead projector, he acknowledged we had chosen the right path amid difficult surroundings. "You go with what you have," he said. "You can't wait for the R&D to catch up with you." And that had been our philosophy from the beginning. If it had been up to MISD [the NYPD MIS division], we would have all been sitting around the Old Policemen's Home before they found a system they liked and could make operational.[13]

In spite of its low-tech beginnings, together the components of HRA's JobStat system perform tasks that achieve a rare and valuable result: They align the policy of welfare reform with the information needed to assess pol-icy implementation, and they do much of the work necessary to implement the policy case by case. This alignment mostly results from how data, data sources, and technology are connected to client activity and agency action.

Client activity (or lack of it) is the basis for agency action in welfare reform, and, conversely, agency action is the basis for client activity. Thus, one of the management information systems that frontline workers in HRA use to manage their cases—which feeds the JobStat database—keeps track of and actually generates much client activity and agency action by automati-cally scheduling appointments for clients and sending them notices, auto-matically sorting and queuing client cases for worker action, initiating new cases, and starting a clock for worker action. This MIS (called New York

City WAY, for Work, Accountability, and You) also prioritizes client activity and agency actions for JobStat data collection, which is necessary because some activities can occur simultaneously, for example, when an aid recipient is both working and going to school.

As data from the NYCWAY system and the WMS financial aid system are converted to JobStat performance indicators, important judgments must be made, judgments that are embedded in the conversion program: Only some client activities and agency actions count for performance, and some activities count more than others. This is one way that welfare reform policy is aligned with the information needed to assess policy implementation. Other judgments are made and refined over time about occurrences of intense policy interest, such as "recidivism"—people who return to the assistance caseload after their cases are closed. This indicator was revised after some experience—including dialogue at JobStat meetings among operations, analysis, and support (fair hearings) staff—to take out of the recidivist count the closed cases that were reopened for aid to continue because recipients asked for fair hearings.

Accuracy Issues

A major accomplishment of JobStat is the alignment of policy with information that can be used to assess policy implementation, but issues of data accuracy are endemic to any performance indicator system and have been the focus of considerable attention in JobStat. Both of JobStat's major feeder data systems, NYCWAY and WMS, were designed to tie workers' ability to take action on a case to submission of information to the system about the case. These systems "kick back" submissions that are detected as erroneous based on built-in parameters for data. The benefit of creating a separate database for JobStat fed by systems with this feature is that many errors in data that JobStat uses are corrected in the feeder systems and are not passed along to JobStat.

The accuracy issue cuts the opposite way as well. HRA's JobStat managers and agency executives have often been challenged by local managers about the accuracy of JobStat data and performance measures or the usefulness of particular measures. These challenges are essential to the process of improving data, data collection, and technology because they are followed up with corrections, development of new capabilities, and technical assistance to local users.

One of the subtle but very important features of JobStat is that many of the performance indicators are composed of proxy measures that are tied to familiar operational decision and reporting events. For example, the JobStat system relies on a data item from the WMS system, "cases closed for earnings," to indicate employment-related successes even though this reporting system is historically known to undercount actual employment and earnings. Most other methods of collecting and reporting employment of welfare recipients, that is, methods not tied to case budgeting, have historically proved to be even less reliable. This underscores the importance for the system's accuracy and usefulness of involving people in the development of Job-Stat who have in-depth operational experience and others who have in-depth experience using operational data. Because frontline supervisors and managers are able to understand and respond to these measures, it also suggests that, to the extent possible, a JobStat system should rely on data that are already collected instead of introducing new forms and data entry tasks. While new data might result in closer approximations of desired performance measures, they also introduce new sources of confusion and error.

On the other hand, although the cost in time, accuracy, and goodwill of new data collection may be steep, there can be advantages to avoiding the use of some existing data. When HRA initiated JobStat, some sources of data for JobStat reports on performance were hand counts from local offices. From office to office, definitions of data items varied, time frames for data collection varied, and accuracy varied. HRA decided that JobStat data based on automated sources would be more consistent and reliable, and thus NYC-WAY was enhanced. This increased the reporting responsibilities of line staff in the Job Centers but ultimately eliminated most center hand tabulations as inputs to the JobStat performance data.

HRA's experience in designing and implementing JobStat underscores the following lessons on data, data collection, and technology:[14]

- Build on existing data systems, rather than starting from scratch with new technology and new data collection requirements, and modify over time.
- Capacity (size) of the system that houses the JobStat database is important because it will grow very rapidly; "history" is needed to construct current indicators and to compare current performance with past performance.
- Before committing to any particular system software, check the availability of trained systems analysts and programmers for the preferred system; some are in very short supply.
- Use the system to make the jobs of the frontline staff easier; this will pay off in performance, accuracy of data, and goodwill.
- Involve people who are experienced in operations and analysis in the design of the system.
- Use data from automated sources (as opposed to manually collected data) to build performance indicators to the extent possible.
- Embed data collection in the welfare agency work process (as opposed to asking for reports after the fact) in order to maximize accuracy.

- Produce indicators for a short while before setting goals. Keep the indicators constant for at least six months.
- Distribute indicator results for all performance units to all other units to encourage constructive competition.
- Define indicators to coincide with the frequency of reporting operational data when operations are optimally performed; that is, operational activities should not have to be reported for JobStat purposes any more often than is best for operational purposes, but JobStat indicators should not lag optimally defined activities by much.
- Create indicators based on short periods of time so that they can be easily redefined to reflect different time periods for analysis based on the work cycles of operational units. (These cycles need to be understood by top-level management. They are not necessarily the same as management cycles. Some operational work cycles are driven by the behavior of the service population, some by the seasons, and some by agency requirements of clients, whereas management cycles may be driven by budget, fiscal years, external review of agency performance, and politics.)
- Decide on indicators first and then look for the data and/or create the data collection systems to support them. Although proxies may be necessary, the availability of data should not be the most important criterion for selecting indicators.
- Provide simple tools such as "work lists" of cases needing attention for all service delivery units based on their needs and requests.
- Place data sources for indicators under the control of the operational units and/or central MIS unit to the maximum feasible extent.
- Reward timely, accurate, and complete data collection as well as performance on goals based on indicators.
- Give lots of credit to agency MIS people for the indicators system, especially when outside consultants are involved.

JOBSTAT IMPLEMENTATION: EARLY, MIDDLE, AND LATE PHASES

HRA started implementing JobStat at a time when the pressures to help clients attain self-sufficiency were increasing. Under the 1996 TANF law, HRA had about three years to get JobStat ready for the "graduation" from welfare of the first group that would reach the TANF-imposed five-year lifetime limit for federal aid. That preparation process began with using a JobStat measure of unengaged clients both as a way to get a handle on the caseload and to get a sense of JobStat's potential to change the way HRA's direct-service units worked. Welfare agency executives starting later with a JobStat-like system may not have the luxury of time to begin with a single "clean-up" measure such as unengaged clients. The same issues, however, are likely to arise when data never before used for any critical purpose become drivers of the day-to-day work of direct-service units and the basis for employee evaluation and compensation. Also, no matter when welfare agencies start building a JobStat system, a similar evolution of JobStat-induced changes in agency operations is likely. Finally, the roles of top-level management and local managers and staff will change over time regardless of when JobStat is introduced.

Early Implementation: When Data Matter for the First Time

"Cleaning" data that have never been used for important purposes takes time and educates welfare agency managers and staff because it draws their attention to processes and categories of cases that may not have been examined with an eye toward the agency's shift in mission. A clear example is how large welfare agencies have historically handled referrals to addiction/substance abuse services or other mental health services, especially when these services were provided by other public agencies. Often, there has been no collaboration between the agencies, nor any agreements about when referrals are appropriate, what services are provided for how long, and what information about clients will be shared and how information will be exchanged. Thus, it was difficult for welfare agency frontline workers to find out whether clients actually used the services, how often, for how long, and with what effect on their employability. Once a goal is set for zero unengaged cases, the incentives are in place for looking closely at these cases.

There are often surprises when old information is studied in a new light. Jack Maple describes surprises revealed when the NYPD's CompStat began to map crime data:

> In New York, mapping showed us that 60 percent of the city's grand larcenies occurred in just three precincts. It showed us that robbers in one Lower East Side precinct worked one side of the neighborhood by day and shifted to the opposite side of the neighborhood at night. It showed us that a rash of rapes in Queens had all taken place within a couple of blocks of one subway line, allowing us to set up stakeouts and take down our man. It proved, when we mapped the home addresses of robbers arrested in Midtown, that the old adage was true: "Manhattan make it, Brooklyn take it." As a result, we started asking Midtown victims to look at more photos of Brooklyn crooks.[15]

An equivalent revelation resulting from JobStat's implementation concerned agency practices. Job Centers were scheduling aid recipients to come in for assessment and/or assignment to work according to the number of time slots available for such appointments rather than on the basis of who actually needed assessment or assignment. Once a case management data system (NYCWAY) was in place that had the ability to create appointment schedules based on recipients' current work status, scheduling was rationalized and produced more "engagement."

When data matter for the first time, there are often instances of "fiddling" the numbers in addition to surprises. The most effective defenses in a Job-Stat-like system are to use only automated sources of data that come from systems with built-in error-detection features and to minimize the opportunities that line staff have to make changes to data without going though a controlled procedure to correct errors.

What accountability means during the early, "data cleaning" phase of Job-Stat implementation is different from what it means later, when key users and analysts agree that the data are reliable and represent what they are purported to represent. In the early phase, managers at all levels should be held accountable for diligent participation in the JobStat process and for their efforts to look behind the numbers, learn about their operations, and take steps to improve. Later, managers should be held accountable for actual performance based on the indicators.

Because the JobStat system is a combination of numbers and talk, talk compensates for a lot of numerical shortcomings. There are always flaws in new indicators. As of the end of 2001, for example, HRA had not recognized that differences in achievement in the components of the JobStat indices for a particular Job Center could result from local variations in the importance of employment, administrative, and self-sufficiency progress measures, in contrast to the standard weights applied to these measures across the centers. Conditions are not "average" in all centers. Employment indicators, in other words, may not truly reflect 45 percent of a given center's relative achievement. The importance of numerical problems is reduced, however, by the way the numbers are used. Evaluated in the context of JobStat meetings, the various components serve principally to focus attention on issues. They are, in a sense, reweighted "on the fly."

JobStat's Effect on Agency Operations over Time

One early result of the heightened interest of HRA agency executives in the Job Centers' performance on case engagement and job placements was a heightened interest on the part of Job Center directors in the performance of the vendor organizations that provide job-search and other employment services. The vendors already worked under performance contracts but accountability was taken to another level with VendorStat. This illustrates a general expectation for early effects of introducing a JobStat system: When managers become newly accountable for the performance of their units, they begin to look at how their performance is affected by other parts of the agency and the bigger system of assistance for low-income people. Often, they move to influence or control these external factors. One of the principles for organizational structure discussed above—making the boundaries of responsibility and authority coterminous to the extent possible—is related to this tendency. When tension erupts within an organization that has introduced a performance accountability system, the troubles are often at the boundaries of organizational units' responsibility and accountability. The challenge for agency leaders is to balance incentives for cooperation and competition so that boundary problems can be resolved.

The effect that the introduction of a JobStat-like system will have on specific welfare agency operations is difficult to predict, but it is nearly certain that operational problems revealed by investigating the causes of poor performance will turn out to be the tip of an iceberg and the effects of starting to investigate will be felt for a long time. In complex systems that have been doing things basically the same way for a long time, operational glitches are often a sign of major structural dysfunction, and the process of "cleaning up" one problem reveals another and another and another. As Peter Senge says, "Today's problems come from yesterday's solutions."[16] The explanation for this phenomenon is that it is difficult to see a whole system by looking at one problem.

An example comes from a Job Center in the early stages of implementing the CenterStat version of JobStat. This center had Error Correction Specialists to whom individual case problems were funneled for investigation and data changes, mostly in WMS. Prior to the introduction of JobStat, the centers had little incentive to analyze patterns in errors or to create feedback loops. The Error Correction Specialists understood their job to be to correct the errors, not to work on the source of the errors. And, prior to the introduction of CenterStat, the centers had limited capability to pinpoint individual staff sources of errors. In the example, once the Job Center director focused on error patterns, it was discovered that a major source of a particular error was actually "upstream" of the Job Center. (The solution to this particular problem entailed crossing organizational boundaries, which JobStat provided new incentives to undertake.)

Like many large welfare agencies, HRA does not actually provide a direct service with respect to the new welfare reform mission because vendors do the work of teaching people how to find jobs, supervising them in work experience, and improving their literacy and vocational skills. HRA manages the flow of cases with the objective of keeping aid recipients engaged in vendor-provided activity that is intended to lead to self-sufficiency, using the persuasive power of financial benefits that depend on aid recipients satisfying requirements for activity. At this writing, HRA was just entering the stage of JobStat implementation that will enable frontline staff and their supervisors to knowledgeably use specific vendor programs as tools of their craft.

For other welfare agencies implementing JobStat, this suggests that an expected effect of JobStat on agency operations over time will be a return to generic line workers who have the lever of activity requirements tied to financial aid *and* program resources at their disposal. Such workers, called Job Opportunity Specialists, were being introduced in HRA Job Centers in late 2001.

The Role of Agency Managers in JobStat over Time

The effectiveness of JobStat as a management tool depends as much on the face-to-face meetings between top-level agency managers and the managers of frontline service units, the Job Centers, as it does on the data and analysis that go into the reports on performance indicators. The role played by the HRA commissioner in these meetings has been critical to the acceptance and credibility of JobStat as a management tool and as the foundation for performance accountability. There is an implicit contract between the agency executive and the Job Center managers that the commissioner has a right to expect commitment and the best possible performance and the center directors have a right to expect his respect and his participation, and to be able to bring their performance issues to his attention directly and receive responses. Every manager in the middle of the HRA hierarchy between the Job Center directors and the commissioner plays a role in helping the Job Centers perform, but the model for these meetings—taken from the NYPD's CompStat, but less aggressive in tone and more dependent on behind-the-scenes assistance to the frontline managers—has the agency executive in an indispensable role indefinitely. While the commissioner's role might be delegated on occasion, it seems unlikely that JobStat would have the same stature in the agency, or work in the same way, if the commissioner did not participate regularly in the JobStat meetings.

Some JobStat functions can be handed off over time, however. For example, while it may be necessary for a deputy commissioner to lead the technology/systems integration work needed to get JobStat going, the executive can delegate ongoing oversight when the system is established and functioning as expected. Similarly, at some point after JobStat is running smoothly, less executive-level attention is required within the internal MIS group.

Other JobStat functions may be reorganized over time. HRA committed significant resources to preparing and supporting Job Center directors who were scheduled to attend and present at JobStat meetings and to technical assistance for center staff on all aspects of JobStat and its use in operations. The need for this wanes as these managers become familiar with JobStat reports and how the performance indicators relate to their operations. According to HRA executives, it was important at the beginning of JobStat not to give analysts to the Job Centers but to provide assistance centrally so that center directors would not delegate the necessary learning to subordinates. After almost three years of experience with JobStat, analysts are going to be assigned to the centers.

JOBSTAT'S ROLE IN TEACHING AND MANAGEMENT EDUCATION

JobStat principles should not be confused with JobStat particulars—the details of what's measured and what's not. JobStat could work with a very different set of indicators than the ones used by HRA in the 1999–2001 period. The key principle is that indicators should be devised to reflect the importance to management of specific features of the assistance process. As objectives change, so should JobStat. Further, the transformative power of information that is intended to support the reconceptualization of the goals, tasks, and functions of an agency derives from what line staff, middle managers, and top-level managers learn from new information about the nature of their work and how to do it. JobStat's performance indicators are valuable tools for teaching and learning because they point to functions that are bottlenecks or trouble spots, units that have management problems, and—in its CenterStat and VendorStat forms—worker groups, individuals, and vendors that should be retrained, reconfigured, or emulated. But the data are only the beginning of the teaching and learning opportunities that JobStat offers.

The process, first of all, encourages a new way of thinking among line staff. In order to adapt to and perform well in the JobStat environment, line supervisors and Job Center directors must become data analysts. In the New York City welfare system, this is a big step because supervisors and managers of Job Centers (previously Income Support Centers) are promoted from within the ranks of line staff. They are accustomed to relying on their experience and operating in a system of minutely prescribed procedures. The training they receive is typically "how to" style focused on new procedures, and, historically, there has been little investment in broadening their perspectives or helping them become better generic managers. The result has been that the effective ones have a good sense of their own operations, but a fairly dim picture of agencywide operations and policy issues, and not much experience studying systems. HRA managers said that getting Job Center directors to begin to think like analysts was the most difficult part of implementation. JobStat offers an education in systems thinking because the performance indicators are built on processes that must be understood in order to understand why measured performance is good or not.

The most complicated part of JobStat's performance indicator approach symbolizes the underlying systems thinking. This is an index score, a single number awarded to every Job Center every month that summarizes how the centers performed on more than 30 measures related to policy-determined goals. The measures that make up the index are weighted according to their policy importance (which changes from time to time), and the index is calculated by distributing 100 points across the achievement categories based on the policy-determined priorities. This scoring system is not transparent nor is it intuitively sensible to many JobStat users because each indicator has parameters set separately for each Job Center to gauge the range of performance from poor to excellent based on varying conditions for the centers. While the elements of the indexing approach may not have much practical value at the front line, it enables HRA to rank the performance of Job Centers, which is intuitively sensible and important to Job Center managers. Every Job Center director knows that the question about performance "compared to what?" has an answer: his or her peers.

JobStat also encourages a different orientation toward action among frontline staff and their supervisors and managers. One of the advantages of all the experience that accrues in Job Centers, because managers are promoted from within, is a keen sense of where the problems are. The performance accountability structure of JobStat provides the incentives for line staff and managers to become problem-solvers, and the JobStat reports provide the means to focus their problem-identification efforts. This is what it means to "empower" frontline staff and managers with information.

An important, but easily underestimated, educational benefit of JobStat is the dialogue and feedback that occurs in the weekly JobStat meetings. These forums are where top-level agency managers learn what Job Center directors and their mid-level operations managers know, and where the directors and managers can connect their knowledge to the overall system or agency perspective, a link missing in the past. The forums are where Job Center directors and mid-level operations managers get the kind of thought-provoking questions and suggestions that do not usually come out of their day-to-day interactions. But the forums are also a significant opportunity for personal growth of the Job Center directors. In New York City's welfare system, these employees have always been considered the base of an organizational pyramid, rather that the customer service group or the group "producing the organization's product" that needs to be supported by the rest of the agency. Consequently, their presentation, participation, and public-speaking skills have not been valued, nor have they been valued as thinkers. JobStat's forums give new importance to these skills and qualities and to their ideas for improving the outcomes of their work.

INSTITUTIONALIZING A NEW APPROACH

Ensuring the endurance of innovations is difficult in the public sector. The benefits are not always quantifiable or clearly attributable. Leadership changes regularly. Politics sometimes outweighs "rational" organization management. Welfare administrators who introduce a JobStat-like system will help the system survive leadership changes if:

- *operations people, especially the "lifers," own it and consider it indispensable.* This requires major investments in educating and supporting frontline and mid-level managers in the use of the system; continuous and effective responses to requests from these managers for modifications or supplements to standard JobStat reports; automated systems that make their work easier, including easier to perform well as measured by JobStat indicators; and embedding maximum opportunities for personal growth in the routine JobStat activities.
- *the technical and analytic capacity to maintain the system exists within the agency infrastructure.* If the brains of JobStat repose in temporary organizational structures or in units that are vulnerable to being reduced, reorganized, or eliminated, the system has not been institutionalized. This means that JobStat should not be dependent on consultants or contractors, nor should it be managed as a policy initiative or project for very long.
- *there is external interest in and support for the system.* External interest is tricky as administrations change and the relative influence of interested outsiders changes. NYPD's CompStat survived Commissioner Bratton's departure and Mayor Giuliani's departure, apparently because of *internal* NYPD support for this way of policing. A widely admired, studied, and replicated innovation has a better chance of survival than one that only agency insiders know about and understand.

THE REAL OUTCOMES

The results of JobStat for the organization that adopts the system and the results for the agency's customers are the real test of its value. JobStat should produce *a more effective organization* and an *increase in self-sufficiency* among recipients of public assistance. Police Commissioner William Bratton's vision of how CompStat would transform the NYPD could apply to any bureaucracy:

> We created a system in which the police commissioner, with his executive core, first empowers and then interrogates the precinct commander, forcing him or her to come up with a plan to attack crime. But it should not stop there. At the next level down, it should be the precinct commander, taking the same role as the commissioner, empowering and interrogating the platoon commander. Then, at the third level, the platoon commander should be asking his sergeants,

"What are we doing to deploy on this tour to address these conditions?" And, finally, you have the sergeant at roll call—"Mitchell, tell me about the last five robberies on your post"; "Carlyle, you think that's funny, it's a joke? Tell me about the last five burglaries"; "Biber, tell me about those stolen cars on your post"—all the way down until everyone in the entire organization is empowered and motivated, active and assessed and successful. It works in all organizations, whether it's 38,000 New York cops or Mayberry R.F.D.[17]

A welfare agency that has such consistency and clarity of accountability from top to bottom also needs consistency and clarity of purpose and widely shared knowledge and excellent practice of its craft. As of this writing, Job-Stat had been demonstrably effective in supporting the agency's purpose. Its role in improving the craft of helping aid recipients become self-sufficient has yet to be tested.

Appendix

JOBSTAT INDICATORS[18]

For most of 2001, there were 32 JobStat indicators, measuring employment, administration, and progress to self-sufficiency. A target range (acceptable to excellent) was established for each indicator for each Job Center. The achievement for each indicator was published for each Job Center each month, along with an index of overall achievement based on a weighted sum of individual indicators that is based on distributing 100 points. HRA's choice of indicators and the points assigned to each reveal a great deal about what top management consider the key features of the assistance process and the most important outcomes.

Table A.1 lists all 32 indicators used in 2001, which can be used to decode the Job Center report shown in table 5.1. The notes in table A.1 explain where each indicator fits into the assistance process and what the indicator measures. In JobStat reports, the indicators are grouped in the categories "Employment," "Administrative," and "Self-Sufficiency Progress." (Because the actual JobStat report had to be shortened to fit as table 5.1, the seven indicators of "self-sufficiency progress," numbers 26–32, are not shown.) Ten indicators (the "Basic 10") are identified by HRA as representing key features of the entire system; they are marked by asterisks in table A.1. The employment indicators account for 45 of the 100 possible points overall; administrative indicators for 40, and the remaining 15 refer to the self-sufficiency goals.

The analysis of JobStat data and the production of JobStat reports has been the responsibility of HRA's Office of Policy and Program Analysis. This agency unit has produced detailed guides for users of the indicators and reports. The *JobStat Reference Guide* (Version 2.0, revised 5/23/01) is the principal resource for the following explanation of 2001 indicators.

EMPLOYMENT INDICATORS

The eight Employment Indicators measure job placement and case closure through employment. The key to this system is an indicator that appears to be bookkeeping: Indicator 3, "Budgets Completed." A Job Center scores in this category if a recipient experiences an earnings increase that requires adjustment of the cash benefit. Inclusion in JobStat scoring of such budget adjustments creates a significant incentive for ensuring that employment gains are identified and recorded. Without a revised budget, a Job Center cannot count Indicators 1 (Closed for Earnings) and 4 (Qualified Reported

Table A.1. Definitions of the JobStat Indicators

Indicator Group

No.	Indicator	Assistance Process	Note
Employment Indicators			
1	Closed for Earnings	Termination	Outcome; ratio of cases closed for earnings to number of cases in undercare status.
2	Not Opened for Earnings	Application	Outcome; ratio of persons referred to SAP (Skills Assessment and Placement) contractor who found jobs and did not open cases to total SAP referrals.
3	Budgets Completed	Receipt	Outcome; ratio of number of cases in which earnings increase requires recalculation of cash benefit to total "engageable" undercare cases.
4	Qualified Reported Placements	Application/ Receipt/ Termination	Outcome; based on indicators 1, 2, and subset of 3 in which earnings increase > $100 per month.
5	3-Month Recidivism Rate	Follow-Up	Ratio of persons under care in current period who were counted under indicators 1 or 2 13 weeks before current period to total persons so counted.
6	Still Off PA at 3 Months	Follow-Up	Absolute number still off PA (Public Assistance).
7	6-Month Recidivism Rate	Follow-Up	Identical to 5, but with longer interval.
8	Still Off PA at 6 Months	Follow-Up	Identical to 6, but with longer interval.
Administrative Indicators			
9*	PA Application Timeliness Rate	Application	Duration of time between filing of application and agency acceptance/ rejection.
10*	FS Application Timeliness Rate	Application	Proportion of FS (Food Stamp) cases processed within mandatory 30 days.
11*	Overdue Face-to-Face Recertification	Receipt	If recertification does not occur within 60 days of due date, FS (Food Stamp) eligibility is lost.
12*	WMS 16-Day Error Weekly Average	Application/ Receipt	Number of such errors/number of WMS (Welfare Management System) transactions.
13*	WMS Total Error Average	Application/ Receipt	Weekly average of all errors per report month/WMS transactions.

(continues)

Table A.1. Continued

Indicator Group

No.	Indicator	Assistance Process	Note
14	Family Assistance Dollar Error Rate	Receipt	Sample-based error assessment; errors weighted by absolute value of payment error (hence under- and over-payments receive equal weight). Samples are too small for valid inference about center.
15	Food Stamps Dollar Error Rate	Receipt	Sample-based error assessment; uses same QC (Quality Control) sample as for indicator 14.
16*	Medicaid Separate Determination Referral Rate	Application	Evaluation of frequency of proper referrals of persons denied or withdrawing from public assistance to Medicaid evaluation.
17*	Access Spot Violation	Application	Results of random checks of center procedures for dealing with help-seekers using decoys ("spotters").
18	Fair Hearing Request Rate	Receipt	Ratio of monthly fair hearing requests to caseload.
19	MDR Impact Rate	Receipt	Ratio of number of fair hearing issues resolved through MDR (Mandatory Dispute Resolution) in month to number of fair hearing issues.
20	MDR Client Accept Rate	Receipt	Proportion of issues resolved at MDR in accord with precipitating center action.
21	Fair Hearing Withdrawal Rate	Receipt	Share of fair hearing issues decided by HRA withdrawal.
22	Fair Hearing Reversal Rate	Receipt	Share of fair hearing issues in which HRA action is reversed.
23	Fair Hearing Win Rate	Receipt	Number of wins (number of wins + number of losses). (Cases remanded to the center for more information are not counted in numerator or denominator.)
24*	Public Assistance Compliance Rate	Receipt/ Termination	Implementation of fair hearing decisions within requisite 30-day period.
25*	Food Stamps Compliance Rate	Receipt/ Termination	Implementation of fair hearing decisions within requisite 15-day period.

(continues)

Table A.1. Continued

Indicator Group

No.	Indicator	Assistance Process	Note
Self-Sufficiency Progress			
26	Transitional Childcare Application Submit Rate	Termination	Ratio of number of clients submitting an application for transitional child care to number of previous users of subsidized childcare who closed due to employment.
27	Percentage Long-Time FA Reduction Rate	Termination	Measures progress toward target reduction in number of cases at risk of reaching five-year time limit.
28*	ISAR Timeouts	Application	Measure of number of cases opened despite failure to comply with application requirements (ISAR = Income Support Application Rejection).
29	FA/TANF Engagement Process Completion Rate	Receipt	Indicator examines all FA clients entering the engagement process each week and calculates the percentage that exits in five weeks or less.
30	SNA Engagement Process Completion Rate	Receipt	Same as 29, but for SNA (Safety Net Assistance) recipients.
31	FA Sanction Process Completion Rate	Receipt	Rate at which cases moved into the sanction process are resolved within six weeks.
32	SNA Sanction Process Completion Rate	Receipt	Same as 31, but for SNA cases.

* "Basic 10" Indicator
Note: Indicators are typically weekly rates averaged over a month.
Source: New York Human Resources Administration, *JobStat Reference Guide, Version 2.0.* (New York: HRA Office of Policy and Program Analysis, 2 July 2001).

Placements) currently and, ultimately, Indicators 6 (Still Off Public Assistance at 3 Months), and 8 (Still Off PA at 6 Months).

ADMINISTRATIVE INDICATORS

The seventeen Administrative Indicators, numbers 9 through 25, measure the management of the public assistance process. Subgroups cover timeliness (9–11), error rates (12–15), and dispute resolution—either through fair hearings or a mediation alternative introduced by HRA to speed up resolution and thus increase engagement (16–25). Indicators 9 and 10 result from a sample audit of cases; Indicator 11 comes directly from administrative data. The agency emphasizes the importance of reducing Welfare Management System errors because WMS data directly influence, by the agency's count, 15 other indicators.

Indicators 14 and 15 are drawn from the case sample HRA uses to estimate the TANF participation rate and errors in food stamp eligibility and payments assessment. The sample is accumulated over the year; the data serve as a check on the 800-case sample the state uses for a similar purpose. While 5,000 is an adequate sample size for statistical inference concerning the characteristics of the city's average monthly caseload over an entire year, the monthly samples for individual Job Centers are too small for use in assessing center performance. In an attempt to compensate, the JobStat indicators are based on the ratio of benefits granted in error to total grants recorded in the sample since the beginning of the current federal fiscal year; the quality of this estimate improves with sample accumulation. "Current" values are also reported; these cover the results over the most recent three months. In fact, even with these adjustments, by the end of the year, the sample sizes are still not large enough to support confident comparative assessment of center performance. The outcome becomes, in terms used by one HRA official, something of a "crap shoot."

Administrative indicators 16 and 17 are products of *Reynolds v. Giuliani*, a 1998 lawsuit challenging HRA's assistance intake procedures on grounds that the city's diversion-oriented benefit application procedures violated federal and state law. Indicator 16 relates to the choice applicants make to either withdraw from consideration for cash benefits or pursue eligibility. If found ineligible, applicants must be reviewed separately for Medicaid. (Similar eligibility reviews are done for Food Stamps.) One of the *Reynolds* contentions was that HRA was denying persons seeking assistance the opportunity to submit an application formally until alternative sources of support were considered. Such delays had real economic consequences because the Food Stamp benefit begins, for eligibles, on the date of signed application. The agency's *Reynolds* compliance plan set up a survey system in which persons are hired by the agency on a temporary basis specifically to visit centers and test for procedural compliance with the plan.

Administrative indicators 18 through 25 refer to the fair hearings process. The fair hearings system is maintained by New York State for applicants or recipients who believe they have been unfairly denied assistance or inappropriately sanctioned for failure to comply with agency regulations. Requests go directly to the New York State Office of Temporary and Disability Assistance (OTDA). OTDA sends lists of the requests to HRA grouped by center and issues.

Each center has a Fair Hearing Group responsible for attempting to resolve the issues. The first steps are informal, but the groups have authority to go to workers for explanation and to require client presentations. If not resolved informally or through mandatory dispute resolution reviews, the case eventually goes for resolution to an administrative law judge. Prior to the introduction of JobStat and related corrective action, the fair hearing decisions overwhelmingly favored clients, often because the agency was unable to assemble adequate documentation to support its decisions or to respond to complaints in timely fashion. For JobStat, HRA created indicators for every stage of the fair hearing process, signaling the importance attached by the agency to consistent application of rules, adequate documentation of enforcement decisions, and commitment to follow-through.

Indicator 28, ISAR Timeouts, is listed among the "self-sufficiency" indicators, but logically it belongs with the other administrative indicators. ISAR is HRA's system for monitoring the application process. (It stands for Income Support Application Rejection; the name is a residual from the days when Job Centers were Income Support offices.) The system creates lists of clients who have failed to comply with one or more public assistance application requirements, including referrals to Eligibility Verification and Review, Child Support Enforcement, and a Skills Assessment and Placement vendor. At the same time, a case action clock is ticking; HRA is obligated to act on cases within 25 days of application acceptance. Action in this process means changing a case to "under care" status, which is supposed to be contingent upon compliance with the various referral requirements. In some instances, however, caseworkers proceed with application processing without checking client compliance. The ISAR indicator is intended to create incentives to ensure that such review occurs. The lower the number of "ISAR timeouts," the better the Job Center's administrative performance.

SELF-SUFFICIENCY PROGRESS INDICATORS

The seven Self-Sufficiency Indicators, numbers 26 through 32, are of two types. The first refers to what HRA views as critical details of the assistance process. The second type is linked to the engagement report. The details judged sufficiently important to include in JobStat involve post-assistance child care and the TANF time limit. The focus on child care is, in part, the result of external criticism; critics have argued that recipients who go to work need, but cannot obtain, child-care assistance. The agency response is to reward centers for high rates of child-care subsidy carryover by people who were subsidy users while receiving assistance. As is true for some other Job-Stat indicators, this "Transitional Childcare Application Submit Rate" has flaws. For example, it refers only to persons who moved from a situation in which they combined work and welfare to work alone. This transition can be the product of a better job or higher earnings—accomplishments that might reduce the need for child-care subsidy. Therefore, a Job Center that was exceptionally adept at achieving job advancement among its clients might actually see its performance on this indicator decline. Perhaps more important is what's missed: The indicator might more accurately reflect its intent if the denominator included *all* persons closing cases for employment, not just those who had previously used the child-care subsidy.

Indicator 27, "Percentage Long-Time FA Reduction Rate," is an example of subpopulation targeting. It is focused on aid recipients "at risk of expiring their five-year time limited Family Assistance (FA)/TANF cash benefits" as described in the *JobStat Reference Guide* (Version 2.0).

NOTES

1. The author gratefully acknowledges contributions to this chapter from Michael Wiseman, Research Professor of Public Policy and Economics at the George Washington University, and Jason Turner, former Commissioner, New York City Human Resources Administration.

2. Dennis Smith with William Bratton, "Performance Management in New York City: Compstat and the Revolution in Police Management" in Dall W. Forsythe, ed., *Quicker Better Cheaper? Managing Performance in American Government* (Albany, N.Y.: Rockefeller Institute of Government, 2002), 456 (figure 1).

3. Smith and Bratton, "Performance Management," 455.

4. Recollections of Jason Turner, September 2003.

5. Andrew Bush, interview, May 31, 2001.

6. Jack Maple with Chris Mitchell, *The Crime Fighter: Putting the Bad Guys Out of Business* (New York: Doubleday, 1999), 93. Jack Maple called the system Comstat in his book, but noted that is was also known as CompStat, the name currently used by the New York City Police Department and by many of the city police departments around the country that have adopted the statistics-driven, crime-fighting approach.

7. The HRA Office of Policy and Program Analysis staffs the data collection and reporting functions of JobStat. This office has no direct line responsibility for operations.

8. Andrew S. Bush, Swati Desai, and Joanna Weissman, "New York City's JobStat Program: Managing for Performance in Large Welfare-to-Work Organizations," presented at the conference "Boosting Effectiveness in Urban Welfare Programs," Washington, D.C., July 19, 2000.

9. Andrew Bush, interview, May 31, 2001.

10. Peter M. Senge, *The Fifth Discipline: The Art and Practice of the Learning Organization* (New York: Currency Doubleday, 1990), 42 of Currency Paperback Edition (1994).

11. Jack Maple with Chris Mitchell, *Crime Fighter*, 134.

12. Reducing welfare case openings as a welfare reform goal has been controversial in New York City and elsewhere. The controversy centers around whether the thrust of "welfare prevention" policies is to divert people in short-term need from a system that is believed to have encouraged long-term dependency or whether needy people eligible for assistance are actively discouraged from applying by bureaucratic procedures and messages. Part of New York City's prevention efforts have focused on

reducing the number of cases opened for people who are not verifiably eligible. Like most welfare agencies that have viewed their mission as providing a safety net for the very poor, HRA has not historically initiated or participated in policies and programs to change the social conditions leading to the need for income support.

13. Jack Maple with Chris Mitchell, *Crime Fighter*, 108.

14. Mike Keating of AMS is credited with many of these lessons. AMS was the principal private sector contractor to HRA for the development and maintenance of JobStat.

15. Jack Maple with Chris Mitchell, *Crime Fighter*, 114.

16. Peter Senge, *Fifth Discipline*, 57.

17. William Bratton with Peter Knobler, *Turnaround: How America's Top Cop Reversed the Crime Epidemic* (New York: Random House, 1998), 239.

18. This description of JobStat indicators was prepared by Michael Wiseman.

6

Achieving "Full Engagement"

Douglas J. Besharov and Peter Germanis

The object of the Human Resources Administration's (HRA) welfare reform program is to engage the entire caseload in activities that reduce dependency and increase employability. It does so by striving to "engage" all eligible recipients in planned, constructive activities. HRA monitors "engagement" to assess and manage its program.

This analysis of engagement and participation trends is based on the agency's Weekly Engagement Reports and various other data sources. The Weekly Engagement Reports classify individuals into two main categories depending on whether they can be "engaged" in various work activities or not. "Engageable" cases are those with an able-bodied adult who is expected to participate in work activities. The reports further subdivide the engageable cases according to whether they are engaged or not and, if engaged, the activities or other engagement categories they are in. "Unengageable" cases are not expected to participate because they are exempt or otherwise excused from participation. The reports subdivide these cases according to the reason they are considered unengageable.

The data on engagement and participation trends are limited. In particular, we had only partial information prior to April 1999 (because Weekly Engagement Reports did not exist before then) and sporadic information afterward. In some cases, we filled in data gaps by relying on other HRA data or data from the Urban Institute's review of New York City's welfare reform efforts.[1] There were, however, some differences in definitions and measurement practices across these data sources, which may have introduced some bias into our assessment of trends over time. For example, the Weekly Engagement Report for October 23, 2000, indicated that there were 16,626

Family Assistance (FA) Work Experience Program (WEP) cases, whereas our extrapolation from an HRA chart suggests that there were only about 16,000 WEP cases. The difference arose because the number of WEP adults in the Weekly Engagement Reports is based on the primary engagement status for cases active at a point in time (every Sunday night), whereas the number in the WEP roster is a count of the number of people in WEP during a given two-week cycle. Similarly, we relied on the Urban Institute's tabulations of HRA data for 1996. The definition of "engaged" as used in the Urban Institute analysis, however, was different from HRA's definition in the later Weekly Engagement Reports. For example, the "needed at home" group was classified as "unengageable" in the Urban Institute, but as "engageable" and participating in community service in the later HRA reports. We adjusted the Urban Institute's data to make the two data sources more consistent with each other, but this was not always possible. Nevertheless, we believe the data problems are relatively minor and do not obscure the broad trends in engagement over time.

"UNENGAGEABLE" CASES

Participation is mandatory for almost all adults receiving either FA or SNA. However, some families are not expected to participate because they are "unengageable." The three major categories of unengageable cases are: "exempt," "child-only," and "active single-issue" cases, described below.

The following discussion usually makes comparisons of caseloads or activities at five points in time: November 1996, April 1999, December 1999, November 2001, and August 2002. The first date was chosen because most data are available only from that point; April 1999 was chosen because it is the first date that Weekly Engagement Reports became available; December 1999 was chosen because that is when full engagement was achieved; November 2001 was used because that is the last month before the first families reached Temporary Assistance for Needy Families' (TANF) five-year time limit and were transferred from the FA program to the SNA program; and August 2002 because that was the last month for which there were data as this report was being prepared.

The number of unengageable FA cases fell sharply between November 1996 and April 1999, as HRA narrowed available exemptions and monitored existing ones more rigorously. The number of unengageable cases declined 74 percent, from 165,150 to 42,870 (see figure 6.1).[2] The most significant factor in this decline was the narrowing of the age-of-child exemption for single mothers, followed by the narrower application of the exemption for those with temporary incapacities. Since the caseload also fell during this period, the percentage of the caseload considered unengageable did not fall quite as rapidly (64 percent), declining from 59 percent of the caseload to 21 percent. Between April 1999 and November 2001, the number of unengageable cases rose from 42,870 (21 percent) to 49,799 (35 percent), due to an increase in child-only and active single-issue cases. (In figure 6.1, for 1996, we labeled as "undetermined" child-only cases, active single-issue cases, and any residual, because we did not have data about the number of cases in these individual categories. Nevertheless, we estimate that a large number of these cases are child-only cases.) Note that the data for August 2002 include the FA cases that, because of the five-year time limit, were transferred to the SNA caseload.

The number of unengageable SNA cases also fell because of HRA's heightened scrutiny of exemptions (see figure 6.2). Between November 1996 and April 1999, the unengageable SNA caseload declined 51 percent, from 74,916 (49 percent of the caseload) to 37,698 (38 percent).[3] The tighter screening of cases claiming a temporary incapacity appears to be an important cause of this decline. This was followed by a period of relative stability.

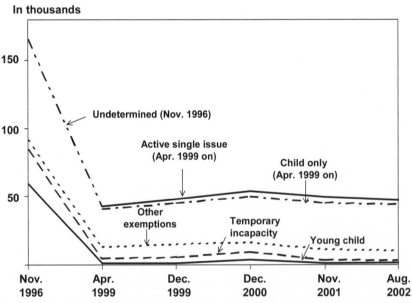

Figure 6.1.   Unengageable Family Assistance Cases in New York City, 1996–2002

Sources: New York City Human Resources Administration, "PA—Weekly Caseload Engagement Status" (New York City: New York City Human Resources Administration, various periods); and Demetra Smith Nightingale et al., *Work and Welfare Reform in New York City During the Giuliani Administration: A Study of Program Implementation* (Washington, D.C.: The Urban Institute, July 2002), B-2.

Note: Before 1998, Family Assistance was called "Aid to Families with Dependent Children" (AFDC). The data for August 2002 includes those FA cases that, because of the five-year time limit, were transferred to the SNA caseload.

In thousands

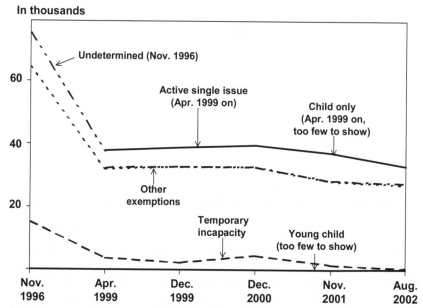

Figure 6.2.   Unengageable Safety Net Assistance Cases in New York City, 1996–2002

Sources: New York City Human Resources Administration, "PA—Weekly Caseload Engagement Status" (New York City: New York City Human Resources Administration, various periods); and Demetra Smith Nightingale et al., *Work and Welfare Reform in New York City During the Giuliani Administration: A Study of Program Implementation* (Washington, D.C.: The Urban Institute, July 2002), B-2.

Note: Before 1998, Safety Net Assistance was called "Home Relief." The data for August 2002 exclude those FA cases that, because of the five-year time limit, were transferred to the SNA caseload.

Between April 1999 and November 2001, it fell just 2 percent, from 37,698 to 37,048, although this represented a larger share of the caseload, growing from 38 percent to 49 percent.

Exempt Cases

Historically, the federal government allowed states to exempt large numbers of welfare recipients from work requirements. Under TANF, however, for purposes of calculating federal participation rates, relatively few adults can be exempted from participation.[4] There are only three limited exceptions. First, states may exclude single parents with a child under twelve months old, but this exclusion is limited to a lifetime maximum of twelve months for any adult. Second, states may exclude families receiving assistance in which an adult has been sanctioned for not complying with work activities, but this exclusion is limited to families that have been under a sanction for no more than three months in the preceding twelve-month period.

Finally, two-parent families that include a disabled parent are not included in the calculation of the higher two-parent participation rate, but they are included in the "all family" requirement.

Although states may exempt any other category of recipients, they must still meet their required participation rates for those not federally exempt, or face financial penalties. But, because federal participation requirements have been so easy for most states to meet under the current version of TANF,[5] most have exempted many more categories of recipients. As of October 1999, the most common exemptions were caring for a young child (forty-four states); disabled or temporary illness or incapacity (thirty-four states); caring for a disabled household member (twenty-eight states); advanced age (twenty-seven states); victim of domestic violence (twenty-four states); child care unavailable (nineteen states); and pregnant (twenty states).[6]

Under TANF, New York State narrowed its exemption policies to mothers with children under three months old, making it one of sixteen states that require parents with children less than a year old to participate. Otherwise, New York retained most of the exemptions that it had before TANF, mainly for those who are ill or injured (for up to three months), sixty years of age or older, under the age of sixteen or under the age of nineteen and in school, disabled or incapacitated, needed in the home to care for another member of the household; pregnant (in the later months of pregnancy or due to a medical assessment determination), or the parent of a child under three months of age in a single-parent home.[7] These same exemptions apply to the SNA program as well, although their relative importance varies due to differences in the characteristics of the two caseloads.

Overall, these changes in New York State's exemption policies resulted in a sharp initial decline in the total number of FA and SNA cases that were considered "exempt" in New York City, followed by a slower, but continued, decline afterwards. For FA cases, between November 1996 and April 1999, the number of exempt cases dropped from 91,380 cases (33 percent) to 13,282 cases (7 percent). Although the number continued to decline in subsequent years, the percentage of the total caseload that these cases comprised actually increased slightly. By November 2001, the number of exempt cases fell to 11,164 cases (8 percent).

For SNA cases, between November 1996 and April 1999, the number of exempt cases dropped from 64,136 cases (42 percent) to 31,967 cases (32 percent). As with the FA caseload, the number continued to decline, but their percentage of the total caseload increased slightly. By November 2001, the number of exempt cases fell to 28,121 cases (38 percent).

Young Child

Narrowing the age-of-child exemption for single parents with a child under six years of age to under three months did more to reduce the number of exempt adults than any other policy change. In November 1996, 59,596 FA cases (21 percent of the total caseload, including child-only cases) were considered exempt because they had a young child in the home. By April 1999 (and probably much sooner), this number had plummeted to just 1,382 cases (less than 1 percent of the caseload) and remained very low through November 2001, when it was just 1,356 cases (1 percent). (See figure 6.1.)

Limiting the age-of-child exemption had almost no effect on the number of exempt adults receiving SNA, because the program has traditionally focused on single adults and childless couples. Families with children applying for public assistance would be referred to the FA program. In November 1996, there were no SNA cases considered exempt because they had a young child in the home. Between April 1999 and November 2001, fewer than 100 cases reported being exempt for this reason in any given month (0 percent of the total caseload). Beginning with December 2001, this number may have increased as families that exhausted their five-year time-limited FA benefits were converted to SNA, but the number is still probably small.

Temporary Incapacity

Temporary exemptions for poor health or disabilities were also narrowed, but through administrative changes rather than legislation. HRA imposed more rigorous assessments of whether such incapacities preclude participation in a work-related activity. According to Jason Turner, HRA commissioner from 1998 through 2001, the agency was able to control the number of exempt cases by following through with third-party medical verifications for families claiming a disability or health problem and by assigning appropriate activities for those with a health or physical problem. HRA changed the focus of these medical evaluations (conducted by an independent contractor, Health Services Systems) from simply identifying those who should be exempt from participation to also focusing on what those with physical or health problems can do and assigning them to appropriate activities, in other words emphasizing what recipients can do, as opposed to what they cannot do. Turner explains that recipients are now given a list of work activities and are asked to identify those they feel they can do and those they cannot do.[8]

As a result of these stricter policies, between November 1996 and April 1999, the number of FA cases that were temporarily exempt due to a health problem or incapacity fell from 24,927 cases (9 percent of the caseload) to 3,423 cases (2 percent). The number of temporarily exempt cases continued to decline along with the rest of the caseload since then. By November 2001, the number had dropped to 3,042 cases and by August 2002 it had fallen further, to 2,305 cases, both representing about 2 percent of the caseload.

The tighter screening process also sharply reduced the number of SNA cases exempt due to a temporary incapacity. Between November 1996 and April 1999, the number of SNA cases that were temporarily exempt due to a health problem or incapacity fell from 15,182 cases (10 percent of the caseload) to 3,670 cases (4 percent). The number of temporarily exempt cases continued to decline along with the rest of the caseload throughout most of the period since then. By November 2001, the number had dropped to 1,960 cases (3 percent).

Some welfare advocates have criticized this stricter approach to recipients with disabilities. Health Services Systems has been criticized for performing perfunctory physical exams and ignoring test results and recommendations by recipients' personal physicians. A report of a bar association committee, for example, questioned the fairness of the treatment given to recipients who claim they should be exempt from work activities due to medical disabilities, accusing the for-profit contractor that evaluates such disability claims of "perfunctory physical examinations using physicians who could not or did not communicate with the clients and . . . disregarded and sometimes discarded their personal physician recommendations and test results."[9] According to the report, "Clients who challenged the employability determinations were rarely able to overturn the city's claims at these sophisticated hearings because they did not possess sufficient documentation, and, due to funding cutbacks for public interest law offices, were unable to obtain legal representation."[10] The same report accused HRA of running a biased hearing process in cases involving work requirements.[11]

HRA, however, defends its strict participation policies on the ground that it provides special activities and services for those with disabilities and other barriers to employment. As to the allegations of unfairness in the medical reviews, HRA officials explain that the third-party review is a de novo assessment, although the recipient's physician's notes are considered in the review process. The medical assessment includes a blood test, health and blood pressure measurements, an interview with the recipient about physical limitations, a drug screen, and additional tests determined to be necessary. Thus, they contend that the reviews allow for a more balanced application of work requirements, because the assessment tools are the same and the same medical vendors provide the results.

Other Exemptions

There was little change in the remaining exemption categories. This includes cases in which the parent or caretaker is elderly, receiving Supplemental Security Income (SSI) or has an SSI application pending, receiving AIDS-related assistance, awaiting assignment to the Personal Roads for Individual Development and Employment program (PRIDE), or is exempt for some unspecified reason.

The number of FA cases in these categories remained relatively stable between November 1996 and November 2001. Between November 1996 and April 1999, the number of such cases actually increased slightly, from 6,857 cases (2 percent) to 8,477 cases (4 percent), possibly reflecting an increase in SSI receipt, as some adults were able to avoid the work requirement. By November 2001, the number fell to 6,324 cases (4 percent). (The percentage rose because the FA caseload was falling during this period.)

The number of SNA cases in these exemption categories declined, but remained a relatively stable fraction of the caseload. Between November 1996 and April 1999, it fell from 48,954 cases (32 percent) to 28,275 cases (29 percent). This appears to be due to a sharp reduction in the number of cases with an adult receiving either SSI or Social Security benefits. By November 2001, the number of cases with one of these exemptions dropped further, to 26,086 cases (35 percent).

Child-Only Cases

Cases in which no adult in the family is receiving assistance, that is, "child-only" cases, are not subject to the participation requirement.[12] In November 2001, for example, there were 34,156 child-only cases in the FA program (about 24 percent of the caseload) that were not subject to a work requirement. Between December 1994 and April 1999, it appears that there was a large drop in the child-only caseload, from about 44,000 cases[13] to 27,814 cases. (Their share of the caseload was the same in both periods—14 percent—because the FA caseload was also falling.) Between April 1999 and November 2001, however, the number of child-only cases grew, from 27,814 to 34,156 in November 2001 (from 14 percent to 24 percent of the caseload). (As mentioned above in figure 6.1, for 1996, we labeled as "undetermined" child-only cases, active single-issue cases, and any residual, because we did not have data about the number of cases in these individual categories. Nevertheless, we estimate that a large number of these cases are child-only cases.)

The initial drop in the number of child-only cases was probably a by-product of the overall caseload decline,[14] but the reason for the turnaround since April 1999 (or earlier) is unclear. One possibility is that some parents may have left the family ("assistance unit") to avoid the new work requirements and put their children in the care of relatives while the child continues to receive welfare. Another possibility is an increase in the number of immigrant families that put their children on welfare (while the adult parents were not eligible). The growth in child-only cases is largely responsible for the steady increase in the proportion of the caseload deemed unengageable.

The number of child-only cases in the SNA program has always been very small, because the program has traditionally focused on single adults and childless couples.[15] Between April 1999 and November 2001, the number of such cases fell from 257 cases to 142 cases, too small to represent even 1 percent of the caseload.

More information is needed on the characteristics of these child-only cases to determine whether the adults in the household can also be "engaged." As Lawrence Mead, professor of politics at New York University, explains: "The idea that only the children receive support in these cases is a fiction. Congress should find a way to bring at least some of these groups under the work test, perhaps by putting the caretakers on the grant. A lesser reform would be to include these cases in the denominator for the work participation rate calculation."[16] For example, some cases may involve children living with immigrant parents not eligible for TANF. Although these parents do not receive assistance, it is possible that they could benefit from participation in various work-related activities. Alternatively, if work requirements cause some parents to leave their children with relatives, this unintended effect should be made known so that policymakers can explore its implications.

Active Single-Issue Cases

Applicants who receive one-time payments instead of going on welfare are considered "active single-issue cases." In most other states, such cases are called "diversion" cases, because the families receive payments to help them meet immediate needs and are thus diverted from welfare. (These cases are typically not counted as part of the caseload, because they receive only a temporary, one-time payment.) Between April 1999 and November 2001, the number of active single-issue FA cases grew from 1,774 cases to 4,479 (from 1 percent to 3 percent of the caseload).[17] One reason for the increase could be that some families may seek periodic one-time payments to avoid the hassle of applying for welfare and the subsequent work requirement. (Caseworkers may encourage families to take these payments for the same reason.) Another reason for the increase could be a reflection of the large number of families that left welfare who are on the borderline between self-sufficiency and dependency, and who may need a one-time payment to meet an immediate, but temporary, need.

In SNA, the number of active single-issue cases also experienced considerable growth. Between April 1999 and November 2001, the number of such cases grew from 5,474 cases (6 percent) to 8,785 cases (12 percent). As with FA cases, this increase could be a reflection of the desire for some recipients to seek periodic one-time payments to avoid the hassle of applying for welfare and the subsequent work requirement.

INCREASE IN "ENGAGEABLE" CASES

These policy changes resulted in large increases in the number and proportion of "engageable" cases, that is, cases with an able-bodied adult who is expected to participate in various work activities. These changes, however, had a much larger effect on FA cases than on SNA cases, as described below.

Family Assistance (FA)

There was a remarkable growth in the number of engageable FA cases, primarily due to the narrowing of the exemption for mothers with young children and the tightening of the process used to determine temporary exemptions due to illness or incapacity (see figure 6.3). Between November 1996 and April 1999, the number grew from 113,682 to 159,078, even as the overall caseload declined from 278,832 to 201,948. As a result, engageable cases nearly doubled as a proportion of the caseload, from 40 percent to 79 percent. By November 2001, the number of engageable cases fell to 91,289, largely due to the decline in the caseload. And the share of caseload considered engageable also fell, to 65 percent, largely due to the increase in child-only cases, as discussed above.

Safety Net Assistance (SNA)

Unlike the FA caseload, there has been a steady decline in the number of engageable SNA cases (see figure 6.4). This is largely because the exemption for parents with young children did not affect many SNA cases, since few of them had children. Between November 1996 and April 1999, the number of engageable cases fell from 77,953 (51 percent of the total caseload) to 60,981 (62 percent), and by November 2001, it dropped to 37,831 (51 percent).

"FULL ENGAGEMENT" ACHIEVED

In November 1996, fully one-third of the engageable FA caseload was unengaged, as was 11 percent of the SNA caseload. By December 1999, this was reduced to zero in both programs, so that "full engagement" was achieved.[18] Under HRA's definition, adults in recipient families are engaged if they are

In thousands

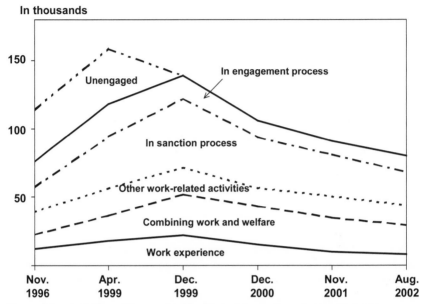

Figure 6.3.   Activities of Engageable Family Assistance Cases in New York City, 1996–2002

Sources: New York City Human Resources Administration, "PA—Weekly Caseload Engagement Status" (New York City: New York City Human Resources Administration, various periods); and Demetra Smith Nightingale et al., *Work and Welfare Reform in New York City During the Giuliani Administration: A Study of Program Implementation* (Washington, D.C.: The Urban Institute, July 2002), B-2.

Note: Before 1998, Family Assistance was called "Aid to Families with Dependent Children" (AFDC). The data for August 2002 include those FA cases that, because of the five-year time limit, were transferred to the SNA caseload.

(1) participating in an approved work-related activity (including specified educational and treatment activities), (2) in the process of being assigned to a work-related activity, or (3) sanctioned or in the process of being sanctioned. (An important qualification, however, is that the city's large number of child-only cases are not subject to participation requirements.) New York City's Independent Budget Office has complained that HRA uses "a fairly loose definition of full engagement."[19] This assessment is somewhat unfair because of the limitations placed on HRA by the absence of a full-family sanction and a true time limit on benefits. As Demetra Nightingale noted in chapter 2,

> "full engagement" merely means that all public assistance recipients are engaged in activities and are accounted for; they are either engaged in employment or work activities, in the assignment or assessment process, sanctioned for noncompliance, or appropriately classified as exempt from work activity.

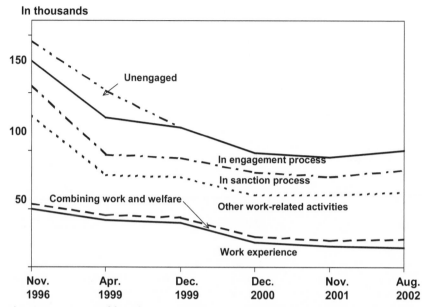

In thousands

Figure 6.4. Engageable Safety Net Assistance Cases in New York City, 1996–2002

Sources: New York City Human Resources Administration, "PA—Weekly Caseload Engagement Status" (New York City: New York City Human Resources Administration, various periods); and Demetra Smith Nightingale et al., *Work and Welfare Reform in New York City During the Giuliani Administration: A Study of Program Implementation* (Washington, D.C.: The Urban Institute, July 2002), B-2.

Note: Before 1998, Safety Net Assistance was called "Home Relief." The data for August 2002 exclude those FA cases that, because of the five-year time limit, were transferred to the SNA caseload.

Family Assistance (FA)

In November 1996, about one-third of the engageable FA caseload was unengaged, and, as mentioned, full engagement was reached in December 1999. In the period November 1996 to November 2001, among the major engagement categories, about 34 percent to 55 percent of all engageable cases were participating in approved work-related activities, about 11 to 17 percent were in the "in engagement process," and about 16 to 38 percent were in the "in sanction process" (see figure 6.5).

Safety Net Assistance (SNA)

As early as November 1996, the SNA caseload was already near full engagement, with just 9 percent of its engageable caseload classified as unen-

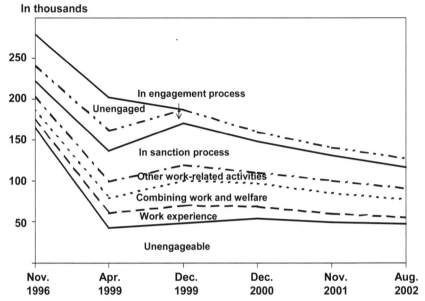

Figure 6.5. Engagement Status of Family Assistance in New York City, 1996–2002

Sources: New York City Human Resources Administration, "PA—Weekly Caseload Engagement Status" (New York City: New York City Human Resources Administration, various periods); and Demetra Smith Nightingale et al., *Work and Welfare Reform in New York City During the Giuliani Administration: A Study of Program Implementation* (Washington, D.C.: The Urban Institute, July 2002), B-2.

Note: Before 1998, Family Assistance was called "Aid to Families with Dependent Children" (AFDC). The data for August 2002 include those FA cases that, because of the five-year time limit, were transferred to the SNA caseload.

gaged. In the period November 1996 to November 2001, about 52 to 66 percent of the engageable cases were participating in approved work-related activities, about 11 to 22 percent were in the "in engagement process," and about 12 to 20 percent were in the "in sanction process" (see figure 6.6).

As for the FA cases that were transferred to SNA (because they exceeded the five-year federal time limit on benefits), in August 2002, for example, this group of then 36,967 families was already fully engaged. About 63 percent of the engageable cases were participating in approved work-related activities, about 11 percent were in the "in engagement process," and about 26 percent were in the "in sanction process." At least in that month, the engagement rates and patterns of this group mirrored FA cases.

Work-Related Activities

Besides actual paid work and work experience activities, HRA counts other activities as work-related, including education, training, and other activities that are related to work.[20]

In thousands

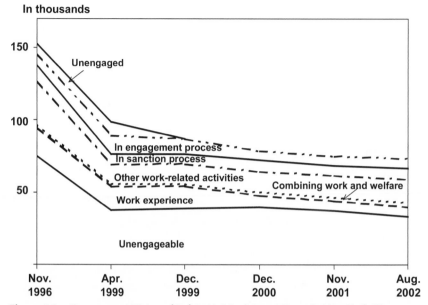

Figure 6.6. Engagement Status of Safety Net Assistance Cases in New York City, 1996–2002

Sources: New York City Human Resources Administration, "PA—Weekly Caseload Engagement Status" (New York City: New York City Human Resources Administration, various periods); and Demetra Smith Nightingale et al., *Work and Welfare Reform in New York City During the Giuliani Administration: A Study of Program Implementation* (Washington, D.C.: The Urban Institute, July 2002), B-2.

Note: Before 1998, Safety Net Assistance was called "Home Relief." The data for August 2002 exclude those FA cases that, because of the five-year time limit, were transferred to the SNA caseload.

- For FA, between November 1996 and April 1999, the percentage of the engageable caseload participating in any activity increased, going from 34 percent (39,251 cases) to 35 percent (56,413 cases). By December 1999, it had jumped to 52 percent (71,671 cases), as full engagement was achieved. In November 2001, the percentage increased further to 55 percent (56,496 cases).

- For SNA, during the same period, the percentage of the engageable caseload participating in any activity initially fell, but then returned to its earlier level. Between November 1996 and April 1999, the percentage of engageable cases participating in a work activity fell from 67 percent (52,278 cases) to 52 percent (31,497 cases). By December 1999, it rebounded to 64 percent (30,964 cases). In November 2001, the percentage increased further, to 66 percent (24,798 cases), nearly matching its November 1996 level.

Work Experience Program

WEP, or workfare, is the centerpiece of New York City's work-based welfare system. In WEP, recipients are assigned to public and private agencies to perform actual work.

- For FA, between November 1996 and April 1999 participation in WEP increased rapidly from 10 percent (11,757 cases) to 14 percent (17,862 cases) of engageable cases. Participation peaked in December 1999, reaching 16 percent of the engageable caseload (21,933 cases). However, the use of WEP then waned, dropping to just 11 percent of engageable cases by November 2001 (and just 10,127 cases). In addition, there was a marked shift from "basic WEP" to WEP combined with other activities. Between April 1999 and November 2001, the percentage of WEP participants in "basic WEP" declined from 86 percent to just 10 percent.

- For SNA in this period, WEP participation cases initially increased more slowly than FA as a percentage of the engageable caseload, but this may be because, compared to the FA caseload, it started at a relatively high level. Between November 1996 and April 1999, it increased from 26 percent (19,982 cases) to 27 percent (16,219 cases) of engageable cases. Participation peaked in December 1999, reaching 32 percent of the engageable caseload (15,320 cases). As with the FA caseload, SNA participation on WEP then declined, dropping to 19 percent of engageable cases by November 2001 (and just 7,186 cases). There was also a similarly large shift in the SNA caseload from "basic WEP" to WEP combined with other activities. Between April 1999 and November 2001, the percentage of WEP participants in "basic WEP" declined from 88 percent to just 12 percent.

Combining Work and Welfare

HRA considers as engaged, welfare recipients who are working, but at such low wages or so few hours that they continue to receive benefits. This may or may not help reduce dependency, as discussed below.

The ability of recipients to work and receive welfare benefits is dependent on the state's "earnings disregard," that is, a threshold of earnings that is not taken into account in determining the welfare grant. Under Aid to Families with Dependent Children (AFDC), the federal government set the amount of the earnings disregard nationally. For all practical purposes, the AFDC earnings disregard was limited to the first $90 in earnings, after which benefits were reduced dollar-for-dollar as earnings increased—a 100 percent marginal tax rate. Under TANF, though, individual states set the amount of their earnings disregards, and most greatly liberalized them. In 1997, New York State expanded the earned income disregards in its FA program to allow families to remain eligible until their gross income reached the poverty level (about $14,250 for a family of three in 2001). In that first year, the disregard was $90 plus 42 percent of the remainder of the family's monthly earned income. Reflecting rises in the federal poverty guidelines (because of inflation), the percentage disregarded has been increased each year and was 50 percent in 2002. These expansions raised the income eligibility limit for recipients with earnings from about 50 percent of the poverty level before 1999 to 100 percent of the poverty level afterward.

- For FA, the largest increase in participation was among those combining work and welfare. Between November 1996 and April 1999, the percentage of the engageable caseload combining work and welfare increased slightly, from 10 percent (11,005 cases) to 12 percent (18,821 cases). The expansion in the earnings disregard, beginning in 1999, seems to be the reason for the rapid increase in the percentage combining work and welfare after April 1999, reaching 22 percent by December 1999 (30,316 cases) and 26 percent (25,106 cases) by November 2001.
- For SNA, the percentage of engageable cases combining work and welfare tripled between November 1996 and November 2001. However, both the absolute number of such combiners and their share of the caseload were relatively small, increasing from 2 percent (1,824 cases) to 6 percent (2,081 cases). We hypothesize that there are so few "combiners" in the SNA program because most recipients were single adults receiving relatively small grants. Those who find work generally have earnings high enough to make them ineligible for cash assistance.

Education and Training Activities

Although TANF emphasizes participation in work and work-related activities in regard to satisfying participation rates/requirements, states are free to require participation in other program components, including education and training activities. HRA considers participation in such activities as engagement—if they are consistent with a recipient's employability plan.

- For FA, between April 1999 and November 2001 the percentage of the engageable FA caseload participating in such activities was relatively stable, falling slightly from 7 percent (11,692 cases) to 6 percent (5,274 cases).[21]

- For SNA during this same period, the percentage of the engageable SNA caseload participating in education and training activities increased, from 1 percent (516 cases) to 4 percent (1,390 cases), although participation in these activities remained relatively low overall.

Treatment Activities

Some welfare recipients cannot participate in work programs because they have serious substance abuse problems. An increasing share of FA and SNA cases is participating in various treatment activities, often in lieu of mandatory work. (Many treatment programs include a work component; see chapter 9.) Among FA cases, there was a marked increase in participation in treatment activities.

- For FA, between April 1999 and November 2001 the percentage of the engageable caseload in treatment programs grew from 0 percent (421 cases) to 2 percent (2,044 cases).
- For SNA there was a similar increase. Between April 1999 and November 2001, the percentage of the engageable caseload participating in treatment activities increased from 19 percent (11,558 cases) to 27 percent (10,311 cases). This increase in participation may reflect improved coordination between HRA and substance-abuse treatment providers.

Wellness/Rehabilitation

Recipients with a short-term medical problem are placed in a wellness/rehab program, where they can receive treatment for their illness and report back in several months. The main focus of the wellness initiative was to address individuals with chronic health problems such as diabetes, high blood pressure, asthma, and so on, who first need to be in a proper health regime and learn how to manage their chronic health problem. The required engagement plan for recipients in this category was prepared by the medical assessment contract provider; it involved having them get medical rehabilitation services and having their condition regularly assessed. Once the condition was stabilized, usually in three to six months, they moved on to a combined work, rehabilitation, and training engagement plan. The wellness plan was mandatory and failure to cooperate resulted in the normal work sanction.

- For FA, between April 1999 and November 2001 the percentage of the engageable FA caseload participating in wellness/rehab activities increased from 0 percent (0 cases) to 2 percent (2,044 cases).

- For SNA during this same period, the percentage of the engageable SNA caseload participating in education and training activities increased from 0 percent (0 cases) to 7 percent (2,667 cases), although participation in these activities remained relatively low overall.

Community Service

Working in a public or nonprofit agency, either for pay or not, is generally considered a form of community service and would ordinarily be an allowable activity under TANF. New York State defines this activity broadly to include caring for family members with impairments or other special needs.[22] Thus, recipients who are "needed at home" are considered to have met their participation requirements. This is not a complete change in policy, because under the old AFDC program, they would have been exempt from participation. However, since federal law no longer provides this as an exemption, counting such activities as participation would help the state meet applicable participation requirements. Foster parents are also considered to be providing a community service.

HRA is apparently careful in granting exemptions in this category, which is both amorphous and easily abused.

- For FA, the percentage of engageable cases classified as "needed at home" remained steady at 5 percent between April 1999 (7,617 cases) and November 2001 (4,638 cases).[23]
- For SNA, the same pattern is evident, with 3 percent of engageable cases "needed at home" in April 1999 (1,606 cases) and in November 2001 (1,025 cases).

Other Activities

Beginning in late 2000, HRA began offering some public assistance recipients temporary, subsidized jobs. For example, under the Job Opportunities Program, HRA developed arrangements with three city agencies to create temporary, one-year jobs paying about $8 to $10 per hour.[24]

- For FA, in November 2001, 3 percent (2,352 cases) of engageable cases were in a subsidized job.
- For SNA, 1 percent (397 cases) of engageable SNA cases were in a subsidized job.

"In Engagement Process"

Even in a "full engagement" program, some people experience periods when they are not participating in any activity and are waiting for an assignment. This generally happens when they either lose an exemption or have completed an activity and have not yet been assigned to a new one. HRA tries to minimize such periods of inactivity by calling nonparticipants into the office within two weeks of a change in status (referred to as "call-in appointment scheduled"). Because recipients are involved with HRA while they are being assessed and assigned to appropriate work activities, this process is also considered a form of engagement and is called the "engagement process."

In the past, it could take weeks, even months, for HRA to assign nonparticipants to program activities. With the adoption of its "full engagement" model, however, HRA also appears to have streamlined the engagement process.

- For FA, between November 1996 and November 2001, the percentage of engageable cases in the engagement process steadily declined from 17 percent (19,173 cases) to 11 percent (10,022 cases). This is a reflection of heightened monitoring and scheduling activities intended to minimize down time.
- For SNA, in contrast to the trend in the FA caseload, the percentage of cases in the engagement process increased. Between November 1996 and November 2001, the percent waiting to be assigned to an activity increased from 10 percent (8,380 cases) to 17 percent (6,528 cases). We assume that this was caused by their greater need for treatment services. It may take longer initially to assess their condition and place them in an appropriate activity, thus leaving them in the engagement process longer.

"In Sanction Process"

Engagement includes both being "sanctioned" or "in the process of being sanctioned." The latter is important because before a sanction can be imposed, HRA must provide individuals an opportunity to resolve in a conciliation conference the problems associated with nonparticipation. If HRA determines that a sanction should be imposed, a recipient can still request a fair hearing and benefits continue until a hearing decision has been made. This process can be time consuming and can delay the time it takes to actually impose a sanction. (For FA cases, a first sanction can be ended when the nonparticipant complies with program requirements. In the case of a second sanction, benefits are reduced for a minimum of three months, and in the case of all subsequent sanctions, benefits are reduced for a minimum of six months. For SNA cases without children, the first and second minimum sanction periods are slightly longer—three months and five months, respectively.)

Between November 1996 and April 1999, the percentage of engageable FA cases "in sanction process" category (including sanctioned cases) increased from 16 percent (17,727 cases) to 24 percent (37,911 cases). By December 1999, it had reached 37 percent (50,743 cases), after which point it seems to have leveled off. In November 2001, for example, 34 percent (30,679 cases) of the engageable caseload was in the sanction process.

For FA cases, most of the growth in this category since April 1999—the earliest period for which detailed data are available—was the result of an increase in the number of cases with a sanction in effect, rather than in the number in the process of being sanctioned, such as being part of the conciliation or fair hearing process. For example, between April 1999 and November 2001 alone the percent of those in the category that were actually under a sanction increased from 20 percent to 51 percent, reflecting HRA's commitment to making the process more efficient.

The large proportion of engaged cases that are under a sanction rather than in a work-related activity raises important concerns. Jo Anne Barnhart and her colleagues call this high level of sanctions a "major barrier faced by NYC in moving case heads into work and self-sufficiency."[25] For example, alternative policies may be needed to bring the "happily sanctioned" into compliance, as discussed below.

The percentage of engageable SNA cases in the sanction process also increased, but was considerably lower than the corresponding percentage for the FA caseload. Between November 1996 and November 2001, the percentage of engageable SNA cases in the sanction process increased from 13 percent (10,386 cases) to 17 percent (6,505 cases). (See figure 6.6.) However, the percentage in November 2001 was half that of the FA caseload (17 percent vs. 34 percent). This relatively low percentage reflects the fact that over 95 percent of SNA cases have traditionally been single adults, where a sanction usually meant case closure. Indeed, the percentage of engageable cases that were in the process of being sanctioned was about the same for the two programs (16 percent for FA and 17 percent for SNA).

LESSONS LEARNED

Almost every objective observer agrees that the implementation of New York City's welfare reform program was a tremendous administrative and management accomplishment—especially given the city's bureaucratic and political environment. The city's Human Resources Administration (HRA) under Mayor Giuliani and Commissioner Turner demonstrated that it is possible to run a large work-experience program that uses a "full engagement" model of case management and requires twenty hours a week of mandatory work experience plus fifteen hours a week of mandatory educational and treatment services.[26] As a result, it is widely seen as a model for how a high-intensity program should be run.[27]

HRA succeeded in establishing a high-participation, work-oriented welfare system largely by using the tools provided under the old Aid to Families with Dependent Children (AFDC) program. It did not have TANF's two best-known components: a full-family sanction or a time limit on benefits. But it did have two other important TANF tools: the ability to deny eligibility to an applicant who fails to perform a job search or comply with other application requirements and the ability to increase the earnings disregard. Therefore, it is useful to consider what lessons that New York City's experience provides.

Participation Rates

- Beginning the engagement process as soon as a family applies for welfare appears to have raised participation rates.
- Careful assessment of illness and disability claims (and services to address them) can substantially reduce the number of exemptions from participation granted for these reasons.
- Narrowing the age-of-child exemption for single parents from those having a child under six years of age to those having a child under three months of age increased the number of adults expected to participate by about 50 percent. HRA's experience suggests that mothers with such young children can work without severe disruption to the family. At the same time, new demands for child care and other support services were created.
- In any high-participation welfare regime, "unsubsidized employment" (combining work and welfare) is likely to be a major activity.
- The growth of child-only cases removed a growing share of the caseload from the engageable caseload; developing strategies to engage this group may be the next big challenge.
- Even New York City, with one of the largest WEP programs in the nation, would not meet the putative 70 percent participation requirement in the pending bills to reauthorize TANF because (as of December 2002) about 17 percent of its engaged cases were "in sanction process" and another 17 percent were in the "in engagement process," neither of which is considered a countable TANF activity. In addition, the nearly 10 percent of its caseload excluded from participation due to age, disability, health, or other problems would become subject to participation

requirements. Combined, these categories would account for about half of the caseload subject to participation requirements.

- The proposed reauthorization of TANF sharply raises participation requirements. In order to meet these new participation requirements (once they are fully phased in), New York City would have to increase by as much as 50 percent the participation in its work experience and other activities (unless more welfare families were placed in separate state programs). (For the United States as a whole, the increase would have to be much larger, because the overall participation rate and the number of adults in work experience are considerably lower in most other states than in New York City.)

"Safety Net" Cases

- The SNA program's full-family sanctions help keep participation rates high and may have a larger smoke-out effect than the partial sanctions in the FA program.
- SNA recipients are much more likely than FA recipients to have substance-abuse problems that limit their full participation in work activities. Among those deemed engageable, about one-third participate in treatment at any point in time.
- Even in the SNA program, careful assessment of illness and disability claims (and services to address them) can reduce the number of exemptions from participation granted for these reasons. Nevertheless, about one-third of the SNA caseload is exempt due to age or disability and is not likely to participate in work activities.
- The benefits of an SNA work experience program are likely to exceed its costs, especially since child-care costs are low and sanction savings are high (due to the full-family sanction for single adults).
- Unsubsidized employment (combining work and welfare) is not a major component of SNA participation, probably because the welfare grant for a single-person household is relatively low.

NOTES

1. Demetra Smith Nightingale, Nancy Pindus, Frederica D. Kramer, John Trutko, Kelly Mikelson, and Michael Egner, *Work and Welfare Reform in New York City during the Giuliani Administration: A Study of Program Implementation* (Washington, D.C.: Urban Institute Labor and Social Policy Center, July 2002).

2. Due to data gaps, the size of the decline is somewhat uncertain. We estimated the number of unengageable cases for November 1996 by relying on data from the Urban Institute. (See Nightingale et al., *Work and Welfare Reform*, B-2.) They estimated the number of unengageable cases for that month at 95,957, but because they

excluded child-only and active single-issue cases, their numbers are not consistent with ours (or HRA's), so this should be viewed as a minimum. Alternatively, we subtracted the number of engageable cases, as reported by the Urban Institute, from the total caseload, as reported by HRA, to derive an estimate of 165,150, which may be somewhat high, since it would mean that about 70,000 cases are unengageable because they are child-only or active single-issue cases. (The Urban Institute did not count "needed at home" as engageable, even though HRA includes them in this category, as we do as well. However, this number was not reported in November 1996, but it is possible that if this number were added back to the engageable group, the number of unengageables would be slightly smaller.) Nevertheless, we use the latter estimate, because it appears to be most consistent with the data in HRA's Weekly Engagement Reports.

3. For November 1996, the Urban Institute estimated the number of unengageable SNA cases at 64,136, but they excluded child-only and active single-issue cases, so this should be viewed as a minimum. Subtracting the number of engageable SNA cases, as reported by the Urban Institute, from the total SNA caseload, as reported by HRA, yields an estimate of 74,916 unengageable SNA cases. The main difference appears to be the treatment of active single-issue cases, since child-only cases are a very small proportion of the caseload. We use this latter estimate since it is most consistent with the data summarized from Weekly Engagement Reports.

4. TANF permits states that had welfare waivers to continue their pre-TANF policies until the waiver expires. These waivers could affect the allowable work activities, hours of participation, and exemptions.

5. See "Statement of Douglas J. Besharov, Professor, University of Maryland School of Public Affairs, College Park, Maryland, and Resident Scholar, Public Policy Research, American Enterprise Institute," before the Committee on Ways and Means, Subcommittee on Human Resources, *Implementation of Welfare Reform Work Requirements and Time Limits*, 107th Cong., 2nd session, March 7, 2002, 69–83.

6. Center for Law and Social Policy and Center on Budget and Policy Priorities, *Work Requirements: Exemptions*, July 2000, available from http://www.spdp.org/tanf/exemptions.pdf, accessed August 1, 2002.

7. The state actually exempts a parent in a single-parent family if the child is under twelve months of age, but the exemption is limited to three months for any one child; so as a practical matter, the exemption is limited to parents with a child under three months. In addition, the exemption is limited to a maximum of twelve months over a parent's lifetime.

8. Jason Turner, former commissioner, New York City Human Resources Administration, conversation with Peter Germanis, January 15, 2002.

9. Association of the Bar of the City of New York (ABCNY), Committee on Social Welfare Law, *Welfare Reform in New York City: The Measure of Success* (New York City: Committee on Social Welfare Law, August 2001), available from http://www.abcny.org/currentarticle/welfare.html, accessed January 11, 2002.

10. ABCNY, *Welfare Reform in New York City.*

11. ABCNY, *Welfare Reform in New York City.*

12. Child-only cases do not include cases where the adult has been removed from

the grant due to a sanction, since such cases would be reflected in the "in sanction" category. Swati Desai, then executive deputy commissioner, Office of Program Reporting, Analysis, and Accountability, New York City Human Resources Administration, e-mail to Douglas Besharov, June 17, 2003.

13. Although we do not have data on FA child-only cases prior to April 1999, we have the number of Public Assistance child-only cases in December 1994 (45,930). Since it appears that over 95 percent of Public Assistance child-only cases have typically been FA cases, we estimate that there were about 44,000 FA child-only cases in December 1994.

14. The caretakers of children in child-only cases, primarily either nonparental relatives or ineligible immigrant parents, presumably benefited from the same strong economic conditions that drove down caseloads generally.

15. Prior to December 2001, the SNA program was primarily limited to single adults and childless couples. However, some FA household heads could be placed in the SNA program as child-only cases if they failed to comply with mandatory drug treatment. Since December 2001, families with children who have exhausted their five-year, time-limited FA benefits have been transferred to the SNA program. As a result, the number of child-only cases could increase, simply because a larger share of the SNA caseload is composed of families with children. Nevertheless, the number is likely to remain small, because most of the transferred cases had a parent or caretaker receiving assistance.

16. Lawrence M. Mead, professor of politics, New York University, Testimony before the Committee on Finance of the United States Senate, "The Reauthorization of TANF," April 10, 2002, 4, available from http://finance.senate.gov/hearings/testimony/041002lmtest.pdf, accessed March 10, 2003.

17. We did not have access to data on the number of active single-issue cases prior to April 1999.

18. Nightingale et al., *Work and Welfare Reform*, 18.

19. Paul Lopatto, "Growing Share of Welfare Caseload Exempt from City's Workfare Program," *Inside the Budget* (Independent Budget Office newsletter), no. 82 (May 4, 2001): 1, available from http://www.ibo.nyc.ny.us/, accessed January 10, 2002.

20. Nightingale and her colleagues report: Once New York City's caseload decline leveled off, administrators revamped their program approaches to allow a broader range of activities to count toward fulfilling the work requirement, rather than just regular employment or unpaid workfare. (Nightingale et al., *Work and Welfare Reform*, ix.)

21. We did not have access to data on the number of cases participating in education, remedial, and treatment activities prior to April 1999.

22. New York's Office of Temporary and Disability Assistance gives localities flexibility in defining community service, but specifies that (an individual needed in the home because another member of the household requires his/her presence due to a verified mental or physical impairment shall be deemed to be engaged in community service to the extent such person is actually providing care for such member of the household. (See New York State Department of Labor, "Section 1300.9: Work Activities and Work Requirements," 9-2, available from http://www.labor.state.ny.us/pdf/13009.pdf, accessed February 3, 2003.)

23. We did not have access to data on the number of cases participating in community service prior to April 1999.

24. Jo Anne Barnhart, Deborah Chassman, and Sandie Hoback, *Moving from Full Engagement to Full Employment: A Program Review of New York City's Welfare Reform* (Klamath Falls, Oreg. American Institute for Full Employment, November 5, 2001), 14.

25. Barnhart, Chassman, and Hoback, *Moving from Full Engagement*, 14.

26. See, for example, Nightingale et al., *Work and Welfare Reform*, vii, stating: "Without question the City's welfare reform is work-centered, with strong emphasis on ensuring that all able-bodied adults are subject to work requirements, rapid imposition of sanctions for those who do not comply, and assignment to WEP jobs for those who are not employed in the regular labor market."

27. Nightingale et al., *Work and Welfare Reform*, iii, stating: "New York City has more welfare recipients than any other city in the nation (one out of every 13 cases nationwide receiving Temporary Assistance for Needy Families [TANF] [FA in New York] in 2001) and represents one of the strictest systems in terms of work participation requirements. As such, the operational experiences suggest lessons important to New York City and to federal welfare policy makers implementing large scale work programs—lessons about restructuring a large and entrenched bureaucracy and about adapting priorities and programs to changing policies, economic conditions, and caseload characteristics."

7

Overcoming Opposition and Giving Work Experience to Welfare Applicants and Recipients

James Clark

A principal element of Mayor Giuliani's welfare reform was the Work Experience Program (WEP). New York has had a mandatory work requirement since 1971, when many single adults receiving Home Relief had to "work off" their grants. Modest in scale at first, and involving only a fraction of those eligible, the program gradually expanded to include other categories of welfare recipients. In keeping with his basic belief that welfare recipients had obligations to society as well as rights, Mayor Giuliani in 1995 adopted a policy of requiring all able-bodied adults on Home Relief to seek employment or work in an expanded public works program. WEP was an attempt by the mayor to restore the work ethic and to help people believe that they could be useful to themselves and society.

Almost immediately the mayor came under attack from advocacy groups. Norman Seigel, the American Civil Liberties Union's executive director, denounced the initiative and said that it would produce a sub-labor workforce working under sub-labor conditions. On the other hand, Stanley Hill, the District Council 37 executive director, voiced his support of the initiative as long as it gave participants training that would lead to real jobs.

Lillian Barrios-Paoli, the city's human resources administrator at that time, proceeded to expand the public works program over the next year. Meanwhile Congress continued to pass welfare reform legislation that President Clinton would veto three times before eventually signing. Without the congressional authority to alter the Aid to Families with Dependent Children (AFDC) program, New York initially focused on Home Relief recipients. By the end of the year, what had been a small program with about 10,000 participants under Giuliani's two predecessors, Mayors Edward Koch and David Dinkins, expanded to include 35,000 people working at various municipal tasks.

HOW WEP WORKS

In operational terms, implementation of the welfare reform had three components. The first level consisted of traditional staff workers, who acted as application specialists and case managers. The second level was composed of vendors who performed the job-search and job-club functions in a six-week effort to find immediate employment. A third level was composed of sub-vendors engaged in short-term training, job referral/placement activities, and medical and psychological reviews. Welfare recipients who failed in their efforts to get a job at the second level would be referred to WEP, where they would work in city agencies and nonprofit organizations that developed openings to provide job experience. The largest agencies operated independent staff training and reporting systems that acted much like small personnel units. Support services in the form of child care or medical examinations were provided by another group of vendors.

When an applicant applied for assistance or a current recipient was reassessed for a continuation of assistance, information was entered into an interactive system that allowed different HRA workers and contractors to access and input data and that facilitated the assignment of participants to various work sites or employment services placement (ESP) vendors. The system was known as the "New York City Way," or NYCWAY, with WAY being an acronym for Work, Accountability, and You. Information about the applicant's skills and circumstances was collected so that he or she could be placed in an appropriate work situation. Thus a person could be identified as an ex-offender or addict, someone without a high school education or a driver's license, or someone who could do only light indoor work. The system tracked individual appointments, sent out letters requesting additional appointments, arranged conciliation meetings, initiated sanctions, and matched an individual who had specific barriers to employment with WEP assignments that accommodated the barriers. An attempt was made to assign people to jobs near their homes to minimize their travel time. Requirements for job and language skills, pre-employment training, and the like were indicated and matched with client skills.

Some recipients "worked" the system; that is, they knew the regulations and the limits of the city's ability to impose penalties. When such recipients were identified, appropriate counseling was initiated. Notice had to be given 10 days before someone's grant could be reduced, and participants could request a conciliation that would further delay any action. If everything always occurred on the last day allowed, it was assumed that the participant was "working" the system. If the recipient agreed to comply, he or she would not be sanctioned. If there were a second noncompliance incident, the regulations required a sanction of several days before reinstatement; a third incident required a longer period of compliance before reinstatement. Non-compliant participants could—and often did—work the system for many months before working at a job. The NYCWAY system gave case managers more information about their clients and helped them move participants into jobs. They could consult the system at any time to find out where a WEP participant was employed and to which of the employment-services vendors he or she was assigned.

FEDERAL WELFARE REFORM

The Personal Responsibility and Work Opportunities Reconciliation Act of 1996 (PRWORA) was signed into law by President Clinton and fundamentally altered both the way people received assistance and federal–state relations. After vetoing several versions of the new law, Clinton agreed with a version that affected only AFDC and excluded Medicaid and the Food Stamp program. The law limited the time that a person or family could receive assistance under the AFDC program to a period of five years in a lifetime. The name, Aid to Families with Dependent Children, which had been in place for 60 years and was seen to imply *continual* aid, was changed to Temporary Assistance to Needy Families (TANF).

The restrictions in the earlier law on how much public work could be required were removed and replaced with a requirement that recipients would have to work a minimum of 20 hours for the first two years the new law was in effect, increasing to 30 hours in 2000. What constituted "work" was defined narrowly and included subsidized employment in the private or public sector, on-the-job training, community service, vocational education, and education required by an employer. General education was limited to people under twenty years old who had not completed high school. Education or training was limited to 12 months. Job search was limited to six weeks a year.

The focus of the new law was on work. It reflected Congress's belief that under the prior law the states had defined activities in a way that allowed too many recipients to be excused from participation. Those who did participate often participated only marginally or in activities that did not result in economic independence. Work advocates proclaimed, "work works," adding that it should be "up-front" and ongoing.

The TANF legislation provided for a grant based on a state's former level of state AFDC expenditures. It required the state to maintain prior funding levels and to spend the grant only on specifically authorized activities. Penalties would be imposed if the state spent less than 80 percent of what it had previously budgeted or spent the block grant on unauthorized activities.

Failure to have enough participants engaged in work activities or engaged for the number of hours that constituted work would also result in penalties. Levels of participation were prescribed, beginning with 25 percent participation the first year and rising to 50 percent in the last year of the five-year, block-grant period. Similarly, participation did not count if the hours per week did not reach 20 in the first year, rising to 30 in 2000. A state could avoid penalties by reducing the number of recipients from the base period; that is, those who left welfare were counted as "participating." For example, a state that cut its welfare rolls in half was credited with 50 percent participation.

GIULIANI, FEDERAL WELFARE REFORM, AND THE CRITICS

The 1996 TANF legislation gave the states and cities flexibility with respect to personal responsibility. Welfare recipients who failed to meet their work obligations could be removed from the rolls. Although this had been true for many years, federal regulatory constraints in the past made it difficult to do. One major change allowed states to impose a "full family sanction": the entire household would be denied assistance if the parent refused to accept employment or otherwise failed to honor the work requirement. Prior to this change, a noncompliant parent could lose his or her grant, but a reduced grant was still provided to the head of the household. This provision for "full family sanction" was adopted by many states, but not by New York.

"Sanctioning" increased after the new law went into effect; advocacy groups saw this as "throwing people off" welfare. In the year before Mayor Giuliani assumed office, 13.1 percent of recipients were removed from welfare for failure to comply with the work requirements; in 1995 and 1996 the rate more than doubled to 30.2 percent.[1]

The TANF legislation also allowed New York to require a work program for participants in the TANF program similar to the one in place for Safety Net Assistance (SNA) recipients, formerly called Home Relief recipients. The potentially explosive expansion of the WEP was seen by the public-employee unions as a direct frontal assault, "union busting," threatening that WEP workers could replace strikers and that the expected growth of union jobs would be curtailed by the employment of welfare recipients. Lawsuits were common, and the city had a contentious relationship with DC 37, the New York affiliate of the American Federation of State, County, and Municipal Employees (AFSCME). Although federal law prohibited the replacement of laid-off workers by welfare recipients, and the mayor said he would not do it, there was not enough trust between the parties.

In the Parks Department, for example, the number of people working in administration fell from 2,786 in 1990 to 1,925 under Mayor Dinkins in 1994 and then to 1,156 under Mayor Giuliani. A critic of WEP who saw such a large workforce reduction and a parallel rise in WEP workers would consider it proof that WEP participants were replacing union workers. For city administrators who were trying to balance the budget and live within their revenue, WEP was a way to get important work done while reinforcing the social contract between city government and its citizens.

In 1996, New York City Transit agreed to use WEP workers as part of its new contract with Transport Workers Union Local 100. On an average day, 200 WEP participants were assigned to the Transit Authority. The union was mollified, however, because hundreds of new civil service positions for cleaners were added, increasing the number of regular cleaner positions to 2,600—almost 300 more than required in the union contract.

Nonetheless, the unions continued their criticism throughout 1996, asserting that the WEP was ill conceived because there were not enough jobs in the private sector for the people assigned to public work, so they would never leave the program.[2] This argument was often raised against workfare programs in general. Opponents of welfare reform argued that most welfare recipients have middle-class aspirations and would like to work if they could; they were on welfare because there were not enough jobs for people with their skills, work experience, and education. The *New York Times*, lamenting the passage of the welfare reform legislation, said it was impossible for the city to move hundreds of thousands of New Yorkers from public assistance to full-time employment.[3]

Stanley Hill, the District Council 37 executive director, had supported Mayor Giuliani in 1995, a position that placed him at odds with AFSCME at the national level, which opposed the welfare reform legislation. Less than a year after Hill agreed to work with Giuliani, however, Congress passed the welfare reform legislation, and as more and more people entered the WEP, Hill's support for the mayor waned. By the end of 1996 he had become an opponent. In the union's newspaper, Hill said WEP was an "accident waiting to happen" and called for a moratorium on future assignments to the program.

According to Hill, the WEP placements were "dead-end jobs" without benefits or decent pay. Participants worked side by side with union members who were paid more. Hill and union members also believed that the city was replacing regular employees with welfare recipients.[4] Hill wanted the mayor to train welfare recipients to become regular city employees and expand the union's membership, hopes that were at odds with the economic realities of a declining tax base and what many considered an already inflated public service corps. The mayor adhered to the original agreement and had not laid off any city workers, but he had not added new positions and had kept some vacated positions unfilled.

Mayor Giuliani met with Hill and others in late September 1996 to address the concerns of the labor unions and the advocacy groups. The mayor agreed to monitor the program and to ensure that the WEP jobs were not taking employment away from union members. The mayor also agreed to hire WEP participants into regular positions as openings occurred for which the recipient was an appropriate candidate; they should be given "substantial consideration for those positions."[5]

A labor-sponsored, public-interest group calling itself "The Workfairness Organization" was formed in 1996. Claiming over a thousand members, it signed up welfare recipients at the location where all WEP work assignments were made. The group claimed the right to serve as a union-type organization representing WEP workers. Its goals were (1) equal pay for equal work; (2) a moratorium against sanctioning nonconforming welfare recipients; (3) reversing the limitations on immigrant welfare receipt; (5) permanent jobs at union wages; and (6) allowing WEP workers to select their work sites.[6]

David Jones, president of the Community Service Society of New York, was another critic of the mayor. Jones argued that the WEP initiative would lower wages or push more low-wage earners into poverty. He claimed the program was a form of indentured servitude and that after two years of operation it had failed to prove that it could find permanent employment for participants. He noted that in the year ending April 1996 only 4,180 recipients left welfare for employment. He argued for more emphasis on education and training.[7]

Welfare reform was of enormous public interest, and the topic was covered intensely and from highly divergent perspectives. The citywide news media, union newspapers, civil-service newspapers, newspapers serving minority groups, neighborhood papers, the counterculture press, and conservative, liberal, and leftist publications all covered every evolving aspect of the program. Most critics seemed to feel that the government was forcing people to do something demeaning and unproductive and was punishing the poor for a fault of the broader society.

The vitriolic responses of opponents to welfare reform in general and WEP in particular often seemed excessive and unsupported by the available data. Certainly, the dire prediction of mothers sleeping on open grates with children clutched to their breasts failed to materialize. The program requirements, such as showing up for work and cleaning the parks, did not resemble slavery in the antebellum South. Yet opponents of public work programs routinely used such terms. For many otherwise well-meaning people in the media and for traditional advocacy groups, the reasons for opposition had emotional roots and were often spewed forth with vehemence and venom. Giuliani would face continuous attacks from advocacy groups, organized labor, and some of the city's media in the ensuing years.

The focus of WEP was to instill confidence in people who thought they could not be hired in the private, unsubsidized sector. The mayor asserted that the goal was to replace "entitlement with enablement." He did not believe there were too few jobs; rather, he saw the problem as too little commitment. He blamed well-meaning "progressives" who supported an expansion of welfare even as it harmed the supposed beneficiaries. WEP became the tool the mayor would use to reestablish the social contract.[8]

The mayor's level of commitment was crucial. In other states and cities the fraction of the caseload in public work programs was about one percent; in New York the figure was nearly 50 percent. This huge difference in participation was the result of program design and leadership. Various officials said the program worked because it came from the mayor; all of his commissioners understood that welfare reform was "carved in stone."

New York's WEP initiative built on the experience of the JOBS legislation that preceded TANF. The initiative differed from the prior programs in that it was ongoing and not optional. It was mandatory for almost all participants and included both former AFDC recipients and Safety Net Assistance (SNA) participants. (The latter were formerly called Home Relief recipients.) Although WEP provided for job-search and job-club activities on the two days the participant was not engaged in public work, these options were part of the public work program not an alternative to it.

Federal Constraints on WEP Implementation

Legal and regulatory issues had yet to be resolved. Welfare advocates railed against the income difference between WEP participants and city employees and lobbied the state legislature and the city council. Laws that conflicted with federal law were enacted at the behest of unions or advocacy groups. In some instances there was conflict between federal laws and agency interpretations of the law. If a WEP participant was to be considered an employee, to what degree would that thinking extend to other employee–employer relations? In Florida in the 1980s, when the food stamp "workfare" pilot program was initiated in Jacksonville, the state was required to purchase workers' compensation insurance for the welfare recipients. The fact that their grant would continue if they were injured on the job and that they were already entitled to free medical care was insufficient reasoning to the lawyers who reviewed the state–city agreement. Concomitantly, there was an issue as to whether the participants were entitled to unemployment insurance should they be "fired" from their work assignment. As irrational as such arguments appeared on the surface, court cases throughout the country were based on them.

Interpretations of federal regulations and laws confounded implementation of workfare programs in almost all states, including New York. The issue of food stamp and Medicaid requirements versus TANF requirements caused continued conflict between the states and the federal government. Although almost all TANF recipients received food stamps and Medicaid, the three programs had different federal administrators. The food stamp and TANF programs had separate laws and regulations governing work requirements, but Medicaid had no work requirements. When someone sought welfare assistance they were screened for all of the available programs; the eligibility worker had to make sure that the process was consistent with all the laws and regulations.

For years state administrators struggled with bizarre differences in federal policies. For example, the food stamp law exempted participation in work programs for parents whose youngest child was under 12, while the AFDC program exempted parents whose youngest child was under six. If a state sanctioned someone for failing to show up for a work requirement in the AFDC program, the penalty or reduction in the grant would be partially offset by an increase in the food stamp allocation—the participant now had less income and was therefore entitled to more food stamps. In the reform legislation of 1988 and 1996, some of these issues were addressed; for example, a state could now consolidate the value of the food stamps and the TANF grant to calculate the number of hours that a person must work.

Federal courts had ruled, and the U.S. Department of Health and Human Services (HHS) policy required, that the mandatory hours of work be calculated by dividing the grant by the minimum wage. Although New York's SNA program was not federally funded and thus was outside the rule-making process that governed Medicaid, food stamps, and AFDC, it still needed to be consistent with state and federal labor laws. By setting the number of hours of assigned work at a level generous enough to capture all possible grants, New York avoided the arduous task of assigning and tracking a unique number of hours for each WEP participant.

WORKING IN WEP

WEP workers were assigned to nonprofit organizations and to government agencies. They could not be assigned to profit-making corporations and be paid directly by the government.

WEP at Nonprofit Agencies

Although the focus of WEP was on employing welfare recipients in public agencies, some 5 to 8 percent were assigned to nonprofit, community-based organizations (see table 7.1). With the exception of Goodwill Industries, most of the contractors were small agencies with limited management and budgeting skills. The CBOs were nongovernment agencies, so they had a formal contractual relationship with the city and not just an agreement, as city agencies had. The relationship was not always harmonious, according to the contracting supervisor in the Human Resources Administration. The nonprofit agencies received payment both for providing a work site and for helping the WEP participants gain unsubsidized employment.

Many nonprofits existed on day-to-day budgets and wanted to be paid quickly. This did not always happen. The contracts required the CBOs to place a specified number of the WEP participants in jobs in addition to providing work experience. The HRA contracts office monitored contract performance and cited the agencies if they failed to meet their performance goals. In many cases the CBOs were not able to meet the requirement and thus they did not receive the expected revenue. As caseloads declined, the nonprofits complained that they could not fulfill the performance goals required by the contract because HRA wasn't sending them enough welfare recipients. If a participant was placed in an unsubsidized job, payment was made only after the person had been working in that job for 90 days. HRA would not pay until the case was closed, and delays often occurred between employment and case closing.

A typical contract required that the nonprofit accept a specific number of referrals from the Office of Employment Services (OES), a subunit of HRA, and that a certain percentage of those people be placed in unsubsidized employment. Thus, for example, the contractor would be expected to maintain work-experience positions for 300 referrals and that in a year 75 people would be placed in unsubsidized jobs for a minimum of 90 days each. In order for a referral to count toward the 300 total, the WEP participant was required to work for the contractor for at least 28 days. The type of work was spelled out by the contract and included such activities as office services, maintenance work, and human or community services. The contract required the person to remain in the work-experience position for a minimum of six months. At any time during the initial 28 days of the assignment, OES could reassign the person to another agency. The CBO also had to agree to consider the WEP assignee for any employment opportunities that arose in the agency. When a WEP participant left for employment, the placement was tracked by the CBO to verify continued employment and then checked by OES.

The CBO was required to offer an orientation to people assigned to them

Table 7.1. WEP Assignments by Agency, Selected Points in Time

Agency	03/26/96	06/30/99	06/30/00	12/31/00
Administration for Children's Services		466	423	284
BEGIN		5,770	5,387	4,193
Board of Education	275	518	258	388
Bronx County Clerk's Office		11	31	5
Business Improvement Districts	28	30	9	11
City Commission on Human Rights		2	2	0
Community Boards		11	17	25
Community Based Organizations		1,662	1,846	1,336
Comptroller's Office		2	2	0
City University of New York	242	132	397	211
Dept. for the Aging	418	968	685	570
Dept. of Citywide Administration	2,611	3,151	2,672	1,209
Dept. of Consumer Affairs		25	22	13
Dept. of Design and Construction		10	9	5
Dept. of Environmental Protection	52	100	24	4
Dept. of Finance		52	43	41
Dept. of Health	209	305	218	180
Dept. of Housing and Preservation	1,499	384	373	239
Dept. of Parks and Recreation	6,259	6,154	4,259	3,852
Dept. of Probation		10	6	0
Dept. of Records and Information		25	19	26
Dept. of Sanitation	4,263	2,912	1,748	1,249
Dept. of Transportation	517	656	425	89
Employment Services and Placement				59
Enhanced				4,450
Financial Information Services		7	0	0
Fire Dept.		41	96	101
Health and Hospitals Corporation	743			
Human Resources Administration	2,135	4,891	8,940	1,434
Landmarks Preservation Commission		9	3	0
Mayor's Office		10	1	1
Metropolitan Transit Authority		319	678	340
Museo del Barrio		27	18	24
Nonprofit organizations	1,686			
New York City Housing Authority	453	1,861	1,550	535
Other Non-city Agencies		132	180	120
Police Dept.	280	411	350	207
State Agencies	318	197	165	76
Taxi and Limousine Commission		66	32	44
Welfare-to-Work				447
Uncategorized	0	0	0	0
TOTAL	21,988	31,327	30,888	21,768

Source: Demetra S. Nightingale, Nancy Pindus, Federica D. Kramer, John Trutko, Kelly Mikelson, and Michael Egner, *Work and Welfare Reform in New York City during the Giuliani Administration* (Washington, D.C.: Urban Institute, July 2002). Based on New York City Mayor's Management Reports.

and to supervise their work. The contracts were for various dollar amounts and had certain reporting and record-keeping requirements: monthly reports, a quarterly meeting, attendance records, and a biweekly attendance roster. Any failure to cooperate or maintain participation on the part of the WEP worker was to be reported to OES. The personnel file on each participant included information on previous employment, child-care arrangements, any absences from the work site, employment contacts made while in the WEP assignment, any resumes that were prepared, personnel evaluations completed during the assignment, and time sheets—the latter being required. A copy of any file change was sent to OES biweekly.

OES staff made unannounced visits to work sites to audit the program. If the contractor did not meet the contract requirements—by failing to submit accurate reports, documents, or program information on time—it was subject to liquidated damages. For each quarter in which the CBO failed to meet reporting or supervisory responsibilities, 10 percent of the monies due could be withheld by HRA. If the contractor failed to make the required number of placements in unsubsidized jobs, 20 percent of the amount due could be withheld at the end of each quarter.

A typical CBO contract might be for $200,000 for one year, including $75,000 for placements into unsubsidized employment, $1,000 paid for each person employed full-time for 90 days, and $500 for each person placed in a part-time job (at least 20 hours a week) for 90 days.

When renewing the CBO contracts, HRA paid nonprofit organizations only for providing work sites and dropped the requirement of placing people in unsubsidized employment. Given the diminishing caseloads and the demand for WEP participants by city agencies, some questioned whether contracts with the nonprofit CBOs were needed at all. Terminating the contracts, however, was difficult as the CBOs are social service agencies with contributors and public support, which make them political forces as well. As a contract administrator noted, "We will have to proceed somewhat gingerly."

Two of the city's leading minority churches, the Abyssinian Baptist Church and Riverside Church, joined with 70 other ministers and churches and denounced WEP for paying too little attention to training and workplace safety. Reverend Ralph Warnock, an assistant pastor at Abyssinian, said that he was concerned that the city was cutting its workforce by more than 20,000 while creating a program with 38,000 workfare participants.[9]

WEP in City Agencies

Joe Gioe, an HRA manager whose unit monitored the CBO contracts and the agreements with the city's departments, believed that WEP worker placements in city departments were more productive than assignments with the nonprofits. The Department of Parks and Recreation was the largest user of WEP workers, and Gioe considered it the best of the city agencies in this respect. The department worked closely with the WEP participants, who felt that their assignments were worthwhile experiences. Gioe said, "A lot of welfare recipients are not prepared to go to work, and there really should be a program like this one." Gioe said the program could be improved if participants made more than they would on welfare and their pay were in the form of a paycheck and not a welfare check. This would be a psychological boost and provide a stronger commitment to the employing agency. (There are serious administrative and budgetary hazards to do this, however, as noted below.)

The HRA agreements with other city departments provided funding that could be used to hire additional staff for training and supervision of the WEP participants. The funding for city agencies came partially from HRA and partially from the agency receiving the WEP participants; all of the funding for the CBOs came from HRA.

The Parks Department was exemplary in its management of WEP. Early in the program, the Parks Department created an internal operations unit to train supervisors and select WEP workers. In 1995 and 1996, the Park Career Training Program (PACT) was small compared to the caseload, only 800 out of 240,000 Safety Net recipients. Participation was voluntary, and 80 percent of the participants were men between the ages of twenty-five and fifty-five. AFDC mothers were not part of the original program. The selection process culled a third of those who sought to enter the program. Volunteers who had language deficiencies, criminal records, little work experience, or were long-term recipients were excluded from the program. PACT had an agreement with the New York City Board of Education to provide GED, ESL, and adult literacy education and drivers' education. Supervisors acted as references for employment, and 40 percent of the participants secured jobs. A follow-up study found that 77 percent were still employed at the end of 90 days. After entering the program, 57 percent were no longer receiving assistance 13 months later. Twenty percent were expelled from the program, primarily for poor attendance. Between April 11, 1994, when the PACT program began, and the end of June 2001, a total of 1,846 WEP participants had obtained employment at an average wage of $10.82 per hour.

PACT provided training for jobs in security, construction, custodial work, horticulture, clerical work, auto mechanics, telecommunications, and MIS support. Volunteers could select the vocational area of most interest to them. The Parks Department hired job-placement specialists to work with the community and the clients. At any time the program had 500 participants, and as vacancies occurred new recruits were brought in. The cost of the PACT program was $4,466,667, with HRA providing three-fourths of the funding and the Parks Department one-fourth. The $3,350,000 from HRA was distributed based on the PACT's performance: $1,000 was paid for each person that entered the program, another $4,000 when the person entered outside employment, and a final $4,000 when the person was employed for 90 days.

The Job Assistance Center (JAC) agreement called for the funding of four such centers, one each in the Bronx, Manhattan, Brooklyn, and Queens. Each was equipped with video cameras, telephones, newspapers, and the other equipment needed to operate a Parks and Recreation Department "job club." Each center had a coordinator, an assistant coordinator, and four job developers. HRA paid $1,000 for each person enrolled in a JAC, up to a maximum of 600 people, and an additional $5,500 for each participant that was placed in an unsubsidized job, up to a maximum of 225 placements. The $5,500 was paid incrementally: $2,200 at the end of 30 days of unsubsidized employment, an additional $1,650 at the end of 90 days, and a final $1,650 if the person remained employed for six months.

Discussions with HRA Work Experience Director Samara Epstein revealed some confusion in the way the agreements and contracts functioned with respect to a participant who was served by both the Parks Department and by one of the employment services contractors. It was unclear whether the city was paying two different providers, the Parks Department and the employment services contractor, for assisting the same WEP participant to become employed. It was also unclear if the bonus funds that accrue to the placement agent were being paid twice or only once.

Work Experience or Education?

Although education initiatives for welfare recipients were greatly restricted by the 1996 welfare reform legislation, welfare advocates blamed the mayor and the city for requiring WEP participants to first meet their work obligation and then pursue their education in the evening. The lack of substantive data to support an emphasis on education over work was not an effective argument to the critics of WEP. David Jones, president of the Community Service Society of New York, said that the mayor had pushed 10,000 welfare recipients out of City College of New York because of the "get a job" mentality of welfare administrators.[10] The other side of the argument was presented in a *Daily News* editorial: "Doing homework is not work experience. . . . Generations of motivated students have held down jobs, raised families, paid their own tuition, and earned their degrees."[11]

Low educational achievement was a common barrier to employment for welfare recipients. About half the TANF recipients lacked a high school diploma, and on standardized tests they scored, on average, at about a sixth-grade level in math and reading. Table 7.2 shows the self-reported educational attainment of welfare recipients.

Table 7.2.   Educational Attainment of Welfare Recipients, Percent

Level of Educational Attainment	TANF	Safety Net
No School	2	2
First to 8th grade	7	9
9th to 11th grade	40	41
HS or post HS	50	48
Unknown	1	1
TOTAL	100	100

In June 1997, Judge Jane Solomon ordered HRA to accommodate college students who were welfare recipients by arranging their work schedules to fit their class schedules.[12] In response to Judge Solomon's order and because TANF law allowed for up to a year of education, HRA established procedures to assist and accommodate students. Out of about 140,000 New York TANF participants over age fifteen in November 2001, roughly 4,000 were pursuing an education. In June 1997 Commissioner Barrios-Paoli, noting that half the recipients lacked a high-school education, said that she intended to increase education and training opportunities. Former New York State Social Services Commissioner Barbara Blum supported Barrios-Paoli and said that the administration's approach, namely, uniform treatment for everyone, was a problem.[13]

Critics often implied that the majority of recipients failed in past educational efforts because of circumstances beyond their resources or abilities. When welfare administrators quoted statistics on the failure of retraining programs and said that most recipients would not succeed in formal education, advocates said they were insensitive to the needs of low-income people and were denying them the tools necessary for independence. Welfare advocates considered all people equally able to obtain and benefit from education and tended to see open discussion of the issue as insensitive and demeaning to people who were already struggling with a diminished self-image.

The new federal time limit added a new dimension to the issue of education as a primary goal of a participant's plan. If the educational effort failed, the participant's allowable welfare time was frittered away, and, while appearing to be compassionate and supportive of education, the caseworker could be accused of subjecting the client to one more depressing experience.

Earlier welfare programs had a much greater emphasis on job search and education. A belief embedded in the federal and state laws passed in the 1980s was that what welfare recipients needed most was literacy and skills training. California's Greater Avenues to Independence (GAIN) program focused on remedial English and training in English as a second language. The experience with such programs was almost universally negative with respect to employment.

In the opinion of many welfare employment and training administrators, the emphasis on education was misplaced and allowed recipients to avoid the challenge of employment. Some recipients benefited from long-term vocational education programs, but follow-up studies indicated that most training programs were short-term and few trainees were working in fields for which they were trained. Many welfare recipients had been through numerous training programs for such jobs as nurses' aides and word-processing clerks only to find that their lack of work experience and employment skills inhibited long-term employment. The results for welfare recipients were not that different from studies of laid-off plant workers and others who entered vocational training programs as adults. Follow-up studies indicated that most trainees were not working in the area of their training three years after the training was complete.

New York has a large immigrant population, and 40 percent of its residents speak a language other than English at home. Only 14 percent of welfare recipients were not U.S. citizens, according to HRA, and speaking broken English was not a significant barrier to employment. Many of the entry-level jobs that formerly went to native-born minorities now went to immigrants who, as a group, were doing better economically than native-born minorities.

Mothers in WEP

An issue that arose early in the debate on welfare reform concerned the best use of a mother's time. Studies of orphans and other children lacking adequate parental care demonstrate that deprivation has serious social and developmental consequences. Child psychologists do not all agree about the degree of nurturing required and who could provide it, but there was general agreement that children needed daily contact with a mother (and/or father) to realize their full potential.

The issue was hotly debated as more and more mothers entered the workforce. Critics of welfare reform cited child development as another reason to keep mothers at home and away from work. Many conservatives who championed the traditional family, with dad working and mom at home with the kids, agreed with them. In the middle were researchers who argued for some middle ground where licensed child care and quality parental time would permit both work and good outcomes for the children.

Workers in the field of child abuse and neglect knew that there is a distressingly large overlap between welfare families and families in which child neglect and abuse occur. In most jurisdictions, half the children under state supervision were from welfare homes. Good child care in these instances might relieve mothers from too much stress. Some studies of developmental child care suggested that for low-income families, child care might actually be a benefit. The Head Start program and some preschool programs were an outcome of this research.

Prior to the growth of the day-care industry, children were often cared for by members of the extended family. Fewer women were in the workforce, and grandmothers, sisters, and older siblings often assumed responsibility for helping mom take care of the baby. In the last 50 years, however, the country saw a breakdown in marriage, two-parent households, and the extended family. These family failures and welfare reform increased the demand for day-care services.

Mothers in TANF who had WEP jobs needed child care. Means-tested day-care funding grew at both the state and federal levels to enable mothers to work. Some formal day-care centers, however, were reluctant to serve children from families on welfare. The state usually paid less than the going rate for child care, thus reducing the center's income. Day-care owners believed that having too many welfare children could, for reasons of race or behavior, drive away paying customers. Children from welfare homes were thought to have more emotional problems and require more care than other children. Finally, most centers found dealing with welfare mothers frustrating because the mothers often failed to pick up their children on time, pay fines for late pick-up, or pay fees for special outings.

These tensions probably spurred the growth of paid child care by relatives and friends, and a new, small, day-care industry grew in the last half of the twentieth century. Although many churches and nonprofits got into the child-care field, there was an increase of what came to be known as family day-care homes. These were homes where unemployed mothers, retired women, and others who had the time, space, and location cared for children other than their own. The cost of such care was often lower than in formal day-care centers, and the family day-care homes also had the advantage of being closer to where the child and mother lived. In some states the relatives of welfare children saw government-funded day care as a new way to earn money. If the welfare mother could channel funds to a relative or neighbor, she got child care while also providing income for those otherwise not eligible for assistance.

Not every welfare recipient needed child care. About two-thirds of the TANF caseload was composed of families whose youngest child was under the age of twelve. Some needed only after-school and summer-vacation care, but many needed infant and toddler care. Children age twelve and older were assumed to be old enough to care for themselves until their parent(s) returned from work.

The Giuliani Administration in 1999 changed the way it provided child care for welfare recipients. In the past, the mother arranged care for her children with a neighbor or relative, the city paid her, and she in turn paid the provider. If she chose a licensed facility, then the payment was made to the facility. Under the changed policy, HRA still allowed the mother to choose the provider, but the payment for the care went to the provider and not to the mother. HRA changed the funding mechanism because in many cases the welfare mothers would pocket the payment and not pay the child-care provider. According to a senior HRA staff member, in 1998 there was a backlog of 2,000 complaints from day-care providers who had not been paid by the mother. Although all funding for child care flowed through one state entity, the city had divided the funding into two streams before the Giuliani Administration took office. People who needed child care obtained it from HRA if they were current welfare recipients or in transition from welfare to work. If they left welfare, however, and were no longer in transition, then child-care funding was provided by the Agency for Child Development, a subunit of the Administration for Children's Services.

HRA improved this arrangement by introducing an automated child-care information and referral system. The system determined eligibility, identified providers, and kept track of available day care. Those receiving child-care services from HRA were able to continue the care through the Agency for Child Development without a break in service or a disruption in the life of the child.

Child-care specialists were now available in HRA field offices. They could work even with women who spoke only Spanish, Chinese, or Russian and were in contact with the five New York child-care information and referral agencies. When a mother needed child care, she was given a planning form and a fact sheet that had the telephone numbers of the agencies. She also was given the names of two possible child-care providers, and two more if necessary. She had to return in a week and tell HRA who was going to be her child-care provider.

WEP and the Sick and Disabled

WEP was limited in its early days by the large number of people who failed to participate because of real or perceived health barriers. Primary among these were welfare recipients who claimed that they were too ill or mentally debilitated to work. Federal regulations allowed them to be excused from work requirements, and the federal reform law passed in 1996 allowed for up to 20 percent of the caseload to be excused. People were also excused if they were caring for someone who was ill, were over the age of fifty-nine, were appealing a disability claim, had a child under three months old, or were receiving Social Security disability insurance.

In the Giuliani Administration, health assessment was enhanced by using an independent contractor, Health Services Systems, which had a three-year, $18-million contract with the city to screen WEP participants who claimed a disability. Conventionally, a note from a licensed physician indicating that the person could not work was all that was required to be excused from participation. The procedure was open to abuse, and welfare administrators knew that some physicians would give such a letter if their patient requested it. An independent contractor would ensure that all people capable of participation were engaged.

At any time there were about 5,000 to 6,000 welfare recipients who claimed a disability and were being assessed. They completed a checklist that indicated why they were disabled or restricted from participation and the degree to which they could participate. If the HRA worker was satisfied, the participant was excused from participation. On the other hand, if the person merely had "a note from a doctor" or if the employee felt that the person should be examined, she was referred to the medical contractor.

Health Services Systems conducted a "functional assessment," which consisted of lab tests, a medical examination, and medical information supplied by the client. If there was evidence of a mental disability, a psychiatrist also examined the client. If the person claimed to be drug dependent, he was tested for that condition. The contractor prepared a "functional assessment outcome report" (FAO) for each individual and gave it to HRA.

Each report classified the individual according to a category of functionality. Those in Category 1 were judged to have no disability that would prevent them from full participation. Category 2 was for those who could participate, with restrictions. (Common restrictions were that the participant couldn't sit for long periods or couldn't lift any object heavier than a certain weight.) Category 3 was a more severe level of restriction. HRA used a "disease-management" approach to match the level of involvement to the person's needs to improve his or her health and functionality. Category 4 was for someone dependent on a legal or illegal drug; it also indicated the degree to which the individual was codependent or mentally ill. Category 5 was for someone who was HIV positive. Many in Category 5 also had drug, mental health, and physical health problems. A special unit within HRA, the HIV/AIDS Services Administration, handled all HIV-related cases. Category 6 was for a temporary condition that would last for a specified period of time.

About 8 percent of the caseload was excused from the work requirements for various health and other reasons; 5.6 percent of this 8 percent was excused only temporarily. Another 14.4 percent of recipients were excused from WEP because they were engaged in other allowable activities. Some were in substance abuse treatment (2 percent), while others were at home caring for someone who was ill or disabled (5 percent). Others (2 percent) were in rehabilitation programs or in educational programs (4 percent).[14]

The health screening by the independent contractor was not infallible. A WEP participant, a fifty-year-old woman, died on the job in a Parks Department office in 1997. This triggered demonstrations and a $10-million negligence suit against the city.[15]

A relatively high percentage of the cases excused from participation were "child-only" cases, which often consisted of relatives caring not for their own children but for grandchildren, nieces, or nephews living in their home; they received a welfare check from the state to care for the children. At best it was less expensive for the state than foster care, and it supported the extended family when the mother was not available to care for her children. At worst, it was a way for aging welfare parents to continue to receive a welfare check when their own children had reached adulthood and left home. In New York and in most states this was about 20 percent of the TANF caseload, and as the welfare population declined, the "child-only" cases grew as a fraction of the remaining caseload.

The city examined the exemption status of those clients who had been exempted because they were caring for a disabled child. State law required the Department of Education to provide services to disabled children, and HRA wanted to ensure that all children eligible for services were receiving them. Adults freed from the need to care for a disabled child might be able to participate in the employment programs.

Four clients selected at random were interviewed to see if they were getting services from the Department of Education and if they were able to work while their children were engaged in educational programs. All were receiving appropriate services for their children, but it was also found that three of the four could participate in WEP if the hours of participation were structured around their child's schooling and treatment. HRA was redesigning the "family care assessment form" (W582A) to identify other people in similar situations who might be available for employment preparation or WEP.

"Work First"

Reflecting the values incorporated in the 1996 federal welfare reform law, immediate employment was the principal goal for a welfare applicant rather than merely engaging him or her in WEP. This was called "up-front" or "work-first" employment in most states. It was to be achieved primarily by Skills Assessment and Placement (SAP) contractors at the Job Centers.

Applicants for public assistance who could not be placed within six weeks entered WEP. WEP was really two concurrent programs. Although public attention focused on the 21 hours a week that a participant worked at an assigned job, most clients spent the other two days of the week in activities tied to their ongoing search for employment, such as efforts to get an unsubsidized job in the private sector or vocational training in clerical skills that would lead to employment. Employment Services Placement (ESP) contractors, different from the SAP contractors, assisted the participant at this stage. Payment to these contractors was greater than at the first level, as it was assumed that this was a more difficult participant to place. The payment to the contractor was made in increments tied to the longevity of employment, and bonuses were paid for placing people in higher-paying positions. Participants were assigned to ESP contractors until they were employed for six months, although in some cases HRA workers extended the time.

One such contractor was Career and Educational Consultants, Inc. (CEC). CEC has a long history of working with welfare clients. In the early years of WEP, during the Koch Administration, CEC worked with referrals on alternating weeks. People would work in a public service job one week and then train for employment the next week. Under Mayor Giuliani the approach was changed to allow for two days of training each week and three days of work experience. CEC staff considered the new method better from a training perspective as it kept the education current. According to a CEC staff member, under Mayor Giuliani the program was better and had more participation than before because everyone got the word that the highest authority in the city, the mayor, wanted it to happen. There was "some static at first," said Ruby Jones, a CEC staffer, but after the 1996 federal legislation, everyone recognized that it was "for real."

Although only half of those assigned to WEP showed up for orientation, the percentage increased to 75 percent for CEC/WEP participation. CEC and the city agency where the worker was assigned received a hard copy and an e-mail list of the following week's assigned participants every Friday. An HRA computer was provided to the contractor, and the contractor was allowed to input certain information directly into the HRA database. Such input of client compliance information by the contractor was unusual; in most states, only government employees could enter information on participation or nonparticipation. This HRA innovation facilitated early sanctioning of uncooperative welfare recipients.

The type of placements sought for WEP participants by CEC was a product of its experience in working with employers and clients. One of the CEC staff, David Burnstein, had worked in human resources on Wall Street and knew of the need for financial operations clerks. He knew the firms and their human resources or personnel staffs that did the hiring. According to Burnstein, financial companies wanted to hire the CEC-trained workers because they were ready to hit the street running, and their financial situation led to high employee retention and low turnover.

CEC worked effectively with the supervisors of the participants at their WEP work sites, coordinating letters of reference and personalized training for the individual, for example. Sometimes work days were rescheduled to fit the training. The bottom line, according to CEC staff, was that the clients had to carry out their WEP assignments. Education and training had to fit around that schedule. People who wanted to take the GED test were allowed, during the two days that they were with CEC, to use computerized adult educational material that prepared them for the test. CEC had three different computer-skill training tracks that were licensed by the State Department of Education. Other programs were provided by the Board of Education, and the participants were made aware of those programs if it appeared that the GED might involve several years of preparation.

According to CEC, 37 percent of the people it placed in jobs were still employed at six months. This does not mean that those not still employed were back on welfare or unemployed. It generally meant that they were not still employed with the employer with whom they were originally placed or that they had not remained in contact with the welfare agency or their contractor. Many people in low-income jobs frequently changed jobs, and in many cases changed residences, and follow-up to determine job retention was difficult. As welfare reform director in Florida and later as director of social services in South Carolina, the author found that 15 to 20 percent of welfare recipients placed in jobs lost or left their jobs or left within 30 days; at 90 days that figure increased to 35 to 50 percent; and at six months it increased to 50 to 65 percent. Follow-up studies in other states indicated that 50 to 60 percent of people who left welfare were employed one year later.

CEC staff believed that a credible penalty for noncompliance—sanctions that reduced the grant—was effective for most of the people they worked with and that people were more willing to participate than they were before welfare reform. CEC staff further believed that requiring compliance for a specified period of time prior to reinstatement would further strengthen the program.

CEC staff also thought that the program was improved because of follow-up. After a client was placed in a WEP job, CEC staff called every week to see how things were going and if there were any problems. Most of what they heard was that the WEP assignment was not in line with the participant's job interests. "We try to blend their WEP experience . . . and to adjust their expectations and desires with our two training programs," said Ruby Jones, the CEC director of admissions.

"One of our contracts is for computer training in word processing and Microsoft Office, the other is in customer service," said another CEC staff member. "We work with the supervisors and the client to try and get the training to support the WEP experience. A lot of the positions we place people into are word-processing type jobs and if we can train people before they get to the job it is very meaningful. Our folks are averaging $10 an hour when they complete the training. That was the key to job retention, a good wage and solid training."

"It takes 35 hours of training each week, for eight to 16 weeks, to complete the training," a CEC trainer explained. "Some of the WEP people take the entire 26 weeks they have with us to complete the training because they were only in training for two days a week. For the folks who were not in WEP we push them through in eight to 16 weeks. In some cases we have to get extensions from the HRA caseworker to the 26-week maximum period for some folks to complete the training."

Although the employment assistance that WEP participants received from CEC was limited to six months, the time spent in WEP with a city agency was not limited. WEP continued for as long as the person continued to receive assistance.

SUCCESS, OPPOSITION, AND A NEW COMMISSIONER

The mayor's perception that the problem was not one of too few jobs appeared to be borne out by historical unemployment data. There was no clear relationship in the past between unemployment figures and welfare receipt, but "work-first" programs appeared to be correlated with lowered unemployment rates. (See figure 7.1.)

Follow-up studies of people who left welfare were carried out by a few states, such as South Carolina, and the results suggest that between 50 and 60 percent of the former recipients were working a year after leaving welfare and believed their lives had improved. Dr. Swati Desai and Andy Bush,

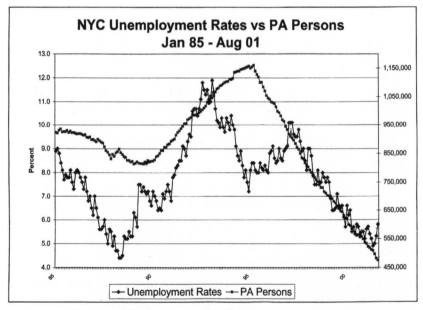

Figure 7.1. Unemployment Rates vs. Number of People on Public Assistance

HRA's research administrators, followed a sample of 126 former welfare recipients six months after leaving the welfare rolls. The results indicated that 54 percent had left for employment and another 21 percent left for various other reasons associated with increased income. An additional 25 percent left because they were sanctioned. Of those working, 88 percent had incomes that were higher than when they were on welfare. (See also chapter 11.)

Some former welfare mothers reestablished two-parent households, and although they were not working, their "significant other" was employed. This should have been expected in that the second most common reason for leaving welfare after "increased income" was reestablishment of a two-parent household. An unintended, but positive, consequence of welfare reform may have been to encourage the formation of two-parent families.

Critics of welfare reform assumed that recipients dropped out of welfare not because they were better off, but because they did not understand the rules, had medical or mental-health problems that limited their involvement, or were caring for their children due to a breakdown in their child-care arrangements. Although all of these reasons may apply to some recipients at some point, it was equally likely that many did not participate because they were already employed. As one worker put it in an interview for this report, they were the "conveniently sanctioned." Another called them "happily sanctioned."

Sanctioned people often worked in what labor officials called "uncovered employment," which included activities such as day labor and domestic labor where the employer illegally did not pay taxes or social security; it also included self-employment in lawful or unlawful pursuits. "Covered employment" included all other forms of employment where contributions for unemployment insurance were made and could be checked. People already employed would not participate in WEP if it meant a reduction in their unreported income. Some argued that the grant level was insufficient to maintain a family and that it was not surprising to find that many recipients had income "off the books."

Many states, but not New York, applied what was called a "full family sanction." This terminated grants to all family members if an adult participant refused to comply with the program requirements. Although such practices mirror real-world employment, where a worker is not paid if he or she does not show up for work, advocates deemed this policy too severe, saying it punished the child for the error of the parent. In states that invoked a full-family sanction, the noncompliance or "no show" rate was no different from states that sanction only the errant parent. This suggested that the severity of the penalty was not the discriminating factor in deciding for or against compliance. Regardless of the sanction method, a person already working could not generally comply with the rules without losing his or her unreported income.

Those who believed they were unfairly treated could appeal the sanction and receive a hearing. When they agreed to comply with the requirements of the program they were reinstated. In some states, with the discretion allowed in the new TANF legislation, people who failed to comply were required to comply for a period of time before their grant was retroactively reinstated.

"No Light at the End of the Tunnel?"

With roughly a third of the cases excused from participation, two-thirds were potentially available for work; these were referred to as "engaged." A third of the "engaged" caseload was in a sanctioned status, however. The bottom line was that many welfare recipients found employment and went to work or were already working when they applied for welfare. Some recipients chose not to participate in WEP because they felt that the reduction in their grant was not as onerous as the inconvenience of a WEP assignment. Critics of welfare reform who claimed there were too few jobs for WEP participants had to confront the fact that large numbers of people relinquished public assistance rather than comply with the work requirements.

With WEP in full swing in 1997, the unions and advocacy groups continued their attacks, protesting that WEP was unfair and did not provide wages and benefits comparable to those earned by regular city workers, and there was no "light at the end of the tunnel" in terms of unsubsidized, permanent employment. Councilman Stephen DiBrienza complained about the program and said there was inadequate follow-up on WEP participants. Commissioner Barrios-Paoli promised to initiate a follow-up study[16] and a small-scale one was conducted in 1998. Over half the former recipients were employed a year after leaving welfare. This was similar to the results found in longitudinal follow-up studies carried out in many states.

Legal challenges to the WEP were also mounted in 1997. Suits brought by the Welfare Law Project and advocacy groups before a sympathetic judge, Jane Solomon, wasted time and resolved little. Judge Solomon ruled that the city should pay WEP participants prevailing wages and that water and easy access to bathrooms had to be provided. Safety equipment and seasonal clothing should not be shared but provided individually to participants. HRA appealed and in time most of Judge Solomon's orders were reversed.

The media was largely sympathetic to the WEP critics, and many of the city's numerous local newspapers ran articles with a pro-welfare, anti-WEP message that challenged the mayor's program. An article in the *Village Voice*, "Facing Welfare: As America Moves to Punish Our Neediest Citizens, Society Suffers," stated "welfare reform was a dangerous effort to legislate morality and social values."[17] The *New York Post*, the conservative city newspaper, and the *Daily News* would occasionally editorialize in favor of the program.

Mark Green, the public advocate and then a leading contender to replace the mayor in the 1998 election, issued a report titled, "Welfare to Work: Getting Lost along the Way." The report complained of unsafe working conditions and a dearth of training and education. Green said, "The city seems less interested in long-term job placements than the immediate reduction in the welfare rolls."[18]

The unions continued to blast the program and meet with the mayor. The New York City Central Labor Council, the umbrella organization for the city's municipal unions, proposed offering associate memberships to WEP participants and argued for equal pay for equal work. Interestingly, Elaine Ryan, an aide to former Governor Mario Cuomo and then director of government affairs for the American Public Welfare Association, cautioned the unions about seeking something that cities could not afford. She said, "What looks to be a kind of fairness on its face might turn out to be a very bad deal for welfare clients."[19]

In June 1997 a crowd of 50 welfare mothers came to the HRA offices to protest WEP and the policy that required participants to leave their children and go to work. Commissioner Barrios-Paoli met with the placard-carrying group and promised to look into their demands for more payment for child care and an end to threats that if they didn't accept the child care offered they would be terminated from the program.[20]

The arguments raised by unions and advocacy groups equated WEP work with the work of regular government employees or employees in nonprofit organizations, but these two kinds of jobs were not comparable. WEP recipients received free medical care and if their WEP job ended they were reassigned to another job; thus they didn't need unemployment insurance. Transportation allowances and day care were provided to WEP recipients but not to civil servants. WEP recipients received food stamps, but regular civil servants generally did not. If WEP participants were injured on the job, their medical bills were paid and they continued to receive TANF benefits until they were able to return to work. A WEP worker who was permanently disabled was, in most instances, eligible for federal and state disability payments. From the perspective of advocates, WEP participants neither received annual nor sick leave, nor accrued retirement benefits. WEP participants who were sick were excused, however, and continued to receive their welfare checks, whereas civil servants were limited to a prescribed number of days accrued over time, otherwise they were not compensated. Although the level of remuneration for WEP workers was tied to the minimum wage and civil servants received a higher level of pay, regular employees did not get public housing or the various other means-tested benefits of welfare recipients. WEP participants were excused from participation when they reached age sixty and continued to receive benefits as long as they remained eligible for

TANF or New York's Safety Net Assistance. Finally, WEP clients participated for 21 hours a week, and civil servants worked 35 hours a week.

One WEP worker said that he had skills that were not being used and were deteriorating from lack of use.[21] Some WEP workers said that the work was demeaning, that they had to pick up syringes discarded by drug users, and that cleaning subway cars or cleaning parks and streets was not preparing them for employment. On the other hand, if the purpose was to train the recipient to show up for work on time, be civil to one's fellow workers and supervisor, and deal appropriately with authority figures, then the experience in the program was appropriate.

Many WEP workers felt they were engaged in productive work. Studies of past public work programs by the Manpower Development Research Center revealed that workers believed their work to be similar and equal in value to that of regular employees. Union officials gave two contradictory arguments: welfare workers were not as qualified as regular employees and therefore were seldom hired into vacant positions, and conversely, that WEP participants took the place of regular workers and WEP was a form of union busting.

WEP park workers reported in interviews that they believed the work they did was valuable and no different from the work carried out by salaried city workers. The city's Parks and Recreation Department confirmed this in two ways. Supervisors whom I interviewed maintained that the work performed by WEP employees made a difference. A park administrator noted that the work was valuable, but may have differed in quality and quantity from the work of the regular employees.

The Department of Parks and Recreation had a long-standing system for evaluating the cleanliness of the city's parks. Each of 59 park districts was monitored for cleanliness and ranked according to a number of criteria. Prior to the advent of the WEP, the parks were collectively rated at 74 percent. After WEP was introduced, the rating of the parks climbed into the high 90s, according to Samara Epstein, the administrator of the Parks Department's WEP. A similar monitoring system of city streets by the Department of Sanitation showed similar improvement. The parks and streets were cleaner by objective standards, and the city was better for it.

Another measure of the value of WEP was the competition between Parks and Sanitation for more WEP workers when the welfare rolls began to decline and fewer workers were available. Interviews with both Parks and Sanitation officials confirmed that WEP workers benefited their agencies.

If the work was making the parks and streets cleaner, why did the workers see it as demeaning and why were the critics comparing it to slavery? Did the perception of the worker as a welfare recipient connote personal failure in the eyes of the worker and those with whom he worked, and did it underscore society's disdain? Was the clothing that identified one as a WEP worker, or treatment by supervisors and HRA staff, demeaning to the participant? If that was the case, perhaps welfare recipients didn't object so much to participation in WEP as to not being respected and being treated as different.

WEP participants interviewed in this study said that paychecks were different from a welfare check. The welfare check carried with it the stigma of public assistance, and recipients preferred a paycheck. In part this was because the paycheck paid more per hour and was a "regular" job and in part it was because recipients and those all around them knew that their WEP job identified them as something less than a regular employee. A stigma was attached to the welfare check but not to the paycheck. All of the interviewees for this report indicated that they wanted to work for the city in a salaried position doing what they were currently doing in WEP.

Welfare officials have known for some time that WEP recipients do not want to be perceived as different; special programs like "work supplementation" in the former JOBS legislation was an attempt to deal with this issue. In the work supplementation program, the welfare check was given to the employer as a way of offsetting the labor costs and to pay the employer for training the welfare recipient. The analogy of work supplementation to WEP is not a direct one because wage supplementation was for the private sector while WEP is a public and nonprofit program.

In September 1997 the mayor responded to union criticism, agreeing to try to place welfare recipients in jobs by hiring contractors who would offer screening, assessment of employability, and short-term vocational training. Contracts for this work would go to nonprofit organizations, city agencies, and private contractors.[22]

HRA documented the increase in the number of job placements each year. In 1997, the second full year of the Giuliani initiative, there were 34,705 TANF placements and 17,436 SNA placements.

In the meantime, Wisconsin Governor Tommy Thompson had established a national reputation in welfare reform. His election in 1987 established the issue for the voters, and since then he had proposed a series of reforms at the rate of about one per year. By 1994 the state legislature enacted a law to eliminate AFDC altogether, and Thompson turned to Jason Turner, formerly the director of the AFDC program at HHS under the first President Bush, to lead the policy group tasked with designing a work-based alternative to the entitlement system. Following the national attention generated by the Wisconsin reforms, by 1998 Mayor Giuliani would recruit Turner to tackle New York City's mammoth welfare bureaucracy.

After she was replaced, Barrios-Paoli said that Giuliani called her in and told her she didn't have the stomach for what they were about to do with welfare. She transferred to another agency, and later she left city government to head United Way.[23] The former commissioner believed that training was the cure for welfare, and a she was a supporter of the welfare training programs that had been created over the years by Congress. The literature did not support that position for the vast majority of welfare recipients, but it was understandable that Barrios-Paoli would side with those institutions and vendors who had traditionally followed and benefited from this prescription.

Public Service Work, Giuliani, and the Unions

The disputes and disagreements that had marked prior years continued in 1998. Mayor Giuliani had been reelected in 1997, and he appointed a new commissioner for HRA, Jason Turner, but he continued to be criticized by the unions and much of the media.

Stanley Hill of DC 37, who had once endorsed WEP, continued the usual criticism when the jobs of unionized hospital workers were threatened. The basic issue was the same. The number of workers required had fallen as bed occupancy in the public hospitals decreased by 25 percent, and the Health and Hospitals Corporation, the administering entity for the public hospitals, was trying to live within its budget by cutting city jobs to match the declining workload. If WEP workers were assigned to a hospital at the same time staff positions were cut, the union membership saw WEP workers as replacing city employees.

In response to a lawsuit that challenged the layoff of 900 employees by the city's Health and Hospitals Corporation (HHC) and alleged that WEP workers were replacing union workers, in April 1998 the city said it was withdrawing the 1,400 WEP workers who were already assigned to hospitals.[24] An editorial in *Queens Newsday* berated the municipal labor leader, Stanley Hill, for referring to workfare as "slavery," called the argument nonsense, and said that change was long overdue.[25] The mayor also heard from the Clinton Administration: The U.S. Secretary of Labor, Alexis Herman, wrote and pointed out that federal law prohibited the replacement of laid-off workers with welfare recipients. Thus WEP workers were denied training that they might have received.

In June 1998 Michael Hood, the head of a union that represented seasonal park workers, claimed that WEP workers were replacing regular workers. He said that before the mayor's WEP, the temporary workers' union membership had slid from 1,700 to 1,100 members. "What we are witnessing in New York City is the growth of a mammoth class of forced laborers," he said.[26]

Another court challenge produced a ruling by Judge Jane Goodman that HRA had to allow WEP participants hearings on the health and safety of their job placement. The mayor said that if people were disabled they should apply for federal SSI assistance and that the judge was inappropriately putting herself in the position of a medical professional. The mayor believed that if a person could work a little, he or she should be offered the opportunity. Jason Turner, the HRA commissioner, said that this approach was in keeping with the spirit of the Americans with Disabilities Act, which advocates the full integration of disabled people into the mainstream.[27]

The rhetorical outbursts continued in 1998. William Mason, cochair of Workfairness, said that the WEP was a declaration of war against the poor. He attacked Commissioner Turner by calling him a proponent of the infamous Nazi phrase on the gates of Auschwitz, *"Arbeit mach frei"* (Work shall make you free).[28]

A study by the city comptroller said that WEP participants who were enrolled in college did as well or better in their coursework than they did before entering the program. An editorial lauded the study and said the critics of the WEP were elitists and racists by suggesting that welfare recipients were less able than others to work and go to college.[29] The decision by HRA to require welfare recipients to work while they attended college remained of interest to the media throughout the year, generating articles and demonstrations. During a multipurpose demonstration in August, protesters carried placards that denounced both Mayor Giuliani's WEP and President Clinton's attack on terrorists in Africa and Afghanistan.[30]

In 1998, Commissioner Turner's first year in office, 35,691 TANF recipients and 10,722 SNA recipients were working in WEP. But finding actual employment in city government for WEP workers was never a goal of an administration that was trying to live within its budget; New York City government employment was larger on a per-capita basis than in any other major city. Still, some WEP participants made the transition: In 1998, 169 WEP workers were hired into permanent city jobs.[31]

This was also the year that the new commissioner launched his initiative to transform welfare offices into Job Centers. Eligibility workers became "financial planners" and "employment planners." By the end of the year, eight of the city's 37 welfare offices had been converted to Job Centers, and an agreement with the Public Housing Authority resulted in a Job Center in one of the public housing projects. The effort not only changed job titles, but it reoriented the workers away from discussions of eligibility to discussions of employment. The mayor said at the opening of a new Job Center in Harlem, "Today we can see real progress as we transform our city from the welfare capital of the world to the work capital of the world."[32]

Turner's plan for WEP was to alter the culture of the agency through his conversion of welfare offices to Job Centers and to increase accountability by paying attention to outcome measures. Equally important, however, was converting the staff's focus from eligibility determination and error rates to employment. Part of this new focus was up-front job search.

New Procedures and Accountability—and Continued Opposition

As 1998 came to a close, New York Transit had a budget surplus and wanted to upgrade service. Part of the plan was to fulfill the promise that the mayor had made to the unions to hire a thousand WEP workers into career service jobs. Transit Authority President Larry Reuter said the WEP workers would be hired as train and station cleaners.[33] The plan, however, was never realized; although cleaners started at an annual salary of $21,382, which rose in three years to $36,000, the Transit Authority was able to hire only 596 cleaners, of whom a mere 45 were former WEP participants. The Transit Authority successfully applied the Parks and Recreation Department's strategy of rewarding line workers with additional pay when they supervised WEP workers, however. The new union contract provided for 150 regular cleaners to receive an additional $1.70 per hour to supervise WEP workers.[34]

Compared to prior years, 1999 was quieter. There were fewer demonstrations and articles attacking the WEP as the new commissioner introduced major management reforms to support his welfare reforms. Principal among these were his new reporting system and implementation of performance goals for each Job Center. A new "JobStat" system tracked activities at each Job Center, and periodic meetings were held to allow questions by central office administrators and an exchange of ideas that could help local offices achieve their goals. JobStat measured everything from sanctions to child-care and job placements, with a heavy emphasis on knowing how many people were properly engaged. Social work managers had never been under such close scrutiny. (See chapter 5 in this volume.)

The hospital employees' union brought suit against the city in 1999. Stanley Hill, who had been criticized by his own union for being too accepting of the mayor's WEP, now spoke out, saying that the city and the Health and Hospitals Corporation (HHC) shouldn't be allowed to exploit welfare recipients. Jane Zimmerman of the HHC said the staff reductions resulted from having fewer patients and had nothing to do with WEP. The union claimed that the city was violating the federal law that prohibited welfare recipients from performing work "the same or equivalent to that of regular civil service employees."[35]

In another lawsuit against the city, a legal aid society obtained an order from Judge Richard F. Braun that HRA could not give job leads and send people out to look for jobs until it had first completed an assessment of their individual needs, goals, and abilities. The *New York Post* upbraided Braun in an editorial, saying that his philosophy was one of "Go to school—get a check! Have a baby—get a check."[36] In his ruling the judge said that the city had flouted state law by forcing mothers on public assistance into WEP

without developing job plans or considering personal employment prefer-
ences.

In May the mayor and Martin Osterreich, the city's commissioner of
Homeless Services, announced their intention to extend WEP to people in
the city shelters. City Councilman Stephen DiBrienza, a WEP critic, accused
Commissioner Osterreich of "doing a great disservice to your own tenet, by
turning people back to the streets if they fail to perform mindless counter-
productive WEP assignments."[37]

In July 1999 another WEP worker died from heat exposure, and his
daughter filed suit against the city for $50 million. City Councilman Bill Per-
kins said, "A horse in Central Park would have been protected from the
heat!"[38] Robert Lawson, a Parks Department spokesman, said, "Every pre-
caution was taken. He was given light duty in the shade."

In September the city council attempted to legislate a new grievance and
appeal procedure for WEP workers. There was already a hearing process
mandated by federal law, but advocates and the unions argued for a "less
bureaucratic" system. In addition, the council called for the creation of
10,000 jobs—6,000 in the public sector and 4,000 in the nonprofit sector.
The proposed legislation was widely denounced in the press with both the
New York Post and the *Daily News*[39] editorializing against the initiative. The
mayor said he would veto it.

The city initiated a plan to engage able-bodied welfare recipients with
HIV in WEP. In the days that followed, advocates complained and said that
individuals with HIV would be forced to work and might miss medical
appointments or be dropped from the rolls for failing to participate. Hayley
Gorenberg, an attorney with Legal Services, said WEP was a "case-closing
sanction machine—a reality very different from trying to lift people out of
poverty." He added that "technically, HIV-positive people have never been
exempt from WEP, but with help from advocates and their contacts in HRA,
most have been able to get around it."[40]

At this point TANF recipients were increasingly cooperative and almost
all were "engaged." In 1999, TANF placements rose to 38,940. In the Safety
Net Assistance program, which benefits single men and women without
dependent children, failure to cooperate caused the grant to be cancelled. As
the rolls declined the number of SNA recipients available to work declined,
and Safety Net placements decreased to 9,980. In six years the number of
welfare cases had dropped from over 1.1 million to 631,000, and the mayor
was rightfully feeling proud of his success. The reductions were in part
related to helping people get jobs and in part the result of new income-
verification procedures and the sanctioning of those who failed to participate. At the end of the year the mayor said, "We said last year that we would
end welfare by the year 2000. We now have everyone engaged."[41] Not all
who were "engaged" were participating in work, however; fully half of the

"engaged population" was in a sanctioned status, which meant that a grant still went to other family members.

The unions attempted an "end run" in 2000 by working with the New York City Council and the state legislature to create 7,500 new, time-limited, public service jobs for WEP participants. The city council allocated $3 million over three years for this purpose; 2,500 jobs would be created each year. Although the creation of the jobs was more symbolic than real, given the number of welfare and WEP recipients, it was important to activists and opponents of WEP. In a more than symbolic way, it also paved the way for a new union that would be made up of welfare recipients. The mayor, in a controversial move, vetoed the legislation.

The mayor said that the Temporary Employment Program (TEP), as it was called, would "featherbed the government workforce with thousands of unneeded positions while fostering a culture of government dependency that our welfare reform efforts have worked so hard to reverse." Lawrence Mead, a professor of politics at New York University and author of several books on welfare, said that the proposal constituted "make work" that taxpayers would have to fund. Mead maintained that the TEP was unfair to the other 32,000 welfare recipients who would continue as WEP workers and that the focus of the Giuliani Administration should not be on growing the public sector but on working with the private sector to grow the tax base and to help people get unsubsidized jobs.[42] Councilman DiBrienza, the author of the TEP legislation, argued that the city was working with the least skilled and hardest to employ and that such a program was needed. The cost of the three-year initiative was estimated at $14 million, some of which would come from the federal government.

A year and a half later, however, HRA did in fact create time-limited jobs for participants who were reaching the end of their five-year entitlement period. The jobs paid more than $9 an hour and participants could work for up to a year as part of a transitional employment period. Surplus TANF funds were available in late 2001 because of the large decline in the number of people enrolled, and the federal government approved their use for this purpose.

In 2000 the equity issue was again brought to the courts. The suit argued that the number of hours of participation should be adjusted downward by using normal and customary pay rather than the minimum wage, resulting in fewer hours of WEP participation. The city responded that the WEP provided work experience, not regular employment, and that if their hours were reduced WEP participants would obtain less work experience. The state's highest court ruled in favor of the city, saying that work experience was not the same as regular employment.[43]

Advocacy groups, legal services entities, and unions accused Mayor Giuliani and HRA Commission Turner of everything from running a public-service sweatshop to creating the conditions that promote, rape, death, and child sexual abuse.[44] City Councilman DiBrienza asserted that a WEP participant who had a "stroke" on the job "lived in fear and died in fear, and it is Jason Turner who is responsible."[45] The abduction of a five-year-old child by a former WEP participant with a criminal record—who two years earlier was a WEP worker in the park from which the child was abducted—resulted in a multimillion dollar suit against the city and its WEP.[46]

As 2000 drew to a close, the city had spared no effort to meet the mayor's welfare goal. That year job placements jumped to 58,787 for all welfare recipients and 30,284 for TANF. All these were entitled to city-sponsored child care. According to HRA, WEP in New York provided child care to an average of 36,644 participants per month at a cost of $133 million. The mayor's *Management Report* stated that for every child who required care to enable a parent to engage in work activity, the parent received child care and assistance in locating care. The federal government provided half the needed funds.

The End of an Era

The acrimony between the city agencies, HRA, and the U.S. Department of Labor was exacerbated in 2001 by HRA's failure to spend federal funds, particularly after the September 11 attack on the World Trade Center. Federal and state labor officials accused HRA of not spending the federal funds quickly enough and endangering their continued flow. Nationally, states rescinded more than $100 million in federal Welfare-to-Work funds that had been targeted to state labor departments. Federal officials warned the mayor that the city was jeopardizing its one-stop-service employment centers because they were focused too much on welfare recipients and not enough on other low-income individuals. There was reason to believe that people in the city administration may have alerted federal authorities about this situation.[47]

The declining number of welfare recipients reduced the claim against federal TANF funds, and there was little need for additional federal funds. But vendors and nonprofits that traditionally offered training and employment assistance through state departments of labor lost "their" money. Although they knew that welfare departments viewed them with suspicion, they chastised state and city welfare administrators who did not "buy" their training and employment programs as preventing poor mothers from getting the training and education that would lift them from poverty. Governors and mayors who were aware of the decidedly modest impact of the training programs nevertheless feared that not drawing down these federal funds would bring criticism from community organizations and minority activist groups. Therefore they generated appropriate rhetoric and programs to snare those funds. For some mayors it was simply an effort to retrieve a portion of the federal taxes collected from their citizens. For others it provided patronage for their supporters.

Another union issue arose in converting the functions of the HRA front-line social workers from establishing eligibility to helping recipients become employed. The HRA strategy was to create a new job classification, Job Opportunity Specialist (JOS), and to offer additional pay as a reward for reaching job-related goals. The unions were divided on the issue; some union officials tried to dissuade their members from changing titles and functions. Some members embraced the new functions and opportunities for additional pay and volunteered for the new, integrated JOS positions; others did not want to change their job functions. In October 2001, District Council 37 filed suit against the city for giving special pay increases to some but not all the employees. Commissioner Turner saw the new JOS position as way to reward workers for specific outcomes without breaking the city budget and also as a way to change the culture of the agency from a myopic focus on error rates and eligibility determination to the broader perspective of employment.

CONCLUSION

The welfare rolls continued to decline. By fall 2001 the number of WEP participants had been reduced to 14,825; of that total, 9,512 were TANF households and 5,313 were single, unemployed people. According to HRA, child-only cases at the end of 2001 were 24 percent of the TANF caseload. (See figure 7.2.)

The first five years of welfare reform confirmed what its advocates predicted. People engaged in work at a rate considerably greater than the work-participation rate of welfare recipients prior to passage of the welfare reform legislation. Thus, when Congress forced "work first" on the states, more people went to work even while they continued to receive assistance.

One issue rarely discussed in terms of the success of work programs was the large fraction of welfare recipients who refuse to accept a WEP placement. No matter how many jobs or WEP work sites were available, some recipients would not accept employment. They were penalized, and the family grant was reduced by the value of the grant to the nonparticipating member. In the Safety Net Assistance program for people without dependent children, when recipients failed to participate in the WEP, their cases were closed and they no longer received cash assistance. There were 77,000 recipients who were engaged and not excused from WEP participation. Of those, 38,000 were in sanction status. The remaining 39,000 were not in sanction status for various reasons.

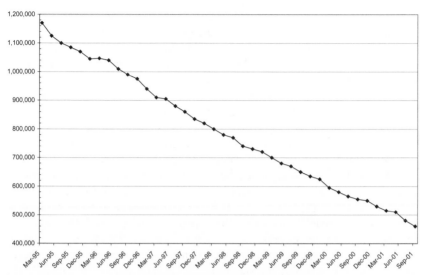

Figure 7.2.   Trend in the Number of Public Assistance Recipients
Source: Human Resources Administration, Public Assistance Caseload Reductions, Chart #1, 1995–2001.

Table 7.3 shows the degree of compliance with WEP assignments and reveals that compliance increased over time. Of the initial assignments in 2000, 42 percent experienced "failure to report"; the corresponding figure for the first half of 2003 was 12 percent. Of the assignments that were started, the fraction that experienced failure to comply—for example, due to insufficient hours or absence—declined from 15 percent to 12 percent.

In 2001 another change in the agreement with the Parks and Recreation Department allowed support services to be directly provided. The Parks Department became an employment and training agency with a personnel

Table 7.3.   WEP Assignments and Compliance

Calendar Year	No. of WEP Assignments	No. Failed to Report[a]	Percent of Assignments	No. Failed to Comply[b]	Percent of Assignments
2000	98,019	41,959	42.81%	14,725	15.02%
2001	80,475	34,666	43.08%	9,452	11.75%
2002	70,904	26,123	36.84%	11,811	16.66%
Jan–June 2003	35,516	11,771	33.14%	4,297	12.10%

Source: HRA records
[a]Failure to report to initial WEP assignment
[b]Failure to comply with WEP assignment after initial report, which can be insufficient hours or lack of attendance
Note: Data refer to assignments and not individuals; an individual can be assigned more than once and fail to report or comply more than once.

section, support services, coordination with child-care providers, skills training, and a work-site job-experience program. The annual cost of the basic WEP agreement with the Parks Department was $14,883,208; this included some $6.2 million for Metro passes. The funding allowed the hiring of 12 timekeepers, 14 coordinators, 20 assistant coordinators, and 367 field supervisors. As noted above, the unions agreed to support the program in part because union workers were given promotions to supervise WEP participants.

In 2001 New York was in conflict with federal food stamp regulations over when the HRA eligibility worker could discuss with the applicant the dollar amount of the food stamps that he or she would receive. Federal officials were displeased that the city first discussed employment opportunities with applicants rather than the amount of food stamps they were entitled to receive. Philosophically the U.S. Department of Agriculture, which administers the food stamp program, saw work requirements and employment as secondary to the applicant's entitlement to food assistance. They believed that federal law required the states first to give relief and then to help the applicant find work. Thus a state was in the untenable position of being allowed to talk to applicants for aid about employment before discussing the TANF grant, but not before telling them about the amount of food stamps they were entitled to receive.

Interviews with WEP Participants

Interviews with WEP supervisory personnel and participants were conducted at one of the city parks in August 2001. Supervisors maintained that the participants had made the parks cleaner and that the program benefited both the city and the participants. According to one supervisor, some participants appeared to have become too close to the program in that they would volunteer to work in the park and "hang around" even after they had been terminated from welfare. Many of the participants interviewed had been with the program for three years on either an intermittent or continuous basis.

The Parks Department program had a higher rate of participation than the Sanitation Department. A senior official in Sanitation said in an interview that initially about 50 percent of the WEP participants who were required to report for work in the streets failed to show up and were subsequently sanctioned. As the number of recipients left welfare and the rolls declined, the "no-show" rate increased to 70 percent. In contrast, the "no-show" rate for WEP workers at the Parks Department was initially about 20 percent, and it remained at that level even as the rolls declined. WEP participants preferred to work in the parks rather than with the Department of Sanitation.

Participants stated that they enjoyed the work, but some complained that while they had been recognized as WEP "Worker-of-the-Month" several times, they were never considered for regular employment. They asserted that their experience should give them priority status when it came to filling regular job vacancies. One participant complained that his eight-year-old drug conviction and jail time were still held against him. He felt that the Parks Department policy of not hiring someone who had been convicted of a felony was unfair and that he had been "blackballed." Another participant felt that the attendance policies were too strict and that he had been unfairly treated because he was late in getting to work. The chief complaint among participants was that changes in the rules or program requirements were not always communicated to them until well after the fact or until they had transgressed a new policy. All the participants felt that they were treated fairly by their caseworkers and that the city cared about what happened to them. They said that they were given uniforms and gloves, and that in inclement weather they were equipped with special clothing. In response to a question regarding safety and concerns for their well-being, the participants interviewed said that Parks Department supervisors were concerned about their safety and that if started to rain or snow they were told to go inside.

The WEP workers interviewed all said that they believed it was appropriate for the city to expect them to work and for them to return something of value to the city in return for their welfare grant. One can assume that those who did not show up for work and chose to be sanctioned felt differently about WEP participation.

The New York Difference

As Mayor Giuliani's term was drawing to a close at the end of 2001, it was appropriate to ask about the changes wrought in the system. One clear message was frequently repeated in interviews with HRA staff and others in other city agencies: The mayor and the commissioner had changed the rules and the management style of the agency. The "word had come down from the highest levels that the mayor expected welfare recipients to work for their checks." They were to get "a hand up and not a hand out." Commissioners in Parks, Health, Sanitation, and other city agencies knew the change was real.

One longtime HRA employee, Joan Randel, said that the new commissioner's approach to management was strikingly different. "We were in the Dark Ages regarding the computers and automation we needed for our jobs, and he made sure we all had the tools to get the job done," she said. "He had a new idea every week, but unlike his predecessors, his approach was to meet with lower-echelon staff, lay out the idea, and ask us how to get it accomplished. We didn't have any of the rigidity and top-down formalism that we were used to." Randel went on to say that the morale of the agency had changed. "It used to be the dumping ground for folks in other agencies who messed up. Today people want to work at HRA."

Commissioner Turner and his top staff met at HRA headquarters with one or two Job Center directors and their respective regional administrators. Attendees received JobStat statistical charts (see chapter 5) so that they could review the center's performance and discuss why it was exceeding, meeting, or failing to meet its placement goals. This "hands-on" approach let staff throughout the HRA know that the commissioner was involved in the day-to-day operations of the agency and cared about them and their work.

New York faced the same problems as other jurisdictions and encountered the same difficulties that kept other agencies from initiating public works programs. In terms of the program's size and complexity, and given the obstacle of aggressive unions, however, New York's task was arguably much more difficult because of opposition from much of the media and suits brought continually by various welfare advocacy groups and other factions.

Although the rest of the country knew about work-experience programs, it was only in New York that the leadership was willing to take the political risks associated with creating a large-scale public employment program. Mayor Giuliani had the courage to bring into his administration someone who shared his vision of the future. The mayor's belief in the program was based on his knowledge of the city and its voters. He understood that many people would support his initiative, even if silently. When he left office he was more popular than ever—due in great measure to his leadership after 9/11, to be sure—but he pointed to his welfare reform program as one of his proudest accomplishments.

Ten Lessons Learned

The following lessons were learned from WEP in New York City:

(1) Placement of welfare recipients into work experience programs may be interpreted as a form of job replacement by unions if at the same time economic problems require the reduction of regular staff.

(2) Except in extreme municipal circumstances, public employee unions view public employment and membership in the union without regard to the city's need for workers and the ability of the city to pay for them. They see their job as securing better pay and benefits for their members and protecting them from downsizing.

(3) Acceptance of work experience programs by the unions can be achieved, to a degree, by offering pay increases to union members who supervise program participants.

(4) Mayors and governors who embark on a public-work service initia-

tive as part of a welfare reform effort can expect to be criticized by liberal media and advocacy groups.

(5) Programs similar to New York's WEP can make a difference in the quality of life for all.

(6) If recipients of public assistance are given WEP assignments that conflict with their underground jobs or other sources of income, they will drop out of the program.

(7) Large agencies can be made accountable, and values that appear to be deeply rooted in the past can be changed.

(8) Legal challenges to public-work initiatives can be expected but can often be overcome.

(9) Having measurable goals for each office and a good reporting system is essential for success.

(10) Leadership and commitment by the governor or mayor is mandatory for a program to be successful.

Epilogue:
Calculating WEP's Costs
and Monetary Benefits

Douglas J. Besharov and Peter Germanis

Although a jurisdiction could well decide that work experience programs are good policy regardless of their cost, in many places fears of high costs have been a barrier to their adoption. Limited data from New York and other jurisdictions suggest that well-run work experience programs result in benefits to the community that can more than match the costs of administration, that probably cover the costs of child care, and that may cover the costs of at least some education and treatment services. (This analysis deals only with the possible monetary benefits of work experience programs; many other benefits, such as increased self-worth of recipients and positive role models for their children, are impossible to quantify in monetary terms and are not discussed here.)

This epilogue refers to costs and monetary benefits from various years, as early as 1993. To facilitate comparison, all dollar amounts are in 2003 constant dollars.

COSTS

The costs of work experience programs vary greatly and depend on several factors, including the number of participants, the average length and intensity of participation, the types of activities in which people participate, the characteristics of participants (age of children, barriers to employment), the extent of participant monitoring and case management, the scope and intensity of support services offered, management practices, overhead costs, and employee wage scales.[48]

Administrative Costs

Actually operating the program, including finding and supervising quality sites, assigning recipients to the sites, and making sure that the recipients actually participate is a major undertaking.

Site Administration

The cost of site administration includes costs for developing work sites, assigning participants to work slots, and monitoring program operations. Researchers from the Manpower Demonstration Research Corporation (MDRC) estimated that in the programs operating in 1993 that they studied, the costs ranged from about $334 up to about $1,245 per participant. Most participants were in a work experience position for three months or less, so the annual cost of keeping a slot filled was generally higher, ranging from about $468 to about $4,076.[49] The mean cost was about $2,042, and the median cost was about $1,771 for single-parent programs.

Jason Turner, then commissioner of the Human Resources Administration (HRA), and his coauthor Professor Thomas Main of Baruch College, estimated the annual cost to administer a HRA WEP slot at about $1,546 in 1999. At that time, they were mostly full-time.[50] This cost estimate largely reflects the costs of operating a full-time, 35 hour per week WEP program, because in 1999 only about 15 to 25 percent of WEP participants combined their work experience participation with another activity.[51] About 67 percent of costs went to payments to other government agencies for direct costs, including timekeepers, coordinators, and field supervisors, as well as for tools and equipment. About another 24 percent was spent for third-party medical assessments, and approximately 9 percent was used for HRA's administrative costs.

The Turner and Main estimate of the cost of site administration is at the low end of the range for the MDRC-evaluated programs (about $1,546 vs. a mean of about $2,042). Moreover, it reflects more hours on assignment: The work obligation in New York City was 35 hours per week, compared with about 20 hours per week in most of the MDRC-evaluated programs.[52] The economies of operating on a large scale may help explain HRA's lower costs. Indeed, the MDRC research indicates that the work experience programs in West Virginia and Cook County, which had the largest number of work experience positions, also had the lowest costs per slot filled.

Participant Monitoring

The MDRC researchers also estimated the costs associated with monitoring participant compliance, primarily the costs associated with the sanctioning process. These costs ranged from about $44 to about $1,194.[53] The annual cost per slot ranged from about $37 to about $5,190. The mean cost was about $2,228, and the median cost was about $2,316.[54] Turner and Main apparently did not include the cost of monitoring recipients and the sanctions process in their cost estimate. We assume that such costs would be at least as high as the costs in the MDRC projects (about $2,234 per slot per year). This assumption may still result in an underestimation of the direct cost of a work experience program, because New York City's sanction process involves a much larger share of the caseload than any of the work experience programs evaluated by MDRC. HRA refined the process to the point that costs per case may be significantly lower than they would be if sanctioning were less frequent. For example, in November 2001 about one-third of the city's engageable caseload either had a sanction in effect or was in the process of being sanctioned. In contrast, Brock, Butler, and Long report that "sanctions were not used extensively at the study sites."[55] Of course, sanctions also reduce the cost of welfare benefits, which ideally should be reflected in the cost of a work experience slot.

As these findings indicate, the estimates of the cost of work experience programs vary considerably, making it difficult to generalize the findings. Nevertheless, because the costs associated with most of the programs were in the middle of this range, many analysts have narrowed this range to develop cost estimates for program administrators and policy analysts exploring federal and state welfare reform options. For example, an MDRC analyst concluded that the cost of filling a work experience position (excluding child-care costs) for one year would be between about $2,546 to about $5,091.[56] A Congressional Budget Office (CBO) analyst estimated that the annual cost of a 20-hour per week work experience slot (excluding child care) would be about $3,300 and that a 40-hour per week slot would cost about $3,700.[57] (Since both estimates relied on earlier MDRC research, it is not surprising that all these estimates are comparable.)

Support Services

The foregoing cost estimates do not include the cost for child care and transportation, often needed if a mother is to work. Some Temporary Assistance for Needy Families (TANF) recipients may also need to resolve other issues such as the lack of stable housing, medical or legal issues, or family or personal problems, in order to participate in activities. Because we have no data on the latter, we offer cost estimates only for child care and transportation.

Child Care

HRA, as well as all other jurisdictions, provides child-care subsidies for mothers who participate in work experience programs. Sheila Dacey at CBO used administrative data on child-care subsidies under the Child Care and Development Fund (CCDF) to estimate child-care costs for work experience programs.[58] She estimated that the annual cost of child care for a child in CCDF-funded child care was about $4,000, including both full-time and part-time child care. The administrative data also indicated that about 1.68 children per family received subsidies, resulting in an estimated annual cost of about $6,720 per family. She further estimated that 86 percent of TANF families included a child under age thirteen and were eligible for a subsidy and that 50 percent of these eligible families would actually use the subsidy. On this basis, Dacey estimated the annual cost of child care for a 24-hour per week work slot would be about $2,900. (Analysts at CLASP estimated the cost of the subsidy as about $3,404 per work slot.)[59] Dacey further estimated that child-care cost for a full-time work slot would be about 10 percent higher, or about $3,200.

New York City's costs per slot are apparently higher than these national estimates. The city's Independent Budget Office, for example, reports that in 2002 the average annual cost of subsidized child care per child in New York City was about $6,605, considerably higher than the $4,000 per child estimate used by the CBO.[60] Applying the CBO's assumptions of 1.68 children per family suggests that the cost per family is about $11,096; applying CBO's assumptions of 86 percent of TANF families with a child under 13 and a 50 percent take-up rate results in an estimated annual child-care cost of about $4,771 per WEP slot. (We have no data on take-up rates or total costs.)

These estimates are rough. For example, whether the cost of a part-time or part-day slot is considerably less expensive than a full-time slot depends on the actual number of hours involved and the availability of child-care providers willing to provide part-time or part-day care. Similarly, the take-up rate might well rise in a full-engagement regime.

Transportation

Recipients may need financial help getting to worksites and to other program activities. HRA assists TANF recipients with transportation. Every two weeks, $34 is added to the welfare checks of WEP participants so that they can buy two weekly unlimited farecards. (The unlimited card has the added advantage of helping recipients who have to make separate stops at child-care providers.)[61] This benefit adds $884 to the annual cost of a WEP slot. There is no assurance, however, that the money is actually spent on transportation. As Seth Diamond explains, "We don't know that they are buying the fare cards, but we hope they are."[62] (Other jurisdictions have helped TANF recipients set up van services to transport participants to activities.)[63]

Education and Treatment Services

Most recipients also took advantage of an extensive array of education and treatment services. We have no information on the costs associated with these services in New York City, but they could easily exceed the cost of work experience activities. For example, Brown compared the costs of various program activities for five welfare-to-work programs. She reported that the cost of "basic education" and "vocational training and college" ranged from about $2,037 to about $8,911 per participant, considerably higher than the about $433 to about $1,782 for work experience in the same programs.[64] As we will see, determining whether the benefits of HRA's WEP program offset its costs depends on how much these services cost.

Total Costs

Based on the foregoing, we estimate that HRA's costs for site administration (about $1,546), participant monitoring (about $2,228), child care (about $4,771), and transportation ($884) total about $9,429 per slot per year. As noted above, even this cost estimate may be low for New York City, because the cost of the sanctioning process may be understated. It also does not take into account the cost of providing other education, training, treatment, or support services that may be associated with WEP.

By way of comparison, both the CBO and CLASP estimates are lower. CBO's Dacey estimates that the annual cost of a 24-hour per week work experience slot, including child care, was about $6,200 and about $6,900 for the cost for a 40-hour per week work experience. The CLASP estimate for 2003 would be about $6,476.[65]

MONETARY BENEFITS

Counterbalancing these costs is (1) the value of the services provided by recipients in the work experience program, plus (2) the possible reductions in welfare caseloads and payments. (We consider benefits to the city, only, not to other levels of government or recipients because of data limitations.)

Value of Services

Based on MDRC studies of 12 programs in seven sites,[66] Brock, Butler, and Long concluded that the work performed by work experience participants was of value to the government and nonprofit organizations where they worked.[67] Most supervisors and participants rated the work as necessary, and almost all of the supervisors surveyed said that the work would be done by regular staff if unpaid welfare recipients were not available.

The researchers estimated that the annual value of the output produced by each participant ranged from about $1,138 to about $5,837. The annual benefit associated with each slot ranged from about $4,231 to about $11,065.[68]

The mean annual value per slot filled was about $6,715, and the median was about $6,163.

By all accounts, HRA's WEP placements resulted in "real work" that provided "real" benefits to the community. Turner and Main report that immediately before the introduction of large numbers of welfare workers in New York City's parks, the parks had an "acceptable cleanliness" rating of 74 percent. With the introduction of welfare workers to a peak of more than 3,000 full-time worker equivalents, the acceptable cleanliness rating of the city's parks climbed to from 74 percent to 95 percent, an increase which they attribute largely to the work experience program.[69]

Community Voices Heard (CVH), a citywide organization of welfare recipients, surveyed 649 WEP participants at 131 worksites in 1999 and 2000, and found that most respondents reported doing the same work as regular municipal employees. CVH also found that WEP workers were performing 35 of the 36 tasks in three union job titles.[70] (The survey included a mix of TANF and SNA recipients, but the findings were not reported separately.)

The maximum number of hours a welfare recipient can be required to work is based on the welfare grant divided by the minimum wage; therefore one way of valuing the output performed by WEP participants is to multiply the minimum wage by the number of hours worked. Thus, a 20-hour per week WEP slot would produce services valued at about $5,150 per year ($5.15 multiplied by 1,000 hours) and a 35-hour per week slot would produce services valued at about $9,000 per year ($5.15 multiplied by 1,750 hours).

The minimum-wage approach to estimating the value of services may substantially underestimate the value of the work produced by WEP participants. Hence, we also could use MDRC's approach, which would apply the hourly cost of a city worker doing the same work. Because at least two surveys indicate that WEP participants perform real work and are nearly as productive as regular city workers performing similar tasks, we could use the salary of a low-level, full-time worker at the Department of Parks and Recreation (about $23,189) as a proxy for the value of the work of WEP participants.[71] (Some would suggest a higher valuation of the services provided based on a comparison of specific services to associated salaries, but we refrain from doing so.) Thus, we estimate that the annual value of work produced by a WEP participant in a 20-hour per week assignment could be about $11,595. For a participant in a 35-hour per week assignment, the value of output produced could be nearly $20,290.

Robert Lerman and Eric Rosenberg of the Urban Institute conducted a rough benefit-cost analysis of the WEP program as it existed in 1996. They interviewed 22 managers at WEP sites in five New York City agencies.[72] The managers rated the quality of the WEP work force only slightly below that of city workers, on average, and they all indicated that they would accept more WEP workers. Lerman and Rosenberg noted that the cost associated with administering WEP was $9.4 million. Using a cost estimate of $29,000 per year for a low-level Parks Department employee, they concluded that the benefits to the program exceeded the costs:

> Since $9.4 million would hire an additional 325 Parks workers, each of the city's 20,000 WEPs would need to be less than 1/30th as efficient as the average city employee (keeping in mind that WEP workers work half-time), for the WEP program to be cost ineffective—the least efficient workers recorded in the departmental survey were one quarter as efficient.[73]

The survey also indicated, however, that WEP workers were performing tasks that were previously done much less often. As a result, although their work may have been important, it may not have been valued as much as the ongoing work of the city. Lerman and Rosenberg explain, "Though the value of having the brass in the city court house polished more often may not have direct economic value, it has the secondary benefit of helping to maintain the dignity and stature of the rule of law."[74] They also suggest that the work may have other, less tangible, benefits: "Cleaner parks and streets improve overall city morale and make for a more pleasant environment in which law abiding citizens can congregate and drive down the number of desolate, abandoned spaces where crimes or criminal dealings can occur."[75] This analysis suggests caution in comparing the value of the work produced by WEP workers with that of other city workers.

Reduced Welfare Payments

Theoretically, a well-functioning work experience program should reduce welfare caseloads and reduce payments to the families that remain on welfare. We can offer only anecdotal evidence on the first and can make only a very rough estimate of the second.

Lower Welfare Caseloads

Many believe that work experience programs discourage families from applying for welfare and encourage those receiving assistance to leave. Work experience programs appear to "smoke out" recipients who are working (usually under the table) and encourage nonworking recipients to find jobs, since their choice is either unpaid work experience or a "real job." One HRA official explains, "By design, WEP was also intended to reduce caseloads by providing participants with job experience and skills necessary to find employment."[76]

Other aspects of HRA's program, however, such as access to quality education and training, might attract families to welfare or at least give them an incentive to stay on. Similarly, it is well documented that pre-TANF "earnings disregards" encouraged families to stay on welfare. Whether families do so under time limits or mandatory participation regimes are still open questions. Given this uncertainty, we do not include such likely effects in our calculations here.

Lower Welfare Payments

Work experience programs can reduce welfare payments by encouraging welfare recipients to find work and by imposing sanctions on those who fail to comply with the participation requirements. Some of the MDRC projects described above, for example, isolated the impact of work experience on welfare expenditures and tax revenues associated with changes in employment and found that benefits exceeded total costs.[77] Unfortunately, we do not have similar data for New York City and cannot include such benefits in our analysis.

Unlike the MDRC projects, however, a large portion of the HRA caseload is under a partial sanction, and it is possible to estimate (very roughly, of course) the amounts saved. In November 2001, 15,738 Family Assistance cases were receiving reduced benefits due to a sanction, compared with just 10,127 Family Assistance cases participating in WEP. Assuming a family of three, each sanction case would bring savings of about $270 in monthly TANF and food stamp benefits. Assuming that all of the sanctions were due to nonparticipation in WEP, the annual savings per WEP slot would be about $5,035. (About $936 of this amount would be in food stamp savings, which would accrue to the federal government, not the city.)

COSTS VS. MONETARY BENEFITS

To recapitulate, we estimate the costs and benefits for HRA's Work Experience Program in table 7.4.

Given the paucity of information and evaluation, the net benefit is necessarily expressed as a range. Another way of viewing the benefits versus costs of HRA's work experience program is as follows: Even using the most conservative estimate of the benefits of work experience (i.e., a part-time slot at the minimum wage, $5,150), because of the savings from sanctions (about $5,035), our estimate is that WEP benefits covered the cost of site administration and participant monitoring (about $3,774) as well as the costs of child care and transportation (about $5,655). This conservative valuation of the services provided by recipients would not exceed total costs, however, once expenditures on ancillary education and treatment services are factored in. The costs of such services would be covered only if the value of the participants' work were set at that of low-level city workers or if the work assignment were full-time.

Table 7.4.   Estimated Costs and Benefits of HRA's Work Experience Program

Costs (2003 $)		
Site administration	$1,546	
Participant monitoring	2,228	
Child care	4,771	
Transportation	884	
Education and treatment	Unknown	
Total Costs	$9,429	
Benefits (2003 $)		
Value of services	$5,150–$20,290	Depending on how services are valued and if 20 or 35 hours of work per week
Reduced caseload	Not available	
Reduced welfare payments	$5,035	Savings from sanctions, but no estimate of savings or costs as recipients combine work and welfare
Total Benefits	$10,185–$25,325	
Net Benefit	$756–15,896[i]	Depending on (1) the costs of education and treatment services, (2) the valuation of the services provided, and (3) the possible caseload reduction

i. Includes $936 in Food Stamp savings that accrue to the federal government.

NOTES

1. Paul Moses, "Thousands Sanctioned Off Welfare," *Queens Newsday*, May 5, 1996, 32.

2. Gregory Heires, "Welfare Reform Is Born in New York," *Public Employee Press*, November 29, 1996, 1.

3. Alan Finder, "Welfare Clients Outnumber Jobs They Might Fill," *New York Times*, August 25, 1996, 1.

4. Stanley Hill, "The Workfare Program Is an Accident Waiting to Happen," *Public Employee Press*, October 4, 1996.

5. Peter Benjaminson, "Forming Joint Committee to Monitor WEP," *Chief*, October 1996.

6. "What's Fair About 'Workfairness'?" *New York Beacon,* November 14–20, 1966.

7. David R. Jones, "Forced Labor No Solution to Joblessness," *Amsterdam News,* October 5, 1996, 1.

8. Rudolph Giuliani, "Why We Will End Welfare by 2000," *New York Post,* July 21, 1998.

9. Steven Greenhouse, "Two Well-Known Churches Say No to Workfare Jobs," *New York Times,* April 13, 1998, 1.

10. David R. Jones, "Education: An Escape Route," *Amsterdam News,* July 6–12, 2000, 1.

11. "Keep Work in CUNY Workfare," *Daily News,* August 8, 1997.

12. "Judge: Don't Interfere with WEPs in College," *Chief-Leader,* June 13, 1997.

13. Paul Moses, "Is Mayor's Workfare Program on the Job?" *Queens Newsday,* June 15, 1997.

14. HRA Weekly Report, August 5, 2001.

15. Joe Sexton, "Woman's Death Prompts Concerns over Workfare," *New York Times,* June 24, 1997; David L. Lewis, "Workfare Woman's Family Seeks 10M for On-Job Death," *Daily News,* August 28, 1997.

16. Robin Epstein, "Commish: City May Test Reality of Welfare-To-Work," *City Limits,* April 7, 1997, 7.

17. Jill Nelson, "Facing Welfare: As America Moves to Punish Our Neediest Citizens, Society Suffers," *Village Voice,* May 6, 1997.

18. *Chief,* August 6, 1997, 1.

19. Paul Moses, "Workfare Rights—Laborers Seek Union Benefits; Officials Balk at Cost," *Queens Newsday,* April 20, 1997, 11.

20. "WEP Moms 'Lobby' Barrios-Paoli on Workfare Childcare," *City Limits,* June 23, 1997.

21. Robert Ratish, "Working in Fear of a Dead End: Workfare Doesn't Utilize Skills, Some Say," *Queens Newsday,* September 1, 1997.

22. Robert Parillo, "Mayor Giuliani Announces Three Welfare to Work Initiatives," *Queens Ledger,* September 25, 1997.

23. LynNell Hancock, *Hands To Work: The Story of Three Families Racing the Welfare Clock* (New York: Harper Collins, 2001).

24. Ian Fisher, "Giuliani Drops Workfare Jobs at the Hospitals," *New York Times,* April 24, 1998.

25. "'Slavery?' Hill's Workfare Charges Are Nonsense." *Queens Newsday,* April 23, 1998.

26. "Cites Rise in WEPs; Parks Phasing Out Paid Staff–Union," *Chief,* June 5, 1998, 1.

27. Mike Allen, "Judge Limits Assignments for Workfare; City Must Consider Health and Safety," *New York Times,* May 10, 1998.

28. J. Zamgba Browne, "Giuliani's Plan to End Welfare Meets Stiff Opposition," *New York Amsterdam News,* July 30, 1998.

29. "The Pleasures of Work," *New York Post,* July 10, 1998.

30. Leonard Greene, "Swipe at Welfare Protest Targets Program, Blasts Missile Strikes," *Queens Newsday,* August 23, 1998.

31. Gregory Heires, "DC 37 Takes on The Challenge of Workfare: Does NYC's Workfare Work?" *Public Employees Press*, June 25, 1999.

32. "City Continues to Transform Welfare Centers into Job Centers," *Brooklyn Heights Courier*, November 16, 1998.

33. James Rutenberg, "TA Maps Upgrades: Eyes More Runs and Cleanliness," *Daily News*, December 3, 1998.

34. M. Daly, "TWU: Transit Jobs up Despite WEPS," *Chief*, March 10, 2000, 1.

35. L. Dicomo, "Hospital Unions File Lawsuit against the City," *New York Amsterdam News*, April 23, 1999.

36. "Why Do You Think They Call It Work?" *New York Post,* April 17, 1999.

37. "Shelter Residents Bound for WEP Assignments," *Chief*, May 14, 1999.

38. Leslie Casimir, "City Sued in Welfare Worker Death," *Daily News*, July 31, 1999.

39. "Workfare's Trojan Horse," *Daily News*, September 16, 1999.

40. Robert Polner, "City: Having HIV Is No Excuse, Wants Welfare Recipients to Work," *Newsday*, November 5, 1999.

41. Associated Press, "Giuliani Touts Workfare," *Staten Island Advance*, December 29, 1999.

42. "No, Plan Is Misguided," *Daily News*, March 20, 2000.

43. Salvatore Arena and Frank Lombardi, "Rudy Wins 1, Loses 1 on Workfare Policy," *Daily News*, February 23, 2000, 4.

44. *Newsday*, June 28, 2000.

45. Thomas J. Lueck, "Workfare Critics Cite the Case of a Woman Who Died on the Job," *New York Times*, August 31, 2000, B3.

46. Helen Peterson, "Kidnapped Boy's Parents Sue City for 75M," *Daily News*, September 28, 2000.

47. Diane Cardwell, "Warning on Funds for Employment Centers," *New York Times*, November 1, 2001, D3.

48. See, for example, Gayle Hamilton and Susan Scrivener, *Promoting Participation: How to Increase Involvement in Welfare-to-Work Activities* (New York: Manpower Demonstration Research Corporation, September 1999), 31–32, available from: http://www.mdrc.org/Reports99/PromotingParticipation.pdf, accessed September 19, 2001.

49. Thomas Brock, David Butler, and David Long, *Unpaid Work Experience for Welfare Recipients: Findings and Lessons from MDRC Research* (New York: Manpower Demonstration Research Corporation, 1993), tables 10 and A.1.

50. Jason Turner and Thomas Main, "Work Experience under Welfare Reform," in Ron Haskins and Rebecca Blank, eds., *The New World of Welfare* (Washington, D.C.: Brookings Institution, 2001), 301.

51. New York City Human Resources Administration, "FA—Weekly Caseload Engagement Status," various reports issued in 1999.

52. Brock, Butler, and Long, *Unpaid Work Experience*, 71.

53. Brock, Butler, and Long, *Unpaid Work Experience*, tables 10 and A.1. The findings for AFDC and AFDC-UP are reported separately in four of the sites studies and are considered separate programs.

54. These figures are for only the single-parent programs. As mentioned above,

there were four sites that had programs for both single-parent and two-parent families. We excluded the cost data for the latter to avoid giving too much weight to the sites with both programs, but the costs across the two programs were almost the same in a given site.

55. Brock, Butler, and Long, *Unpaid Work Experience*, 73.

56. Amy Brown, *Work First: How to Implement an Employment-Focused Welfare Reform* (Washington, D.C.: Manpower Demonstration Research Corporation, March 1997), 55. The Center for Law and Social Policy used the midpoint of this range, $3,000, for its 2002 analysis of the Bush Administration's TANF work participation proposal (also excluding child-care costs). By not adjusting the MDRC estimate for inflation from 1993 to 2002, the CLASP analysis may understate the annual cost of a work experience position by over $600. See Mark Greenberg, Elise Richer, Jennifer Mezey, Steve Savner, and Rachel Schumacher, *At What Price? A Cost Analysis for the Administration's Temporary Assistance for Needy Families (TANF) Work Participation Proposal* (Washington, D.C.: CLASP, April 15, 2002), 18, available from http://www.clasp.org/DMS/Documents/1023208530.14/At_What_Price_anaylsis.pdf, accessed March 5, 2003.

57. Sheila Dacey, Congressional Budget Office, conversation with Peter Germanis, January 27, 2003.

58. Dacey, conversation with Peter Germanis.

59. Greenberg et al., *At What Price?*, 21.

60. Paul Lopatto, "Where Have All the New Child Care Dollars Gone?" *Inside the Budget*, no. 111 (December 12, 2002): 1.

61. Seth Diamond, former deputy commissioner for Operations, New York City Human Resources Administration, conversation with Marie Cohen, December 20, 2001.

62. Diamond, conversation with Cohen.

63. For more ideas, see Carolyn Jeskey, *Linking People to the Workplace* (Washington, D.C.: Community Transportation Association of America [CTAA], revised January 2001), available from http://www.ctaa.org/ntrc/atj/toolkit, accessed September 19, 2001; Community Transportation Association of America, *Access to Jobs: A Guide to Innovative Practices in Welfare-to-Work Transportation* (Washington, D.C.: CTAA, updated July 1999), available from http://www.ctaa.org/ntrc/atj/pubs/innovative/, accessed September 19, 2001; Margy Waller and Mark Allen Hughes, *Working Far From Home: Transportation and Welfare Reform in the Ten Big States* (Philadelphia: Public/Private Ventures, and Washington, D.C.: Progressive Policy Institute, July 1999), available from http://www.ppionline.org/documents/far_from_home.pdf, accessed September 19, 2001.

64. Brown, *Work First*, 55.

65. Greenberg et al., *At What Price?*, 21.

66. The findings for AFDC and AFDC-UP are reported separately in four of the programs evaluated.

67. Brock, Butler, and Long, *Unpaid Work Experience*, 32. Their assessment also includes findings from the four programs targeted to two-parent families.

68. Authors' calculations based on Brock, Butler, and Long, *Unpaid Work Experience*, tables 11 and 13.

69. Turner and Main, "Work Experience," 302.

70. Community Voices Heard, *Welfare to Work: Is It Working? The Failure of Current Welfare-to-Work Strategies To Move the Hardest To Employ Into Jobs* (New York City: Community Voices Heard, 1999), 6, available from http://www.cvhaction.org/Publications.html, accessed January 23, 2002.

71. According to Elizabeth Zeldin, an assistant budget and policy analyst in New York City's Independent Budget Office, a low-level, full-time worker at the Department of Parks and Recreation earned about $21,000 in 1999. See Elizabeth Zeldin, "Use of Work Experience Program Participants at the Department of Parks and Recreation," *Inside the Budget*, no. 72 (November 1, 2000): 3. But see Robert Lerman and Eric Rosenberg, "The Benefits and Costs of New York City Workfare" (unpublished paper, January 2, 1997), suggesting that, in the mid-1990s, "the cost of one low level Parks employee is approximately $29,000 per year."

72. Lerman and Rosenberg, 1997. The work in the paper was completed at a time when most WEP participants were recipients of Home Relief (New York City's general assistance program), not AFDC.

73. Lerman and Rosenberg, "Benefits and Costs," 18–19. The work in the paper was completed at a time when most WEP participants were recipients of Home Relief (New York City's general assistance program), not AFDC.

74. Lerman and Rosenberg, "Benefits and Costs," 16.

75. Lerman and Rosenberg, "Benefits and Costs," 16.

76. Swati Desai, then executive deputy commissioner, Office of Program Reporting, Analysis, and Accountability, New York City Human Resources Administration, e-mail to Douglas Besharov, June 17, 2003.

77. Most of the programs combined work experience with other services and could not isolate the impact of work experience alone. Total benefits exceeded total costs in two of the three programs for single parents, with a net gain of $1,001 in West Virginia and $997 in San Diego ($1,275 and $1,270, respectively). [Brock, Butler, and Long, *Unpaid Work Experience*, table A.2.] Reductions in welfare expenditures and increases in tax revenues accounted for about 12 percent to the net gain in West Virginia and about 60 percent of the net gain in San Diego.

8

Placing Welfare Applicants and Recipients in Jobs through Performance-Based Contracting

Burt S. Barnow and John Trutko

The last few years have seen major changes in the way that New York City manages and operates its human service programs and a major decline in New York City's public assistance caseload. According to Human Resources Administration (HRA) data, between March 1995 and September 2001 the caseload dropped from 1,161,000 to 464,000—a drop of over 60 percent. Several factors are responsible for the decline.[1] This chapter analyzes the effects of a management tool, performance-based contracting, on the welfare caseload in New York City.

As is often the case, programs being analyzed are constantly changing. This project examines the performance-based contracting system in effect in the last six months of 2001, based on interviews conducted mostly between November 2001 and March 2002. Michael Bloomberg was elected mayor of New York City in November 2001, and a number of changes were made subsequently in HRA's programs. The epilogue documents those changes.

INTRODUCTION

In this section, we present the purpose of the study and describe the general approach. Major caveats are stated, and the section concludes with a guide to the rest of the report.

Purpose of Study

We examine the role that one of the reforms instituted during the Giuliani Administration, performance-based contracting, has had on the decline in the public assistance caseload, by providing evidence from interviews with knowledgeable parties about the effects of performance-based contracting on caseload changes and services to HRA clients. We had originally hoped to be able to develop numerical estimates of the impact, but for reasons described below, we had to use this more qualitative approach to analyze the effects of performance-based contracting.

ORGANIZATION OF THE CHAPTER

We review the background of performance management and performance-based contracting, including findings in the literature on the impact of performance-based contracting on employment and earnings in employment and training programs. Next, we describe the HRA public assistance programs, with an emphasis on the Temporary Assistance for Needy Families (TANF) program. The section indicates how the program was administered prior to the implementation of performance-based contracting and the many changes that were implemented at roughly the same time that performance-based contracting was implemented.

This is followed by a review of academic studies and stories from the popular press on the effects of performance-based contracting in HRA programs. Then we interviewed HRA officials, federal and state government officials, and contracted service providers with a variety of perspectives on performance-based contracting. (See the appendix for a list of interviewees.) All but one of the interviews were conducted in person. Individuals who were interviewed were guaranteed anonymity so that they would share their views candidly. The subsequent section summarizes the findings from our interviews, and the final section presents our conclusions.

Caveats

Qualitative studies are generally better at capturing the general effects and the direction of change rather than the magnitude of a change. Our intent had been to supplement the interviews with quantitative analyses to estimate the effect of performance-based contracting on the size of the public assistance caseload.[2] As we describe below, the problem with using a quantitative approach is that so many other aspects of the public assistance program and its management changed at the same time that we considered it unlikely that a quantitative analysis would be able to isolate the impact of performance-based contracting. HRA research officials concurred in our decision to abandon the quantitative component of the analysis.

Qualitative analyses are not free of risk either. In particular, there is a risk that respondents will give merely self-serving answers. Although this may have occurred to some degree, we were pleasantly surprised at the consistency of the answers on factual matters. Both vendors and HRA officials were in close agreement on the problems experienced and the effects of performance-based contracting. Sometimes there was disagreement on whether the changes due to performance-based contracting were desirable or not. For example, virtually every interviewee agreed that performance-based contracting led to more emphasis on placing clients in jobs and less emphasis on providing education and training; respondents often disagreed, however, if this was an improvement or not. That is, some people disagreed with the goals of the program. Not surprisingly, therefore, there was disagreement when we asked HRA respondents to rank performance-based contracting in relation to other management and program reforms that were implemented at roughly the same time. Much of what we heard is also consistent with the popular research literature on the use of performance-based contracting by HRA.

PERFORMANCE MANAGEMENT AND PERFORMANCE-BASED CONTRACTING

The National Performance Review defined performance management as "[t]he use of performance measurement information to help set agreed-upon performance goals, allocate and prioritize resources, inform managers to either confirm or change current policy or program directions to meet these goals, and report on the success in meeting those goals."[3] Thus, performance management is a broad category of techniques that can be used by a government (or private) organization to help manage its subcomponents or contractors it has retained to deliver services. HRA's use of JobStat (Job Statistics) and VendorStat (Vendor Statistics) to track the accomplishments of its Job Centers and vendors, respectively, are good examples of performance management that will be discussed below. Barnow noted that a performance management system generally has three components: (1) performance measures against which the performance of the entity being monitored can be judged, (2) standards of acceptable performance for the measures, (3) and rewards and sanctions to encourage the units being judged to meet or exceed the performance standards.[4]

Performance-Based Contracting

Performance-based contracting is a special case of performance management where a vendor is retained to deliver services for the organization that issues the contract. We adopt the definition of performance-based contracting proposed by Kettner and Martin: "A contract that uses performance specifications and ties at least a portion of a contractor's compensation to their achievement."[5]

There are several reasons to rely on performance-based contracting, but the primary reason is to align the vendor's interests with those of the party that issued the contract, commonly referred to as the "principal-agent" problem.[6] In the absence of a performance-based contract, a vendor may pursue interests other than the issuer's primary goal or the contractor may have a different view on how to achieve goals that are shared. For example, in employment and training programs focusing on welfare recipients and other disadvantaged groups, there are different philosophies and conflicting evidence about whether it is better to try to get participants into jobs quickly (the "labor force attachment" model) or to provide them with education and training so that they can qualify for better-paying and more permanent jobs (the "human capital" model). A performance-based contract can provide strong incentives for the contractor to adopt not only the objectives but also the means of the contract issuer. In HRA's case, the Employment Services and Placement (ESP) contracts have strong incentives for placement and retention; the Skills Assessment and Placement (SAP) contracts include milestone payments (for assessment and engagement of participants in work-related activities) as well as performance incentive funding for placements and retention.

In the human services field, there are differences of opinion on how to measure HRA vendors' performance. Peter Cove, the founder of one of HRA's for-profit ESP vendors (America Works), argues strongly that the service an HRA vendor is providing is job placements, and vendors should receive payment only if they produce value for HRA by getting their clients placed and retained in employment.[7] He argues that if a defense contractor delivered 20 planes and only four could fly, it would not make sense for the government to pay for the nonfunctioning planes.

On the other hand, some observers argue that providing human services is different than manufacturing goods, especially when one is dealing with the disadvantaged populations served by HRA. They note that many of the clients have severe barriers to employment and that a vendor cannot be expected to achieve a high rate of success in placing such individuals in jobs. Ironically, while a strong economy can result in high success rates initially, after a while only the most unemployable individuals will remain jobless, and it will be more difficult to find such individuals jobs. Proponents of this view argue that payment to vendors should be based on services provided rather than on job placements and retention.

Performance-based contracting can lead to several effects:

- It can lead to "creaming," whereby the vendors concentrate most or all of their resources on clients who are most job ready and ignore those most in need.
- By paying vendors for events that occur long after services are provided (e.g., job retention), smaller organizations that lack substantial capitalization may be effectively barred from participating. On the other hand, advocates of such contracting point out that this may be a normal evolutionary development in this industry and not necessarily bad.
- Vendors have an incentive to provide the least expensive services that will result in a placement, thus emphasizing job search over education and training. This is consistent, however, with the new federal, state, and local policy.

The issues raised here are not unique to HRA. As the Social Security Administration is developing policies to implement the "Ticket to Work program" to enable the disabled to receive education, training, and other rehabilitation services, it must decide on the right balance between pay for performance and pay for services.

Performance-Based Contracting in Employment and Training Programs

Although there are many anecdotes about the virtues of performance-based contracting, there are surprisingly few rigorous evaluations in the employment and training field.[8] In this section, we review findings from some of the relevant studies.[9] Several recent studies analyze the relationship between the use of performance-based contracting and outcomes in Job Training Partnership Act (JTPA) programs.

Dickinson et al., studying the impact of performance-based contracting in the JTPA program, hypothesized that performance-based contracting would result in "creaming" by local programs, that is, selecting participants with the lowest barriers to employment.[10] Their empirical work, based on a survey of local programs, did not support the theory very well. The use of performance-based contracting was *not* associated with increased creaming, but contracts with high wage standards did result in creaming; the amount of payment at risk was not associated with a clear pattern in selecting participants.

Heinrich and Lynn unexpectedly found a statistically significant *negative* relationship between use of performance-based contracting and program outcomes.[11] In another study, however, Heinrich found large, statistically significant *positive* impacts on outcomes in one county. More recently, Spaulding analyzed the impact of performance-based contracting on placements and earnings of JTPA participants across the country.[12] She found that the use of performance-based contracting is associated with increased employment and earnings for participants, with stronger results for employment than earnings.

In a study involving case studies of performance-based contracting in welfare programs, Vinson found that performance-based contracting was associated with reduced cost per placement and improved placement rates.[13]

In summary, more often than not, studies support the hypothesis that performance-based contracting improves performance, but the number of analytical studies is limited and the evidence is not strong enough to draw unambiguously firm conclusions.

Consolidation of Contracts under SAP and ESP Vendors

A critical action under the welfare reform initiative was replacing many contracts with vendors of various sizes with fewer than 20 substantially larger contracts with Skills Assessment and Placement (SAP) vendors and Employment Services and Placement (ESP) vendors. HRA entered into performance-based contracts (explained below in greater detail) with four SAP providers and 11 ESP providers for employment preparation and employment services. (Four of the ESP were also SAP providers.) The vendors provide individualized assessment services to determine each participant's background, capabilities, and interests. They then work with applicants and participants in a combination of work, training, work experience, job search and placement, and other support services that are intended to lead quickly to employment.

HRA contracted with four SAP vendors—Arbor, Curtis and Associates, Federation Employment and Guidance Services (FEGS), and Goodwill Industries of Greater New York—to work with FA and SNA applicants while their public assistance applications were pending (i.e., prior to receiving benefits).[14] The services are aimed at quickly assessing individual needs and interests, providing job-readiness skills, and attempting to attach applicants to jobs as quickly as possible before welfare assistance is approved. Each SAP provider is assigned to serve specific Job Centers, and each Job Center is served by just one SAP vendor. Job Centers and SAP providers work out the specifics of client flow into and through SAP services. SAP providers may or may not locate staff directly at Job Centers for intake and initial assessment. Applicants are typically assigned to SAP vendors for a period of four to six weeks while their applications for public assistance are pending. Although the process flow of services varies somewhat by vendor, the following is fairly typical:

- Job Centers refer new FA and SNA clients to the SAP vendor daily (about 100 per week for this vendor).

- During the first week, participants attend a group orientation (two to three hours) and a three-day assessment at the Job Center. The assessment is a group activity that includes taking the Test of Adult Basic Education, completing an interest inventory test, and developing an employability plan.
- During the second week, participants attend a job-readiness workshop at the SAP vendor's principal office. The workshop, which runs for three and a half hours a day for five days, provides instruction and interactive group activities focusing on goal setting, resume development, job-search skills, and interviewing skills. During the remaining hours in the 35-hour simulated workweek, participants are given varying assignments to facilitate job search and placement (e.g., obtaining identification, spending time researching and identifying skills needed to enter occupations of interest, and preparing and submitting job applications).
- At the end of the second week, participants are referred to the vendor's Job Search Unit. On the following Monday, participants receive an orientation and a job-search booklet. Each day, they attend a half-day workshop to assist with job-search techniques; the other half-day is spent searching for a job with the help of a job developer who may provide job leads and do whatever is necessary to eliminate barriers to successful job search. These job-search activities go on for about two to four more weeks until the individual obtains a job or begins to receive FA or SNA benefits.
- If an individual is placed in a job, the SAP vendor assigns a job-retention specialist to track the individual and help him or her retain the job. This retention specialist talks with the participant during the first week of employment, encourages the individual to keep in contact, and periodically contacts each individual during the first 180 days of employment. During the first three months, participants are given a $17 MetroCard for mass transit fares; at the 90-day benchmark, the vendor provides a monthly MetroCard and makes the participant aware that an individual training account (ITA) voucher is available for upgrading skills. The vendor also operates a "Call Before You Quit" 24-hour hotline, as a last-gasp measure for job retention.

When the SAP effort is unsuccessful, applicants become active beneficiaries and most are reassigned to ESP vendors to receive services for up to two days per week while they participate in a work experience program three days per week. Initially, HRA contracted with 12 ESP vendors to serve TANF/SNA recipients across the city's five boroughs: America Works of New York, Career and Educational Consultants, Consortium for Worker Education, Curtis and Associates, Federation Employment and Guidance

Services, Goodwill Industries of Greater New York, MAXIMUS, New York Urban League, New York Association for New Americans, Non-Profit Assistance Corporation, RF/CUNY/LaGuardia Community College, and Wildcat Services Corporation.[15] New TANF/SNA recipients (who have not been exempted from work requirements) are assigned randomly to ESP contractors (generally within their home borough).[16] In addition to new cases, ESP contractors receive assignments of existing TANF/SNA beneficiaries and also provide contractual services for non–public assistance (non-PA) cases.[17] ESP vendors are encouraged to subcontract with other community-based providers to assign PA (and non-PA) participants to receive the same blend of services (e.g., one of the ESP providers we visited subcontracts with ten other local organizations, which together serve an estimated 40 percent of the individuals referred by HRA to this ESP provider). ESP providers select subcontractors, negotiate subcontracts (including payment terms), monitor subcontractor performance, submit subcontractor invoices for payment by HRA, and reimburse subcontractors after they are paid by HRA.

Participants are generally assigned to ESP providers for up to six months, at which time their status is reassessed by HRA and a decision is made whether to keep the individual with the current ESP provider or move the individual to another ESP provider or a special HRA program. Usually, within about three months, most of the individuals assigned to an ESP provider are either placed in jobs or are returned to Job Centers for sanctioning and/or reassignment to another vendor or special HRA program (e.g., for failure to report for services or to comply with work requirements). The blend of services varies by vendor, although in all cases there is a clear emphasis on rapid work attachment; relatively few vendors are engaged in job-training activities, and if they are, it is typically short-term training. If FA/SNA participants have not yet been placed in a job after working intensively with the ESP vendor for about two weeks, they are assigned to the Work Experience Program (WEP) through HRA. The WEP assignment typically covers three days of the work requirement (although it is reduced in accord with FA/SNA and food-stamp benefit levels so that the Fair Labor Standards Act is not violated), and the remaining two days the individual is to report to the ESP provider for job-readiness, search, and placement activities. This blended approach—three days of WEP and two days of ESP activity—is designed so that recipients do not languish in WEP assignments indefinitely (which are considered temporary) but are engaged in ongoing activities to gain unsubsidized employment. Although it varies by vendor, the basic client flow through one vendor's ESP services is as follows:

- Every two weeks, HRA gives the vendor a list of about 150 FA/SNA participants who are to receive ESP services (about 60 percent of whom show up for orientation at the vendor). In addition, the vendor mounts his own recruitment efforts, which result in recruiting non-PA individuals interested in and in need of employment and training services. About one-fourth of FA/SNA referrals are passed on to one of the ESP vendor's seven subcontractors, based primarily on the expertise of the subcontractor.

- On the first day, the participant attends an orientation session about the program, completes various intake and assessment forms, and takes the Test of Adult Basic Education.
- On the second day, the individual returns for an in-depth interview with one of the vendor's case managers. During this session, the case manager assesses the individual's capabilities and interests and comes up with a service plan and goals.
- The next eight days (days three through ten), the individual attends an all-day pre-employment job-readiness workshop. This focuses on learning effective job-search techniques, completing job applications, practicing interviews, preparing resumes, and generally preparing the individual for the world of work.
- WEP assignments come in about two weeks after assignment of the individual to the ESP provider. So, following the job-readiness workshop, the participant is shifted to a simulated workweek, which generally involves a WEP assignment for three days each week and then going to the ESP vendor the other two days a week for job-search/placement assistance, short-term training, and an array of other services to facilitate transition from welfare into work.
- Short-term training (generally involving less than six weeks) that leads directly to a job is offered to a small proportion of those assigned to the ESP vendor. Examples of limited training are for jobs such as home health care aide (about three weeks), security guard, food-service worker, copy-machine repairer, medical billing/records worker, and emergency medical services (EMS) worker.[18]
- When individuals are placed in jobs, case managers periodically check with the participant on how work is going and provide retention services as needed to reduce chances of job loss. Employed participants are also eligible to receive transportation vouchers (bus/subway passes) and ITAs to upgrade skills while working.

Institution of Performance-Based Contracting

HRA, which had formerly contracted for services primarily on a cost basis (using line-item contracting), instituted performance-based contracting with SAP and ESP vendors. Negotiated acquisition contracts with built-in performance incentives are awarded on a fixed-price basis to each contractor. Payments are contingent upon meeting performance criteria closely tied to placement and retention of participants in jobs. Higher payment levels are also provided for placing individuals in higher-paying jobs and for assisting individuals to leave and remain off of public assistance. Clearly, payment is tied closely to moving welfare participants into jobs and promoting self-sufficiency. The payment points (referred to as "milestones" within contracts) are different for ESP and SAP contracts, although each has milestone payments for job placement and retention. In addition, actual payment rates for each milestone vary across vendors (within ESP and SAP contracts) to reflect slightly different blends of services and rate structures across contractors. Below, as an illustration, we provide details from the ESP contract of one vendor we visited (terms in other ESP contracts are similar, although payment amounts vary slightly):

- HRA agrees to pay up to an overall maximum to the ESP contractor over the three-year period of performance under the negotiated acquisition contract. This payment is based on the contractor reaching maximum payments for each of the milestones included in the contract. For example, one ESP vendor we visited had an overall contract maximum of $30,630,000. Neither HRA nor vendors anticipated that they would achieve the maximum contract amount. In managing ESP and SAP contracts, HRA obligates a portion of the total maximum to the contractor on an incremental basis and, as needed, increases the obligation as reimbursement is made.
- Compensation is on "a unit price basis." The payment amount assumes that the ESP contractor shall be responsible for all direct costs associated with the program. Under the payment methodology, ESP providers are paid for achievement of specific "milestones" in serving each participant. For each ESP contractor, a "base rate" is established for each participant if all milestones are achieved; the base rate for one vendor is $4,641. HRA pays ESP vendors for each milestone achieved in serving each participant. In the case of the sample vendor, payment is made at the following points:
  - Job placement: 40 percent of the base rate ($1,856) is paid per job placement.
  - 13-week job retention: 30 percent of the base rate ($1,392) is paid for each participant employed during the 13th week in which the 90th day following job placement occurs.
  - 13-week high wage retention bonus: In addition, 10 percent of the base rate ($464) is paid for each participant employed who receives high wages at the 13th week of employment. High wages are defined in the contract for the particular vendor as an average weekly wage of $344.25.
  - 26-week job retention: The vendor is paid the following percentages

and amounts for each participant employed in an unsubsidized position during or after the 26th week after job placement: (a) 30 percent of the base rate ($1,392) for each participant formerly receiving public assistance benefits who is no longer receiving such benefits; or (similarly) 30 percent of that rate for each participant who, while not a PA recipient, is placed in a high-wage job; (b) 10 percent of the base rate ($464) for each participant who receives public assistance benefits who cannot be removed from public assistance following job placement; or (similarly) 10 percent of the base rate ($464) for each participant who is not a public assistance recipient, but is placed in a job that does not pay high wages.

- Vendors may place a participant into multiple jobs, but can be compensated only once for the placement milestone and each of the retention milestones for any particular participant within a 12-month period.

The concept of paying when milestones are achieved is the same for SAP contractors as ESP contractors, but specific milestones and payment amounts are quite different. In addition, the first two milestone payments under SAP contracts are tied to completion of the client assessment process and full engagement of the participant in a simulated workweek, rather than participant outcomes. Under SAP contacts, there are five potential payment points; amounts shown are for one of the vendors we visited and vary slightly by vendor:

- Completion of client assessment: $250;
- Full engagement (based on five days of attendance in SAP activities): $500;
- Job placement: $1,250 for full-time employment (31 or more hours) or $750 for part-time employment;
- Job retention at 90 days: $250;
- Public assistance case closure because of earnings: $1,500.

Finally, ESP and SAP vendors are encouraged to bring in smaller subcontractors. In each case, the vendors negotiate milestones and unit prices with each subcontractor and monitor their performance. Subcontracting agencies submit invoices for payment by HRA through their ESP or SAP vendor and are paid directly by that vendor.

Table 8.1 shows the results of the vendors' activities as well as the responsiveness of the individuals referred to the various SAP and ESP vendors.

Implementation of Enhanced Electronic Tracking and Payment Systems

As part of its overall efforts to enhance program performance and tracking of welfare recipients through the wide array of services provided under wel-

Table 8.1. Average Monthly SAP and ESP Activity Levels by Vendor, 2001

SAP Vendor	Number of referrals	Percent of referrals who fail to report	Percent of referrals seen by vendor	Percent of referrals placed into jobs[a]	Percent of referrals seen who are placed into jobs[a]
Arbor	440	25	74	26	40
Curtis & Associates	943	30	68	20	33
Federation Employment & Guidance Services	781	20	78	18	29
Goodwill Industries of Greater N.Y.	1,007	22	75	23	34
TOTAL	3,171	24	73	21	33
ESP Vendor					
America Works of New York	205	22	77	21	27
Career & Educational Consultants	229	42	58	22	38
Consortium for Worker Education	297	34	65	21	32
Curtis & Associates	220	44	56	21	37
Federation Employment and Guidance Services	200	39	60	20	34
Goodwill Industries of Greater New York	612	23	77	18	23
New York Urban League	151	26	74	15	20
New York Association for New Americans	91	33	67	20	30
Non-Profit Assistance Corporation	230	26	73	20	27
Research Foundation	388	25	75	20	27
Wildcat Services Corporation	839	14	86	26	30
TOTAL	3,460	26	74	21	29

Source: D. S. Nightingale et al., *Work and Welfare Reform in New York City during the Giuliani Administration* (Washington, D.C.: Urban Institute, July 2002).
[a] Average monthly percentage for 2000–2001.
Note: One firm listed earlier in the text was not under contract at this time.

fare reform, HRA initiated major efforts to enhance information flow and technology through the introduction of JobStat, VendorStat, NYCWAY (New York City Work, Accountability, and You), and PACS (Payment and Claims System). These systems provide critical structural underpinning for monitoring vendor performance without which HRA would have had a very difficult—if not impossible—time in implementing performance-based contracting. These systems provide information necessary for assigning individuals to vendors, for vendors to track individuals and submit information for payment, and for HRA to verify payment claims and process invoices in a timely manner.

VendorStat (Vendor Statistics) is vitally important for monitoring performance of ESP and SAP vendors. It enables HRA (as well as each ESP and SAP vendor) to monitor vendor performance across a set of agreed-upon performance indicators. VendorStat reports are generated every month for each vendor site in the city (i.e., if vendors have more than one site location, they receive a report on each location). The performance indicators in the report are calculated for the site, the vendor as a whole, and the city (all vendors together). For each performance indicator, there is a rank that indicates how well the site (or the vendor) is performing in comparison to other sites (or vendors) for the most recent month and for the year to date. VendorStat reports are reviewed at periodic meetings (several meetings each year with each vendor) with HRA administrators and representatives of each vendor.

Though similar in purpose and general appearance, VendorStat reports have different performance indicators for SAP and ESP vendors. For example, the ESP VendorStat reports show outcome indicators, length-of-stay indicators (which measure the average time taken by a vendor to achieve an outcome), administrative indicators (which measure administrative timeliness), and statistical indicators (which are raw numbers and are averaged for different outcome indicators). The ESP VendorStat report displays the following seven outcome indicators:

- Placed and Closed Cases: This outcome is defined as the number of cases that were placed and had their public assistance (PA) case closed divided by the sum of all outcomes.
- Placed and Still Open: This outcome is defined as the number of cases that were placed but are still on PA divided by the sum of all outcomes.
- Fail to Comply (FTC): This outcome is defined as the number of cases that failed to comply divided by the sum of all outcomes.
- De-Assigned or Closed: This outcome is defined as the number of cases that were deassigned or closed for a reason other than employment divided by the sum of all outcomes.
- Still Open No Job: This outcome is defined as the number of cases that

are still with the vendor and do not yet have a placement divided by the sum of all outcomes.

- Returns: This outcome is defined as the number of cases that were returned to the center divided by the sum of all outcomes.
- Non-Fail to Comply (FTC)/De-Assign (DA)/Returned Placed: This outcome is the ratio of all cases that were placed to all outcomes minus the FTC, deassigned, and those who got returned.

The Payment and Claims System (PACS) is also fundamentally important to ESP and SAP providers, for it makes milestone payments to vendors for participants served. NYCWAY (New York City Work, Accountability, and You) provides HRA and vendors with the capability to track the status of each public assistance recipient and to assign individuals to ESP and SAP vendors for services. Finally, the JobStat system (Job Statistics), much like the VendorStat system, provides HRA with performance data to monitor the performance of each Job Center using standardized measures. (See chapter 5 in this volume.)

HRA Responsibility for the Workforce Investment Act

HRA was given responsibility for administering Workforce Investment Act (WIA) funds and programs for adults in New York City, and therefore it had flexibility in funding a range of employment, training, and support service for low-income and welfare recipients. HRA was able to use the same ESP and SAP vendors and performance-based contracts—including the same milestones and payment amounts—to serve both public assistance and non–public assistance individuals. HRA has also been able to make available (as needed and appropriate) Individual Training Accounts (ITA) or training vouchers for PA participants in need of training to upgrade skills and advance to higher-paying (and more secure) jobs. Under Mayor Bloomberg, however, New York City transferred responsibility for administering WIA back to the Department of Employment (DOE), which had administered WIA prior to its transfer to HRA in the Giuliani Administration.[19]

PERFORMANCE-BASED CONTRACTING IN HRA PROGRAMS

Although not extensive, there is some literature assessing the impact of performance-based contracting in HRA programs. For the reasons noted above, all of the articles are based on qualitative assessments rather than statistical analyses.

A study released in December 2000 by City Project of 152 contracts with

77 nonprofit organizations in New York City identified several concerns that have been directed at HRA in other studies.[20] It notes that the city is generally slow to pay community-based organizations (CBOs), with an average waiting time of about four months for the first payment after contract award. The city was even slower, however, in paying HRA contractors; the latter had an average waiting time of 4.5 months.

City Limits Article

An article by Kathleen McGowan appraises the changes to New York City's welfare programs in the late 1990s.[21] Based on interviews with current and former city officials and vendors, the article discusses the changes in the city's welfare program and their likely impacts.

The shift in emphasis from enhancing human capital to job placement and retention leads to several of the most commonly voiced criticisms of performance-based contracting. First, the article notes "performance-based contracting can be tough on nonprofits." Payments based on accomplishments mean that there is a delay between provision of services and receipt of cash for meeting contract requirements. (A critic's rebuttal is that the goal of this effort is neither to ease the life of nonprofits nor to pay for results that were promised but not yet accomplished.) McGowan concludes that this payment policy favors for-profit organizations, although she does not indicate why a well capitalized nonprofit might not also prosper and why a small for-profit organization might not suffer. McGowan's second major charge is that performance-based contracting leads to the provision of services to those who are most job ready while ignoring others: "the dirty little secret of welfare-to-work is creaming—finding a way to get clients who are more talented, better educated, or more motivated than the general pool, and thereby boosting a program's success rates. Everybody accuses everybody else of doing it. But nobody will own up to it and it's very hard to prove." McGowan does admit, however, that after several years of welfare reform, much of the cream is long gone from the welfare rolls. If there is a desire to avoid creaming, then the incentive system can be structured so that rewards are greater or standards are lower for serving individuals with more barriers to employment.

McGowan also claims that the emphasis on job retention can be contrary to a client's interests. Specifically, she quotes a worker at a for-profit HRA vendor as saying that she would sometimes try to keep a client employed by a "sleazy employer" rather than risk losing their pay. Based on the contract language, this criticism appears misguided. The HRA contracts require a retention payment for employment after the initial placement, but there is no requirement that the subsequent employment be with the original employer.

Center for an Urban Future Article

This article explores how the welfare reforms have affected vendors and clients.[22] Although issued by the same organization, Center for an Urban Future (CUF), as *City Limits,* it has more depth and balance than the article reviewed above. In addition to providing comments on the likely effects of welfare reforms, the article describes very well the organization of the work-force development system. It states, "The first year of prime contracts and performance-based compensation has been a virtual debacle, characterized by inept assessments, tardy reimbursements, overly strict regulations, unrealistic goals, and Kafkaesque record-keeping requirements." The report acknowledges that some vendors, such as America Works, praised the shift in emphasis. In addition, the trend has clearly been toward improved functioning of the system: "The prime and subcontracting agencies who spoke with CUF generally found consensus around two points: The system has functioned more smoothly over time, and the lines of communication with HRA have generally remained open, with the agency largely responsive to providers' concerns and complaints."

Another concern raised by the report is that through December 2000, the vendors had filled only 26 percent of their contractual maximum, but that again the trend was toward improvement. Low placement rates relative to the contract specifications could reflect a number of potential problems. It could indicate that either the population was too difficult to serve or that the vendors were ineffective. Another potential problem is that if the placement and retention rates are low and the contract ceilings are not periodically adjusted, the agency might not spend its entire allocation. We explored these issues in our interviews, and our findings are presented in the next section.

As was the case for the *City Limits* study, the Center for an Urban Future found that vendors who built on existing infrastructure—usually large and experienced organizations—fared better than others. A major concern raised by the study is whether small community-based organizations (CBOs), which typically function as subcontractors under the system, will be able to survive under the new performance requirements and cash-flow constraints: It conjectures, "If CBOs decide that they cannot earn enough money to stay in business as subcontractors under this system, their departure could open a hole in the bottom of the system, weakening its ability to serve the hardest cases."

The article further notes that the system presents the vendors with a number of uncertainties, all of which threaten the cash flow to the vendors:

> In a nutshell, the problem those training providers face is pretty simple. They have little idea of how many referrals they will receive from the stop before them in the system. . . . Then, they have no real way of knowing just how ready

for work the referred clients will be when they arrive. Finally, when they do manage to train and place clients in jobs, they must wait for payment to flow first from HRA, and then, in the case of the subcontractors, through the prime.[23]

The Center for an Urban Future report concludes by offering five recommendations to improve operation of the system:

- The city should revisit the Welfare-to-Work contracts, convening a panel of providers, employers, and clients to determine what is and isn't working for all parties. The two biggest concerns of CUF are that SAP providers are not performing enough assessment for the people they do not place, and that the city should determine ways to allow the ESP providers to spend more time and resources on the hardest-to-serve clients.
- Government officials and individual training providers should do everything they can to ensure that clients are getting skills, training, and placement that leads not just to short-term work but to career-track positions paying a living wage.[24]
- To assist providers concerned about cash flow while adapting to performance-based contracts and voucher-driven referrals, HRA and the Workforce Investment Board (WIB) should consider creating and funding a nonprofit organization to assist vendors with cash flow problems.[25]
- When drawing up contracts, HRA and the WIB should offer incentives for CBOs to work together by sharing resources and offering training programs that are complementary.
- CBOs should look for ways to become leaner and more efficient.

These recommendations deal with the common themes we encountered throughout our study: adequacy of the initial client assessment, dealing with cash flow, and assuring that those with the greatest barriers are provided enough services.

When the Private Sector Competes Article

Bryna Sanger's article differs from the studies cited above because New York City is one of four jurisdictions analyzed rather than the sole focus of the study. She looks at what happens in four local jurisdictions (Houston, Milwaukee, New York City, and San Diego County) when the private sector is used to deliver services to welfare recipients. Pressure due to the national welfare reform legislation (PRWORA) to increase services and job placements to recipients led some cities to "contract with large, experienced, well-financed organizations" to avoid long-term commitments to public employ-

ees and to "harness market forces to provide services in a manner that some
public officials believe is cheaper and more efficient."[26]

Three of four sites she studied (Milwaukee, New York City, and San
Diego County) used performance-based contracting. Agency officials in
these sites claimed that performance-based contracting provides incentives
for contractors to place their clients in stable, well-paying jobs because payments to the contractors are based on placements and retention. Critics at
the sites told a different story. Citing the "cream-skimming" argument, they
told Sanger that performance-based contracting induces "fewer and lower
quality services and encourages contractors to select easier-to-place clients
over those who are more difficult (and more expensive) to serve." She also
notes that because payments are determined more by placements than by
retention, the contractors focus more on getting clients into jobs than on
long-term prospects for retention and advancement. This presumed shortcoming could be overcome by changing the payment schedule.

Sanger's concerns go beyond performance-based contracting. She believes
that transferring responsibility for managing service delivery from government agencies to a small number of large vendors that oversee the delivery
of services provided by smaller vendors may lead to dereliction of responsibility by the cities without necessarily improving services to the clients.

> New York, in effect, relinquished much of its authority and responsibility for
> oversight to third parties when it selected contractors whose role now included
> insuring the performance of their subcontractors. There is little evidence that
> public officials in New York and elsewhere have improved their oversight or
> increased their personnel commitments to ensure the long-term well being of
> clients.[27]

But Sanger's fears may be premature. Although New York City clearly has
shed much of the direct responsibility to the vendors, HRA has adopted a
number of management strategies to identify weak performers. In particular,
the VendorStat program enables HRA officials to monitor the performance
of its direct contractors. Sanger's concern may be valid, however, at the subcontractor level where considerable service delivery takes place. By looking
only at aggregate contract performance, HRA leaves it up to the prime contractors to identify and remove or improve weak performing subcontractors.
It is, of course, in the financial interest of prime contractors to monitor the
performance of their subcontractors and remove poor performers or reduce
their role.[28]

Sanger notes that it is too early to draw conclusions about the effectiveness
of different types of providers, but she finds that the contract arrangement
adopted by New York City and other cities in her sample threatens the ability of nonprofit organizations to place the needs of the client first: "A major

dilemma for large, stable nonprofits is whether they will compromise their missions of putting the client first and meeting individual needs. Performance-based contracts and current payment levels favor rapid placement of clients and few specialized services." She also expresses concern that HRA contracts provide no incentive for long-term investment and that the contracts pay only a small portion of the cost of effectively serving a client with major barriers. Since Sanger's paper was prepared, HRA has partially met this concern by offering the vendors the opportunity to issue individual training accounts (ITAs), which do not come from their contractual payments.[29] Also, an HRA official pointed out that TANF recipients with the most severe barriers are referred to vendors serving "special populations," such as those with literacy problems or who are disabled, and these vendors have different incentive structures that better enable them to provide more services.

Sanger noted the pattern of moving responsibility for service provision and monitoring performance away from the government and toward large, well-capitalized for-profit and nonprofit organizations, with performance-based contracting generally used as a tool for promoting the goals of placement and cost efficiency. Her conclusions on the success of such efforts are mixed:

- Market incentives generated by performance-based contracting are inducing innovation and desirable management changes in many nonprofit providers but they are producing distortions of contractual intent by motivating . . . contractors to make service delivery choices that may compromise the well-being of clients in order to minimize costs. Minimizing costs may inadvertently be threatening service quality and ultimately client outcomes.
- The future of mission-driven nonprofits is uncertain and worrisome.[30]
- Market forces alone are likely to drive the large national for-profits to arenas where their comparative advantages make them dominant. This could lead to a void.
- The competition for talent in stronger nonprofits and private organizations may drain people from the public sector.[31]

FINDINGS FROM INTERVIEWS

This project focuses on documenting the goals, design, implementation, and effects of performance-based contracting in HRA's effort to reform the welfare system. In this section we report on our interviews with HRA officials and ESP/SAP vendors. The interviews were conducted with ten administrators at HRA and administrators and staff at four SAP providers and six ESP providers (see appendix for a list of interviewees).[32] HRA identified individuals knowledgeable about the design or implementation of performance-based contracting that we should interview as part of the study; as the project proceeded we added others to our list of interviewees. The following section discusses interviews with (1) ESP and SAP vendors and (2) HRA administrators.

Interviews with ESP and SAP Vendors

According to our interviews with ESP and SAP vendors, the implementation of performance-based contracting—coupled with the other changes introduced under welfare reform—has had a profound effect on ESP/SAP contractors' program goals, structure and types of services delivered, project staffing, and overall operations. The general patterns reported by vendors are as follows:

- SAP contractors are generally more satisfied with performance-based contracting than ESP contractors.
- Among ESP vendors, for-profit contractors appear generally more satisfied with performance-based contracting than their nonprofit counterparts.
- Some concerns of vendors are not solely tied to performance-based contracting, but are linked to wider policies and events—such as timely processing of reimbursement claims.

Several of the contractors interviewed have both SAP and ESP contracts. The vendors invariably prefer the SAP contract arrangements for several reasons. First, the population is generally easier to serve: All applicants are first assigned to SAP vendors; those who do not obtain employment through SAP services are then assigned to ESP vendors. Hence, SAP providers filter out the most employable individuals, leaving ESP providers with those who face steeper barriers to employment.

Second, SAP providers we interviewed consider SAP milestones and payment levels generally fair. In comparison to ESP contracts (which are entirely performance-based), the first two (of five) milestones under SAP contacts are based on delivery of services. Regardless of whether an individual served by an SAP provider is eventually successful in securing a job, SAP providers receive some payment if enrolled individuals complete the assessment process and become fully engaged (i.e., meet work requirements). SAP vendors can achieve these two milestones within the first two weeks of providing services to individuals assigned by Job Centers. ESP contractors receive payment for a particular individual only if that individual is placed in a job, regardless of the staff time and resources expended on serving the individual.

Third, cash flow can be better for SAP providers because the assignment of participants is for a much shorter period (typically four to six weeks), and vendors receive a portion of their payment as they complete processes such as assessment. While it is possible for ESP vendors to achieve the first milestone (job placement) within a short period (within several days to several weeks), if the placement process is drawn out, the reimbursement process is stretched out over many weeks or months. If they are ultimately unsuccessful in placing the individual in a job, not only has the ESP provider spent several months working with the individual, but the potential for realizing other milestone payments (for job retention, "high-wage" employment, and termination of welfare receipt) disappear. Comments by several SAP contractors reveal their general satisfaction with performance-based contracting:

- One SAP contractor notes that SAP works pretty well: "the mix of payments is pretty good—would keep it." This vendor also observes that ESP vendors have a "trickier population to serve" and have to wait a long time before payment is received.
- Another SAP vendor indicates that performance-based contracting helps to "focus the staff on placement and retention . . . under line-item contracting you are not as placement oriented." This SAP vendor has done well under the contract—expecting to reach close to its contract maximum. If there is any area in which the payment system might be changed, this vendor suggests that the job-retention payment rate is relatively low compared to other milestones; increasing the payment level would create greater incentives for SAP vendors to concentrate on job retention.

Among ESP vendors, opinion varied substantially about the merits of performance-based contracting. Even those ESP providers who expressed enthusiasm about performance-based contracting acknowledged some of the difficulties the system imposes on contractors, particularly the long delays between providing services and receiving payments, and the risk that vendors would provide services but receive no compensation if the client fails to achieve the specified milestones. Under a payment system that rewards contractors solely for job placement, job retention, "high-wage" employment, and termination of welfare benefits, prospects for contractors can be particularly perilous in times of high unemployment and deteriorating economic conditions. In general, for-profit vendors seemed to be more enthusiastic about performance-based contracting than nonprofits.

The main arguments made by one ESP contractor (a for-profit firm) for performance-based contracting, which were echoed (though perhaps not quite as enthusiastically) by other ESP vendors, are as follows:

- "We like the freedom and flexibility we have to run the program." This vendor (and others we interviewed, including those less enthusiastic about performance-based contracting) noted that a major advantage of such a system is that vendors can hire whom they want and provide the services they think are needed.

- "With performance-based contracting you are paying for results, not process." This particular vendor (and other for-profit vendors) likes the private-sector spirit of performance-based contracting and hires staff that is similarly inclined. Two vendors we interviewed indicated that they pay staff commissions related to successful outcomes for participants. Paying for performance, according to vendors, concentrates program staff and participants directly on primary goals of the program (i.e., getting and keeping a job and leaving welfare).

The ESP vendors that support performance-based contracting also observe that several of the criticisms against performance-based contracting are unwarranted. For example, one vendor (a for-profit that strongly supports performance-based contracting) said that concerns about contractors not spending funds is not the fault of performance-based contracting, but result from contracts not being set up correctly in the first place (e.g., milestones and payment amounts are not calibrated correctly or contractors fail to anticipate costs correctly and hence do not bid payment rates at proper levels).

Second, some critics leveled the charge that performance-based contracting will lead contractors to "cream" by selecting and focusing services on those who are most likely to achieve milestones. One contractor noted that random assignment of participants by HRA went a long way to alleviate this problem: "We don't know the cream from the sour cream." If such problems persist, this vendor argues that contracts should be adjusted to deal with the problem, but performance-based contracting is not at fault.

A third criticism leveled against performance-based contracting centers on cash flow, namely, that contractors are required to make large expenditures prior to being reimbursed and under risky conditions they may not be able to recoup costs. While supporters of performance-based contracting acknowledge that this may have been an initial problem, they note that HRA has introduced a system for providing cash advances and changes (especially the Payment and Claims System) that deliver reimbursement in a more timely and accurate manner to vendors.

Even the most ardent supporters of the system (mostly for-profits) have some criticisms of performance-based contracting and think it could be improved:

- *HRA should, to the extent possible, reduce paperwork requirements.* According to one vendor, "HRA has created a paperwork nightmare in setting up requirements for documentation because people did not trust performance-based contracting." Paperwork includes documentation of attendance, case notes, notification of caseworkers, and documentation of placements.

- *Documentation of placements is not always easy.* HRA holds vendors to a high standard in documenting job placements and retention, producing either a pay stub or a verification letter on employer letterhead. Once placed, however, some clients may lose the incentive to return to contractors and may be reluctant to bring in their pay stub. As an incentive for workers to come in with their documentation, HRA will give them transportation vouchers for six months. In addition, in the absence of pay stubs, businesses that hire program participants may not want to waste time writing a letter verifying employment, and small businesses may not even have stationery.

- *Contracts do not take into consideration local economic conditions.* If the economy deteriorates, it is harder to place people in jobs, but the contract terms remain the same. Contractors have to expend more time and resources to place individuals in jobs, and for some individuals job placement may not be possible regardless of the efforts made.

- *Vendors are at the mercy of HRA referrals.* Without a steady and sufficient flow of referrals, vendors cannot achieve milestones. In our interviews, ESP vendors indicated that they receive biweekly lists of referrals from HRA and, thus far, the flow has been generally adequate and steady. HRA clients, however, often do not show up or are not motivated to find a job. Vendors also worry that as welfare rolls decline, so will the flow of referrals to vendors for ESP/SAP services. Several vendors we interviewed indicated that the ability to serve non-PA walk-ins has been a big help in terms of meeting participant goals and realizing placement and retention milestones.

Compared to their for-profit counterparts, nonprofit ESP vendors expressed somewhat greater concern about their performance-based contracts. One nonprofit ESP vendor indicated that it had initially selected subcontractors based on their expertise in training, but in fact, under the performance-based contract that focused on job placement and retention, their subcontractors had little or no opportunity to offer participants training. Another nonprofit indicated that it was doing well at placements but poorly at retention. This vendor felt it could do better on the retention milestones if ESP contractors could provide more in the way of training and basic skills to enhance employability. According to this vendor, the payment system provides no incentives to train, to the detriment of some participants: "One size does not fit all; the ability to offer training is important. There needs to be leeway to provide training if needed . . . some need more work experience and others need training. The case manager is in the position to make this determination. Under Work First, the pendulum has swung too far." Although ESP providers have always been able to refer participants to training available under WIA (formerly JTPA) and HRA has made it much easier for vendors to make ITAs available to participants (especially once they are working), the milestone payments under performance-based contracting provide virtually no incentive for training. In fact, the provision of anything but short-term training may result in delays in realizing milestone payments.

. Nonprofits report the same problems as for-profits in getting verification of placements. As one nonprofit said: "It is very hard to get retention information from employers. . . . In addition, participants often do not want to be bothered once they are employed." Several nonprofits also indicate that reimbursement rates are too low and milestones are too back-loaded (toward retention): "We are losing money on this contract . . . we are way below capacity on both 90- and 180-day retentions. We lay out the dollars before we get paid . . . reimbursement comes in months and months after providing the service. It is very tough to break even on ESP . . . SAP is okay. Under our ESP contract, we would like a higher initial placement payment rate."

Discussions with one subcontractor raised many of the same issues as were raised in Bryna Sanger's study. Specifically, the staff interviewed felt that by having subcontracting arrangements, the actual providers of services did not receive sufficient reimbursement because the prime contractors retained a substantial portion of the funds for themselves. Staff at the subcontractor felt strongly that that the system was unfair because even though they delivered the services to clients, they were isolated from HRA staff and were unable to negotiate with HRA on terms and conditions. This subcontractor was so dissatisfied with their relations with one of the prime contractors that they ultimately broke off relations with that contractor.[33] As we noted above, reducing the number of direct contractors produces some advantages for the city in dealing with a more manageable number of contractors, but the disadvantages include isolation from some of the ultimate service providers and the potential for abuse of the subcontractors. This is the perennial principal-agent problem.

Interviews with HRA and State Officials

The interviews under this project were with officials who implement policy rather than set it. HRA officials note that during the Giuliani–Turner years there was a strong emphasis on the Work First philosophy. This is the underlying philosophy of PRWORA, and New York City pushed work activities very strongly.[34] HRA officials recognize many of the same benefits and problems with performance-based contracting as the vendor community; where possible, they have made a concerted effort to eliminate the problems.

HRA officials argue that the advantages of performance-based contracting far outweigh the disadvantages. They cited the many benefits of performance-based contracting. First, the government and vendors spend substantially less time documenting the process of serving clients and focus instead on outcomes such as job placement and retention. Formerly, under cost-based (line-item) contracts, HRA spent a great deal of time monitoring how vendors delivered services; now the focus is clearly on results. Line-item contracting required HRA to authorize many different types of changes, even small ones relating to staffing and acquisition of equipment and supplies. HRA officials point out that "micromanaging" line-item contracts is a huge administrative burden. Under performance-based contracts, vendors can easily change their staffing without HRA approval, for example, hiring more staff to meet an increased client flow. Hence, performance-based contracting has placed HRA in a less adversarial role with vendors. Vendors are free to design their service-delivery systems to be most effective for the participant and profitable to the agency.

Second, performance-based contracting spurred vendors to move participants quickly into jobs, a major goal of welfare reform. The placement process is speeded up because vendors do not receive payment until an individual is placed in a job (with the exception of the small payment made to SAP vendors for assessment and engagement milestones). Formerly (under the JOBS program), vendors in New York City were providing much more training (six or more months) to prepare participants for jobs; performance-based milestones place the focus squarely on getting clients into jobs quickly.

Third, milestone payments encourage vendors to keep working with participants; they are reluctant to return participants to HRA because they forfeit their ability to obtain milestone payments in the future on these (returned/deassigned) individuals. Typically, ESP providers have about six months to work with participants—if at the end of six months they are not placed in jobs (and have not been sanctioned), HRA reassigns participants to different program activities (e.g., BEGIN [Begin Employment, Gain Independence Now], PRIDE [Personal Roads for Individual Development and Employment], or other special initiatives).

Finally, the introduction of performance-based contracting has made it easier and less costly for both HRA and vendors to manage contracts and determine which programs and vendors are operating effectively. In the past, vendor performance was evaluated not just on placements, but also on many other factors. Under performance-based contracting, job placements and retentions are what matter most—this makes it easier for HRA and vendors to manage contracts to achieve agreed-upon results.

Despite the overall advantages—which HRA officials argue far outweigh the disadvantages—HRA officials acknowledge that there are some problems inherent in performance-based contracting and risks of potential abuses if contracts are not carefully monitored. HRA officials identified several problems or potential problems with performance-based contracting. First, there is a possible overlap between programs administered by the city (e.g., the local TANF program) and the state (e.g., the Welfare-to-Work program), resulting in a double payment for placing the same individual. In fact, there is currently an investigation to determine if there have been multiple payments made to vendors for the same job placements or retentions. Similarly, HRA worries that two vendors may bill for the same individual being placed in a job. The need for FA/SNA participants to be engaged 35 hours in the simulated workweek means a lower likelihood of duplicate payment, because it is unlikely that an individual will have time to participate in more than one employment services program. Careful tracking of cases through NYCWAY is another way HRA attempts to minimize this problem.

Second, performance-based contracting can make it difficult to subcontract with vendors to serve subpopulations that are particularly difficult to place (i.e., where the potential for job placement is limited). For example, HRA would like to have one of its ESP contractors cover Riker's Island (where a prison facility it located), but under the existing milestone payments (where job placement and retention are the key payment points), the contractor would likely realize few milestone payments. In such a case, it may make sense to provide an existing contractor with a line-item budget to cover the cost of serving this special location and population, but a separate contract is necessary because of HRA contracting constraints on mixing performance-based and line-item payments in the same vendor contract.

Third, HRA officials acknowledge that cash flow was initially a problem for some vendors, although HRA offered cash advances to ease cash-flow problems under the initial contracts with ESP and SAP providers. As noted earlier in the literature review, some analysts argue that performance-based contracting requires a substantial organization. This is not necessarily a problem, particularly since small vendors can work as subcontractors. Because we did not interview vendors who formerly received HRA funding to serve welfare recipients, but no longer do, we do not know if there are small vendors who feel shut out of the process.

Fourth, performance-based contracting does not create an incentive for vendors to train and upgrade the skills of participants. HRA officials recognize that under the current system few participants undertake training, but they do not view this as a disadvantage and note that it is consistent with the Work First philosophy that underpins welfare reform: "We do not view this as a downside . . . we've moved away from development of human capital to moving people into the labor market. Also, we have lots of training opportunities available through other programs (e.g., WIA)." As welfare reform evolved, HRA recognized that in some instances training is desirable, and it has made ITAs available to the ESP vendors.

Fifth, one HRA official notes it is possible that some participants might benefit from several vendors working together toward job placement. Collaboration between vendors is difficult (if not impossible) under the structure of the payment system because of fears that two vendors will claim milestone payments for the same individual.

Sixth, obtaining needed documentation to verify placements and retention can be difficult and time-consuming for vendors, as noted above. HRA officials feel, however, that the integrity of the system requires a high standard for documenting each milestone.

Finally, it appears to some HRA officials that ESP vendors have concentrated more on initial job placement during the first year of their contracts, perhaps at the expense of job retention. This may be one reason that retention rates have lagged (though there are other factors, such as the deteriorating local economy). Only recently have contractors seemed to focus on retention. To get contractors to emphasize retention, HRA actively promoted the availability of six months of transportation/carfare payments and ITAs for upgrading skills of individuals.

We also interviewed a New York State Department of Labor official to obtain his views on HRA's performance-based contracting system.[35] He indicated that the state is supportive of performance-based contracting. The state did have concerns, however, about some aspects of HRA's specific approach. In particular, the state was concerned that HRA's system puts too much emphasis on placement and retention; the state would prefer to see a system with more milestone payments for services provided instead of putting the entire weight on placements and retentions.

CONCLUSIONS

Our interviews have led to a consistent set of responses about the effects of performance-based contracting. There were, however, a variety of opinions about whether the changes bring net benefits to the human resource system and participants. Major study findings are the following:

- *Performance-based contracting has greatly increased emphasis on getting clients placed in jobs quickly.* Everyone we talked to, both vendors and HRA officials, agreed that by paying vendors mostly (in the case of SAPs) or entirely (for ESPs) on the basis of placements and retention, vendors have responded by shifting their attention to getting their clients placed, and as quickly as possible.
- *Performance-based contracting is one of the reasons that the welfare caseload declined dramatically in New York City, but it is impossible to deter-*

mine what share of the decline should be attributed to performance-based
contracting. Many other changes were instituted at the same time, including the reorganization of HRA services through Job Centers, the great
reduction in the number of vendors from several hundred to under 20,
the implementation of JobStat and VendorStat to track performance of
HRA Job Centers and vendors, and improvements in the city's management information systems to track the status of clients and to speed
payments. The welfare caseload decline in New York City was commensurate with the declines in most states; the strong economy undoubtedly
played a major role in the decline in New York City as it did in other
parts of the country that did not use performance-based contracting.
One HRA executive opined that performance-based contracting was the
third-ranking cause of the caseload decline, following the reorganization
of HRA staff into Job Centers and the decision to greatly reduce the
number of vendors and carefully manage their performance.

- *SAP vendors whose contracts included some payments for services as well
  as for performance-based results were much more satisfied with performance-based contracting than were ESP vendors.* For the most part, the
  SAP vendors believed that the payment levels were fair, that the cash
  flow pattern was reasonable, and that the mix of performance-based
  payments and service-based payments was reasonable. The SAP vendors
  also had easier-to-place clients than the ESP vendors, and the uncertainty resulting from the ESP caseload may have contributed to ESP
  concerns.

- *Among the ESP vendors, the for-profit organizations were enthusiastic
  about performance-based contracting, but the nonprofit vendors had
  more reservations.* For-profit vendors liked the concept of pay for performance, and they frequently paid their staff on a commission basis.
  The nonprofit vendors, however, were oriented toward assisting the client in the manner they believe is most appropriate rather than emphasizing immediate job placement. Often the nonprofit vendors were
  frustrated because they had to get jobs immediately for clients when
  they believed that providing education, job training, and social services
  were more appropriate initial activities. In short, they disagreed with the
  blanket application of federal, state, and city policy in effect at this time.

- *There was agreement among vendors and HRA officials that there were
  start-up problems in moving toward performance-based contracting and
  other management reforms, but everyone agreed that HRA understood
  the problems and that matters improved somewhat over time.* Problems
  frequently mentioned by vendors include slowness in receiving payment and excessive paperwork and documentation for placements.
  HRA has improved the cash flow through advance payments and has
  moved to a sampling system for documenting placements. Some con-

cerns have not yet materialized, and may present problems later. For example, if economic conditions worsen and jobs become harder to find, the original contract terms may no longer be appropriate, and if the caseload drops, vendors may not receive enough clients to operate at the scale contemplated when the contract was signed. This latter concern may be more important because HRA no longer is responsible for the Workforce Investment Act, and it may no longer be possible for vendors to serve walk-ins.

• *Many vendors and observers expressed concern that performance-based contracting leads to "creaming" and thereby results in too little service to those most in need, and that there are incentives to push people into jobs when—the vendors and observers believe—they need education or vocational training.* Unless adjustments are made, performance-based contracting creates incentives to serve those who are most likely to succeed with little help, but one vendor said it is not so simple to identify the cream, and HRA's goal is to obtain employment for all welfare recipients and applicants. HRA concurred that there is a bias against providing training, and it recently made individual training accounts (ITAs), which are essentially training vouchers, available for ESP clients at no cost to the vendors. This reduces the incentives to avoid training, but because training delays placement and payment to the vendor, some incentive to avoid training still exists.

In summary, the management reforms introduced by HRA in recent years have simplified the system, made it easier to identify the performance of the vendors, and oriented the system toward job placement rather than long-term human capital development or the provision of social services. The performance-based contracting implemented by HRA clearly played a key part in changing the system and reducing the caseload. HRA has recognized the complexity of the system and has made changes to make sure that vendors receive payments in a timelier manner. Some issues involve more than management, however. In particular, there is a national debate on how effective job training is for welfare recipients, and even if training can boost earnings, how much the system should invest in training rather than emphasize immediate placement. In addition, Sanger and others raised concerns about whether the contracting system and structure used by HRA is draining human resources from the government and driving the small community-based organizations—that have traditionally served the disadvantaged—out of business.[36] With a new administration in place, HRA must take stock of its philosophy on services to welfare recipients. This study indicates that performance-based contracting can provide important management tools for achieving the administration's goals, but care must be taken to make sure that the incentives are properly structured.

EPILOGUE: SUBSEQUENT CHANGES

Most of the interviews for this project were conducted between November 2001 and March 2002. Michael Bloomburg was elected mayor of New York City in November 2001 and took office the following January; Verna Eggelston was appointed HRA commissioner in early 2002. The change in administrations was not a change in parties, so the changes in HRA's programs were not as significant as they might have been had a new party come to office. There were, however, several important changes that occurred after we completed our interviews:

- The base payments for ESP contracts increased slightly to an average of $5,500. The new payment amounts are 25 percent for the initial placement, 45 percent for 13-week retention, and 30 percent for 26-week retention. This reflects increased importance to job retention, as the corresponding percentages before were 40 percent, 30 percent, and 30 percent, respectively.
- The SAP contracts have also been modified to emphasize job retention rather than placement. Payment for full engagement and assessment remain about the same, but payment for job placement has been reduced from $1,250 to $875 while job retention at 90 days after employment has increased from $250 under the old terms to $875.
- Several of the contractors have stopped participating, either voluntarily or because HRA dropped them. Among the SAP contractors, MAXIMUS no longer participates, and among the ESP contractors, MAXIMUS and the Urban League no longer participate.
- HRA no longer administers major components of the Workforce Investment Act (WIA) programs. The program is now administered by the Department of Employment. An important effect of this change is that HRA no longer has authority to provide WIA support for training and other activities to non–public assistance customers. Vendors can no longer augment their pool of participants through outreach to poor non–public assistance individuals and now must rely exclusively on referrals from HRA to fulfill their contracts.
- HRA is continuing to fine-tune its system for monitoring Job Centers and vendors. The agency will be tracking monthly status of clients in more detail through modifications to JobStat and VendorStat.

No doubt the system will continue to evolve over time.

The authors are grateful for comments received from Swati Desai, Toby Herr, E. S. Savas, and Jason Turner.

Appendix

Individuals in the following organizations and positions were interviewed:

Human Resources Administration: four central office administrators
HRA Resource Development: director and two deputy directors
HRA Business Link: executive director; senior account manager; and the director of Grant Diversion and Employee Contract Hiring
New York State Department of Labor
Arbor (SAP Vendor): SAP project coordinator (Manhattan office); comptroller
Curtis and Associates(SAP and ESP Vendor): SAP director; Job Center liaison; supervisor of the SAP program at the Waverly Job Center; workshop facilitator of the SAP program at the Waverly Job Center
Goodwill Industries (SAP and ESP Vendor): manager of quality control; case manager (SAP); two case managers (ESP); coordinator (ESP)
Federation Employment and Guidance Services (FEGS) (SAP and ESP Vendor): senior vice president and SAP/ESP project coordinator; assistant vice president (BEGIN and WtW project coordinator); assistant vice president (ESP supervisor)
America Works (ESP Vendor): founder; chief executive officer
Career and Educational Consultants (CEC) (ESP Vendor): president (ESP project coordinator); executive
Wildcat Services Corporation (ESP Vendor): vice president (ESP project coordinator)
Berks Trade and Business School (ESP Subcontractor to Wildcat): director; job developer; case manager
Parks Department (WEP Provider): Manhattan coordinator, WEP; WEP crew chief
Waverly and Melrose Job Centers of HRA: Interviews conducted with variety of Job Center administrators, supervisors, and workers
WHEDCO (Subcontractor to ESP and SAP contractors and Special Population Contractor): president; two vice Presidents

NOTES

1. All states have experienced significant caseload declines in recent years. New York's decline appears to be similar to the declines in many other states. See http://

www.acf.dhhs.gov/news/stats/case-fam.htm as of February 15, 2002 for state-by-state comparisons from 1993 through 2000.

2. In broad terms, we planned to use regression analysis in a "difference in differences" framework. In somewhat simplified terms, the change in caseload for New York City from before the use of performance-based contracting would be estimated as a function of economic conditions and other factors expected to influence the size of the caseload. To identify the effect of performance-based contracting, we would compare the change in the caseload in New York City with the change in nearby areas experiencing the same economic conditions but not implementing performance-based contracting.

3. *From Red Tape to Results: Creating a Government That Works Better & Costs Less*, Report of the National Performance Review, Washington, D.C., 1993.

4. Burt S. Barnow, "The Effects of Performance Standards on State and Local Programs," in C. Manski and I. Garfinkel, eds., *Evaluating Welfare and Training Programs* (Cambridge: Harvard University Press, 1992).

5. See S. Spaulding, *Performance-based Contracting under the Job Training Partnership Act* (master's thesis, Johns Hopkins University, Baltimore, 2001); and P. M. Kettner and Lawrence L. Martin, "Performance, Accountability, and Purchase of Service Contracting," *Administration in Social Work* 17, no. 1 (1993): 61–79.

6. For a discussion of the principal-agent model applied to employment and training programs, see G. Marschke, "The Economics of Performance Incentives in Government with Evidence from a Federal Job Training Program," in Dall W. Forsythe, ed., *Quicker, Better, Cheaper? Managing Performance in American Government* (Albany, N.Y.: Rockefeller Institute Press, 2001), 61–97; and Burt S. Barnow, "Exploring the Relationship Between Performance Management and Program Impact: A Case Study of the Job Training Partnership Act," *Journal of Policy Analysis and Management* 19, no. 1 (2000): 118–41.

7. See Peter Cove, "Making Welfare-to-Work Fly," *Civic Bulletin*, Center for Civic Innovation, Manhattan Institute, New York, 2000.

8. Performance-based contracting is one of the approaches recommended by Osborne and Gaebler for "reinventing government." See David E. Osborne and Ted Gaebler, *Reinventing Government: How the Entrepreneurial Spirit Is Transforming the Public Sector* (Reading, Pa.: Addison-Wesley, 1992).

9. This section is based on Spaulding, *Performance-based Contracting*, which provides more detail on the studies. We discuss only studies dealing with performance-based contracting here.

10. See K. Dickinson, R. West, D. Kogan, D. Drury, M. Franks, L. Schlictmann, and M. Vencil, *JTPA Performance Standards: Effects on Clients, Services, and Costs* (Washington, D.C.: National Commission for Employment Policy, 1988).

11. C. Heinrich and L. Lynn, "Government and Performance: The Influence of Program Structure and Performance on the Job Training Partnership Act (JTPA) Program Outcomes," in C. Heinrich and L. Lynn, eds., *Government and Performance: New Perspectives* (Washington, D.C.: Georgetown University Press), 75–123.

12. See S. Spaulding, *Performance-based contracting*.

13. See E. Vinson, *Performance Contracting in Six State Human Service Agencies* (Washington, D.C.: Urban Institute, 1999).

14. At the time of our fieldwork on this study (late 2001), MAXIMUS was no longer providing SAP services. As noted in the epilogue, HRA did not contract with MAXIMUS as part of the second round of SAP contracts; hence, as of December 2002, there were four SAP vendors.

15. At the time of our field work on this study (late 2001), MAXIMUS was no longer providing ESP services. As noted in the Epilogue, HRA did not contract with MAXIMUS or New York Urban League as part of the second round of ESP contracts; hence, as of December 2002, there were 11 ESP vendors.

16. Able-bodied individuals (those not exempted from work requirements) are assigned to ESP. For example, individuals with low basic skills (below sixth grade) are assigned to BEGIN; individuals who have been assessed by Certified Alcoholism and Substance Abuse Counselors (CASAC) as having substance abuse problems are mandated into treatment programs (for a minimum of 15 hours per week for up to 90 days, whereupon they are reassessed for ongoing treatment needs and employability). In addition, HRA has contracted with a variety of organizations to provide services for special populations (e.g., such as the PRIDE program, which provides vocational rehabilitation, work-based education, SSI counseling, and other services for individuals with physical limitations, medical conditions, or other factors that have limited or prevented past involvement of individuals in work).

17. ESP vendors also serve substantial numbers of non–public assistance cases. Vendors receive walk-ins and conduct their own recruitment efforts to attract these non-PA individuals. These individuals—covered under the Workforce Investment Act (WIA)—are typically served alongside PA recipients and receive the same blend of services.

18. Our understanding is that access to vocational training through the use of individual training accounts (ITAs) funded through the Workforce Investment Act (WIA) and other sources increased over time.

19. "Job Dollars: In New York It's Wait and Switch," *City Limits,* February 25, 2002.

20. S. Buttenwieser, ed., "Focus on Contracting," *City Project Bulletin,* December 2000.

21. K. McGowan, "The Welfare Estate," *City Limits,* June 1999. Much of the article is not relevant to the subject of this report.

22. *Center for an Urban Future,* Spring 2001.

23. On the other hand, critics argue that the more capable organizations will survive and thrive while others will not.

24. A skeptical reviewer noted that government already has such a program; it's called elementary and secondary education.

25. We discussed the cash-flow issue with HRA officials and vendors. There was agreement that although there were initially cash-flow problems for vendors, HRA responded by making cash advances when needed and by improving the participant tracking system so that payments could be accelerated. Thus, none of the people we interviewed saw a need for a new organization to improve cash flow.

26. M. B. Sanger, "When the Private Sector Competes," *Reform Watch,* no. 3, Brookings Institution, Washington, D.C., 2001.

27. Ibid.

28. We are grateful to E. S. Savas for pointing this out to us.

29. There is still an incentive to avoid long-term training, however, because the vendor does not get paid until after the client is placed.

30. Savas points out that this can be said of practically any organization.

31. One of our reviewers questioned the merits of this conclusion, noting that the purpose of the programs is to accomplish their mission efficiently, not to retain workers in the public sector, and that if workers move to jobs that are more satisfying outside the public sector that is not a bad result.

32. Several of the SAP/ESP vendors interviewed for this project were also interviewed as part of another HRA-sponsored study (documenting employment services provided under welfare reform in New York City) conducted by the Urban Institute.

33. It is a good management principle that subcontractors should not try to bypass the prime contractor and negotiate directly with the agency, and they *should* withdraw if they find the prime contractor unsatisfactory and beyond redemption.

34. Before being appointed HRA Commissioner, Jason Turner was head of welfare in Wisconsin where the idea of "full engagement" was a key component of welfare reform.

35. In New York, the State Department of Labor is responsible for overseeing work activity programs administered by the counties for welfare recipients.

36. Sanger, "When the Private Sector Competes."

9

Engaging Drug and Alcohol Abusers

Sally Satel

The 1996 Personal Responsibility and Work Opportunity Reconciliation Act (P.L. 104-193) represented an historic shift in the emphasis of federal public aid. No longer would the government provide virtually unfettered cash assistance to individuals for an indefinite period of time. Instead, under a new block grant called Temporary Assistance to Needy Families (TANF), recipients, mostly single mothers with children, were expected to become self-sufficient within five years. Welfare was thus transformed from an entitlement addressing individuals' needs into a social contract that emphasized their obligations.

Within this new environment of expectations and time limits, barriers to self-sufficiency took on great significance. From the start, policymakers, administrators, and social services advocates assumed that recipients who abused illicit drugs and alcohol would be among those least able to become self-sufficient within five years. Estimates of the afflicted reached as high as 37 percent, though the most commonly cited estimates were 15 to 20 percent.[1] Joseph Califano, former secretary of Health Education and Welfare, sounded the alert: "All the financial lures and prods and all the job training in the world will do precious little to make employable the hundreds of thousands of welfare recipients who are addicts and abusers."[2]

Expecting such high levels of disabling substance abuse, the Human Resources Administration of New York City implemented an array of programs and provided treatment for individuals with drug and alcohol problems. The effort began with the New York State Welfare Reform Act of 1997 and required two major agencies—the Human Resources Administration (HRA) and the New York State Office of Alcoholism and Substance Abuse

257

Services (OASAS)—to alter their institutional cultures in fundamental ways.[3] They would need to revise their roles within the larger context of public aid, from functioning as unaccountable conduits of services to shapers of recipient behavior. Yardsticks for measuring success would need to be recalibrated as well. This was a special challenge for HRA, because welfare reform changed the rules only for welfare agencies, not for substance abuse treatment agencies. Without some leverage over agencies like OASAS, the HRA would face an even more difficult challenge in reforming its approach to substance-abusing clients. Absent the legal means to mandate participation in treatment and thus regulate the flow of referrals (currently, HRA does not have contracts with programs), it would have been nearly impossible for HRA to exert any influence whatsoever over programs.

While federal welfare reform was the subject of national headlines, changes in New York City's own general assistance program, called Safety Net Assistance (SNA, formerly known as Home Relief, financed equally by state and city revenues), were already under way. In April 1996, HRA began tracking public aid recipients who abused substances and determining their employability. When substance abuse was deemed a reason an applicant could not work and needed public assistance, he was required by the New York State Social Services law to participate in treatment as a condition of receiving payments.

The purpose of this chapter is to document the Human Resources Administration's efforts to help individuals with substance abuse disorders become work-ready. It offers preliminary data on the scope of substance abuse among the public assistance population, outlines the major features of new programs, and describes the political backdrop against which those innovations took place.

Traditionally, welfare offices in New York and elsewhere had not played a major role in identifying substance abuse among recipients. Previously, if HRA became aware of an individual's drug or alcohol problem (typically because the client mentioned it), the case was put aside, she was exempted from work requirements and minimal efforts at rehabilitation were made. In the wake of reform, applicants and recipients of public assistance whose primary need for that assistance stemmed from drug or alcohol abuse or dependence (collectively referred to as substance abuse disorders) were required by the Office of Temporary and Disability Assistance to participate in a licensed treatment program as a condition of eligibility to receive benefits.

All states perform some kind of screening for substance abuse, but New York is one of the few states that also assigns individuals to mandatory treatment.[4] In 2002, between 12,000 and 15,000 recipients of TANF and SNA (the latter representing about 6.5 percent of all welfare beneficiaries) attended mandated treatment in New York City on a given day.[5]

SUBSTANCE ABUSE AND WELFARE: LITERATURE REVIEW

"Substance use" refers to any intake of drugs or alcohol. "Substance abuse," as defined by the *Diagnostic and Statistical Manual IV* of the American Psychiatric Association, refers to problem use of drugs or alcohol.[6] To meet diagnostic criteria, an individual must use the substance recurrently and experience a decline in function in one or several areas, including occupation, health, legal, or interpersonal domains within a 12-month period.

There is considerable variation in the amount of drugs or alcohol that qualify an individual for the diagnosis of substance abuse. That is why usage patterns (e.g., amount of alcohol consumed in a single episode of drinking) alone cannot determine an individual's ability to work. Moreover, a diagnosis of abuse does not necessarily mean that the user cannot work or that treatment is required to control the substance problem.

"Substance dependence" is considered a more serious form of substance use and is characterized as compulsive use despite negative consequences, usually accompanied by physical manifestations such as tolerance (needing increasingly higher doses for intended effect) and withdrawal. Diagnostic criteria include three or more of the following features for a period of 12 months: tolerance; withdrawal; excessive amounts of time spent obtaining, using, or recovering from the substance; use of greater amounts than intended; and unsuccessful efforts to cut down.

Note that the term "addiction" is synonymous with dependence. It is reasonable to assume that many dependent individuals could not function responsibly at a job, would not able to hold a job or function optimally in the home, and would probably—though not always—need formal treatment to reduce or stop use. The term "substance use disorder" refers to either abuse or dependence; "addict" refers to someone who is dependent on drugs.

Estimates of Prevalence of Problem Substance Use

The volume of welfare applicants whose use of drugs or alcohol interferes with participation in work has become a subject of considerable—and unexpected—speculation. More generally, data from the 1992 National Household Survey of Drug Abuse, one of the few annual nationwide surveys that include information on mental health, substance abuse, and welfare receipt, estimated that 15.5 percent of AFDC recipients were impacted by drugs or alcohol; twice the rate of nonrecipients. Many welfare planners anticipated at least that extent of impairment among TANF recipients.[7] They speculated that only the most debilitated applicants and recipients would be undeterred by TANF's more stringent policies, the tight labor market of the late 1990s, and other incentives such as an expanded Earned Income Tax Credit and more generous health coverage for the working poor. Presumably this would flush out substantial numbers of people with substance abuse problems and thereby trigger a pressing demand for treatment.[8]

Yet this does not appear to have happened. Instead the level of overall disadvantage among welfare recipients—including substance abuse problems—did not increase as the TANF caseloads declined.[9] The General Accounting Office, for example, estimated between 3 and 12 percent of TANF recipients were substance abusers.[10] Even more conservative numbers are provided by Nakashian and Moore, who contend that TANF recipients' self-reporting of substance abuse to welfare staff nationwide range from 1 percent to 3 percent.[11] Data from several states show that less than 5 percent of enrollees are referred for substance abuse treatment.[12] Researchers at the Public Health Institute in Berkeley, California, found that only 2.1 percent of a sample of Alameda County TANF recipients believed they needed drug treatment, while a RAND analysis found that county referral rates rarely reached 5 percent, with less than 1 percent of the California TANF population admitted to treatment in 1998.[13]

Some analyses have even found that recipients did not differ from nonrecipients with respect to substance abuse problems. A random survey of 728 single TANF mothers in Michigan found recipients were no more likely to meet criteria for alcohol or substance dependence than were adult women in the general population.[14] "Despite the popular view that many women on welfare abuse drugs and alcohol, only 3.3 percent of the sample met *DSM-III* screening criteria for drug dependence and 2.7 percent for alcohol dependence," the researchers wrote. Along these lines, the Fragile Families and Child Wellbeing Study found that in the post-TANF era, 3 percent of unmarried mothers who live in large cities self-reported a drug or alcohol problem that interfered with either their ability to work or with their personal relationships.[15]

If these estimates are reliable, substance abuse problems may not pose a large hindrance to work, as data from the National Longitudinal Study of Youth suggests. Kaestner determined that few individuals were receiving public aid as a result of substance problems. If such problems were eliminated altogether, he predicted that only 3 to 5 percent of individuals would end up leaving the rolls.[16] Pollack and colleagues reached similar conclusions after reviewing the literature and examining data from a Michigan sample:

> [C]hemical dependency is far less prevalent than many other threats to recipient well-being [like depression and physical illness]. Although drug use is one risk factor for welfare receipt, the observed association is weaker than one finds for race, region, unmarried teen pregnancy or measured academic skill. If all welfare recipients were to stop using illicit drugs, multivariate logistic models indicate that the size of the welfare population would remain essentially unchanged.[17]

Other evaluations, however, revealed a substance abuse problem of greater magnitude. Green, Fujiwara, Morris, Kappagoda, Driscoll, and Speiglman interviewed more than 500 TANF recipients in Alameda County, California. Depending upon whether substance abuse was defined narrowly or broadly, the researchers found that between 10 and 22 percent of the beneficiaries had substance abuse problems substantial enough to pose a barrier to work.[18] In Oregon, which started integrating substance abuse treatment six years before the passage of welfare reform, 19 percent of its recipients were identified as having drug or alcohol problems.[19] When trained interviewers conducted screenings in North Carolina, the identification rate was about 23 percent (vs. 11 percent when regular welfare workers did it).[20]

As expected, rates of use exceed rates of abuse (i.e., negative consequences of use) and dependence (e.g., compulsive use; physiological symptoms). Using data from the 1993 National Longitudinal Alcohol Epidemiological Survey, Grant and Dawson found that 9.7 percent of AFDC recipients used illicit drugs at least once in the past year, but only 3.3 percent met criteria for drug abuse or dependence and 7.3 percent for alcohol abuse or dependence.[21] An examination of 1994–1995 data from the National Household Survey of Drug Abuse found that 10 percent reported using an illicit substance (other than marijuana) within the last year; 6 percent used cocaine.[22] Using 1998 Household Survey data (the last year for which data are currently available), Pollack, Danziger, Jayakody, et al., found 6 percent were alcohol dependent and 5.1 percent were dependent upon illicit drugs.[23]

Detection of Substance Abuse

Self-reports of drug use are notoriously unreliable and may underestimate the actual rates of substance abuse.[24] In New Jersey, for example, where welfare applicants receive a standard screening instrument called the CAGE questionnaire—which asks four questions related to severity of current use—only 1 percent were positive.[25] Subsequent hair testing on the group showed that more than 25 percent tested positive for cocaine, though only 12 percent reported using it within the six months prior to testing.

The inadequacy of self-reporting in the social service setting reflects several possibilities. Whether or not their fears are realistic, some women worry that admission of a drug problem will result in the loss of their children to protective services or denial of benefits.[26] In some cases, individuals minimize their substance use and its consequences because they do not want to be sent to a treatment program, especially to residential care, which would likely require separation from their children. Furthermore, the workers doing the screening may not be skilled at eliciting the information. Finally, screening instruments may not be sensitive or specific enough because they were originally developed for and statistically validated on subjects studied in a health-care setting, not a welfare-agency setting. Since the validity and reliability of these instruments depends on the nature of the population for which they were first developed, using them could yield inaccurate results.

In general, detection rates are higher when screens are administered by a substance abuse professional rather than a welfare worker. Targeting obvious high-risk women, such as those requesting emergency assistance or in the criminal justice system or child welfare system, may increase the detection rates.[27] Sanctioned recipients are another natural high-risk group, as discussed below. These factors appear to be more relevant to the identification process than does the particular type of screen used.[28] How often recipients "pass" the screen but fail to attain job placement—or function poorly in jobs they do get—because of substance abuse remains an open question.

Would routine, universal toxicology screening of applicants enhance the detection process? Yes—to the extent that it can pick up recent drug use (hair analysis, in contrast to the more commonly used urine test, can point to use within the previous three months). However, when these tests are administered only once during the intake process, they yield limited information. A positive result obtained at the time of application does not indicate severity of use, only that use has occurred. Nor can one-time tests of any kind reveal whether someone is dependent or whether her use of drugs constitutes a barrier to work. At best, a positive result suggests that more detailed assessment is indicated.

From a legal standpoint, the issue of universal testing has not been resolved. The 1996 federal welfare act authorized some degree of testing, but in October 1999 when Michigan tried to implement a policy that applicants' refusal to submit to random drug testing would mean denial of income support and other benefits, the ACLU of Michigan filed a federal class action suit on behalf of all welfare applicants, charging unreasonable search and seizure. One month after it went into effect, the federal court enjoined testing, contending that it was unconstitutional under the Fourth Amendment. During that brief testing period, 258 recipients were urine-screened and 21 were positive. Of those, 18 were positive only for marijuana.[29] In October 2002, the Sixth Circuit Court of Appeals upheld Michigan's use of mandatory testing to determine eligibility for public aid.[30]

Difficulty detecting substance problems among the welfare population is only partly responsible for the inconsistency of the data on prevalence. Still unresolved is the basic question of who decides to show up at the door of the welfare office. For example, some women with serious substance abuse problems may be too disorganized or too fearful of being reported to child protective services to apply. Others may forego application for public assistance because they can generate enough income from undocumented (legal and illegal) work. In New York City, welfare recipients with substance abuse problems who are also HIV-positive or have AIDS are not required to attend substance treatment.[31]

Linkage between Substance Use and Welfare Behavior

Excessive use of drugs or alcohol is more prevalent in recipients who are failing in work assignments and who come to the attention of child welfare officials. For example, a comparison of Michigan TANF recipients working 20 hours per week and those not working 20 hours per week revealed that none of the workers and 6.4 percent of the nonworkers were dependent upon illicit substances. Twenty percent of those working and 32 percent of those not working were either alcohol dependent or had a psychiatric disorder. Among respondents to the 1998 National Longitudinal Survey of Youth, 45 percent of women over age thirty-three who had used cocaine within the past month had received public assistance for at least five years.[32]

Exit from the welfare rolls is also linked to substance abuse. Michigan researchers found that TANF recipients who were on the rolls for at least a year had twice the rate of drug dependence (*DSM III-R*) as those who managed to get off within that period.[33] A six-year longitudinal study of welfare recipients found that 52 percent of recipients without substance abuse problems left welfare for employment, while only 30 percent of substance-abusing welfare recipients did so.[34]

Sanctioning, too, appears associated with drugs and alcohol. Families in Boston, Chicago, and San Antonio who were facing sanctions were more likely to report substance problems than their unsanctioned counterparts.[35] Likewise, another study found that 49 percent of all sanctioned beneficiaries in one New Jersey county were diagnosed with drug or alcohol problems.[36]

It is possible, however, that some individuals who are being sanctioned will overemphasize a drug or alcohol problem in order to be routed into treatment and thus preserve their benefits. In addition, some patients may exaggerate their substance use in an attempt to win a work exemption or if the idea of a structured setting with room and board is attractive to them. Homelessness may play a role in the latter scenario. The extent to which these strategies are employed is unknown, but if popular, they would make the number of abusers and addicts among the sanctioned appear larger than it is. On the other hand, if substance problems result in noncompliance and ultimately termination, the numbers of abusers and addicts on the rolls will drop. It is useful to keep in mind that substance abuse can represent a primary obstacle to progress, but it can also be proxy for a third factor that is equally, if not more, disabling: deficiencies of character or personal organization that, in turn, affect work performance.

In view of the accumulating data on welfare "stayers," the New York City experience was startling. From October 1 to mid-November 2001, HRA reevaluated between 6,000 and 8,000 TANF beneficiaries who were approaching the fifth and final year of federal support ("timing-out") and were already undergoing sanction. Roughly half of the recipients kept their appointment for reassessment. To the surprise of HRA, however, drug or alcohol problems were detected in *less than 3 percent* of those reporting.[37] Detection of mental or physical health symptoms was somewhat greater, at around 9 percent. There are several ways to understand this. Perhaps TANF women with significant drug problems are too disorganized to keep appointments or to remain connected to the TANF program altogether. Possibly they do not have a stable address at which to receive notices, or they decided to forego public assistance because they managed to generate enough income from undocumented (legal and illegal) work or are supported by partners or others.

Engagement in Treatment

Despite a substantiated drug problem, many individuals may be resistant to participating in treatment. Indeed, the limited data on engagement in treatment are not particularly encouraging. A RAND report notes that "welfare reform programs around the country have experienced low utilization" of substance abuse services after referral, consistent with a low rate of use of other TANF services as well."[38] The Manpower Demonstration Research Corporation took particular note of the state of Kansas, which, it says, "did a good job of identifying and referring participants [with substance abuse problems], most [of whom] either did not enter or did not complete treatment."[39]

Morgenstern and colleagues randomly assigned 146 New Jersey TANF recipients who had been identified as needing substance abuse treatment to either the usual management program, called Care Coordination, or a more aggressive supervision program, called Intensive Case Management.[40] Women in the latter program were assigned a case-management team that identified obstacles to entering and remaining in treatment (e.g., transportation, child care). They also received vouchers as rewards for attending treatment that could be redeemed for items such as cosmetics or children's toys. While women receiving intensive management had good rates of entry into treatment (88 percent vs. 65 percent in the control group), their retention rate was disappointing—they attended only 42 percent of the treatment days. But this figure is still almost twice the control group's retention rate of 22 percent. Thus, the impact of intensive case management was high, but the overall effect was relatively modest.

Preliminary data from HRA suggest modest to good results based on reported participation. Data show an enrollment rate of about 67 percent by the new referrals.[41] Breakdown by type of treatment reveals that a high percentage of those referred to methadone and drug-free outpatient care actually enrolled (80 percent) but that less than half (46 percent) of those assigned to residential treatment were admitted. Once enrolled in treatment, there is fairly good retention at the three-month point. Overall, more than half of all TANF and SNA recipients participating in treatment at the one-month point were still active 60 days later.[42] Almost half the patients in residential care at 30 days were still in treatment at 90 days (410 clients at 30 days vs. 193 at 90 days); about 60 percent of methadone patients present at 30 days remained at 90 days (349 to 228); 50 percent remained in outpatient treatment for drug abuse at 90 days (200 to 106) and about 45 percent remained in outpatient treatment for alcohol abuse at the 90-day mark (196 to 87).[43]

How does this compare to national samples? The Drug Abuse Treatment Outcome Study (DATOS) followed over 10,000 patients in 96 programs in 11 cities from 1991 to 1993 and is considered a reliable national sample.[44] Published in 1997, DATOS found that between one-third and one-half of patients admitted to residential care stayed 92 days or longer (this estimate includes court-referred as well as voluntary patients). Among those in outpatient treatment about one-third to one-half remained for at least 91 days (50 percent of all admissions were court-referred), and almost half of all methadone patients (very few of whom were court referred) stayed an entire year. Taking into account some drop out within the first 30 days, the HRA data for treatment are comparable to national retention data. Length of stay in methadone, however, is much shorter among recipients of New York City public assistance than it is in the general population.

This abbreviated review raises questions. First, what is the best way to determine the scope of the problem? In screening for evidence of a condition, examiners cast a wide net with tiny mesh, so that even individuals who are only mildly affected are "caught." Subsequently, more refined assessment identifies the individuals who need help. Thus, screening tests tend to overestimate the size of a problem. The current situation with welfare recipients may well be that the screen applied to them is not very effective. A second question is, even when substance use is detected, does it necessarily signal a substance disorder, and if so, does the disorder necessarily pose an obstacle to work, especially when sanctions and time limits are in effect? Third, if substance abuse does pose an obstacle to work, is treatment always required to overcome the obstacle? Fourth, when individuals are required to get treatment, do they participate, and if they do, how are their work-readiness and performance affected?

These were among the questions that challenged the New York City welfare planners. HRA is in the process of collecting data on these and other questions. Given the state's legal mandate to require treatment for those recipients of public assistance whose primary need for that assistance stems from drug or alcohol abuse, it is important to distinguish between individuals who require assistance and also happen to abuse those substances from those who require assistance *because* they abuse drugs or alcohol.

THE WELFARE-TO-WORK PROGRAM FOR PEOPLE WITH SUBSTANCE DISORDERS

HRA regards public assistance recipients with substance use disorders as a special-needs population, meaning they receive specialized services and reasonable accommodations. The development of these services and accommodations was guided by several principles:

- The presence of a drug or alcohol problem does not preclude expectation that an individual should become self-sufficient.
- Work itself is therapeutic and should be undertaken concurrently with treatment, which it complements, rather than after treatment is completed.
- Outcome measures of a successful drug treatment must include employment, not simply reduced substance use or even abstinence.
- Treatment providers whose costs are covered by Medicaid (in the context of TANF or SNA) should be accountable for efforts to help patients progress to self-sufficiency.

What Is Addiction?

Since the mid-1990s, a popular formulation of addiction has been that addiction is a chronic and relapsing brain disease. This slogan was coined by the National Institute on Drug Abuse and has since been promoted by the American Society of Addiction Medicine, Physicians on Drug Leadership, and others. It would seem that HRA's new welfare policies are at odds with the "chronic and relapsing brain disease" model. After all, the brain disease model implies that addiction is a disability as concrete as multiple sclerosis, schizophrenia, or a brain tumor. It implies that volition plays a minimal role in the perpetuation of the condition and that a lifelong series of relapses is virtually guaranteed. None of these attributes is especially conducive to a program of accountability and personal responsibility. Indeed, prior to welfare reform, addicts were regarded as essentially hopeless cases.

Today, under welfare reform in New York City, the guiding standard is that addiction is "a temporary, treatable condition," as the New York City Office of Employment Services put it.[45] This is not to say that HRA is unwilling to manage relapses, quite the opposite, but the very fact that sanctions are employed means planners recognize that the course of addiction can be influenced by sanctions and incentives. And because the imposition of sanctions and incentives are triggered by specific behaviors (e.g., positive urine tests, missed sessions, good compliance), addiction can be understood as a behavior whose perpetuation is modified by its own consequences. By contrast, the symptoms and progression of true "brain diseases," like multiple sclerosis or schizophrenia, cannot be influenced by the social responses they provoke. Thus, addiction has a considerable voluntary dimension that clinicians and welfare administrators alike can exploit for the benefit of the individual.

HRA recognizes clinical realities. It acknowledges, in particular, that substance abusers generally do not quit overnight after the first treatment session, and on the road to recovery resumption of use may occur. This understanding, however, is a far cry from the expectation that patients will relapse over and over, and from the failure to hold anyone or any institution accountable when such relapses occur. Indeed, it is precisely because addiction is, at bottom, a behavioral condition—meaning it generally responds to the consequences it engenders—that HRA's special-needs approach to substance disorders is so promising.

Role of Social Institutions in Leveraging the Effect of Drug Treatment

A major irony in the effort to shape addicts' behavior is the fact that the treatment system is probably the one sound institution least equipped to change problem behaviors in unmotivated individuals. The entity with the largest influence is the criminal justice system. This is because so many hardcore users end up committing crime at some point. The criminal justice system has been using mandated treatment in the service of rehabilitating addicts for more than 70 years. The experience has yielded the vital clinical lesson that addicts need not be internally motivated at the outset of treatment in order to benefit from it. Indeed, addicts who are legally pressured into treatment may outperform voluntary patients; they are more likely to stay in treatment longer and are more likely to graduate. As retention in treatment is the best predictor of outcome, mechanisms that ensure retention tend to be associated with better outcomes.

In the employment setting, organizations called Employee Assistance Programs (EAPs) are also promising. The standard arrangement entails EAP notification of the employer if the patient/worker does not comply with the treatment contract; the penalty is loss of job. From the standpoint of the clinician, built-in limits and definitions of compliance can be an invaluable asset. When they are imposed and monitored by an external entity (e.g., judge, employer, welfare agency, or treatment program, rather than the counselor himself) and made clear to the patient at the start of treatment, the clinician and patient do not waste time bargaining over what constitutes compliance. The clinician does not have to risk straining the treatment relationship by threatening the patient with an infraction. Instead, with externally imposed expectations, the clinician's role is simplified. He is an ally, helping the addict develop strategies to resist relapse and ultimately discovering larger reasons for her to stay clean, even if the initial reasons are purely to avoid sanction.

Theoretically, the welfare agency could serve a treatment-enhancing function through the application of sanctions, but at this time the impact of sanctions on treatment retention is largely unknown. It is possible that incarceration or job loss, respectively, are more aversive to criminals and workers than the reduction or loss of welfare benefits is to a recipient. As described elsewhere in this chapter, the impact of sanctions is muted by the fact that benefits are reduced only partially and that implementing sanctions is a slow process.

Finally, where there is leverage, there will inevitably be unwilling subjects of that leverage. Not surprisingly, some potential recipients are so resistant to mandatory treatment that they simply decline public assistance altogether. Others may have little interest but reluctantly comply rather than face sanction. Many clinicians believe, mistakenly, that a patient must desire drug treatment in order to benefit from it, that she must first "hit bottom" and that she must want to undertake treatment for herself and not as a result of any outside pressure. Indeed, there is ample evidence that addicts who are required to attend treatment perform as well or better than those who volunteered: the reason is that they stayed in treatment longer.[46]

Numerous surveys have shown that the typical drop-out rate from outpatient treatment is 90 to 95 percent. That is, if 100 patients enter treatment on January 1, only 5 to 10 remain on December 31. In residential settings, perhaps 10 percent complete the 16- to 24-month programs. Overall, about half of voluntary patients drop out within the first three months. These drop-out rates are not hard to understand. In the early months of a residential treatment, patients often rebel against the rigid structure. For patients in treatment, ambivalence about relinquishing drugs is powerful. Even patients with a strong desire to stop using drugs experience flagging resolve, momentary disillusionment, or intense cravings. If a patient succumbs to these pressures and leaves treatment prematurely, she may have gained some benefit from the exposure to treatment but is at high risk of relapse.

Work Itself Is Therapeutic

Engagement in employment is one of the strongest correlates of post-treatment abstinence.[47] Wickizer conducted an analysis that looked at welfare recipients in particular. He examined outcomes for Washington State welfare recipients who were either in residential treatment or in methadone treatment and compared them to a group of people who did not receive treatment.[48] Among individuals who received intensive residential treatment, 64 percent more were employed than those in the comparison group. Similarly, of those who received methadone maintenance, 50 percent more were employed than those in the comparison group. In this study, as in most observational welfare analyses, the treated and nontreated groups were not randomly assigned. Thus, while the results may be inflated, they are still useful.

Granted, these outcomes may reflect an independent, third factor—the combination of motivation to secure a job and conscientiousness required to hold it—that is also associated with abstinence. Unfortunately, there are no studies comparing outcomes for patients randomly assigned to treatment alone as opposed to treatment plus work—a gold standard for concluding that the concurrent model is superior. Nonetheless, there are aspects of work itself that reduce the risk of relapse, such as busyness, daily structure, absorption in tasks, opportunity to develop social relationships with people who do not use drugs, and enhanced feelings of self-worth or enjoyment through productivity. Once work becomes gratifying in and of itself, the threat of its loss can also constitute incentive for abstinence.

Practical Innovations

STARS

In order to translate HRA's ideas into daily practice, some vital changes needed to be made. Central to the transformation was a management information system, hence the development of the Substance Abuse Tracking and Reporting System, or STARS. This is an Internet-enabled computer application designed to facilitate the exchange of information between HRA and treatment programs that enroll HRA beneficiaries. It was a breakthrough in management, as no computerized tracking system existed before. (There was, and still is, a paper-based tracking system that is being superceded by STARS.) In fact, according to the Government Accounting Office, many states lack the computer systems necessary to aggregate and analyze data for managing caseloads.[49] Through STARS, programs can submit patient participation information such as attendance, urine-screen results, employment information, and data on retention, completion, and discharge. It can also broker transfer requests to other treatment programs. STARS enables HRA to monitor employability, clinical progress, and treatment compliance through the submission of monthly reports and rosters. As of January 11, 2002, STARS was operating in 185 outpatient treatment programs, or more than half of all outpatient programs serving HRA clients.

Another virtue of STARS is its potential to help HRA fulfill the related task, mandated by the state welfare act of 1997, of keeping track of all Medicaid recipients assigned to the substance abuse treatment system irrespective of whether or not they are TANF beneficiaries. With between 60,000 and 70,000 patients in New York City in treatment at any given time (over half of whom are on public assistance and/or Medicaid), there are tens of thousands more individuals that HRA should be following. Thus far, HRA has not made much progress on tracking Medicaid-only recipients, but the intention was to halt the cycle of detoxifications. Clinicians and especially emergency room staff are familiar with the addicted patients who come to the hospital every few months to get detoxified. For heroin users this is sometimes a way to reduce the intensity of their habit, because tolerance for heroin predictably diminishes after detoxification; for others the detoxification is a form of respite care. After several days in the hospital, these patients often resume use. Consequently, HRA will be monitoring such "revolving door" patients and will require them to enter treatment.[50]

Clinical Program Standards

In September 1999, HRA produced the *Clinical Practice Guidelines for Moving Clients with Substance Use Disorders from Welfare to Work* (renamed *Program Standards for Moving . . .* in May 2001). Special-needs planners point to the concordance between their program and the treatment principles set forth by the National Institute on Drug Abuse. Its 1999 publication, *Principles of Drug Addiction Treatment—A Research-Based Guide*, documents the research supporting the following tenets of treatment: no single treatment is appropriate for all individuals; effective treatment attends to patients' multiple needs; patients should be reevaluated periodically and treatment plans need to be flexible to accommodate changing needs; adequate length of stay is necessary to good outcomes; treatment does not need to be voluntary to be effective; possible drug use during treatment must be monitored.[51]

An integral part of the guidelines was the importance of work as both an element and a goal of treatment. It is a well-established though often-overlooked fact that treatment programs are more successful when they offer social services.[52]

The emphasis on employment has channeled funds into Vocational Rehabilitation and Employment Services (VRES), a part of OASAS. Since 1999 HRA has provided OASAS with about $1.7 million annually so that treatment programs can hire vocational rehabilitation counselors. Before welfare reform was enacted, vocational rehabilitation and employment funding was vulnerable whenever budget cuts to OASAS were made.[53] After reform, when vocational preparation became more clearly a responsibility of treatment, the rehabilitation and vocational services agency was able to expand its services considerably. Even so, many treatment programs never accepted the notion that vocational preparation was one of their responsibilities. This was a central point of disagreement between HRA and OASAS, as described below. Ideally, patients are assigned both a treatment counselor and a vocational counselor, and engagement with vocational services begins early in treatment rather than when the patient is about to be discharged.

Plans of Self-Support

If welfare benefits cease once a recipient starts working, Medicaid payments to treatment programs will terminate as well. Consequently, treatment programs have a major fiscal incentive to defer patients' employment. To help maintain newly employed substance abusers in treatment, HRA obtained permission from the New York State Department of Health and Office of Temporary Disability Assistance (OTDA) to introduce Medicaid Plans of Self-Support. When they are used more widely they will enable SNA beneficiaries who earn under $21,000 a year through employment to receive Medicaid for at least one year after they are hired, thus ensuring access to substance abuse treatment. A further advantage of remaining in treatment while beginning work is that counseling and group therapy can provide assistance during what may be a fragile period, especially for individuals who have not worked in a long time.

The Human Resources Administration also received permission from OTDA to use Public Assistance Plans of Self-Support for patients in residential treatment with secure jobs. For both TANF and Safety Net recipients, this benefit allows those mandated into residential care to retain all or part of their public assistance payment once employed. Individuals may earn up to $8,350 annually while in treatment without HRA rebudgeting their public assistance. In addition, the programs' congregate-care payments will not be reduced when the patient earns money. Earnings up to the $8,350 limit must be put in accounts maintained by the treatment programs, and withdrawals may be used only for approved purposes such as housing (e.g., deposit for an apartment when the patient leaves residential care) or work-related expenses (e.g., car repairs so the person can get to work).

PATHWAY THROUGH THE PROGRAM

A process has been established for screening welfare applicants and recipients, assessing those found to have a substance disorder, determining what actions to take and the level of any required care, determining employability or exemption from work, and, if indicated, deciding about sanctions.

Screening

As of November 1997, all individuals applying for public assistance at Job Centers around the city were screened for drug and alcohol disorders using the Alcohol/Substance Abuse Verbal Screening Instrument, developed by OASAS. The nine-item screen was administered by welfare workers as part of the public assistance application process.

An instrument that allows for a somewhat more detailed assessment is replacing the screen. The new screen was developed jointly by OASAS, OTDA, and representatives of local social service districts including HRA. The new screen, completed by the interviewer, was created at the state's initiative because the old screen, completed by the client herself, was not capturing many individuals. The screen is used for first-time applicants as well as for recipients undergoing recertification. In addition, applicants must answer ten questions about substance use. The individual administering the screen records observations of the respondent's appearance (e.g., glassy eyes, pinpoint pupils, track marks or abscesses, odor of alcohol on breath). In addition, the screener inquires about recent social history: Is the respondent (1) homeless, (2) involved with the child welfare system, (3) sanctioned by the Human Resources Administration, (4) under supervision of the criminal justice system within the last two years, or (5) on welfare more than once in the last two years? Individuals answering "yes" to any two or more questions or "yes" to one of the six queries that relate to the presence of active, problem substance use (e.g., "Have you felt the need to take a drink or use drugs when you awaken?") are given a positive score and referred for further assessment.

The rate of detection of potential problem use by the old screen was about 3 to 4 percent for TANF applicants and 10 to 12 percent for SNA applicants. It is important to keep in mind that positive responses do not necessarily mean a person is a substance abuser, or is dependent on drugs or alcohol, or that substance use is a barrier to work. In fact, HRA has found that between 11 and 13 percent of applicants who screen positive at intake are found not to require treatment upon subsequent assessment.[54]

Assessment of Applicants Following Screening

If an applicant's screening indicates a possible substance abuse problem, she is sent for more detailed assessment to the Substance Abuse Centralized Assessment Program (SACAP). At SACAP, three factors are assessed: the severity of the addiction, employability, and the level of care required should treatment be needed. In Fiscal Year 2001, SACAP conducted 36,492 assessments. At SACAP, Certified Alcoholism and Substance Abuse Counselors (on loan from the OASAS) perform the assessment. HRA hopes eventually to contract directly for those services. This interview asks questions about job-related functioning: housing and living arrangements; family and social relationships; substance-use patterns; and medical, psychiatric, legal, and social consequences of substance use. The individual's level of daily function within each of these domains is then rated as either "highly effective," "moderately effective," or "severely impaired." Upon subsequent detailed assessment, 11 percent of individuals require no treatment, 42 percent require treatment with a concurrent work activity, and 45 percent will generally be determined to have a substance abuse disorder that interferes with their employability. These individuals are typically referred to a treatment program. In New York City, intensive treatment (more than 15 hours a week) is considered a "work activity" even if the individual is not yet assigned to WEP or other job. The term "work activity" is used because the patients can engage in a fairly wide number of activities to meet their work requirement.

By law, the HRA has 45 days to determine Safety Net eligibility and 30 days to determine TANF eligibility. During this time, the applicant's engagement with the various requirements (e.g., keeping treatment appointments, completing application process) is a major determinant of her final status. According to the Mayor's Management Report, 41 percent of all public assistance applications are rejected and 3 percent are withdrawn.

Disposition Following Assessment

There are five basic dispositions of individuals who are assessed:

(1) If the applicant judged to have a substance abuse disorder refuses treatment, the application is rejected. If she still wants public assistance she must return to the Job Center of origin to reapply. If she is already a recipient, she receives a "notice of intent" that can result in a sanction and can ask to be scheduled for a fair hearing if she disagrees with the agency's action.

(2) If a mild to moderate substance abuse problem is detected, the individual must engage in a work activity while attending treatment up to 15 hours a week.

(3) If a serious substance problem exists, the applicant is required to participate in intensive treatment (minimum 15 hours a week), and work activity may be temporarily postponed.

(4) If the applicant or recipient does not abuse drugs or alcohol but appears to have a medical or psychiatric condition that precludes work, she is referred to the Health Services System (a medical contractor) for further diagnostic assessment. Those who are assigned to

treatment have their first appointment at the treatment program within two days of referral.

(5) A person deemed not to have a substance abuse problem or other barrier is referred directly to job preparation and placement or work activities.

Levels of Care

A level-of-care manual has been produced by SACAP. Levels of care intensity are defined as follows:

- No treatment referral: no substance use or minimal use without consequences.
- Nonintensive outpatient treatment with work requirement: occasional use or sporadic use with some functional consequences (e.g., has housing, partial or full employment, minimal or no legal issues).
- Intensive outpatient treatment without work requirement: regular use with consequences (e.g., has housing, some social supports, some motivation for treatment, unemployed, legal involvement).
- Full-time residential treatment: habitual use (e.g., lacks stable housing, little interest in treatment, all associates use drugs or alcohol heavily), prior unsuccessful attempt at any level of treatment.

Detoxification is available for patients who are undergoing withdrawal symptoms during the assessment interview; who claim, from personal experience, that abrupt cessation of use tends to result in a difficult withdrawal (e.g., hallucinations or seizures); or report that they have chronic medical or psychiatric problems that make unsupervised withdrawal complicated. After detoxification is completed, the patient is sent to a treatment program.

Preliminary data indicate that about 87 percent of applicants and 84 percent of recipients who screened positive were referred to treatment. Of the applicants and recipients who were not in treatment at assessment, the referral pattern for treatment was as follows: 9 percent to residential; 12 percent to methadone maintenance; 30 percent to drug-free outpatient; 31 percent to (alcohol) outpatient; 15 percent to alcohol inpatient; and 4 percent to shelter-based programs.[55]

Of the applicants and recipients who were in treatment at assessment, the referral pattern was as follows: 28 percent to residential; 38 percent to methadone maintenance; 14 percent to drug-free outpatient; 13 percent to (alcohol) outpatient; 0.5 percent to alcohol inpatient; and 6 percent to shelter-based programs. HRA provides case management services to encourage substance abusers to remain in treatment and to assist them in complying with HRA (and other) requirements. Several case-management organizations serve HRA:

the Visiting Nurse Service, the National Association for Drug Abuse Problems, and University Behavioral Associates. Their function is to provide comprehensive evaluation and coordination of multiple services (treatment, vocational preparation, legal assistance, housing, etc.). Case managers report compliance failure to HRA. Failure to participate in treatment (or to meet other HRA requirements) sets in motion the sequence of actions leading to sanction. The mechanism for the case managers' reporting to HRA was pending resolution of evidentiary issues related to fair hearings.

The Visiting Nurse Service case managers specialize in working with individuals who also have mental illness. Depression, in particular, may accompany substance abuse. Substance abuse can be a way to "self-medicate" depression, though the nature of relationship between mood disorders and substance use is not always clear. For example, women may get depressed because they lose a job and must resort to public assistance, or they might have lost a job in the first place because depression caused absenteeism or lackluster work performance. Or perhaps merely being on welfare generates demoralization and boredom (easily picked up on mental screens as depression). Turning to drugs or alcohol in an effort to self-medicate depression is not uncommon; conversely, regular use of substances like cocaine and alcohol can themselves alter mood. Whatever the genesis of depressed mood, it increases the likelihood that recipients will have trouble moving from welfare to work.[56]

After an individual has been in treatment for 90 days, a CASAC evaluates treatment need and employability status. HRA assumes that at this point most individuals will be able to participate in approved work activities but also recognizes that some people will need an extension of their work exemption.[57] SACAP estimates that roughly half of the clients seen need extensions after the first 90 days of treatment. Providers, however, considered this 90-day period too short. They lobbied HRA for a longer period during which a recipient could attend treatment before being judged work-ready, but they were unsuccessful.[58]

Determining Employability and Work Exemption

Recipients requiring more than 15 hours of treatment per week are temporarily exempt from work. At the 90-day mark, individuals are reassessed to determine whether they are ready to assume work full-time, require treatment in addition to part-time work, or need continued full-time treatment for another 30, 60, or 90 days before they are able to work.

Work Readiness

Another point of friction between HRA and some treatment providers was whether a patient needed to be abstinent before beginning her work assignment. From a clinical standpoint, HRA's position is justifiable since (1) people may be able to work at some jobs despite their drug use; (2) practically speaking, some of these individuals may never completely abandon illicit drug use; and most important, (3) work itself is therapeutic.

The assumption that clients have to be clean before they can work is a basic tenet of most treatment providers, however. They maintain that patients will be too fragile to endure the stresses of the workplace. If the counselor communicates his pessimism about work-readiness to the patient, he can inadvertently relay the expectation that the latter will not be able to handle a work assignment. While such a forecast might well apply to specific patients, it should not be imposed uniformly. This author's own clinical experience has been that counselors who are too protective of patients and try to shield them from potential anxieties are often, themselves, clinging rather tenuously to their own recovery. Such counselors tend to identify too closely with the patient, and thus, if they imagine that work would have been too stressful for them prior to attaining full abstinence, they assume it will be too stressful for their patient. They clearly mean well, but, in the end, such a rigid and self-referential stance only keeps patients from moving forward. This is not to say that the occasional patient might not feel overwhelmed by work and thus maintain or even increase substance use, but if this is the case, it should alert treatment and HRA staff to the need for additional interventions and to consider likely comorbidity, mental illness, or cognitive deficits.

Triggers for Sanctions

Noncompliance (see examples below) results in the suspension of benefits. The first sanction is for 45 days; the second for 120 days and the third and all subsequent ones are for 180 days. There is no limit on the number of sanctions a person can accumulate. Treatment providers are required to notify HRA of noncompliance through monthly rosters and quarterly progress reports. (Note that during a treatment sanction, Medicaid remains active for TANF recipients but not for those receiving Safety Net Assistance. If a sanctioned SNA beneficiary reenters treatment or becomes treatment-compliant, his Medicaid case can be reopened upon reapplication.) When the administration is notified of a client's failure to comply with treatment, it can reject her application for public assistance or impose a sanction.

Attendance requirements differ between the early phase of treatment (days 0 to 30) and days 30 and afterward. During the first phase no more than one unexcused absence per week is acceptable; thereafter no more than two unexcused absences are allowed per month.

During the course of the treatment plan, patients are required to refrain from criminal behaviors such as threatening violence or selling drugs, and they must attend treatment sessions, engage in vocational rehabilitation, and attempt to resolve problems in other areas such as housing, child welfare, and legal matters.

The drug-testing procedure is as follows: During the first 90 days, individuals must submit to weekly random urine tests. After that, monthly random tests are required, with resumption of weekly tests if a test is positive. In all phases, one or more "positives" results in reassessment or new intervention, intensification of treatment, or transfer to a different level of treatment. If the new intervention does not work, the patient may be reassessed by HRA to review the diagnosis and the appropriateness of treatment intensity, transferred to a more intense level of care, or lose benefits. The decision by HRA is based on information from the treatment provider.

The use of sanctions is essential to any accountability system, yet several factors limit the effectiveness of sanctions under welfare reform. First, the sanctions are rather weak. Reducing the monthly payment may not be seen as highly aversive, especially when the income can be supplemented by off-the-books work or support from a friend. Second, there is typically a lengthy time lag between infraction and consequence. Several weeks can pass before someone who has been deemed noncompliant is notified of pending sanction. Several months can elapse between notification and actual action on benefits, in part due to bureaucratic inertia and in part due to procrastination by the recipient himself. This delay violates the basic principle of behavioral modification: Sanctions must be swift and certain if they are to have a constructive impact on behavior. Otherwise, the process will seem arbitrary and the system will be resented for being unfair. Another impediment is the lenient attitudes of many of the administrative law judges who preside over fair hearings. Finally, individuals who have lost benefits can reapply for public assistance.[59]

In principle, consequences should follow action as quickly as possible, but several factors must be considered. First, there is a seemingly unavoidable delay in getting information to HRA from the treatment program. Second, the sanctioning process is cumbersome by its quasi-judicial nature and due-process requirement. Third, administrative law judges conducting the fair hearings are guided by state regulations and policies that have become unfavorable to HRA in recent years.

THE POLITICS OF REFORM: INTERAGENCY CONFLICT

Prior to reform, treatment providers designed their own programs (in accordance with OASAS regulatory guidelines) and shared information only case by case (e.g., with a patient's probation officer). Their performance was never subject to systematic oversight by a large referral entity like HRA. Welfare reform dramatically changed the relationship between HRA and treatment providers: When the welfare agency began mandating that recipients enter treatment, it created a legal means for eventually monitoring individuals' treatment compliance. By controlling referrals to the treatment programs, HRA can exclude particular providers.

Considerable enmity quickly developed between HRA and the entire treatment community—as represented by OASAS, the provider coalitions, and the treatment programs themselves. At the time of greatest animosity, welfare planners regarded the treatment community as intransigent, while the latter regarded HRA as disrespectful of its expertise, intrusive, and cold-heartedly eager to push people off the welfare rolls.

In 1999 HRA asked OASAS to convene a work group of treatment provider coalitions to collaborate in the development of *Clinical Practice Guidelines for Moving Individuals with Substance Use Disorders from Welfare to Work* (since renamed *Program Standards for Moving Clients with Substance Use Disorders from Welfare to Work*). In the spring of 2001—on two separate occasions—HRA asked providers to sign a letter of agreement so it could determine whether their programs would remain on HRA's master list of approved programs. Under this agreement, programs would

- seek to satisfy HRA's clinical guidelines (*Program Standards . . .*);
- report monthly on the status of enrolled recipients and submit a quarterly report for each;
- use the computerized Substance Abuse Tracking and Reporting System to report client information to HRA; and
- obtain HRA approval to transfer patients to another provider.

The agreement was not accepted readily either time it was proposed. In March 2001, HRA informed treatment providers of requirements they would have to meet in order to keep getting referrals from HRA. Two days later OASAS sent letters to providers discouraging them from agreeing to those requirements, strenuously objecting to new administrative costs the programs were likely to incur, and expressing great distress about the guidelines. "OASAS is committed to protecting the integrity of the clinical practice of treatment providers," the office wrote. "[We] are solely empowered to define and regulate the provision of treatment. . . . OASAS never endorsed the *Clinical Practice Guidelines* distributed by HRA."

Also warning New York City treatment providers not to sign the agreement was the Albany-based coalition of treatment providers called New York Alcoholism and Substance Abuse Providers (ASAP), which represents more than 300 treatment agencies, trade organizations, and smaller advocacy coalitions.[60] According to ASAP, its constituents claimed they had no input into the program standards (yet HRA staff claim they did), disapproved of the standards as they existed, and would not sign the letter. ASAP members also worried that their state funding would be jeopardized if any of it were spent using STARS to track public assistance patients.

Whether or not providers had input into the standards was a subject of hot dispute. HRA maintained that "despite their current denial, both OASAS and ASAP were actively involved in the work group that developed and negotiated the standards." After almost one year of discussion, ASAP and OASAS withdrew from the process, claiming that the standards imposed a variety of unfunded mandates, including weekly random drug testing. HRA notes that it has offered to pay the costs of the drug tests conducted by any program unable to afford them, but OASAS repeatedly declined this offer.

The treatment-tracking program, STARS, also posed a problem to ASAP.[61] The organization was concerned that the program was basically another unfunded mandate and that its use put patient confidentiality at risk. "It is essential," ASAP told the providers, "that we unite as a field and stand together in opposition to the implementation of the STARS project."

This objection prompted HRA to remind ASAP that its reservations seemed premature, as representatives of the coalition had not yet received a formal demonstration of treatment tracking.[62] The administration pointed out that training in STARS is free, as is the software, and that time spent entering data would be more than offset by the efficiency gained by eliminating paper reporting. Also, HRA had offered funds to upgrade the technological capacity of treatment programs, but OASAS responded that amending program contracts with HRA to reflect this would be too cumbersome. Complaints about not having the hardware in place were questionable, though, in view of a survey conducted by Baruch College suggesting that many providers already had the equipment needed to use STARS.

Another problem ASAP identified was a breach of confidentiality regarding patient records. Briefly, early versions of a STARS training manual used actual patient names. When this was brought to HRA's attention, those manuals were recalled and subsequent training material used only dummy names and data. HRA formally apologized for the lapse in judgment and hired the Legal Action Center, an advocacy group, to conduct training sessions in confidentiality.

In May 2001 the stalemate over the standards reached the governor's office. The disagreement was finally resolved when some adjustments were made to the standards. A joint letter signed by the commissioner of OASAS, HRA Commissioner Turner, and the commissioner of the Office of Temporary and Disability Assistance (a state agency) was sent to providers recommending that they sign the agreement if they wished to receive referrals. A notably conciliatory tone was used regarding STARS: "We are hopeful that technology such as HRA's STARS . . . will make it easier for this goal [of client self-sufficiency] to be realized." By mid-summer of 2001, 98 percent of the providers had signed this second letter, which was signed by all three commissioners.

Indeed, in an interview, the ASAP executive director sounded enthusiastic about welfare reform, recalling that when some members of his coalition said that the patients were "too debilitated" for employment, he and others vigorously disagreed and endorsed the thrust of HRA's policies. He was especially grateful for the additional vocational resources the HRA gave to treatment programs and enthusiastic about the "plans of self-support," which enable individuals and programs to continue benefits and reimbursement for treatment, respectively.

Largely sharing this optimism is the Legal Action Center.[63] The LAC is a New York City–based advocacy group representing the rights of treatment providers and people actively using drugs and protecting those in recovery from discrimination. It gets modest funding from OASAS, which some observers have suggested can be a conflict of interest insofar as LAC lobbies government agencies on behalf of treatment providers. In representing the providers, the center made it clear to HRA that welfare planners should not try to "micromanage" treatment programs. The major "sticking point" in the HRA provider agreement, according to LAC, was the issue of who decides whether or not a patient should be sanctioned.

Like OASAS and ASAP, LAC felt this prerogative should be the provider's. In the final agreement, specific compliance determinants were set forth, and it was decided that HRA would make the final determination of whether sanctions—versus intensified treatment plans—would be applied to noncompliant individuals on a case-by-case basis, based on information provided by the treatment providers. Despite these reservations, LAC confirmed that the center agrees with the "big picture," namely that drug-abusing welfare recipients should be moving toward work, that sanctions are in order when patients are not making progress, and that performance-based contracting with providers is appropriate. Performance-based contracting was a major thrust of the Giuliani Administration.

Despite the signed agreement and fading resistance by the treatment community to HRA's impositions, antagonism toward HRA by some welfare rights groups is still very much alive and well. As one welfare rights organization put it, HRA "discriminat[es] against persons with substance abuse problems" by "discarding the rights of the recipients and ignoring the judgment of treatment providers," referring to HRA's expectation that treatment programs would adhere to HRA-developed program standards.[64] They condemned the regular use of urinalysis and sanctions as "punitive." As of August 2001, the group was still charging that "HRA has yet to develop practical and humane treatment programs . . . preferring to rely on punitive measures."[65]

COMMENTS

The ultimate goal of both welfare reform and drug treatment is self-reliance. The Human Resources Administration blueprint for serving recipients with substance abuse problems is ambitious and clinically enlightened. It is undergirded by the principle that public aid should be a vehicle for recovery and self-sufficiency rather than an indefinite entitlement to be disbursed no matter how the recipient behaves. This resolve is more demanding than the prereform practice of simply mailing checks and assuming beneficiaries are incapable of or uninterested in self-improvement—it is also more optimistic about their capacity for change.

Still unanswered, however, is whether the hundreds of hours spent negotiating standards and agreements and identifying, treating, and tracking this subgroup justified the creation and cost of a new bureaucracy. The verdict will depend upon whether some acceptable percentage of the treated population was finally able to function in jobs and ultimately left the welfare rolls. In other words, was the cost of meeting the special needs of this group offset by welfare savings?

To date it appears that the number of individuals whose drug or alcohol problems interfere with their employability is relatively small, representing about five to ten percent of all applicants and beneficiaries. This might argue for a "work-first" approach, wherein all recipients engage in job searches with short-term assistance if needed. Those who do not succeed in finding jobs would then be required to participate in services focused on the problems keeping them from working. Some individuals will be helped by these services and move into work activity; those still having trouble would be sent for more intensive aid. With more targeted spending, individuals who have already shown themselves incapable of responding to the basic demands of reform could be assigned to intensive, costly, "last resort" supervisory programs like long-term residential family programs.

Another early result of reform efforts is the significant rate of drop-out from treatment. As noted earlier, one of the most potent determinants of treatment success is the length of time patients are exposed to it, irrespective of whether attendance is voluntary or mandatory. Indeed, the virtue of mandating treatment is its effect on keeping patients in care longer. Typically, it is the criminal justice system—not the welfare system—that sends individuals to mandated treatment; the offender has an incentive to stay in the treatment program to avoid being incarcerated. Though the HRA treatment mandate incorporates sanctions, it seems unlikely that the consequences for poor performance (e.g., a partial reduction in benefit) are potent enough to serve disciplinary or deterrent functions. Furthermore, the sanctions are not yet imposed in a predictable and timely fashion. As behaviorists have long known, swiftness and certainty are essential for shaping response, and when they are applied reliably, the importance of sanction severity diminishes. Thus, it is possible that a relatively weak sanction could still be effective if it is delivered quickly and surely.

Experience managing drug abusers in the criminal justice system suggests that swift and certain sanctions are an excellent supplement to treatment and, for a subgroup of addicted individuals, can sometimes replace treatment altogether in shaping addict behavior. Conceivably, this latter group could be "treated" only with drug testing coupled with swift-and-certain sanctions. This option has several benefits: saving money on drug treatment, sparing recipients the imposition (as many of them see it) of counseling and group therapy, and freeing up more of their time for work activities. As an interesting experiment, HRA could randomly assign half of the individuals who would normally be assigned to the lowest intensity treatment to "sanction and testing only" management. Variations on the design could theoretically include incentives as well as sanctions. For example, small cash payments (prorated from the monthly cash allowance) could be distributed several times a week when the individual turns in a negative drug test. HRA must operate within the limits established by the state Social Services Law and the relevant state and federal regulations. (See the discussion of sanctions above for some of the limits on agency authority.) The coerced absence model may not be applicable to the population HRA serves.

How to distinguish between the truly incapable and the fundamentally unmotivated is an enduring challenge for social service workers. Confronted with those who have still not initiated work within a five-year period, many welfare academics and advocates will surely invoke the notion of "hidden barriers," that is, obstacles to work that are not initially obvious to welfare workers because they are either purposely concealed (e.g., substance abuse) or are not even recognized by the individual as a problem (e.g., learning disability, depression). Granted, "hidden" impediments are real and can pose problems, but planners and policymakers should be skeptical of advocates and academics who excuse stagnating recipients by attributing their poor performance to previously unrecognized barriers. In the case of individuals with substance use problems, we should be especially suspicious of claims that clients' problems are so serious that they defy conventional treatment and now require an even stronger "dose" of therapy or exemption from the welfare time limits.

At one time, the ideological touchstone of the War on Poverty was the assumption that the removal of external barriers (e.g., child care, transportation, housing) would galvanize recipients' work ethic, and innate productive drive would thrive. Welfare scholar Lawrence Mead calls this the "competence assumption." Like the homeless, who it was once said "were just like you and me," and for whom the solution was supposed to be "homes, homes, homes"—a remedy that overlooked completely their gross internal disorganization (at times, psychosis)—welfare recipients were seen by reformers as stymied by structural impediments; to be sure, some—but not most—were.

Now, the idea of barriers includes internal obstacles to employability such as depression, learning disability, or addiction. As University of Michigan researchers state, "policy makers . . . are increasingly using the language of public health to determine who is 'employable' and who is not." It will be interesting to see how such policymakers and academics "diagnose" recipients for whom no disability has been found by doctors, for whom all obvious external barriers have been eliminated or ameliorated, but who still claim to need public support. Mead refers to these individuals as having "psychic inhibitions" to social and economic mobility. Descriptors such as "passivity" or even the indelicate adjective "laziness" might apply as well.

Policy responses take two basic forms. The first is to release these individuals from the federal welfare rolls. The rationale for such a disposition is that poverty alone—especially when it results from bad choices—should not constitute a government-funded entitlement to income. Why insulate individuals from the consequences of their actions?

The second response—apparently motivated by concern for the children—is to strengthen supervisory constraints on these individuals. For drug-abusing women and their children, this could mean mandated living in a highly regimented residential treatment program with supported employment as developed for rehabilitating people with mental illness or cognitive deficits.

With that in mind, welfare planners and politicians are well advised to be vigilant about the trend toward medicalizing internal obstacles. Mead's prediction that the prevailing conceptualization is shifting from a competence model to a disability model (in which barriers are simply redefined as internal, and "psychic inhibitions," being one of those barriers, are recast as psychiatric disorders) is a compelling one. Should the disability models win out and the five-year time limit be waived, welfare agencies must still hold recipients to some kind of contract, whether or not it means some kind of work effort.

RECOMMENDATIONS

Based on the history of HRA's attempt to provide effective drug treatment, four lines of action should be pursued unless new evidence suggests otherwise:

Recipients should undertake treatment and work experience and/or training concurrently.

(1) Strong efforts should be made to impose sanctions in a timely and predictable manner.
(2) If substance-abusing recipients fail to obtain work after receiving treatment (at least twice within a five-year episode, for example), they should be regarded as noncompliant and considered for termination from the rolls.
(3) Local treatment programs should be encouraged to experiment with contingency management protocols with the cooperation of the welfare agency.

Further analysis is forthcoming regarding the size and characteristics of the problem population, whether services actually reach individuals who needed them, and an assessment of the value of the treatment itself. These questions will be answered over time, and the current programs may require amendment. Presumably, the Human Resources Administration will continue to promote the ideals of welfare reform.

NOTES

1. Kirstan Olson and LaDonna Pavetti, *Personal and Family Challenges to Successful Transition from Welfare to Work* (Washington, D.C.: Urban Institute, 1996); N. K. Young and Center for Substance Abuse Treatment, *Alcohol and Other Drug Treatment: Policy Choices in Welfare Reform* (Washington, D.C.: National Association of State Alcohol and Drug Abuse Directors, Government Printing Office, 1999); C. B. Sisco and C. L. Pearson, "Prevalence of Alcoholism and Drug Abuse among Female AFDC Recipients," *Health and Social Work* 19 (1994): 75–77; Center on Addiction and Substance Abuse at Columbia University, *Substance Abuse and Women on Welfare* (New York: CASA, 1994).

2. Joseph Califano, "It's Drugs Stupid," *New York Times Magazine*, March 19, 1995, 40–41.

3. HRA and OASAS were brought together in their capacity as two major systems that offer services to substance abusers under the direction of the New York State Office of Temporary Disability and Assistance.

4. Rebecca Brown, *Issue Brief: Addressing Substance Abuse and Mental Health Problems under Welfare Reform: State Issues and Strategies* (Washington, D.C.: National Governor's Association, 1999).

5. As of January 4, 2002, there were 197,818 total beneficiaries (108,964 TANF/22,904 TANF exhaustees/Safety Net 65,960).

6. American Psychological Association, *Diagnostic and Statistical Manual IV* (Washington, D.C.: APA, 1994).

7. U.S. Department of Health and Human Services, *Patterns of Substance Use*

and Substance-Related Impairment among Participants in Aid to Families with Dependent Children (Washington, D.C.: Office of the Assistant Secretary for Planning and Evaluation and the Substance Abuse and Mental Health Services Administration, 1994).

8. U.S. Department of Health and Human Services, *Functional Impairments of AFDC Clients* (Washington, D.C.: Office of the Inspector General, 1992); Legal Action Center, *State, Local Welfare Officials See Important Role for Drugs and Alcohol Treatment in Welfare Reform* (Washington, D.C.: Legal Action Center, 1995).

9. S. R. Zedlewski and P. Loprest, "Will TANF Work For The Most Disadvantaged?" in Ron Haskins, ed., *The New World of Welfare* (Washington, D.C.: Brookings Institution Press, 2001); H. A. Pollack, S. Danziger, R. Jaykody, et al., "Substance Use among Welfare Recipients: Trends and Policy Responses," *Social Services Review* 25 (2002): 623–51.

10. General Accounting Office, *Welfare Reform: Moving Hard-to-Employ Recipients into the Workforce, GAO-01-368* (Washington, D.C.: GAO, 2001). The studies summarized by the GAO were published between 1997 and 1999.

11. M. R. Nakashian and E. A. Moore, "Identifying Substance Abuse among TANF Eligible Families," 2001.

12. J. Morgenstern, "Why Are Screening and Treatment Referral Rates Lower Than Expected in the New Jersey Substance Abuse Initiative," paper presented at the *Improving the Identification and Referral Process Between the Welfare and Substance Abuse Systems* conference, Washington, D.C., 1999 (as cited in Pollack, Danziger, Jayakody, et al.).

13. J. A. Klerman, G. L. Zellman, T. Chung, et al., "Substance Abuse, Mental Illness and Domestic Services," in *Welfare Reform in California: State and County Implementation of CalWorks in the Second Year* (Santa Monica, Calif.: RAND, 2000); R. Speiglman, L. Fujiwara, J. Norris, et al., *Alameda County CalWORKs Needs Assessment: A Look at Potential Health Related Barriers to Self-Sufficiency* (Berkeley, Calif.: Health Institute, 1999).

14. S. K. Danziger, M. Corcoran, S. Danziger, et al., "Barriers to the Employment of Welfare Recipients," in R. Cherry and W. Rodgers, eds., *The Impact of Tight Labor Markets on Black Employment* (New York: Russell Sage, 2000), 239–69.

15. S. McLanahan, I. Garfinkel, and R. B. Mincy, *Fragile Families, Welfare Reform and Marriage: Brookings Policy Brief 10* (Washington, D.C.: Brookings Press, 2001).

16. R. Kaestner, "Drug Use and AFDC Participation. Is There a Connection?" *Journal of Policy Analysis and Management* 17, no. 3 (1998): 493–520.

17. H. A. Pollack, S. Danziger, R. Jaykody, et al., "Substance Use among Welfare Recipients: Trends and Policy Responses," *Social Services Review* 25 (2002): 623–51.

18. R. Green, L. Fujiwara, J. Morris, et al., *Alameda County CalWORKS Needs Assessment, Barriers to Working and Summaries of Baseline Status* (Berkeley, Calif.: Public Health Institute, 2000).

19. J. Morgenstern, "Why Are Screening and Treatment Referral Rates Lower Than Expected in the New Jersey Substance Abuse Initiative," 1999.

20. Wolstenholme, personal communication, cited in M. R. Nakashian and E. A. Moore, "Identifying Substance Abuse among TANF Eligible Families," 2001.

21. B. F. Grant and A. D. Dawson, "Alcohol and Drug Use, Abuse, and Depen-

dence among Welfare Recipients," *American Journal of Public Health* 86, no. 10 (1996): 1450–54.

22. R. Jayakody, S. Danziger, and H. Pollack, "Welfare Reform, Substance Abuse and Mental Health," *Journal of Health Politics, Policy and Law* 25, no. 4 (2000): 623–52.

23. H. A. Pollack, S. Danziger, R. Jaykody, et al., "Substance Use among Welfare Recipients: Trends and Policy Responses," 2002.

24. National Institute on Drug Abuse, *National Pregnancy and Health Survey: Drug Use Among Women Delivering Live Births* (Rockville, Md.: National Institutes of Health, 1992); L. Harrison and A. Hughes, *The Validity of Self-Reported Drug Use: Improving the Accuracy of Survey Estimates* (Washington, D.C.: NIDA Research Monograph 167, 1997); S. Magura and S. Kang, "Validity of Self-Reported Drug Use on High Risk Populations: A Meta-analytical Review," *Substance Use and Misuse* 31, no. 9 (1996): 1131–53.

25. A. Kline, C. Bruzios, G. Rodrigues, et al., *Substance Abuse Needs Assessment Survey of Recipients of Temporary Assistance for Needy Families (TANF)* (Trenton, N.J.: New Jersey Department of Health, 1998).

26. James N. Dertouzos and Patricia A. Eberner, *A Profile of San Bernardino County CalWORKS Caseload, DB-304-SBC,* 2000.

27. J. Morgenstern, A. Riordan, D. Delphilippis, et al., *Specialized Screening Approaches Can Substantially Increase the Identification of Substance Abuse Problems among Welfare Recipients, Research Notes* (Washington, D.C.: Department of Health and Human Services, Administration for Children and Families, 2001). The authors discuss only women applying for emergency assistance.

28. Starleen Scott Robbins, branch head for Women's and Children's Services in the Division of Mental Health Disability and Substance Abuse Services for the State of North Carolina, personal communication.

29. H. A. Pollack, S. Danziger, R. Jaykody, et al., "Substance Use among Welfare Recipients: Trends and Policy Responses," 2002.

30. Kim North Shine, "Court OK's Drug Tests For People on Welfare; Michigan Can Deny Benefits to Those Who Fail," *Detroit Free Press,* October 19, 2002.

31. Joan Randell, associate commissioner for Special Needs Planning and Program Development, HRA, personal communication.

32. H. A. Pollack, S. Danziger, R. Jaykody, et al., "Substance Use Among Welfare Recipients: Trends and Policy Responses," 2002.

33. S. K. Danziger, M. Corcoran, S. Danziger, et al., "Barriers to the Employment of Welfare Recipients," in *The Impact of Tight Labor Markets on Black Employment.*

34. L. Schmidt, C. Weisner, and J. Wiley, "Substance Abuse and the Course of Welfare Dependency," *American Journal of Public Health* 88 (1998): 1616–22.

35. Columbia University, *Three-City Findings Reveal Unexpected Diversity Among Welfare Leavers and Stayers* (New York: Mailman School of Public Health, Columbia University, 2000), 3.

36. J. Morgenstern, A. Riordan, D. Delphilippis, et al., *Specialized Screening Approaches Can Substantially Increase the Identification of Substance Abuse Problems among Welfare Recipients, Research Notes.*

37. Instrument used was the SACAP assessment, described in "Pathway" section of this paper.

38. J. A. Klerman, G. L. Zellman, T. Chung, et al., "Substance Abuse, Mental Illness and Domestic Services," in *Welfare Reform in California: State and County Implementation of CalWorks in the Second Year*, 279.

39. Amy Brown, *Beyond Work-First: How to Help Hard-to-Employ Individuals Get Jobs and Succeed in the Work Force* (New York: Manpower Demonstration Research Corporation, 2001).

40. J. Morgenstern, A. Riordan, B. S. McCrady, et al., *Intensive Case Management Improves Welfare Clients' Rates of Entry and Retention in Substance Abuse Treatment, Research Notes* (Washington, D.C.: Department of Health and Human Services, Administration for Children and Families, 2001).

41. SACAP (July 2000–June 2001) composite unpublished data.

42. Swati Desai, HRA, "Treatment Types and Outcomes for Active Recipients Starting Substance Abuse Treatment in July, August or September 2000," unpublished data.

43. Sample includes public assistance recipients mandated into treatment by HRA from July 1, 2000, to September 30, 2000, whose PA cases were active at some point in the three-month period. Not included were recipients mandated into short-term alcohol detoxification. All other treatment modalities are included, resulting in a sample of 1,845.

44. D. D. Simpson, G. W. Joe, and B. S. Brown, "Treatment Retention and Follow-Up Outcomes in the Drug Abuse Treatment Outcome Study," *Psychology of Addictive Behaviors* 11, no. 4 (1997): 294–307.

45. Brian M. O'Neill (Office of Employment Services, Systems Operation) "Mayor's anti-drug strategy information request," memo to Fred Patrick, May 13, 1998.

46. S. L. Satel, *Drug Treatment: The Case for Coercion* (Washington, D.C.: American Enterprise Institute Press, 1999).

47. S. S. Martin, C. A. Butzin, C. A. Saum, and J. A. Inciardi, "Three-year Outcomes of Therapeutic Community Treatment for Drug-Involved Offenders in Delaware: From Prison to Work Release to Aftercare," *Prison Journal* 79, no. 3 (1999): 294–320.

48. T. M. Wickizer, K. Campbell, A. Krupski, et al, "Employment Outcomes among AFDC Recipients Treated for Substance Abuse in Washington State," *Milbank Quarterly* 78, no. 4 (2000): 585–608.

49. General Accounting Office, *Welfare Reform: Moving Hard-to-Employ Recipients into the Workforce, GAO-01-368*, 27.

50. Mark Hoover, HRA, personal communication; HRA staff subsequently informed me that the only way to close the revolving door would be to review medical assistance records to determine who is entering treatment without an HRA assessment and mandate. Access to medical records for this purpose is not acceptable to the responsible state agencies so the plan could well be blocked.

51. National Institutes of Health, *Principles of Drug Addiction Treatment—A Research Based Guide, no. 99-4180* (Rockville, Md.: NIH, 1999).

52. A. T. McLellan, L. Arndt, D. S. Metzger, et al. "The Effects of Psychosocial Services in Substance Abuse Treatment," *Journal of the American Medical Association* 269, no. 15 (1993): 1953–59; P. Crits-Cristoph, L. Siqueland, J. Blaine, et al., "Psychosocial Treatments for Cocaine Dependence: Results of the NIDA Cocaine Collaboration Study," *Archives of General Psychiatry* 56, no. 6 (1999): 493–502.

53. Belinda Greenfield, VRES director, personal communication.

54. Joan Randell, personal communication.

55. Swati Desai, HRA, "Treatment Types and Outcomes for Active Recipients Starting Substance Abuse Treatment in July, August or September 2000" and SACAP (July 2000–June 2001) composite unpublished data.

56. S. Danziger, M. Corcoran, H. Danziger, et al., "Barriers to Employment of Welfare Recipients," in Robert D. Cherry and William M. Rodgers, *Prosperity For All? The Economic Boom and African Americans* (New York: Russell Sage Foundation, 2000). In the Women Employment Survey sample, Michigan women who met diagnostic screening criteria for major depression were significantly less likely to be working at least 20 hours per week compared to those who were not depressed.

57. J. A. Turner and F. R. Lipton, *Program Standards for Moving Individuals with Substance Use Disorders from Welfare to Work* (New York: Human Resources Administration, 2001).

58. John Coppola, personal communication.

59. Bronx Comprehensive Services Center, mission statement, 3.

60. John Coppola, ASAPNYS director, letter to President, Board of Directors NYC Treatment Providers, March 23, 2000.

61. Similar letter, Dec. 19, 2000.

62. Frank Lipton, MD, letter to John Coppola.

63. Paul Samuels, personal communication.

64. Committee on Social Welfare Law, "Welfare Reform in New York City: The Measure of Success," August 2001, http://www.abcny.org/currentarticle/welfare.html.

65. Committee on Social Welfare Law, 6.

10

Housing the Homeless

Thomas J. Main

When the census count of the homeless rises at New York City's shelters, homelessness once again becomes front-page news.[1] The city agency with primary responsibility to provide shelter for the homeless is the Department of Homeless Services (DHS), which was established when HRA's homeless operations were spun off as an independent agency. Yet HRA takes the lead in servicing certain special homeless populations. For example, under Local Law 49 of 1997, HRA is responsible for providing shelter for homeless people with AIDS. And there are other areas where HRA, though not mandated by law, deals with homeless people. For example, HRA also plays an important role in diverting "pre-homeless" families from the DHS shelter system and in identifying permanent housing for homeless families. Additionally, HRA aids families that are homeless as a result of domestic violence (DV). Hence, HRA is an indispensable contributor to the city's homeless policy.

OVERVIEW OF HRA AND ITS SERVICES TO THE HOMELESS

HRA's core operations—those that serve the non-homeless public assistance (PA) population—have gone through striking changes during the Giuliani Administration. The introduction of the JobStat system, the sharp reduction in the PA caseloads, the restructuring of the critical tasks of the agency's frontline operators (who now include the new "job opportunity specialists"), and even a greatly improved physical plant all testify to a dramatic reinvention effort. Further, during this time the city's homeless system has also been thoroughly reinvented, most notably by the privatization of much of its shelter operations and by the development of rehabilitative programs in many of its shelters for single men.[2] Both these institutional makeovers were aimed at engaging clients in some positive activity: work, in the case of HRA's clients, and rehabilitation of various sorts for the single men of DHS. Thus HRA's services to the homeless are a set of activities wedged, as it were, between two foci of institutional change. While not themselves an epicenter of change, HRA's homeless operations have had to support and reinforce the changes taking place around them.

But adapting its homeless services to reinforce the turn toward supervision and engagement has not been easy for HRA. The city's services to the homeless are very much constrained by a set of court actions, such as the *Callahan* consent decree, which covers homeless individuals, and the *McCain* decision, which applies to homeless families. And Local Law 49 mandates services to HIV/AIDS patients. A few words need to be said here about the court cases and legal mandates that concern homeless individuals and families and how they influence policy. (Local Law 49 will be discussed later.)

The city's contemporary homeless policy began with the signing of the *Callahan v. Carey* consent decree in 1981. *Callahan* was brought under the New York State constitution against the state and city governments by a Legal Aid attorney and later by Robert Hayes, counsel for Coalition for the Homeless (CFTH). Hayes argued that a provision of the state constitution required the state and the city to provide shelter to whatever homeless man requested it. The court never ruled on whether there was a state constitutional right to shelter. The case led to a consent decree between the city and state and the representatives of the homeless, the key provision of which was that any applicant was to be provided shelter if he met the need standard to qualify for Home Relief or if, because of physical, mental, or social dysfunction, he needed temporary shelter.[3] The decree also set detailed quality standards that city shelters had to meet. In 1982 the right to shelter secured for men under the *Callahan* decree was extended to women in *Eldridge v. Koch*. And in *Lamboy v. Gross* and *McCain v. Koch*, advocates "established a judicially enforceable right to immediate provision of appropriate emergency shelter to homeless families and their children."[4]

Throughout the 1980s, city homeless policy was largely driven by the pressure of CFTH and other advocates to have every provision of the *Callahan* decree and the various judicial findings implemented generously and by the city's resistance to that pressure on the ground that it was doing everything it could. Shelter policy focused on expanding the supply of emergency shelter to which clients were entitled through the various court rulings.[5]

The Dinkins Administration fully embraced the expansion of access to shelter and, at least for homeless families, sought to move clients from emergency shelter to permanent shelter. During the spring and summer of 1990, the Dinkins Administration began relocating hundreds of homeless families from shelters and "welfare hotels" directly into refurbished, city-owned, permanent apartments. Entries into the family shelter system then went up, from about 530 families per month in April 1990 to about 650 in July.[6] The absolute increase was small, but it strained the city's supply of family shelters and welfare hotels. Before long, former homeless advocates now in the Dinkins Administration, such as Cesar A. Perales and Nancy Wackstein, began to worry that the city might not be able to manage the increased demand for shelter that purely rights-oriented policy had apparently stimulated.

A mayoral commission led by Andrew Cuomo addressed these concerns in a February 1992 report titled, *The Way Home: A New Direction in Social Policy*. One of the lessons that the commission drew from the experience of the Dinkins Administration was that since resources are limited, "government should not, and cannot, be expected to provide housing to everyone who asks for it."[7] The report also urged that "[t]he emergency shelter system must incorporate a balance of rights and responsibilities. A social contract and a mutuality of obligation must exist between those receiving help and society-at-large."[8]

Thus, homeless policy in New York City has come to oscillate between two contrasting paradigms. One paradigm is rooted in the *Callahan* consent decree and other legal documents and sees homeless policy as an effort to provide and extend services to which clients are entitled. On the other hand, at least since the publication of *The Way Home,* mayors and commissioners have struggled to regulate access to, and strengthen their management over, the shelter system. One paradigm sees homeless policy as a rights-based struggle to provide services. The other frames policy as a managerial effort to organize the system for better support and stricter governance of clients.

In the case of homeless individuals, DHS remade its operations along management-oriented lines. It did so by establishing a two-tier system of publicly operated and privately operated shelters. Access to the publicly operated shelter system is indeed open to all, with few strings attached, but access to the privately operated "program" shelters is contingent on faithful participation in their various rehabilitative regimes. However, to date a similar administrative structure for encouraging engagement has not been developed for homeless families. Efforts to impose work requirements or other forms of engagement on heads of homeless families have not been successful, as failure to participate still leaves a client with her right to shelter. Managers of HRA's homeless operations therefore face a dilemma: They must support, or at least not undermine, the various efforts of DHS and HRA to engage their clients in work or rehabilitative activities, even though various legal mandates prevent the enforcement of mandatory participation for most homeless clients. HRA's services to the homeless in general can be understood as an effort to square the policy circle of permissive legal mandates and an enforcement orientation.

ENGAGEMENT AND PREVENTION

When possible, HRA has tried straightforwardly to engage its homeless clients in work, or work-related, activities. Toward that end HRA assigned all its single homeless clients to be served by a single Job Center, Riverview. In theory, homeless people who receive benefits under the state's Safety Net Assistance (SNA) program could be obliged to participate in some kind of work-related activity and could be sanctioned should they fail to do so. But shelter residents are eligible under Safety Net only for a small personal allowance, and the administrative costs involved make imposing sanctions an unrealistic option. Consequently, while in theory single homeless people are required to respond when they are called to the Riverview Job Center to participate in work activities, few do so. Thus, designation of Riverview as the sole Job Center for single homeless HRA clients amounts to no more than making work activities available on a voluntary basis, but at least those homeless individuals who wish to participate can do so.

To encourage work among homeless families, HRA developed the Employment Incentive Housing Program (EIHP). The essence of the program is that homeless families receiving Temporary Assistance for Needy Families (TANF) are given a rent supplement payment in return for agreeing to participate in work-related activities. TANF families are in principle required to participate in such activities, but as homeless families are spread out throughout the shelter system, keeping track of them and enforcing work requirements is difficult. EIHP represents an effort to engage such families with positive incentives rather than sanctions. It also has the happy effect of removing families from the crowded shelter system. But few families are enrolled in the program, partly because to be eligible families must have at least 20 months left on their TANF eligibility.

As the cases of the Riverview Job Center and EIHP indicate, straightforward efforts to engage homeless clients in work have had limited success. But in other less direct ways, HRA has tried to make sure that its services to the homeless reinforce the general policy direction toward stronger work mandates. Perhaps the best work effort welfare families can make is to maintain themselves in their own housing and so avoid the shelter system altogether. HRA has thus over recent years put great effort into preventing homelessness. HRA first established "homelessness diversion teams" in 1992, and they are now located in all Job Centers. Each team consists of three to nine job opportunity specialists whose main task to prevent homelessness and thus divert families from the DHS shelter system. Team members work with the central Rental Assistance Unit, which operates in the agency's main office, and with the agency's Housing Court Liaison, which has staff at every housing court in the five boroughs.

The homelessness diversion teams at the Job Centers evaluate clients who come to the centers and are at risk of homelessness. Among the things they evaluate is whether the client can pay his or her arrears. The teams can also sometimes locate alternate resources from the community or the client's family. The team also looks to see if a client has a dispossess order or needs some form of emergency assistance. The diversion team then draws up an intervention plan for clients who are determined to be at risk of homelessness.

Once the outreach worker prepares a plan of intervention, the team supervisor reviews the plan, and then the Rental Assistance Unit, which approves arrears for payment by HRA, reviews it. Debts are often paid through an aid package that combines money from HRA, community organizations, and the client. When the homelessness diversion teams started in 1992, they did not make nearly as much use of family and community money in as they do now. After 1998, the teams were especially energetic in insisting that community organizations and the family contribute as much money as possible. HRA estimates that 15 percent of clients who come to the EAU are diverted from the shelter system by the teams.[9]

Part of the Homelessness Diversion Program is the Rental Arrears Alert (RAA), which helps welfare clients put together a package of aid to cover their arrears. RAA operates at 24 Job Centers. Among the sources of aid the RAA can access are the Bridge Fund, which makes interest-free loans, and the Federal Emergency Management Administration (FEMA). RAA began in May 1999, and as of August 2001 HRA estimates that it has prevented 4,864 evictions.[10] The strategy of the RAA is to negotiate directly with the landlord, demonstrate that whatever concerns he has will be dealt with quickly, and thus convince him to continuing to rent to a struggling family.

The use of housing court liaisons was another HRA initiative aimed at preventing homelessness. The liaisons existed since 1987. They used to provide information to tenants in court and would refer them to the income unit of the Job Centers for counseling. Under Commissioner Turner, however, HRA worked closely with housing court judges in a pilot program in the Bronx. Program staff got the housing court calendar five days in advance. They looked for cases involving people on public assistance and then prepared for those cases. For example, they looked for clerical problems that could easily be solved by HRA without taking up court time. On former HRA Commissioner Jason Turner's initiative, the agency put much effort into the Bronx pilot program. The main innovation was getting the calendar ahead of time and preparing an intervention in advance. It is easier to develop an intervention plan in court—rather than before or after—because the landlord's attorneys are there and negotiations are possible. The object is to reduce court expenditures and avoid evictions. This program existed only in the Bronx because that is where most evictions took place.

Another of Commission Turner's HRA initiatives was a program to work with the Community Justice Center in Harlem. The center provides "one-stop shopping" for people coming in contact with the court system. A single judge handles both family court and housing court matters. As in the Bronx, HRA staff coordinated with the court to avoid outcomes that put families at risk of homelessness. HRA also has contracts with five community-based organizations to provide homelessness prevention services and with seven legal service providers for anti-eviction assistance.

HRA also works with the New York City Housing Authority (NYCHA) to stop evictions and to resolve nonpayment claims before they go to court. Further, since the 1980s HRA has had a unique protocol with city marshals regarding the execution of civil processes, including eviction. The protocol provides that if a marshal who is knocking at a door and has reason to believe that the person on whom he is serving an eviction process meets the profile of someone who is in danger of becoming homeless, then the marshal must refer the case to HRA and stop the eviction process for ten business days.

HRA SERVICES FOR DOMESTIC VIOLENCE VICTIMS

HRA's domestic violence (DV) shelter system includes emergency shelters and tier-two units, each capable of accommodating three people. The emergency beds are for women with immediate shelter needs. Under state regulations, a woman's stay there is limited to 135 days (90 days plus a possible extension of 45 days). Tier-two units are for women with longer-term needs and are available only to women already in the emergency system. Again, state regulations limit a woman's stay in the tier-two shelters to six months. Emergency beds are provided by 31 nonprofit organizations, which are reimbursed on a per-diem basis, and by the city itself, which runs one emergency shelter, New Day. (HRA also provides services to about 50 families in an alternative-to-shelter program.) Clients typically enter the HRA domestic violence system after calling and being referred by the DV hotline, though some clients enter through the DHS system, as discussed below.

Domestic violence victims who are driven from their homes by their abusers present a challenge to HRA's efforts to build an engagement-oriented system. Again, whatever the legal niceties of the matter may be, the *McCain* court decision creates a de facto right to shelter for homeless families and prevents HRA from imposing work requirements on such families. And diversion, in the sense of encouraging a family to stay in its own place, is obviously not a suitable policy in the case of current victims of domestic violence. Instead, the agency's policy has been to divert such families from the DHS system to the HRA system, which is better designed to meet their needs. Thus HRA's goal has been to move all domestic violence victims into its system and out of the DHS shelter system, which is often overcrowded in any case.

In order to accommodate all families displaced by domestic violence, HRA has expanded its DV shelter system greatly between 1994 and 2002. In FY 1992 there were 653 beds[11] in the emergency DV system, and 87 tier-two units. In 2002 there were 1,450 emergency beds and 155 tier-two units.[12] HRA officials estimate that the number of DV victims in DHS shelters dropped from about 1,000 in 1999 to about 400 in 2002. Relocating the DV population into a separate shelter system was accomplished by placing an HRA team in the DHS Emergency Assistance Unit (EAU), which is the main entry point to the "ordinary" homeless system. This HRA team is also known as the NOVA (No Violence Again) Unit. Anyone who enters the EAU and reports to DHS staff that she has experienced domestic violence at any point in her life is sent to the NOVA Unit, which will refer her to the DV system if she turns out to be currently a victim.

Unfortunately, this effort to place DV victims in a system designed for them has run into a snag. DV shelters enforce a set of rules designed to protect their residents. These rules include strict curfews, a ban on men in the shelter, and an absolute prohibition on revealing the location of the shelter. Potential clients, for whatever reason, sometimes balk at these rules and so cannot stay in a DV shelter. Even though these women have, in effect, turned down an offer of appropriate shelter, they retain, under the *McCain* court decision, a right to shelter. Thus they end up in the overtaxed DHS system, which is not designed to meet their needs. Developing a procedure for moving all families who are homeless primarily because of domestic violence to the appropriate shelter system is one of the main challenges faced by the current HRA commissioner.

SERVING HOMELESS CLIENTS WITH HIV/AIDS

One of HRA's most troublesome and troubled programs is the HIV/AIDS Services Administration (HASA). Formerly known as the Division of AIDS Services and Income Support (DASIS), HASA is in charge of HRA's efforts to provide social services, including housing, to those infected with the HIV virus or suffering from AIDS. In doing so HASA has had to cope with strong advocacy groups, such as Housing Works; with the courts; and with considerable media interest. How has HRA coped with this array of outside pressures, which are so typical of policymaking in New York City?

Much of what HASA does is related to housing clients. Many clients come to HASA already homeless, and others eventually fall into homelessness. HASA's central office at 400 Eighth Avenue has an Emergency Placement Unit (EPU) that seeks to place homeless clients in shelter on the same day they make their request. Achieving that goal is perhaps HASA's most difficult task. But, according to the courts, it is one HASA cannot avoid.

The origins of this obligation in some ways reach back to the early days of the Giuliani Administration. A budgetary review of all mayoral agencies opened the possibility that HASA (then DASIS) might be reorganized out of existence. In 1997 the city council foreclosed this option by passing Local Law 49, which mandated the existence of HASA within HRA. Among the services the law required HASA to provide was "medically appropriate transitional and permanent housing," which must include medical refrigeration storage and a locking, private bathroom.[13] Thus HASA is limited in the facilities it can use. For example, no HASA client can be placed in an ordinary congregate homeless shelter. Over the years, the city's supply of single-room occupancy (SRO) hotels declined; many closed down or were converted to serve new populations, including tourists. HASA therefore often has not been able to find enough SRO units to meet its needs and has not always been able to provide clients with suitable shelter immediately.

The AIDS advocacy group Housing Works responded to HRA's dilemma by suing the agency. In the case, *Hannah v. Turner,* among other matters was whether Local Law 49 required HASA to make housing placements on the same day the request is made. The one-day deadline had been in HASA's own manual as a desirable goal, though it was not specifically mentioned in the law. The judge held that HASA was required to make placements within the same day. Richard O'Halloran, acting general counsel of the Office of Legal Affairs, observed "We were hoist on our petard because we had it in our procedures."

HASA was able to handle the same-day requirement effectively until the summer of 2000. In August 2000 demand for housing went up for unknown reasons and HASA was overwhelmed. In April 2001 Housing Works moved to hold Commissioner Turner and Deputy Commissioner Caldwell in contempt of the *Hannah* court order. Whether there actually was contempt of the order depended partly on how perfectly one can expect any order to be followed. The contempt charges were based on 17 people who, for various reasons, had not been placed in medically appropriate beds on the same day they applied for them. Some were given the wrong address by a HASA worker. One person did not have money to get to the place he had been assigned. Some clients, on reaching the Holiday Inns to which they had been sent, were told there were no rooms available, probably because the hotel staff looked at their bedraggled appearance and decided not to rent the rooms to them. According to HRA, 17 people alleged that such circumstances occurred, but as some of them experienced several such incidents, there were more than 17 incidents in all. Housing Works argued that this pattern of failing to provide assistance on a timely basis was widespread at HASA.

HRA entered the contempt hearings optimistically, since even assuming that all the allegations were true (and not all of them were supported by agency records), nonetheless the large majority of the thousands of people who requested shelter got it within one day. O'Halloran said: "We would argue that we were doing pretty well."

Nevertheless, the court held Turner and Caldwell in contempt, thus in effect holding HRA to a strict liability standard in meeting the court's orders. Agency officials reported that they were willing to try and meet such an exacting test. HASA realized it has a responsibility to provide appropriate housing, and one official in the agency argued that it is not dangerous for HIV/AIDS people to spend a night in a standard shelter.

Some useful developments did come out of the legal process. For example, the court suggested that some of the clients who were turned away when they reached the hotels they had been assigned to could have been assigned elsewhere if there were an after-hours telephone number for them to call. There is such a number now. In addition, contracts with shelter providers were amended to include incentives for moving clients from shelters to private apartments. HASA has 11 contract facilities for supportive housing. They receive $1,500 for each client moved from temporary to permanent housing.

RECOMMENDATIONS

As we have seen, much of the city's homeless policy is driven by legal mandates, which—in the short term at least—cannot be changed. And as we have also seen, HRA has taken such steps as it can to either keep families out of the shelter system altogether, engage them in positive activities should they enter the homeless system, or at least make sure they are in the right homeless system. Further steps in these directions could include negotiating with the *McCain* court and advocacy groups for more leeway to impose work-related requirements on suitable families, extending of housing court liaisons to all boroughs, and contining to expand HRA's DV shelter system.

Special attention should be paid to HASA. The physical debility of many of its clients makes both engagement- and diversion-oriented strategies inappropriate for HASA. The legal mandates for virtually instantaneous placement of those with HIV/AIDS are based not on court decisions or state regulations but on New York City Council legislation. These should be challenged. If a challenge is unsuccessful and the mandate continues, reorganization of HASA so it more regularly meets the mandate seems necessary.

It is widely believed that a relative handful of mentally ill, extremely disabled, or otherwise hard-to-place clients make up a disproportionate percentage of the shelter requests to which HASA must respond. Creating an "elite" and specially trained corps of caseworkers to identify and deal with such special-need cases may be appropriate. Local schools of social work may be able to provide interns to help staff such an operation. Further, the use of civil commitment procedures for the most nonfunctional clients should be explored. Also, the process of locating hotel rooms for emergency placement can be improved by such means as having HASA make rent payments directly to the hotel (rather than to clients, from whom the hotel must then collect) and by booking rooms for busy three-day weekends far in advance.

Future HRA commissioners will continue to find homeless services to be a particularly intractable policy area, even by New York standards. Managing by muddling through, however frustrating that may be, will continue to be the order of the day.

NOTES

1. Nina Bernstein, "Homeless Shelters in New York Fill to Highest Level Since 80's," *New York Times,* February 8, 2001, A1.

2. Thomas J. Main, "Homeless Men in New York City: Toward Paternalism through Privatization" in Lawrence M. Mead, ed., *The New Paternalism: Supervisory Approaches to Poverty* (Washington, D.C.: Brookings Institution Press, 1997), 161–81.

3. *Callahan v. Carey et al.,* Supreme Court of the State of New York, New York County, Index No.: 42582/79 Final Judgment by Consent, August 26, 1981.

4. New York City, Mayor's Office on Homelessness and SRO Housing, "Revised and Updated Plan for Housing and Assisting Homeless Single Adults and Families," March 1993, 3.

5. Thomas Main, "The Homeless of New York," *Public Interest,* no. 73 (Summer 1983): 3–28.

6. Thomas Main, "Hard Lessons About Homelessness: The Education of David Dinkins," *City Journal,* Summer 1993, 30–39.

7. New York City Commission on the Homeless, Andrew M. Cuomo, chairman, *The Way Home: A New Direction in Social Policy,* February 1992, 81.

8. New York City Commission, *The Way Home,* 15.

9. Memorandum of Tom Devine, City of New York Human Resources Administration, August 17, 2001, 2.

10. Devine, Memorandum, 3.

11. City of New York, *Reengineering Municipal Services 1994-2001: Mayor's Management Report,* Fiscal 2001, 86.

12. City of New York, *Mayor's Management Report: Volume I—Agency Narratives,* Fiscal 2001, 339.

13. New York City Charter and Administrative Code, Annotated, Title 21, Sec. 21–128.

III

RESULTS OF WELFARE REFORM

11

The Welfare Revolution in New York City

June O'Neill and Sanders Korenman

The Personal Responsibility and Work Opportunity Reconciliation Act (PRWORA), enacted in 1996, marked the first true sea change in the nation's welfare system since the creation of the Aid to Families with Dependent Children (AFDC) program in 1935. It terminated AFDC and replaced it with the Temporary Assistance for Needy Families (TANF) program.

The two programs are radically different. AFDC was an entitlement, under which a family lacking the support of a father could receive assistance as long as its income remained low enough to be eligible and it included a child under the age of eighteen. Families could remain on welfare for many years. About half of those who ever went on the program eventually accumulated five or more years of welfare receipt (counting multiple spells); a third accumulated eight or more years.[1] A primary goal of the 1996 welfare reform was to reduce welfare dependence and encourage self-sufficiency. In keeping with that goal, TANF provides short-term transitional assistance. Federally funded benefits are subject to a five-year lifetime limit as an adult. And while on welfare, an increasing proportion of able-bodied adults face work requirements.

The role of state and local government has also changed. Federal funding for TANF takes the form of a block grant to each state. States now have broad authority to determine conditions of eligibility and the menu of services they will offer.

New York State, and especially New York City, traditionally has been relatively generous in providing social welfare assistance. In terms of per capita state and local spending on public welfare (public assistance plus medical and other spending on the poor), New York State on the whole has usually ranked at or near the top, spending close to twice the national average.[2] With respect to the proportion of the population on welfare, New York City has long ranked well above the rest of the state and the nation as a whole. In 1996, 10 percent of the New York City population received AFDC benefits compared to only 3 percent of the balance of New York State and 5 percent of the U.S. population as a whole.

In view of its welfare history, New York City could be expected to confront particular difficulties in implementing TANF and meeting federal requirements for work engagement of the welfare caseload.[3] Nonetheless, despite the opposition of vocal and litigious advocacy groups, the city did succeed in making significant changes in the operation of its welfare program. Welfare offices under AFDC had primarily focused on determining eligibility and paying out benefits. Under TANF the focus shifted to moving adult recipients into jobs and assisting with job-related support services, such as child care.[4] To underscore the philosophical and pragmatic changes, welfare centers were converted into Job Centers, a change that began in the spring of 1998.

New York State did not enact a plan for implementing TANF until the fall of 1997, about a year later than a majority of states. Yet, over the past several years the number of families on welfare fell dramatically in New York City, matching the decline experienced in the rest of the country (figure 11.1). Between August 1996, when PRWORA was signed into law, and December 2001, the TANF caseload declined by 52 percent in the United States as a whole while it declined by 58 percent in New York City and by 54 percent in the balance of New York State.

TANF caseload data, however, have begun to understate the total number of families receiving welfare assistance in New York and other states that are committed to providing benefits to families who have reached the five-year time limit. Such benefits are the result of state, not federal policy, and are funded by state and local governments. We do not have information on the practices of all the states in this regard. But data are available for New York, where, starting in December 2001, families began to reach the time limit and were transferred from TANF to the Safety Net Assistance program (SNA). SNA is the successor to Home Relief, a long-standing program unique to New York. Like Home Relief, it is wholly funded by state and local funds and provides benefits to childless individuals and couples ineligible for federal welfare. In addition, SNA is authorized to continue providing assistance to families reaching the TANF limit, although the assistance is in a less generous form.

If the cases transferred from TANF to SNA were counted as part of the caseload, the welfare decline in NYC would be smaller, but still impressive—

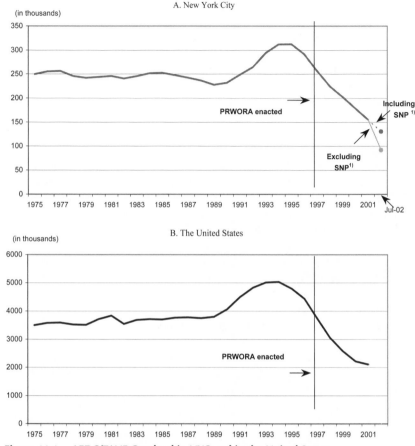

Figure 11.1. AFDC/TANF Caseload in NYC and in the United States

Sources: Caseload data shown above are the annual average number of cases in a calendar year. The New York City data are from the Office of Program Reporting, Analysis and Accountability, New York City Human Resources Administration; United States data are from the U.S. Department of Health and Human Services (HHS) Administration for Children and Families.

about a 50 percent reduction from mid-1996 to December 2001. Measured either way, however, the caseload in New York City has continued to decline since 2001 despite higher unemployment. As of December 2002, the TANF caseload had declined by 69 percent from mid-1996; counting the conversions to SNA as part of the caseload lowers that reduction to 55 percent.

The dramatic decline in the welfare caseload in NYC, as in the nation as a whole, has exceeded the predictions of most analysts. It has also raised natural questions about the corresponding changes in well-being that might have occurred as welfare participation declined. In this chapter we address some of those questions. We focus on changes in New York City among single mother families—the demographic group most strongly affected by welfare reform. Our chapter has two parts. The first provides an overview of changes in welfare and work participation and in the earnings, incomes, and poverty status that have accompanied the shrinking welfare caseload. We compare the changes that have occurred in New York City with those of all other central cities in the United States. We also address the question of the extent to which these changes can be attributed to welfare reform as opposed to the buoyant economy and low unemployment of the 1990s. This part of the study relies on data from the Current Population Survey (CPS), collected by the U.S. Bureau of the Census. Where possible we calculate annual averages from the outgoing rotation groups (ORG) of the CPS for each month of the year. Because questions on annual welfare benefits and other sources of cash and non-cash income are asked only in the March survey (for the prior calendar year), we use the March data for estimating welfare participation, family income, and poverty.

In the second part of the chapter we examine specifically the effects of time-limited benefits. Using data from a sample of NYC welfare mothers interviewed in 1996, combined with administrative data provided by the Human Resources Administration (HRA), we describe the correlates of long-term welfare use under welfare reform. We identify the characteristics of those most likely to exhaust eligibility for federal TANF assistance. In addition to describing the predictors of long-term welfare use, we examine the validity of two hypotheses regarding the exhaustion of eligibility for benefits: (1) that those who have high barriers to welfare exit tend to exhaust eligibility, and (2) that those with low incentive to leave welfare will tend to exhaust. Although the literature about the effects of time limits typically emphasizes the first explanation, we find evidence to support both hypotheses.

THE WELFARE AND WORK PARTICIPATION
OF SINGLE MOTHERS

We first turn to an examination of trends in the welfare and work participation of single mothers. The twin goals of welfare reform were to reduce welfare dependence and increase self-sufficiency through greater participation in the workforce. By those criteria, welfare reform appears to have been successful. As we can see in figure 11.2, the proportion of single mothers on welfare during the year declined sharply in New York City after 1996 while at the same time the proportion who worked climbed impressively, and by about the same amount.

The pattern and timing of change in welfare and work participation in

Figure 11.2. Work and Welfare Participation Rates of Single Mothers in New York City

Note: Percent employed and percent on welfare during the year are calculated from micro data files, CPS March Supplement (for single mothers, ages eighteen to fifty-five).

New York has been roughly similar to that experienced in the rest of the country. This point is made in figure 11.3, which compares the welfare and employment participation rates of single mothers in New York City and in all central cities of the United States during the period from 1984 through 2000.

Work participation is shown using two measures. One refers to whether a person was employed anytime during the year, a measure that is comparable to welfare participation, which is also reported on the basis of anytime during the year. The other measure refers to employment in the week before the monthly survey and is an average of responses from 12 monthly surveys. Work participation (the term we use to refer to these measures) is lower under the second measure because it is more restrictive. But the patterns of change are similar. In New York City and in all cities, the work participation of single mothers, after changing little for many years, rose dramatically starting in the mid 1990s and welfare participation declined.

It is also striking that the increase in work participation rates among single mothers is very different than the pattern of change in the work participation of other women (figure 11.4). In both New York City and other central cities in the United States, it is only single mothers who experience a sharp rise in work participation in the latter half of the 1990s. Married mothers and women without children experience only a mild and gradual increase. In fact, the increase in work participation rates is so much greater among single mothers that they rose from a level distinctly below that of other women to

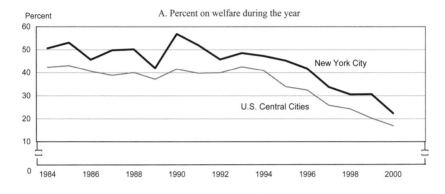

A. Percent on welfare during the year

B. Percent of single mothers who worked during the year

C. Percent of single mothers who worked last week (12 month average)

Figure 11.3.   Comparing Welfare and Work Participation Rates of Single Mothers in New York City and in All Central Cities, 1984–2001

Sources: Percent receiving welfare and percent who ever worked during the year are calculated from micro data files, CPS March, and refer to participation on the previous calendar year. The percent employed last week is based on a monthly question in the CPS, Outgoing Rotation Groups (ORG). The 12-month average of the responses is shown. Single mothers are restricted to those ages eighteen to fifty-five with children under age eighteen.

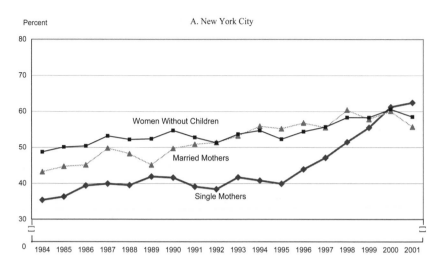

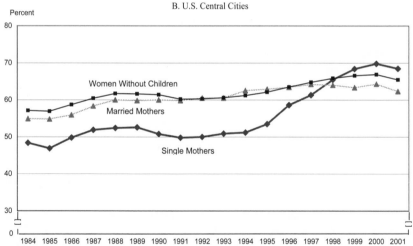

Figure 11.4.   Percent of Women Employed Last Week by Marital and Fertility Status

Sources: Calculated from micro data files, CPS Outgoing Rotation Groups (ORG), for women ages eighteen to fifty-nine. Employment is based on monthly reports of labor force status and the annual numbers show an average of the 12 months. The percent employed last week is based on a monthly question in the CPS, Outgoing Rotation Groups (ORG).

a higher rate of participation by the end of the decade. One obvious explanation for the sharp diversion in behavior between the different groups of women is that welfare reform primarily affected single mothers. That is a question to which we later return.

Despite the significant changes in New York, it remains the case that welfare participation is always higher and work participation is always lower in New York City than in other central cities. The difference in welfare participation between New York and the rest of the country ranges from 5 to 12 percent over the years 1991 to 2000 with similar differences in work participation rates.

Differences between New York and Other Central Cities

Why does New York have higher welfare participation and lower work participation? The potential candidates for explaining these differentials include the following: differences in demographic characteristics that affect the ability to earn an income (e.g., education and immigrant status); differences in the economy, such as wage rates and unemployment; and differences in welfare policy. We examine each in turn.

Characteristics

The relevant characteristics of single mothers and all women, ages twenty to fifty-five, are detailed in table 11.1 for NYC and all central cities in the United States, for the years 1995/1996 and 2000/2001.[5] The first period is the eve of the passage of national welfare reform, and the second two-year period is several years after reform was implemented in all states. The following points are noteworthy:

- The proportion of women who are single mothers is similar in NYC and all central cities in both periods. (In 2000/2001 it was 12.8 percent in NYC and 13.4 percent in all cities.) That proportion declined somewhat in both areas over the five years, although the decline was somewhat larger in NYC than in all central cities.
- Among all women the marital/fertility status and educational distributions are roughly similar in NYC and all cities. However, NYC has a much larger foreign-born population. In 2000/2001 only 53 percent of all women in NYC were native born compared to 74 percent in all central cities. (Sixty percent or more of the foreign born were noncitizens in both places.)
- With respect to racial and ethnic characteristics, the percentage of women who are black is about the same in NYC as in all central cities. The percent Hispanic is now somewhat higher in NYC—26 percent versus 22 percent; the percent Asian is 50 percent higher in NYC than in all cities but is still only 11.6 percent.
- The Hispanic origin and education of single mothers differ much more sharply between NYC and all central cities than was the case for the population of all women. Thus in 2000/2001, 37 percent of single moth-

ers in NYC were Hispanic, compared to only 22 percent in all cities. Evidently, Hispanic women in New York are more likely to become single mothers than is the case elsewhere.[6]

- Similarly, although the percentage of all women who are high school dropouts was only somewhat higher in NYC than in all cities, that percentage was 10 percentage points higher among single mothers (34 percent in NYC versus 24 percent in all cities). At the other end of the educational distribution, a much smaller percentage of single mothers are college graduates than the population at large, but women in NYC are somewhat more likely to be college graduates, whether single mothers or not.

- Single mothers in NYC are much more likely to be foreign born than single mothers in all cities. But that differential is no greater for single mothers than it was for all women.

Can differences in their characteristics account for the seemingly higher proportion of single mothers on welfare and the lower proportion working in NYC than in other central cities? We later address that question with multivariate regression analysis. But a preliminary and negative answer is suggested in tables 11.2 and 11.3.

Table 11.2 shows the percent of single mothers receiving welfare in NYC and in all cities at different levels of education and for different racial/ethnic and nativity/citizenship groups. Within each category, the percent of single mothers on welfare is almost always higher in NYC than elsewhere in both 1995/1996 and 2000/2001.[7] The NYC/all-cities differential is particularly large among Hispanics and high school dropouts, the two groups with unusually high participation in welfare overall. Between 1995/1996 and 1999/2000, however, the welfare participation of Hispanic single mothers and mothers who are high school dropouts declined considerably. That decline was larger in NYC when measured in percentage point differences, and about the same in both places when measured as the percent change in the percentages. (See table 11.2.)

The story with respect to employment is generally similar. As shown in table 11.3, even within demographic groups, the percentage of single mothers who work remains lower in New York City than in all cities. (The exceptions are for white non-Hispanic women and college graduates, two groups with almost the same employment rates in 2000/2001.) Again, Hispanic women and high school dropouts made the largest gains in New York City, increasing their work participation by 91 percent and 120 percent, respectively. These huge gains reduced but did not eliminate the differential in employment rates between single mothers in New York and in all central cities.

Table 11.1.   Characteristics of All Women and Single Mothers in New York City and in All Central Cities

| | 1995/1996 | | 2000/2001 | |
	NYC	All Central Cities	NYC	All Central Cities
All Women				
Marital/Fertility Status				
Married mother	20.8	23.0	21.9	23.1
Married, no children	33.6	36.5	35.4	37.7
Single mother	15.3	14.7	12.8	13.4
Single, no children	30.3	25.8	29.9	25.8
Race/Ethnicity				
Hispanic	27.3	19.2	26.3	21.6
Black, non-Hispanic	26.5	27.3	25.7	25.6
White, non-Hispanic	38.0	47.1	36.1	44.4
Asian	7.6	5.6	11.6	7.7
Others	0.6	0.8	0.3	0.7
Education				
High school dropout	21.3	19.0	19.8	17.7
High school graduate	33.0	31.1	29.0	29.6
Some college	22.0	29.5	23.3	29.1
College graduate	23.7	20.4	27.9	23.6
Nativity/Citizenship				
Native born	59.3	78.8	53.0	74.4
Foreign born, citizen	12.3	5.3	18.6	8.7
Foreign born, not a citizen	28.5	15.9	28.4	16.9
Single Mothers				
Race/Ethnicity				
Hispanic	39.6	19.9	37.4	21.5
Black, non-Hispanic	44.2	49.1	41.9	46.8
White, non-Hispanic	14.2	28.4	17.0	28.0
Asian	1.6	1.6	3.6	3.0
Others	0.4	0.9	0.1	0.8
Education				
High school dropout	35.3	26.0	33.6	23.5
High school graduate	33.7	34.4	27.5	35.2
Some college	21.6	30.5	26.3	31.2
College graduate	9.3	9.1	12.6	10.1
Nativity/Citizenship				
Native born	63.0	85.7	58.1	83.3
Foreign born, citizen	9.5	3.0	17.0	5.4
Foreign born, not a citizen	27.5	11.3	25.0	11.3

Source: Calculated from micro data files, CPS Outgoing Rotation Groups. Population refers to women ages eighteen to fifty-five. Percentage distributions shown above are weighted.

Table 11.2. Percent of Single Mothers Who Received Welfare during the Year in New York City and in All Central Cities, by Race, Education, and Citizenship

| | 1995/1996 | | 1999–2000 | | Change: 1999/2000–1995/1996 | | | |
| | | | | | Percentage Point Change | | Percent Change | |
	NYC	All Central Cities	NYC	All Central Cities	NYC	All Central Cities	NYC	All Central Cities
All Single Mothers	43.5	33.3	27.0	18.8	−16.5	−14.5	−37.9	−43.5
Race/Ethinicity[1]								
Hispanic	56.7	39.8	36.4	24.4	−20.3	−15.4	−35.8	−38.7
Black, non-Hispanic	41.9	37.4	25.2	21.0	−16.7	−16.4	−39.9	−43.9
White, non-Hispanic	18.4	22.3	12.4	10.7	−6.0	−11.6	−32.6	−52.0
Education								
High school dropout	67.5	51.5	44.8	34.4	−22.7	−17.1	−33.6	−33.2
High school graduate	34.4	31.9	23.1	17.8	−11.3	−14.1	−32.8	−44.2
One year college or more	26.0	20.9	13.3	10.3	−12.7	−10.6	−48.8	−50.7
Nativity/Citizenship								
Native born	45.8	33.4	27.7	18.6	−18.1	−14.8	−39.5	−44.3
Foreign born, citizen	37.2	29.1	21.1	16.8	−16.1	−12.3	−43.3	−42.3
Foreign born, not a citizen	41.2	33.9	27.9	19.7	−13.3	−14.2	−32.3	−41.9

Source: Calculated from micro data files, CPS March for single mothers ages eighteen to fifty-five.
[1] Women reporting a race other than those enumerated are not shown separately because of sample size limitations. They are, however, included in the totals and other categories.

The Economic Environment: Unemployment and Wage Rates

The economic environment in NYC is not obviously more or less favorable to the work participation of single mothers than other places. The unemployment rate in New York City and in New York State was higher than in the United States as a whole during the 1990s, but lower in much of the 1980s (figure 11.5). In contrast to the economy as a whole, the recession of the early 1990s appears to have had a larger negative impact on New York than the 1982 recession. Although unemployment ultimately declined sharply in New York in the late 1990s, the rate never returned to the lows of the late 1980s. However, the late 1980s saw little change in either the work or welfare participation of single mothers, suggesting that the low unemployment of the 1990s is not likely to be the major factor underlying the work and welfare changes of the 1990s.

Wage rates, another potentially important impetus for work participation, are higher in NYC than nationwide.[8] As shown in figure 11.6, hourly wages

Table 11.3.   Percent of Single Mothers Who Were Employed Last Week in NYC and in All Central Cities, by Race, Education, and Citizenship

| | | | | | *Change: 2000/2001–1995/1996* | | | |
| | *1995/1996* | | *2000–2001* | | *Percentage Point Change* | | *Percent Change* | |
	NYC	*All Central Cities*	NYC	*All Central Cities*	NYC	*All Central Cities*	NYC	*All Central Cities*
All Single Mothers	42.1	56.1	61.8	69.3	19.7	13.2	46.8	23.5
Race/Ethinicity[1]								
Hispanic	29.8	45.4	56.1	63.1	26.3	17.7	88.3	39.0
Black, non-Hispanic	47.1	54.0	60.6	67.9	13.5	13.9	28.7	25.7
White, non-Hispanic	59.9	67.6	77.7	76.7	17.8	8.9	29.7	13.5
Asian	—	51.0	—	68.3	—	17.3	—	33.9
Education								
High school drop.	18.8	31.3	40.9	49.4	22.1	18.1	117.6	57.8
High school grad.	48.6	56.6	62.1	68.5	13.5	11.9	27.8	21.0
Some college	55.3	68.4	75.5	79.8	20.2	11.4	36.5	16.7
College graduate	78.8	88.9	89.2	88.3	10.4	−0.6	13.2	−0.7
Nativity/Citizenship								
Native born	41.1	57.1	60.9	69.9	19.8	12.8	48.2	22.4
Foreign born, citizen	61.4	66.5	76.8	80.4	15.4	13.9	25.1	20.9
Foreign born, not a citizen	37.9	45.3	54.0	59.2	16.1	13.9	42.5	30.7

Source: Calculated from microdata files, CPS outgoing rotation groups (ORG) for single mothers ages eighteen to fifty-five.

[1] Single mothers reporting a race other than those enumerated are not shown separately because of sample size limitations. They are, however, included in the totals and other categories. The employment rate is not given for Asians when the sample size in a category was below 50.

have been higher in NYC than in all central cities for all women and single mothers over the entire period from 1984 to 2001. Moreover, the wage premium in NYC is not due to the educational mix. As demonstrated in table 11.4, the wage rate is higher in NYC at all education levels for all women, single women, and for men.

At the high school dropout level the hourly wage rate of single mothers in NYC declined somewhat between 1995/1996 and 2000/2001, although it was still 8 percent higher than the wage for the same group in other cities. However, that decline may be the result of a surge of less-educated single mothers into the workforce in NYC during those years. The work participation of single mothers who were high school dropouts increased by 120 percent over this period, implying a relatively large increase in new entrants. Because new entrants generally start at lower pay than would be received by experienced workers, a large increase in their numbers would have put downward pres-

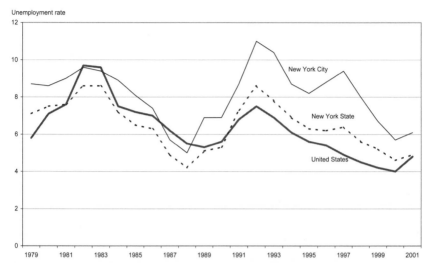

Figure 11.5.   Annual Unemployment Rate in NYC, NY State, and the United States.

Source: Data are from Local Area Unemployment Statistics, the U.S. Bureau of Labor Statistics.

sure on the pay of high school dropouts. At all other levels of schooling the wage rate of single mothers rose in NYC as well as in all cities.

Welfare Policy

As we have seen, the characteristics of single mothers and the economic environment are different in New York City than they are in other cities, and the strength of those differences has varied over time. It is more difficult to measure policy differences between New York and other cities. Although TANF was eventually implemented nationwide, states, and cities within states, frequently operate their programs very differently. It would be a formidable task to measure those differences with any degree of accuracy.[9]

One policy variable that is more easily measured is the size of the welfare benefit available in each state for a family with no other income. The basic benefit in both AFDC and its successor, TANF, historically has been higher in New York than in most other states and remains so. In 2000, the maximum welfare grant for a family of three in New York City was 37 percent above that of the median state in the United States. However, food stamp benefits are income related and as a result partly compensate for the lower welfare benefit in low benefit states. Still, the maximum benefit from welfare and food stamps combined in New York City was 22 percent above that of the median state (again in 2000 for a family of three). It is possible that cities with relatively generous benefits would also adopt less restrictive policies

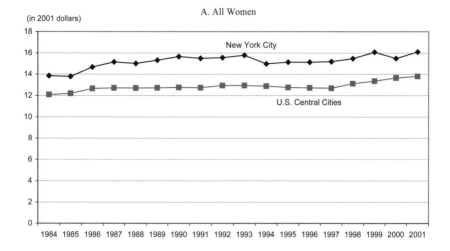

A. All Women

(in 2001 dollars)

New York City

U.S. Central Cities

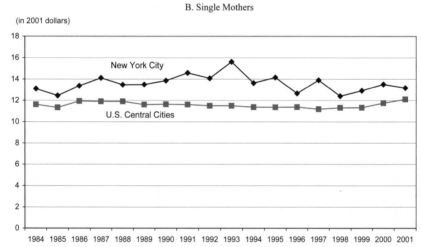

B. Single Mothers

(in 2001 dollars)

New York City

U.S. Central Cities

Figure 11.6. Hourly Wage Rates of All Working Women and of Working Single Mothers, Ages Twenty to Fifty-five

Source: Calculated from micro data files, CPS Outgoing Rotation Groups.
Note: Hourly wage rates including workers paid hourly and weekly.

Table 11.4. Mean Hourly Wage of All Women, Single Mothers, and Men by Education (in 2001 dollars)

| | 1995/1996 | | 2000/2001 | | Ratio: NYC/All Central Cities | |
	NYC	All Central Cities	NYC	All Central Cities	1995/ 1996	2000/ 2001
All Women						
Total	**15.13**	**12.74**	**15.79**	**13.72**	**1.19**	**1.15**
High School Dropout	8.60	7.76	8.75	8.20	1.11	1.07
High School Graduate	11.60	10.30	11.75	11.00	1.13	1.07
One year college or more	18.55	15.02	19.42	16.30	1.24	1.19
Some college	13.79	12.05	13.72	12.87	1.14	1.07
College graduate	22.50	19.15	24.08	20.64	1.17	1.17
Single Mothers						
Total	**13.35**	**11.36**	**13.34**	**11.92**	**1.18**	**1.12**
High School Dropout	9.17	7.62	8.80	8.17	1.20	1.08
High School Graduate	11.42	9.83	12.06	10.46	1.16	1.15
One year college or more	16.44	13.48	15.90	14.26	1.22	1.12
All Men						
Total	**16.97**	**15.35**	**18.52**	**17.02**	**1.11**	**1.09**
High School Dropout	9.83	9.60	10.22	10.23	1.02	1.00
High School Graduate	14.75	12.92	14.54	13.76	1.14	1.06
One year college or more	20.57	18.54	23.15	20.84	1.11	1.11
Some college	15.33	14.65	15.82	15.70	1.05	1.01
College graduate	24.36	22.79	27.98	25.77	1.07	1.09

Source: CPS monthly data for the Outgoing Rotation Groups (ORG).
Note: The hourly wage is the reported wage for those paid by the hour, and it is estimated for those paid on another basis using reported usual weekly earnings and usual weekly hours. Population refers to those aged twenty to fifty-five.

concerning aspects of benefit eligibility. In the regression analysis reported below, we explore the role of policy differences in accounting for differential welfare and work participation between New York City and other cities.

Higher Welfare Participation and Lower Work Participation

To what extent can policy differences as opposed to differences in the economy or in personal characteristics explain why single mothers living in New York City are more likely to receive welfare and less likely to work than single mothers in other central cities? We approach these questions using multiple regression analysis to control for various factors expected to influence welfare and work participation. The explanatory variables fall into three categories: (1) demographic characteristics that might affect the ability of single mothers to become self-sufficient (e.g., age, race, Hispanic origin, education, number and ages of children); (2) differences in the local economy that could affect the ability to earn an income (unemployment and wage rates); and (3) the level of welfare benefits. By controlling for these variables we can determine whether the welfare participation of single mothers in New York City remains significantly higher than elsewhere, even when we compare similarly situated women with respect to demographic and economic characteristics, the state of the local economy, and benefit levels. A significant remaining differential would suggest that unmeasured policy factors encourage welfare participation in New York City. A similar procedure is followed for analyzing employment differences.

The Differential in Welfare Participation

For the analysis of welfare participation we use the March Current Population Survey (CPS) micro data and conduct a series of cross-sectional regressions for each year from 1993 through 2000. The regressions therefore cover several years before and after the replacement of AFDC with TANF. This allows us to observe whether the effect of living in New York City on welfare participation has changed over time and if the implementation of TANF coincides with any such change.

The sample population is restricted to single mothers with children under age eighteen, living in central cities. (There are about 1300 to 1800 single mothers in the sample each year.) The dependent variable is a binary variable indicating whether or not a single mother received welfare during the year. The effect of living in New York, the explanatory variable of major interest, is measured as a binary variable indicating whether or not the single mother is living in New York City. The analysis uses weighted linear regression, where the weights have been rescaled to the original sample size.

The results for each year, 1993–2000, are depicted in table 11.5. As shown in the first column, the welfare participation rate of single mothers living in central cities other than New York declined from 41 percent in 1993 to 16 percent in 2000. The unadjusted difference in the welfare participation rate between New York City and all other central cities—which we will refer to as the "New York differential"—is positive and statistically significant each year, ranging from 7 to 13 percentage points above the average for other cities (column 2). The next three columns show the effect on the New York differential of adding groups of variables. Thus column 3 shows the effect of adjusting for the demographic variables, column 4 adds the economic variables, and column 5 includes all of the preceding variables plus the value of the combined welfare/food stamp benefit.

Table 11.5. Explaining the Relatively High Welfare Participation in New York City: Percentage Point Difference between New York City and All Other Central Cities in the Probability of Receiving Welfare Benefits during a Year

		New York differential after adjusting for:		
Year	*% on welfare in other central cities*	*Observed (Unadjusted) New York Differential*	*Characteristics only[1]*	*Unemployment, wage rates, and characteristics*	*Combined welfare/ food stamp benefit level, unemployment, wage rates, and characteristics*
1993	41.2	9.8***	9.4***	7.0**	5.3
1994	39.7	8.7**	9.0***	5.8	3.1
1995	32.6	11.3***	10.7***	8.0**	6.3*
1996	31.3	9.1***	7.7**	5.6	7.6
1997	24.7	9.7***	10.0***	7.8**	4.3
1998	23.4	7.7**	8.6***	5.2	1.9
1999	18.5	13.1***	10.5***	8.2**	4.3
2000	16.0	7.4**	6.2**	3.3	3.2

[1] Individual characteristics include age, race, Hispanic origin, immigration/citizenship, education, marital status, and number and ages of children as reported in March of the following year.

Source: Derived from multiple regression analysis of a sample of approximately 1300 to 1800 single mothers in the March Current Population Survey (CPS) each year. Receipt of welfare is reported in the CPS for the prior calendar year.

Note: Restricted to single mothers ages eighteen to fifty-nine, with children under eighteen in March of the following year. The year listed is the year of welfare receipt. Results shown are based on weighted sample data. Starred figures denote that the differential is statistically significant at the following level:

* 10 percent level;
** 5 percent level;
*** 1 percent level.

The results shown in table 11.5 indicate that demographic characteristics account for little of the New York differential. In fact, in three of the years the characteristics of single mothers in New York are less likely to be associated with welfare participation, and adjustment for them widens the differential. However, the inclusion of area unemployment and wage rates more strongly reduces the New York differential, leaving it statistically insignificant in half of the years. When the benefit level is also added to the set of explanatory variables, the New York differential is reduced further, and remains statistically significant in only one year (1995). The difference falls essentially to zero in the last two years, 1999 and 2000. The pattern of results suggests that policy differences as measured by benefit levels have been an important reason for New York's relatively high welfare caseloads over the years. However, unmeasured policy differences may be correlated with benefit levels and help account for that effect. Nonetheless, an effect of zero in the last two years is at least suggestive of a TANF-related change in the differential.

The Differential in Work Participation

We follow a similar procedure for analyzing the determinants of work participation. However, our data set for work participation is the CPS outgoing rotation group file (CPS ORG), which contains data for each month of the year.[10] The sample size is considerably larger and includes 3900 to 4700 single mothers each year. Our dependent variable is a binary variable indicating whether or not a single mother was employed last week. The explanatory variables are defined as in the welfare analysis. The results of the work participation analysis are displayed in table 11.6 for each year from 1994 through 2001.

The percentage of single mothers employed in central cities other than New York increased from 53 percent in 1994 to 71.1 percent in 2000 and then declined to 69.5 percent in the 2001 recession year (column 1). Before any adjustment, the percent of single mothers who work was substantially lower in New York than in other central cities from 1994 through 1999, a statistically significant differential of about 14 to 18 percentage points (col-

Table 11.6.   Explaining the Relatively Low Work Participation in New York City: Percentage Point Difference between New York City and All Other Central Cities in the Probability of Employment during the Prior Survey Week

			New York differential after adjusting for:		
Year	% employed in other central cities	Observed (Unadjusted) Differential	Characteristics only[1]	Unemployment, wage rates, and characteristics	Combined welfare/ food stamp benefit level, unemployment, wage rates, and characteristics
1994	53.0	−13.6***	−12.8***	−11.7***	−7.7***
1995	55.6	−16.3***	−13.5***	−8.5***	−6.5**
1996	61.0	−17.9***	−13.8***	−12.1***	−10.0***
1997	63.4	−16.4***	−13.9***	−11.6***	−11.8***
1998	67.7	−18.1***	−15.1***	−13.9***	−12.7***
1999	70.4	−16.7***	−13.5***	−12.3***	−12.0***
2000	71.1	−11.0***	−8.0***	−8.4***	−5.8**
2001	69.5	−7.8***	−6.9***	−6.8***	−5.2*

[1] Individual characteristics include age, race, Hispanic origin, immigration/citizenship, education, marital status, and number and ages of children as updated in March of the following year.
Source: Derived from multiple regression analysis of a sample of approximately 3900 to 4700 single mothers in the March Current Population Survey (CPS) each year.
Note: Restricted to single mothers ages eighteen to fifty-nine, with children under eighteen in current survey month of CPS Outgoing Rotation Groups (ORG). Results shown are based on weighted sample data. Starred figures denote that the differential is statistically significant at the following levels:
    * 10 percent level;
  ** 5 percent level;
*** 1 percent level.

umn 2). That differential declined to 11 percentage points in 2000 and about 8 in 2001. Differences in the characteristics of single mothers account for a portion of the New York employment differential, reducing it by less than 20 percent in most years (column 2). The differential is further reduced after accounting for unemployment and wage rate differences (column 3), and declines again with adjustment for differences in the combined welfare/food stamp benefit level (column 4).

Even after accounting for differences in characteristics, the economy, and benefit levels, however, the work participation of single mothers remains lower in New York than in other central cities and that remaining difference is statistically significant and substantively large in most years. It is particularly substantial in the period 1997–1999, the first years of implementation of welfare reform, but greatly narrows in 2000 and 2001, when the statistical significance of the effect also fades. This pattern may reflect the fact that New York was slower to implement reform than other states and that the provisions adopted were more lenient than those adopted in other states. (For example, New York imposes milder sanctions than many other states and will in many instances continue to pay benefits of needy families who exhaust their federal benefits.)

In New York City there was considerable opposition to reform. Welfare rights advocates attempted to go through the courts to block changes in the administration of the welfare program planned by the Giuliani Administration. For example, the plaintiffs in the case of *Lakisha Reynolds et al. v. Giuliani* sought to derail the conversion of Income Support Centers—the old welfare offices—into Job Centers.[11] The conversion represented a philosophical as well as an organizational change. Eventually the Human Resources Administration (HRA) was given judicial approval to fully implement its plans, but only with substantial delay. It may be that welfare exits and work participation accelerated once the welfare commissioner in New York City gained more control over the process.

The results of the employment analysis are roughly consistent with this explanation, showing a convergence of employment between New York and other cities in 2000, with virtually no difference in 1999 and 2000, once all the measured factors are taken into account. The welfare participation results are more erratic than the employment results, however, in part because the CPS March samples of single mothers are relatively small compared to those in the CPS ORG, which was the basis for the work participation analysis. Moreover, the measure of welfare participation is a weaker one as it is based on the receipt of welfare over during the preceding year. Work participation is measured each month and is based on current behavior.

The Effect of Welfare Reform on Welfare and Work Participation

The pattern and timing of changes in both the welfare and work participation of single mothers suggest that welfare reform was a major factor spurring these changes in New York City and in other cities. Other factors, however, such as the decline in unemployment during the 1990s and the increase in the size of the Earned Income Tax Credit (EITC) for low-income families are also likely to have played a role. We therefore turn to multiple regression analysis to estimate the net effect of welfare reform. The regression analysis spans the period 1984–2000, and separate analyses are conducted for New York and for all other central cities.

Our analysis first addresses the question: Other things the same, what is the effect of PRWORA on the probability that a single mother is on welfare? "Other things" that could have a significant impact on welfare or work participation include changes in the unemployment rate, wage rate, and the AFDC (TANF)/food stamp benefit level in the mother's state of residence; the value of the Earned Income Tax Credit (EITC); the mother's demographic characteristics (her age, race, number and ages of children, and education); and a time trend. We conduct a similar analysis of the probability that a single mother is employed. The strategy of the analysis is to measure the extent to which welfare or work participation differs in the years after 1996 from the years before 1996 after controlling for those factors that might have changed during the same time period and that could be expected to have some effect on welfare or work.[12]

The results (displayed in table 11.7) show that welfare reform, as measured by a "dummy" variable indicating the years when PRWORA was operative, had a strong negative effect on welfare participation in both New York City and in other cities. Passage of PRWORA was associated with a 16 percentage point reduction in the welfare participation rate in New York City and a 10 percentage point reduction in other cities (both effects statistically significant at the 1 percent level). These are very large effects suggesting that enactment of PRWORA was a key factor in the decline in welfare participation. (The total decline in the welfare participation rate of single mothers between 1996 and 2000 was 19.4 percentage points in New York City and 15.5 percentage points in other cities.) Changes in the unemployment rate apparently had no significant effect on welfare participation in New York. However, in other central cities, a 1 percentage point increase in the unemployment rate was associated with a 0.7 percentage point increase in the welfare participation rate, and in years in which the level of unemployment was below 5 percent, welfare participation was about 3 percentage points lower than in years in which the level was higher. These results, although statistically significant and larger than those for New York City, still indicate a much more modest effect of unemployment than of welfare reform on welfare participation in the 1996–2000 period.[13]

The passage of PRWORA appears to have played a smaller role in the rise in work participation of single mothers in New York than it did in the

Table 11.7. Estimated Impact of PRWORA and Unemployment on the Welfare/Work Participation of Single Mothers in New York City and in All Other Central Cities, 1984–2001

	Welfare Participation[1]		Work Participation[2]	
	New York City	All Other Central Cities	New York City	All Other Central Cities
Percentage Point Change in Welfare/Work Participation Associated with a Unit Change in:				
PRWORA (a variable including if the year [month] was post-August 1996)	−16.1***	−10.4***	4.0*	5.9***
Unemployment				
unemployment rate (%)	0.3	0.7**	−0.7	−1.1***
unemployment rate is less than 5.0%	0.4	−3.4***	2.2	2.8***
unemployment rate is more than 7.5%	0.1	−0.7	−0.1	0.3
Mean participation rate (%)	*50.2*	*35.0*	*42.7*	*57.4*
Sample size	*4,974*	*28,153*	*10,328*	*70,082*

[1] The welfare model controls for the following variables in addition to PRWORA and unemployment: demographic characteristics (the mother's age, age and number of children, education, and race), hourly rates of pay for women with high school or less and for more than high school in the state, AFDC/food stamp benefit level, EITC max for a one-child and for a two-child (or more) family, and a time trend. For the U.S. central cities excluding NYC, we control for state fixed effects and trend interactions as well. The data are from micro data files of the March CPS, 1983–2001, referring to welfare receipt in calendar years 1982–2000. The sample population is restricted to single mothers ages eighteen to fifty-nine with children under age eighteen.

[2] The employment model controls for the same variables as the welfare model noted above. The data are from micro data files of the CPS ORG, 1984–2001. The sample population is restricted to single mothers ages eighteen to fifty-nine with children under age eighteen. Employment status and characteristics are monthly observations for each year in each locality.
*statistically significant at the 10% level;
**statistically significant at the 5% level;
***statistically significant at the 1% level.

decline in their welfare participation. The percent of single mothers working increased by 18 percentage points between 1996 and 2001. The regression results reported in table 11.7 indicate a 4 percentage-point increase associated with the passage of PRWORA, which would account for about a quarter of the actual increase. The effect of unemployment is not statistically significant in New York and would in any event account for a very small share of the actual rise in employment. The regression results for other U.S. cities indicate that PRWORA raised the work participation rate of single mothers by 6 percentage points, which would account for 60 percent of the

10 percentage-point rise in work participation actually attained between 1996 and 2001. The effect of lower unemployment in other cities is statistically significant and relatively substantial as it can account for about one-third of the rise in work participation among single mothers in the post-PRWORA years.

In interpreting the results of table 11.7, it should be kept in mind that it can be difficult to account statistically for changes in one variable, such as welfare or work participation, when a number of plausible explanatory factors are changing at the same time. Some variables may have lagged effects; others (for example, PRWORA) may have anticipatory effects; and many are difficult to measure accurately. Measurement is particularly difficult when it comes to the precise contents and actual timing of the effective implementation of welfare reform as undertaken in different cities in different states. Nevertheless, while the contribution of welfare reform to the welfare participation and employment gains of single mothers probably cannot be determined precisely, the results of our analysis are consistent with other evidence we have examined. The many charts and tables show the unprecedented changes in the employment (and welfare participation) of single mothers during a period when welfare policy was radically transformed.

CHANGES IN THE ECONOMIC WELL-BEING OF SINGLE MOTHERS

The immediate goal of welfare reform—to reduce welfare reliance and increase the work participation of single mothers—seems to have been realized in New York. In these respects, New York appears to have made at least as much progress as other central cities. But to be fully successful the expectation has always been that the transition would result in higher incomes and a reduction in poverty for families that left welfare, as well as for those who might have gone on welfare if not for the reform. We examine the changes in poverty and in household income and its components among single mothers in New York City and compare the results with those in all U.S. cities.

Poverty

Single mothers and their families historically have been much more likely to be in poverty than married-couple families with children. That difference is as evident in New York City as it is in all U.S. cities (figure 11.7). In 1996, 50.3 percent of single-mother households in New York were in poverty based on the standard definition that includes as income only cash income sources. The comparable poverty rate for two-parent households in New York was 10.6 percent.

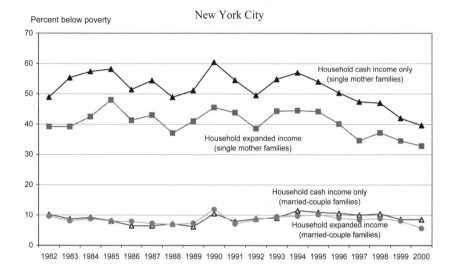

New York City

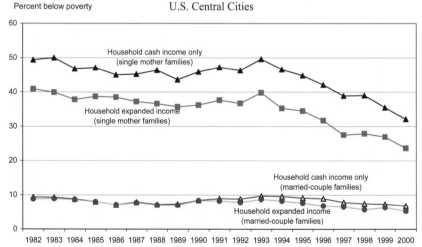

U.S. Central Cities

Figure 11.7.   Poverty Rates (under two definitions) of Single Mother and Married-Couple Families in New York City and in All Central Cities, 1982–2000

Note: Calculated from micro data files, March CPS. Mothers are restricted to those ages eighteen to fifty-five with own children under eighteen years of age. Non-cash income is based on Census Bureau valuations and includes employer contributions for health insurance, housing subsidies, food stamps, school lunch, Medicare, and Medicaid. The value of the EITC is included, and estimated tax payments (federal and state) are subtracted out.

Table 11.8.   Poverty Rates (in Percent) of Single Mother Families and Married-Couple Families in New York City and in All Central Cities, 1993/1994, 1995/1996, 2000/2001

| | 1993/1994 | | 1995/1996 | | 2000/2001 | | *Change: 2000/2001–1995/1996* | | | |
| | | | | | | | *Percentage Point Change* | | *Percent Change* | |
	NYC	*All Central Cities*	NYC	*All Central Cities*	NYC	*All Central Cities*	NYC	*All Central Cities*	NYC	*All Central Cities*
Single mother families (with own children under 18)										
based on household cash income only	55.8	48.1	52.1	43.4	40.8	33.8	−11.3	−9.6	−21.7	−22.1
based on household cash income after taxes plus non-cash benefits	41.4	35.5	38.3	31.1	30.8	23.8	−7.5	−7.3	−19.6	−23.5
Married-couple families (with own children under 18)										
based on household cash income only	10.3	9.6	10.7	9.0	8.5	7.0	−2.2	−2.0	−20.6	−22.2
based on household cash income after taxes plus non-cash benefits	9.6	8.4	9.5	7.2	6.8	5.8	−2.7	−1.4	−28.4	−19.4

Source: Micro data files, March CPS for women ages eighteen to fifty-five.

Note: Net taxes paid include federal income tax, state income tax, social security payroll tax, and EITC. Non-cash benefits include the following: employer contributions to health insurance, market value of housing subsidy, market value of food stamps, market value of school lunch, fungible value of Medicare, fungible value of Medicaid, and the amount of energy assistance. Estimates of the value of non-cash benefits and the taxes paid are based on Census valuations reported in the CPS.

At the time of passage of PRWORA many feared that the poverty status of single mothers would worsen as they left welfare and were unable to find jobs paying enough to compensate for lost welfare benefits. Fortunately that did not happen. Welfare participation plummeted, but as we show below, income associated with increased employment and other sources grew and more than compensated for the lost welfare benefits. Consequently, poverty declined among the households of single mothers in New York City and in all central cities. As shown in figure 11.7, their poverty rates declined considerably below the levels reached during the boom of the late 1980s or any other year since 1982.[14] The decline is evident whether poverty status is based on cash income only—the "official" definition—or whether it is based on an expanded definition of income that includes the estimated value of non-cash benefits and the EITC and also adjusts for federal and state taxes paid. Poverty declined more moderately among married-couple families with children after 1994, not surprising in view of the expanding economy. The decline for two-parent families, however, appears to be more of a cyclical phenomenon and does not dip much below levels attained in the past.

Despite the strong reduction in poverty among single mothers in New York City, their poverty rates remain higher than those of single mothers in other cities. Between 1995/1996 (averaged to enlarge sample size) and 1999/2000 the poverty rate (cash income definition) of single mothers in New York declined from about 52 percent to 41 percent (table 11.8). That was a decline of 11 percentage points or, expressed as a percent, a 22 percent decline in the poverty rate. Although the percentage point difference between New York and other cities narrowed somewhat, the poverty rate in New York City was still 7 points above the rate in all central cities. Presumably the higher poverty rates in New York City stem from the higher rates of welfare participation and lower employment rates of single mothers in New York.

Changes in Cash and Non-Cash Sources of Income

The dramatic changes in welfare and work participation among single mothers during the 1990s were likely to produce changes in the composition of their own income and of that of the households they share with others. We examine these changes in the composition of income of single mothers in New York City and in all central cities in tables 11.9, 11.10, and 11.11.

The total household income of single mothers can change because the likelihood of a mother receiving earnings, welfare, and other sources of income changes, and because the amount received by recipients of each income source changes. Total household income is also strongly influenced by changes in the composition of the household and the incomes of other household members. Young single mothers frequently live with a parent or grandparent. It has also become more common for single mothers to live with a male partner.

Cash Income

We begin by decomposing the single mother's own cash income, looking at the details for 1993/1994, 1995/1996, and 1999/2000 (table 11.9). The following trends are notable:

- The percentage of single mothers reporting earnings in New York City increased dramatically, from 46 percent in 1993/1994 to 69 percent in

Table 11.9. Changes in the Receipt, Amount, and Share of Single Mother's Own Annual Cash Income and Its Components: Single Mothers (Ages Eighteen to Fifty-five) Living in New York City and in All Central Cities (Income in 2001 dollars)

| | Percent receiving income from source | | | | | | Mean amount received by recipients | | | | | |
| | 1993/1994 | | 1995/1996 | | 1999/2000 | | 1993/1994 | | 1995/1996 | | 1999/2000 | |
	NYC	All Central Cities	NYC	All Central Cities	NYC	All Central Cities	NYC	All Central Cities	NYC	All Central Cities	NYC	All Central Cities
Income Source:												
Earnings	45.8	62.1	50.6	67.1	69.2	79.1	23,561	18,811	24,750	19,623	21,819	20,624
EITC[1]	29.0	44.2	33.4	49.7	48.8	59.1	1,376	1,398	1,731	1,957	1,931	2,069
Welfare	48.0	41.8	43.5	33.3	26.6	18.7	5,739	4,978	5,232	4,823	3,826	3,789
SSI/Social Security	5.7	6.3	5.6	5.4	5.6	5.1	5,616	5,346	7,027	6,061	7,044	5,674
Child support[2]	14.1	20.2	13.0	22.4	16.6	23.6	5,110	4,496	6,541	4,692	4,161	4,376
Other cash income	32.0	38.1	33.4	38.1	32.6	37.1	4,137	3,524	4,044	3,474	3,670	3,186
Any cash including EITC	**94.9**	**95.3**	**93.8**	**94.7**	**93.2**	**94.0**	**17,181**	**17,812**	**19,152**	**19,485**	**20,743**	**22,067**

(continues)

Table 11.9. Continued

| Income Source: | Mean cash income including those with zero income from source | | | | | | Share of aggregate cash income from cash source | | | | | |
| | 1993/1994 | | 1995/1996 | | 1999/2000 | | 1993/1994 | | 1995/1996 | | 1999/2000 | |
	NYC	All Central Cities	NYC	All Central Cities	NYC	All Central Cities	NYC	All Central Cities	NYC	All Central Cities	NYC	All Central Cities
Earnings	10,782	11,689	12,525	13,172	15,096	16,308	66.1	68.8	69.7	71.4	78.1	78.6
EITC[1]	398	617	577	972	943	1,224	2.4	3.6	3.2	5.3	4.9	5.9
Welfare	2,754	2,082	2,274	1,605	1,019	707	16.9	12.3	12.7	8.7	5.3	3.4
SSI/Social Security	320	337	392	324	395	289	2.0	2.0	2.2	1.8	2.0	1.4
Child support[2]	722	909	853	1,051	692	1,032	4.4	5.4	4.7	5.7	3.6	5.0
Other cash income	1,325	1,343	1,351	1,322	1,196	1,183	8.1	7.9	7.5	7.2	6.2	5.7
Any cash including EITC	**16,302**	**16,978**	**17,973**	**18,447**	**19,341**	**20,743**	**100.0**	**100.0**	**100.0**	**100.0**	**100.0**	**100.0**

[1] EITC excludes NY supplement to EITC.
[2] Item includes alimony.
Source: Calculated from micro data files, March CPS.

Table 11.10. Non-Cash Benefits Received by Single Mother Households in New York City and in All Central Cities (Income in 2001 dollars)

| | Percent receiving non-cash from source | | | | | | Mean amount received by recipients | | | | | |
| | 1993/1994 | | 1995/1996 | | 1999/2000 | | 1993/1994 | | 1995/1996 | | 1999/2000 | |
	NYC	All Central Cities	NYC	All Central Cities	NYC	All Central Cities	NYC	All Central Cities	NYC	All Central Cities	NYC	All Central Cities
Income Source:												
Energy Assistance	21.1	14.7	9.2	9.7	7.1	7.2	139	273	122	231	159	277
Food stamps	55.2	52.7	49.4	44.6	37.9	30.5	3,018	2,827	2,864	2,788	2,424	2,383
School lunch	63.9	65.1	70.2	66.0	68.1	63.7	646	580	556	552	550	512
Medicare	4.0	5.4	7.6	5.4	7.2	6.9	4,322	4,700	4,794	4,916	6,768	6,063
Medicaid	33.8	32.5	30.5	31.7	31.3	28.1	4,780	3,600	4,010	3,413	4,340	3,096
Housing subsidy	34.9	24.0	34.9	21.2	36.2	20.9	2,520	2,277	2,619	2,223	2,493	2,043
Empoyer contribution to health insurance	29.0	34.7	31.9	40.0	39.4	46.8	4,526	4,127	4,728	4,192	4,012	3,602
Total Non-cash	**94.0**	**95.4**	**96.0**	**94.2**	**94.1**	**93.8**	**6,482**	**5,570**	**6,077**	**5,439**	**5,985**	**4,767**

(continues)

Table 11.10. Continued

Income Source:	Mean income including those with zero income from source						Share of aggregate non-cash income from source					
	1993/1994		1995/1996		1999/2000		1993/1994		1995/1996		1999/2000	
	NYC	All Central Cities	NYC	All Central Cities	NYC	All Central Cities	NYC	All Central Cities	NYC	All Central Cities	NYC	All Central Cities
Energy Assistance	29	40	11	22	11	20	0.5	0.8	0.2	0.4	0.2	0.4
Food stamps	1,666	1,489	1,414	1,243	918	726	27.3	28.0	24.2	24.3	16.3	16.2
School lunch	412	378	390	365	375	326	6.8	7.1	6.7	7.1	6.7	7.3
Medicare	173	256	366	266	488	420	2.8	4.8	6.3	5.2	8.7	9.4
Medicaid	1,618	1,169	1,225	1,083	1,359	870	26.6	22.0	21.0	21.1	24.1	19.5
Housing subsidy	882	549	918	468	900	423	14.5	10.3	15.7	9.1	16.0	9.5
Empoyer contribution to health insurance	1,313	1,433	1,510	1,677	1,581	1,686	21.5	27.0	25.9	32.7	28.1	37.7
Total Non-cash	6,093	5,314	5,834	5,124	5,632	4,471	100.0	100.0	100.0	100.0	100.0	100.0

Source: Micro data files, March CPS. Estimates of non-cash benefits are based on Census Bureau valuations (see text).

1999/2000, with most of the change occurring after 1995/1996. The percentage estimated to receive the EITC also increased and almost half received that supplement in 1999/2000. Although earnings receipt by single mothers also increased in all central cities, the gain was not as large as in New York.

- The average annual earnings of single mothers with earnings in New York declined by close to 12 percent (adjusted for inflation) between 1995/1996 and 1999/2000 after rising in the prior two years. It is likely that the decline reflects a compositional change in the experience and skills of working single mothers as a flood of welfare leavers joined the work force.[15] New entrants typically earn much less than experienced workers. As they gain experience, their earnings will begin to catch up with the earnings of other single mothers.[16] In all central cities the earnings of recipients did increase in real terms. Other cities, however, did not experience as large a surge of welfare leavers into the labor force as was the case in New York City.

- The average annual earnings of single mothers in New York, counting those with zero income, increased by about $4,300 between 1993/1994 and 1999/2000 (adjusted for inflation). That large increase occurred because the percent with earnings rose so dramatically that it greatly offset the decline in average earnings among those with earnings. To this should be added the increase in income from the EITC, for which single mothers with low earnings are usually entitled. The average single mother, including those with no earnings or EITC, gained an additional $550 annually from the EITC over the same period.[17]

- The gain in earnings plus the EITC of close to $5,000 annually more than compensated for the loss in reported welfare benefits between 1993/1994 and 1999/2000, which came to about $1,700 annually, averaged over all single mothers, including those with zero welfare income.

- Although the percentage of single mothers receiving child support in New York increased slightly over the 1990s, the amount received by recipients declined. On balance the average single mother in New York lost a little in child support. Single mothers in other cities, however, appear to have gained a little from this source.

- Counting all cash sources of income and including women with no reported cash income from any source, the income of single mothers in New York increased from $16,302 in 1993/1994 to $19,341 in 1999/2000, a gain of about 19 percent. The gain in income experienced in other cities was somewhat larger.

- As a result of these changes, the composition of a single mother's income changed significantly during the 1990s. In 1993/1994, single mothers in New York on average received 17 percent of their income from welfare and 68 percent from their own earnings plus the EITC. In

1999/2000, welfare contributed only 5 percent and earnings plus the EITC grew to 83 percent.

Non-Cash Income

Non-cash benefits include government provided benefits such as food stamps, Medicare, Medicaid, energy assistance, and housing and school lunch subsidies. These are primarily means-tested benefits and they are typically based on family or household income. Thus the proportion of single-mother households receiving non-cash benefits from the government is likely to decline as income rises and is likely to rise during cyclical downturns. Many workers receive non-cash benefits from their employers—health insurance being the primary such benefit—and receipt of those benefits by single mothers is likely to rise as their employment increases. One offsetting development, however, is the increase in income limits for Medicaid legislated in recent years. Although expanded eligibility for Medicaid has primarily affected children, some states have extended benefits to parents as well. In addition, transition benefits are provided to those who leave welfare.

Table 11.10 details the changes in the amount of different types of non-cash benefits received by single-mother households between 1993/1994 and 1999/2000. We have calculated the value of non-cash benefits received based on information reported to the CPS. In some instances—for example, food stamps—the cash value of the benefit is reported by the respondent to the CPS and is probably close to the value that the recipient would place on the benefit. However, in the case of programs such as those involving medical benefits, the value of the benefit to the recipient is less clear and may or may not be equal to the cost of providing the benefit. We mainly use the Census Bureau estimates of the value of the various non-cash benefits.[18]

The major findings are as follows:

- Most single-mother households—94 percent to 96 percent—receive some form of non-cash benefit, and that has continued to be true in New York as well as in all central cities in 1993/1994, 1995/1996, and 1999/2000, despite a slight decline in receipt of these benefits over this period.
- Non-cash benefits that are means tested are likely to fluctuate with changes in income. Consequently it is not surprising that the percentage of single mothers receiving food stamps and energy assistance (and the average amount received by recipients) declined between 1993/1994 and 1999/2000 as their incomes rose.
- The receipt of housing and school lunch subsidies by single-mother households, however, did not decline in New York City, although we find a small decline in the receipt of these benefits in all central cities.

New York continues to provide housing subsidies to a relatively large percentage of single mothers, and the difference in that percentage between New York and all cities widened during the 1990s. In 1999/2000, 31 percent of single-mother households in New York City received housing benefits compared to 21 percent in all cities. The average benefit was also somewhat higher in New York.

- Medicaid is means tested and automatically provided to welfare recipients. Yet despite the large decline in welfare participation, the percentage of single-mother households covered by Medicaid declined only a little in New York City—from 34 percent in 1993/1994 to 31 percent in 1999/2000. (In all central cities, the decline in Medicaid participation over the same period was somewhat larger—from 33 percent to 28 percent.) An increasing proportion of families, however, have become eligible to receive Medicaid after leaving welfare through programs that provide transitional benefits to welfare leavers and through provisions that have allowed states to provide benefits to lower-income families with no ties to welfare.[19]

- As the employment participation of single mothers has grown, a larger proportion of their households gained employer-provided health insurance benefits. In New York City the proportion of single-mother households receiving these benefits increased from 29 percent to 39 percent between 1993/1994 and 1999/2000; in all cities the proportion was higher throughout the period and the gain somewhat larger (from 35 percent to 47 percent).

- Overall, the average non-cash benefit, including those with zero benefits, declined by 7.5 percent in New York and by 16 percent in all cities. The composition of non-cash benefits has changed, however. Food stamps was the single program with the largest absolute decline. In both New York and in all cities it accounted for only about 16 percent of the average non-cash benefit total, down from about 27 to 28 percent in 1993/1994.

- Health benefits from government and employer-provided fringe benefits combined have made up an increasingly large share of non-cash income and in 1999/2000 accounted for 61 percent of all non-cash benefits in New York and 67 percent in all central cities. However, employer-provided benefits have become an increasingly large source of health benefits as more single mothers gain employment. In all cities employer-provided benefits accounted for 58 percent of all health benefits in 1999/2000; in New York that percentage was 46 percent.

Changes in Net Household Income

In table 11.11 we provide estimates of net household income, which consists of all cash and non-cash income and takes into account the taxes

Table 11.11. Full Household Income and Its Major Components: Single Mother Families (Income in 2001 Dollars)

	Percent receiving income from source						Mean amount received by recipients					
	1993/1994		1995/1996		1999/2000		1993/1994		1995/1996		1999/2000	
	NYC	All Central Cities	NYC	All Central Cities	NYC	All Central Cities	NYC	All Central Cities	NYC	All Central Cities	NYC	All Central Cities
Mother's own cash income	95.0	95.3	93.8	94.7	93.2	94.0	16,740	17,164	18,537	18,457	19,732	20,756
Cash income from partner and/or other household members	36.0	43.1	36.9	44.8	45.0	47.5	20,185	22,187	23,677	24,219	30,914	27,597
Household total EITC	32.5	48.7	36.1	54.5	51.6	63.3	1,390	1,482	1,776	2,027	2,052	2,157
Household total taxes paid[1]	55.4	72.2	60.3	77.3	76.4	87.1	5,877	4,754	7,530	5,025	6,641	5,484
Household non-cash benefits[2]	94.0	95.4	96.0	94.2	94.1	93.8	6,482	5,570	6,077	5,439	5,985	4,767
Total household after-tax cash and non-cash income	99.8	99.7	99.9	99.7	99.7	99.6	26,515	28,618	28,092	30,754	34,025	33,812

(continues)

Table 11.11. Continued

| | Mean income including those with zero income from source | | | | | | Share of aggregate cash and non-cash income from source | | | | | |
| | 1993/1994 | | 1995/1996 | | 1999/2000 | | 1993/1994 | | 1995/1996 | | 1999/2000 | |
	NYC	All Central Cities	NYC	All Central Cities	NYC	All Central Cities	NYC	All Central Cities	NYC	All Central Cities	NYC	All Central Cities
Mother's own cash income	15,903	16,363	17,396	17,473	18,398	19,520	60.1	57.3	62.0	57.0	54.2	58.0
Cash income from partner and/or other household members	7,273	9,566	8,729	10,844	13,910	13,097	27.5	33.5	31.1	35.4	41.0	38.9
Household total EITC	452	722	642	1,104	1,059	1,365	1.7	2.5	2.3	3.6	3.1	4.1
Household total taxes paid[1]	3,259	3,433	4,537	3,883	5,076	4,776	− 12.3	− 12.0	− 16.2	− 12.7	− 15.0	− 14.2
Household non-cash benefits[2]	6093	5314	5834	5124	5632	4471	23.0	18.6	20.8	16.7	16.6	13.3
Total household after-tax cash and non-cash income	26,462	28,532	28,064	30,662	33,923	33,677	100.0	100.0	100.0	100.0	100.0	100.0

[1] Taxes paid include federal income tax, state income tax, and social security payroll tax. Tax payments are based on estimates of the Bureau of the Census reported in the CPS.
[2] Non-cash benefits are based on Census Bureau valuations.
Source: Calculated from micro data files, March CPS. Families are restricted to those with single mother age eighteen to fifty-five.

deducted from income. The elements of income included are the single mother's own personal cash income, cash income from a partner and other household members, the combined income from the EITC of all household members, and the value of the household's total non-cash benefits. The household's total tax payments include federal and state income tax payments and social security payroll taxes.

In 1999/2000 the average net income of single-mother households in New York reached about $34,000, an increase of 28 percent over 1993/1994. (The income figures cited here, as throughout the chapter, are in constant 2001 dollars.) That was a larger increase than experienced in all central cities and brought New York slightly above the all-city average, which it had previously lagged by about $2,000. Over this period the personal cash income of single mothers (not counting the EITC) grew by 16 percent in New York. Although this was a significant increase, it was well below the gain in average income from all sources. As a result, the share of net total income from the single mother's own cash income declined from 60 percent in 1992/1994 to 54 percent in 1999/2000. In all central cities the single mother's income grew at about the same rate as total household income, and so the share of that income attributable to the single mother's own cash income increased slightly, from 57 percent to 58 percent.

The major source of the relatively large gain in the household income of single mothers in New York was a sharp (91 percent) rise in the average cash income received from a partner and/or other household members. That increase was in turn due to a large increase in both the percent of single-mother households reporting income from a partner and other household members, and a large (53 percent) increase in the income of these household members. It should be noted, however, that single-mother households in New York City are still less likely to report income from a partner and other household members than those in all central cities, where this source of income did not increase nearly as rapidly. As a result of the changes described, the share of net total income from partners and other household members increased in New York City from 28 percent to 41 percent between 1993/1994 and 1999/2000.[20] Over the same period that share rose from 34 percent to 39 percent in all central cities.

As discussed above, non-cash benefits provided to single mothers declined somewhat during the 1990s. Since other sources of income were rising, the share of aggregate household income from non-cash benefits declined over the period—from 23 percent to 17 percent in New York and from 19 percent to 13 percent in all central cities.

Because the taxable income of single mothers—particularly earnings—grew during the 1990s, tax payments increased. The average tax payment of single-mother households increased by 56 percent from 1993/1994 to 1999/2000 in New York City and by 40 percent in all central cities. The EITC grew even faster, however, and offset some of the tax increase. Net of the EITC, tax payments increased by 43 percent in New York and by 26 percent in all cities.

DETERMINANTS OF STAYING ON WELFARE TO THE LIMIT

This section assesses the effects of the 1996 welfare reforms on individual welfare participants in New York City. Here we study a unique sample of mothers who were interviewed in New York City welfare-to-work offices in late 1995 and early 1996, prior to national welfare reform, and whose records were matched to administrative records in 2001. We examine the demographic and socioeconomic determinants of long-term welfare use and investigate the effects of these characteristics on the probability of remaining on welfare up to the five-year time limit, the date when federally funded benefits are exhausted. The administrative match allows us to determine who remains on welfare long-term, but also includes a count of months of eligibility for federal TANF assistance used (toward the five-year limit), permitting a more refined analysis of the determinants of exhaustion of welfare benefits under welfare reform.

The results only partly confirm the popular expectation that recipients with significant "barriers to employment" are more likely to remain on the program until they exhaust benefits. Thus we find evidence that low education levels and the presence of young children are associated with a higher probability of staying on welfare up to the limit. But there is little evidence to support the importance of other characteristics considered impediments to employment and welfare leaving (such as having a disabled child, having little work experience, being a long-term recipient, or having health problems). Furthermore, some of our results suggest that recipients with weak financial incentives to leave welfare are, in fact, less likely to leave. For example, older recipients (with older children), who would have few years of eligibility remaining even without time limits, are far less likely to leave than younger recipients. Younger recipients who may anticipate having additional preschool-aged children in the future have a greater incentive to "bank" eligibility for federal assistance.

Incentives to leave welfare have generally been neglected in the literature on benefit exhaustion under welfare reform. To the extent that incentives rather than barriers to employment are important determinants of long-term welfare use, the shrinking caseload is less likely to become dominated by recipients that are hard-to-employ than would be the case if only those with substantial barriers to employment remain on the caseload long-term.[21]

The Available Data

Ideally, we would have a sample of AFDC recipients prior to welfare reform and observe how their behavior was affected by welfare reform. Although we do not have such a sample, we do have a detailed baseline survey of women receiving AFDC before welfare reform that were eligible for or participating in welfare-to-work programs in New York City. And, using administrative records, we have the ability to determine whether they were still collecting benefits nearly five years after the beginning of welfare reform.

The welfare participants were interviewed in eight offices of the HRA's BEGIN program and at the offices of America Works, Inc. (a private contractor that provides welfare-to-work services) between December 1995 and May 1996. The BEGIN offices included in the survey were located in four of the five boroughs (Staten Island offices were excluded). Most women surveyed were required to report to BEGIN offices for assignment to a welfare-to-work program overseen by BEGIN. At America Works offices, virtually all participants who were present were interviewed. Thus, the sampling strategy is intended to produce a sample representative of women on welfare who were eligible for or participating in welfare-to-work programs in four of the five boroughs of New York City in late 1995 and early 1996.

Interviews lasted about one and one-quarter hour, and were conducted in either English or Spanish, depending on respondent preference. In all, 4,966 women were interviewed. Because we are interested in the long-term use of welfare and the exhaustion of eligibility for federal assistance under TANF, we used social security numbers to match the sample survey cases to the New York TANF caseload in January, April, and July 2001 (about four and one-half years after the baseline interviews were conducted). We chose July 2001 as the final month in order to construct a long-term follow up that is not affected by loss of cases that reach the federal time limit (that is, exhausting 60 months of eligibility). As of July 2001, recipients could have used at most 56 months of eligibility for federal TANF assistance. Although we cannot study complete exhaustion of benefits, we can, nonetheless, identify cases that have nearly exhausted eligibility for federal assistance. We also chose to terminate our follow-up at July 2001 because we did not want the caseload data to be affected in any way by the attack on the World Trade Center in September 2001.[22]

Of the 4,966 women interviewed in the BEGIN[23] sample, 4,252 provided information needed for matching to the TANF caseload and, at baseline, had non-missing age information, were at least fifteen years old, and reported having at least one child. Of these, 197 or 4.6 percent were matched to the NYC TANF caseload as of the first week of July 2001, meaning that they received TANF benefits at that time. A total of 271 or 6.4 percent were matched to the caseload in January, April, or July 2001. Clearly, nearly all had managed to exit welfare between early 1996 and 2001. While much research on recent welfare reform has followed those who managed to leave TANF, this study examines the correlates of remaining on TANF long-term, and to the point of exhausting benefits.

Descriptive Statistics

Although they represent a small percentage of women on welfare in 1996, the roughly 6 percent who remain on welfare long term between 1996 and 2001 are of particular concern because they are in danger of exhausting their TANF eligibility. We examine three indicators of long-term welfare use: being on the caseload in January, April, or July 2001, which we refer to as "On TANF" in 2001; being on TANF in one of those months and having used up four of five years of eligibility, which we refer to as "nearly exhausting" benefits (having less than one year of remaining TANF eligibility); and being on TANF in July 2001 and having less than six months eligibility remaining, which we refer to as "exhausting benefits." Among the subsample of the BEGIN sample that remained on the TANF caseload in July 2001, almost two-thirds had nearly exhausted their 60 months of federal TANF eligibility (see table 11.12), and nearly half had used the maximum possible by that date, having only four months of eligibility remaining. This pattern is repeated each month: in January and April, about two-thirds were in a three-month category of maximum usage (i.e., used up 48–50 months as of January 2001; used up 51–53 months as of April 2001; used up 54–56 months as of July 2001).

The significance of exhausting benefits depends, in part, on why recipients exhaust benefits. On the one hand, benefit exhaustion may be a concern if

Table 11.12.   Eligibility Used (in Months) of BEGIN Sample on TANF in January, April, and July 2001

Duration (months)	January (%)	Cum. (%)	April (%)	Cum. (%)	July (%)	Cum. (%)
<12	0.8	0.8	0.4	0.4	2.5	2.5
12–23	5.3	6.1	5.5	5.9	4.6	7.1
24–35	9.8	15.9	5.5	11.4	5.1	12.2
36–47	17.0	32.9	16.1	27.5	10.6	22.8
48–50	67.1	100.0	6.0	33.5	5.1	27.9
51–53			66.5	100.0	6.6	34.5
54–56					65.5	100.0
Sample size	246		236		197	

women exhaust benefits because they are unable or unwilling to find jobs. The dominant view is that those who remain on welfare under threat of termination of benefits are the most disadvantaged, that is, those with the least employment experience and job skills, and others with substantial barriers to employment such as a physical disability or a child with a disability. On the other hand, if those who exhaust benefits have relatively little incentive to leave welfare (for example, if their children are approaching age eighteen when they would lose eligibility) or little need for benefits (for example, if they or their children qualify for disability or old-age other benefits that can replace TANF benefits), then the loss of eligibility may be of less consequence. In the literature on time limits and the potential for exhaustion of benefits under welfare reform, much less attention has been paid to the incentives to leave or remain on welfare as compared to barriers to employment.

Results of the Analysis

In this section we identify correlates of remaining on TANF in 2001, of remaining on TANF and having less than one year of remaining eligibility for assistance, and of exhausting benefits (less than six months of eligibility). Table 11.13 presents basic descriptive information. The four columns of the table refer, respectively, to the full BEGIN sample, "long-term users" (the subsample on TANF in 2001 January, April, or July), "near exhaustees" (the subsample of those on TANF with less than one year of eligibility remaining in January, April, or July 2001), and "exhaustees" (the subsample on TANF in July 2001 that has less than six months of eligibility remaining).

Some striking differences emerge. Long-term TANF users, near exhaustees, and exhaustees tend to be older than the typical BEGIN sample member: exhaustees are twice as likely to be fifty years old or older (14.7 percent versus 6.5 percent) and one-seventh as likely to be under thirty (2.3 percent versus 16.3 percent). Exhaustees and other long-term TANF users are less likely to have either a high school degree or a GED: 53 percent of exhaustees versus 44 percent in the full sample (at baseline). Exhaustees are also more likely to be black (non-Hispanic). Long-term TANF users (though, surprisingly, not exhaustees) are somewhat more likely to have had their first birth before age eighteen. They are also more likely, at baseline, to have been a long-term welfare user or a public housing resident. The public housing difference may reflect priority given to public assistance recipients in the allocation of public housing units. TANF users and exhaustees are less likely to have been married or formerly married at baseline, and more likely never to have been married (with or without a partner in residence). Furthermore, they were more likely to report intergenerational welfare receipt, defined as moving directly from one's mother's welfare benefit to a welfare benefit of one's own.

Table 11.13. Sample Statistics

| | | | Percents unless specified | |
| | | | Remaining TANF Eligibility: | |
	All	*On TANF[1]*	*<1 year[2]*	*<6 months[3]*
In 2001:				
On TANF	6.4	100.0	100.0	100.0
Remaining eligibility:				
<1 year	4.5	70.1	100.0	100.0
<6 months, 7/01	3.0	47.6	67.8	100.0
Number of obs.	4252	271	190	129
Age				
20–29	16.3	8.5	5.8	2.3
30–39	46.4	47.6	45.8	40.3
40–49	30.8	34.7	37.4	42.6
50+	6.5	9.2	11.1	14.7
Baseline characteristics				
Race/Hispanic origin:				
Black, non-Hispanic	57.3	60.9	60.0	65.1
Hispanic, non-black	25.6	21.4	23.7	21.7
Black and Hispanic	9.4	10.3	11.1	9.3
No GED, no HS degree	43.9	50.9	53.6	52.7
GED only	18.3	16.6	18.4	19.4
Has phone	81.5	76.6	78.4	82.2
Lives in public housing	29.1	32.6	36.0	38.4
Poor health	24.0	23.6	23.7	24.0
Heath limits work	17.2	16.4	16.9	15.6
Ever work	74.5	74.9	73.2	76.0
Work in last 3 years	32.7	33.6	30.9	29.9
Age 14 family structure:				
Two parent	47.9	47.6	51.6	51.2
Single mother	35.9	39.1	37.4	38.0
Other/missing	16.2	13.3	11.1	10.9
Intergenerational AFDC	20.2	24.8	30.4	28.1
Married	3.0	2.6	1.6	0.1
Separated, Divorced	35.2	29.9	28.9	28.7
Never married, no partner	59.4	63.1	65.3	65.1
Never married, live w/partner	2.0	4.1	4.2	5.4
Missing marital status	0.4	0.4	0.0	0.0

(continues)

Table 11.13.　Continued

			Percents unless specified	
		On	*Remaining TANF Eligibility:*	
	All	*TANF¹*	*<1 year²*	*<6 months³*
Age at first birth:				
<18 years	36.2	40.6	42.5	36.6
18–19 years	23.9	22.7	20.4	22.8
Missing	5	5.5	4.7	4.7
Number of children	2.0	2.1	2.1	2.1
Any children <5 yrs.	54.2	57.1	55.9	54.8
Child in poor health	3.5	2.2	3.2	3.9
Child in special ed.	20.5	20.6	22.3	18.0
Receive child support	9.4	6.7	7.4	7.0
Duration of AFDC use:				
<2 years	16.7	12.5	10.5	10.9
2–4 years	22.9	16.6	16.3	16.3
4–8 years	30.8	34.3	33.7	35.7
8+ years	29.0	33.6	39.4	38.0
Missing	5.3	8.9	7.4	7.0
America Works	8.2	4.4	2.6	2.3

¹ On TANF in January, April, or July 2001.
² On TANF in January, April, or July 2001 and less than one year of eligibility remaining.
³ On TANF in July 2001 and less than six months of eligibility remaining.

Given the differences in marital status at baseline, long-term and intergenerational welfare use, and public housing, differences in parent's family structure when the recipient was aged fourteen are surprisingly slight. In the full sample, and in the subsamples of TANF users and exhaustees, about 35 percent lived with a single mother and about 50 percent lived with two parents at age fourteen. Thus, conditional on welfare use at baseline, parental welfare use (proxied by intergenerational welfare receipt), public housing, and long-term receipt at baseline appear much more predictive of long-term welfare use and of exhaustion of benefits than does family structure at age fourteen.

Other differences across the columns of the table are more modest. For example, there was little difference at baseline associated with remaining on the caseload or exhausting benefits in the following factors: the number of children; the presence of a young child; having a child who is in poor health or in special education; the mother's health status (self report of poor health or a work-inhibiting health limitation); mother's work history (ever worked or worked in the last three years); or mother's having a telephone. On the surface, at least, the lack of association between remaining on welfare or exhaustion of benefits and these "barriers to exit/employment" suggest caution about the importance of such barriers to exhausting eligibility for TANF benefits.

Finally, being an "America Works" client is associated with a reduced chance that a recipient will be on welfare or exhaust her eligibility for benefits (2.3 percent of exhausters were America Works clients versus 8.2 percent of the full sample).[24]

Since many of these characteristics are correlated, however, a multiple regression framework is required to identify the contribution of each. For example, we noted that older women and long-term users of welfare were both more likely to exhaust eligibility for TANF benefits. Since age and long-term use are correlated, a multiple regression is needed to determine whether age or long-term welfare use is the more important predictor of benefit exhaustion.

We estimated a series of linear regression models to examine the correlates of TANF receipt in 2001. Table 11.14 displays results for three models with three different dependent variables related to long-term welfare use and/or exhaustion of benefits.

The regression results are summarized in the three columns of table 11.14, one for each dependent variable, respectively, as follows:

(1) Long-term welfare user: "On TANF in either January, April, or July 2001" versus not on in any of these months;
(2) Near Exhaustee: "On TANF in January, April, or July 2001, and has less than one year of TANF eligibility remaining at that time"; and
(3) Exhaustee: "On TANF July 2001 and has less than six months eligibility remaining at that time."

Results are from linear probability models estimated by least squares regression. We present linear probability models for ease of interpretation. (Tables with the corresponding logistic regression models are available from the authors. Inferences are not affected by the choice of linear or logistic regression.)

In the body of the table are coefficients from linear probability models and indicators of statistical significance. The coefficients are interpreted as percentage point differences in the outcome between the category indicated and the reference category. Each column corresponds to a separate regression model. A single asterisk (*) indicates that the estimated effect is significant at the 0.10 level or below, and a double asterisk (**) indicates significance at the 0.05 level or below.

The controls/covariates are listed in the left-hand column. The coefficients in the first column indicate that remaining on TANF increases sharply with age, is not statistically related to racial/Hispanic identification, and is higher for those who lack both a high school degree and a GED. Although never-married women are more likely than those married at baseline to remain on

Table 11.14. Regression Models of Long-Term Use of TANF Benefits

Covariates (at baseline unless indicated)	Long-term user: On TANF in 2001 (Jan., April, or July)	Near Exhaustee: On TANF in 2001, < 1 yr. eligibility remains	Exhaustee: On TANF in July 2001, < 6 months eligibility
Age as of 7/2001			
<30	ref	ref	ref
30–39	5.2**	4.4**	3.7**
40–49	7.3**	6.9**	6.7**
50+	10.0**	9.9**	10.0**
Race/Hispanic Origin			
Non-black, non-Hispanic	ref	ref	ref
Black, non-Hispanic	−0.1	0.9	1.4
Hispanic, non-black	−1.3	0.5	0.8
Black and Hispanic	0.4	1.8	1.4
Education			
HS degree or beyond	ref	ref	ref
GED only	0.2	1.0	1.1
No GED, no HS degree	1.6*	1.6*	1.5*
Marital Status			
Married	ref	ref	ref
Divorced or Separated	−0.1	1.0	1.1
Never married, no partner	1.8	2.8	2.7*
Never married, live w/partner	9.6**	8.9**	9.0**
AFDC duration (baseline)			
<2 years/none	ref	ref	ref
2–4 years	−0.1	0.4	0.4
4–8 years	1.8*	1.5*	1.4*
8+ years	1.0	1.5	0.7
Missing	4.9**	2.3	1.3
Barriers to employment/exit			
No work in last 3 years	−1.7*	−1.1	−0.6
Health limits work	−1.1	−1.0	−1.1
Child in poor health	−3.0	−1.0	0.3
Child in special ed.	0.0	0.2	−0.6
No phone	1.6	0.3	−0.6
Public housing	0.6	1.0	0.9
Intergenerational AFDC	0.8	2.1**	1.1
No child support	1.5	0.7	0.5
Number of children	−0.0	−0.1	−0.3
Any child <5?	2.5*	2.3*	1.9**

(continues)

Table 11.14.   Continued

	Estimated Effects (percentage points) Dependent Variables		
Covariates (at baseline unless indicated)	Long-term user: On TANF in 2001 (Jan., April, or July)	Near Exhaustee: On TANF in 2001, < 1 yr. eligibility remains	Exhaustee: On TANF in July 2001, < 6 months eligibility
Age at first birth			
20 or older	ref	ref	ref
<18	2.0**	1.6*	0.7
18–19	0.8	0.1	0.4
Family structure, age 14			
Two parent	ref	ref	ref
Single mother	0.6	−0.3	0.1
Other/missing	−1.1	−1.7*	−1.0
America Works	−2.8**	−2.9*	−2.2**

** p-value <0.05;
* 0.05<p-value <0.10;
Sample size is 4273.
Notes:
1. Coefficients from linear probability models.
2. P-values are from t-tests using robust standard errors.
3. Models also include indicators for missing marital status, missing age at first birth.

TANF, the difference is not statistically significant, unless the never-married woman also reported living with a partner at baseline.

Controls for duration of welfare receipt at baseline should capture any heterogeneity or duration dependence in welfare use. In other words, women who are long-term users of welfare are expected to have a lower chance of exiting welfare both because they have characteristics (such as disadvantaged family background or poor job skills) that make welfare exit more difficult, and because long-term welfare use changes women in some way to make welfare exit less likely (true welfare dependence). Whatever the explanation, prior research has found strong negative duration dependence in welfare exit rates.[25]

We find only modest evidence of duration dependence. For example, there is no evidence that women who had been on welfare two to four years at baseline are at greater risk of remaining on TANF than those who had been on less than two years. Those on welfare four to eight years at baseline have about 2 percentage points greater chance of remaining on TANF than those on fewer than two years at baseline, and this difference is significant. However, those on eight or more years at baseline are no more likely to remain on TANF than those on fewer than two years, controlling for age, race, and marital status. Since welfare reform was intended to decrease welfare dependency, this pattern of modest duration dependence may indicate the success of welfare reform in reducing long-term welfare use.

The model also includes an extensive set of covariates thought to predict long-term welfare use and employability. Significant effects are found for not having worked in the three years prior to the baseline interview (although lack of work participation is associated with *lower* chance of remaining on welfare), the presence of a young child at baseline (coefficient = 2.5), of first birth prior to age eighteen (versus age twenty or later), and of being an America Works client (in accordance with its reputation as one of the better training and placement organizations). Family structure at age fourteen (single versus two parent) is essentially unrelated to remaining on welfare.

Given the expectation that barriers to work would be important predictors of remaining on TANF, the absence of many significant effects (as well as some effects in the unexpected direction) is surprising. For example, little work experience, health limitations, and having a child in poor health, or having many children are all associated with reduced chances of remaining on TANF, although only the effect of no work experience is significant. On the other hand, not having a phone, being a public housing resident or an intergenerational welfare recipient, and not receiving child support are associated with remaining on TANF, but these effects are not statistically significant.

In the second column of the table we turn to the correlates of remaining on TANF to the point of "near-exhaustion" (less than one year remaining) of eligibility for federal assistance. About two-thirds of those in the BEGIN sample who remained on TANF in January, April, or July 2001 have less than one year of eligibility remaining. Therefore, we should not be surprised if the results for this outcome do not differ greatly from those for simply remaining on TANF. While this is true generally, there are a few noteworthy differences between the results in columns 1 and 2. Lacking a high school degree and GED remain significant predictors of nearly exhausting benefits, but now the effect of having only a GED is significant. The effect of being never married (without a partner) is now also significant. The unexpected effect of lack of recent work experience at baseline is no longer significant, and the effect of intergenerational welfare is a significant predictor of nearly exhausting benefits. The America Works effect remains significant.

Finally, in the third column of table 11.14 we examine the correlates of "exhausting" benefits: being on TANF in July 2001 and having less than six months of eligibility remaining. The results are similar to those in columns 1 and 2, and, in fact, reinforce nearly every conclusion drawn from the earlier analyses. The only substantial changes are that the effect of young age at first birth and intergenerational AFDC weaken and are not statistically significant. The main results (strong effects of age, significant effects of education, being never married, especially with a coresident partner, having a young child, being an America Works client, and only weak evidence of duration dependence in welfare use) are common to the three outcomes studied.

A potential source of bias in estimates from the above analyses is that some people who are not on the caseload as of January, April, or July 2001 nevertheless have used TANF long term or are near exhausting benefits. For example, some recipients who have nearly exhausted eligibility may have left welfare and do not appear on the caseload in any of these months. Perhaps we have biased our results by failing to count these welfare leavers as "near exhaustees." Our approach to gauging the importance of this potential source of bias is to take advantage of the insight that everyone who has used up the maximum number of months of eligibility possible as of July 2001 (56) must necessarily be on the caseload in July 2001 (and virtually all those who have used up 54 or 55 months of benefits must also be on the caseload in July 2001). To explore the sensitivity of our results to this potential source of selectivity bias, we conducted a final set of analyses in which the outcome is whether or not the recipient has been on welfare essentially constantly since the TANF time-limit clock began ticking until July 2001 (used up 54 to 56 months of benefits). The results were very similar to those reported in column 3 of table 11.14.

CONCLUSION

In the 1990s, welfare reform revolutionized economic life for many single mothers in New York City and the nation. Their employment and earnings increased substantially. Welfare as a share of single mothers' family income fell by more than two thirds, from about 17 percent to about 5 percent. Yet the income of single mothers increased and poverty rates fell.

The late 1990s was a boom time for both the national and local economy. In the years before the 1996 welfare reform was enacted, however, the employment and welfare participation of single mothers was only weakly responsive to the ups and downs of the economy. Thus, while the unemployment rate in New York City declined to lower levels in the 1980s expansion than it did in the 1990s expansion, the 1980s saw little decline in the proportion of single mothers on welfare, little rise in the proportion employed, and little decline in their poverty rate. The experience of single mothers in the 1990s expansion stands in contrast to these earlier expansions that were only of modest economic benefit to single mothers. What appears to have made the difference was work-oriented welfare reform, which spurred an increase in the attachment of single mothers to the labor force and enabled them to benefit substantially from the 1990s expansion.

Although this pattern was repeated in all cities, the strengthening of the connection of single mothers to the economy is particularly significant in

New York City. Until the late 1990s, single mothers in New York City had much higher rates of welfare use than single mothers in other cities, and commensurately weak attachment to the labor force, and therefore to the city's economy.

Moving the focus from single mothers to welfare recipients more specifically, it is well documented that large numbers of welfare recipients left the welfare rolls in New York City since the passage of welfare reform. (The number of families receiving TANF or "safety net" benefits fell by 55 percent between mid-1996 and December 2002.) In studying the minority who remained on welfare long term we find that some, as predicted, appear to have substantial barriers to employment or welfare exit. Others, however, appear to have stayed because they faced relatively low incentives to leave. For example, older women who would have had little future eligibility for welfare even without the imposition of time limits were far more likely than younger women to stay on welfare to the point of exhausting eligibility for federal assistance.

How are New York's single mothers faring in the recession that has gripped the region in the early part of this decade as a result of the national recession, the particular decline in the financial sector, and the attack on the World Trade Center? Surprisingly, New York's welfare caseload continued to decline through 2002, even though New York continues to provide "safety net" benefits from state and local funds to families who have reached the five-year time limit and are no longer eligible for federal benefits. Also, the employment of single mothers in New York increased slightly through 2001, the most recent year for which we have data. Nonetheless, it will be several years before we can determine whether other behaviors of populations once vulnerable to long-term welfare use have in fact changed in more fundamental ways. For example, will young women delay childbearing, stay in school longer, and prepare for employment that will enable them to avoid welfare and poverty?

Our findings have raised an interesting possibility that would be worthwhile to pursue in future analyses: the end of New York welfare exceptionalism. Historically, welfare use has been higher and employment lower among single mothers in New York City, even in comparison to similar single mothers in other urban areas with similar economic conditions. The 1990s saw a substantial convergence in economic outcomes between New York single mothers and those in other cities. Whether this is a temporary or permanent development remains to be seen. We believe that if political support for work-oriented welfare reform can be sustained, single mothers—and the disadvantaged more generally—should remain as connected or could become more connected to the local economy in New York than in other major American cities. It will be critical, however, to maintain the impetus of the policy changes in New York. That change is based on the view that the most effective way to reduce poverty is to assure that the poor are connected to one of the world's most dynamic economies through employment. The old welfare system provided a long-term entitlement to a guaranteed but limited income, resulting in isolation from the economic mainstream.

NOTES

1. Estimates of welfare duration can vary depending on the measurement used and the data source. The data cited refer to the authors' calculations of actual years of welfare receipt reported by women participants in the National Longitudinal Survey of Youth, born 1957–1965. These data cover welfare receipt over the period 1979 to 2000. (Also see June O'Neill and M. Anne Hill, "Gaining Ground, Moving Up: The Change in the Economic Status of Single Mothers Under Welfare Reform," New York: Manhattan Institute, Civic Report No. 35, 2003).

The NLSY cohort may still accumulate more years on welfare. Moreover, in the absence of welfare reform they likely would have remained on welfare longer. Although welfare duration can certainly change from one generation to the next, it is noteworthy that the NLSY data cited are remarkably close to estimates made by Ellwood. (David T. Ellwood, "Targeting 'Would-Be' Long-Term Recipients of AFDC," Mathematica Policy Research, 1986.) He estimated that close to 50 percent of persons beginning a first spell on welfare would eventually accumulate five years or more on AFDC and 30 percent would accumulate eight or more years. Also note that current welfare recipients, observed at a point in time, typically have much longer welfare duration than those who had ever been on welfare because the latter group includes a large number of persons who go on and leave after a short time and are therefore less likely to be represented in a current snapshot. Ellwood estimated that 65 percent of persons on the caseload at a point in time could be expected to have been on for eight or more years, and again that is close to the actual numbers observed for the NLSY cohort.

2. In 1987, per capita state and local spending on public welfare in New York was about 95 percent above the national average and New York ranked first among the states. The situation was much the same in 1997. (Based on data from the Census Bureau on state and local government expenditures and revenues.)

3. For a concise description of the issues surrounding the TANF implementing legislation proposed by Governor Pataki, the Democratic opposition and the final compromise, see Irene Lurie, "Welfare Reform in New York State" *Policy Research News* 2, no. 1 (1998).

4. Significant changes were made by the Giuliani Administration in the operation of the welfare program in New York City, as described in this volume.

5. The data for adjacent years are combined to enlarge the samples, particularly for New York City. The number of single mothers 18–55 in the March CPS sample for New York City varies from year to year (e.g., it was 330 in 1995 and 196 in 2001). The samples for NYC from the CPS outgoing rotation groups (ORG) for all 12 months are much larger, for example, 620 single mothers in 1995; 485 in 2001. Of course, the sample for single mothers in all central cities is always much larger—1,343 in March 2001; 3,955 in the ORG in 2001.

6. The national origin of Hispanics in New York City differs from Hispanics in other parts of the country. A larger proportion of those in NYC are of Puerto Rican or Dominican Republic origin and fewer are from Cuba or Mexico.

7. We show the average for 1999/2000 instead of for 2000/2001 because welfare statistics are available only in the CPS in March and refer to the prior calendar year. The latest available data was from the March 2001 survey when this analysis was conducted.

8. If the cost of living is higher in New York as is commonly believed, the real wage differential between NYC and other places would of course be smaller than the unadjusted dollar difference. However, geographic cost of living differences are difficult to measure.

9. See Rebecca M. Blank, "Evaluating Welfare Reform in the United States," *Journal of Economic Literature* 40, no. 4 (2003): 1105–66; Robert A. Moffitt, "The Temporary Assistance for Needy Families Program," NBER Working Paper 8749, January 2002.

10. Note that work participation refers to the week before the survey week in each month. Welfare participation is reported only in March and refers to the preceding calendar year. Certain characteristics of respondents (e.g., marital status, number of children) may have been different in the prior year and current welfare participation also may have changed. These possible discrepancies are not relevant for the reporting of work participation.

11. See the *Reynolds Decision, July 21, 2000,* United States District Court, Southern District of New York, Lakisha Reynolds et al., against Rudolph Giuliani et al., William H. Pauley III, District Judge. Plaintiffs alleged that HRA's staff at Job Centers were improperly denying benefits to welfare applicants at Job Centers and in December 1998 sought a temporary restraining order enjoining the conversion of additional income support centers to Job Centers. Judge Pauley issued a stay on further conversions. A series of court proceedings followed, resulting in permission for further conversions followed by another stay on conversions. Ultimately the court allowed the city to complete its conversion plan.

12. See table 11.7 for additional information. Full details of the measurement of the variables and the actual regression results are available from the authors on request.

13. Between 1996 and 2000 the welfare participation rate of single mothers declined by 19.4 percentage points in New York City and 15.5 percentage points in other central cities. PRWORA, as reported in table 11.7, reduced welfare participation by 16 percentage points in New York (10 percentage points in other cities), thus accounting for about 80 percent of the decline in New York (close to two-thirds in other cities). The unemployment rate declined by about 3 percentage points in New York City between 1996 and 2000, but never fell below 5 percent. The decline in unemployment in other central cities was smaller but the rate was below 5 percent in 2000. Putting these changes in unemployment together with the coefficients reported in table 11.7 yields a very small effect of unemployment on welfare participation in New York. But in other cities the change in unemployment is enough to account for about a 4 percentage-point reduction in welfare participation, which is about 25 percent of the total reduction.

14. Historical data from the Current Population Survey for female-headed families with children show that the poverty rate in 2000 was the lowest ever for this group since the government started measuring poverty in 1959. Although it rose by one percentage point in 2001, the poverty rate for this group remained well below the 1996 level. The decline in poverty rates was even more dramatic for single parent families headed by black and Hispanic women.

15. Several researchers have drawn a similar conclusion from an analogous episode when the entrance of married women with relatively little work experience into the labor force during the '60s and '70s diluted the work-related skills of the female labor force. See Claudia Goldin, *Understanding the Gender Gap: An Economic History of American Women* (New York: Oxford University Press, 1990); James P. Smith and Michael P. Ward, "Women in the Labor Market and in the Family," *Journal of Economic Perspectives* 3 (1989): 9–24. Consequently, the gender gap in pay did not narrow during a time when women's labor force participation was rising rapidly. See June O'Neill, "The Trend in the Male-Female Wage Gap in the United States," *Journal of Labor Economics* 33 (1985): S91–S116. See also Timothy Bartik, "Aggregate Effects in Local Labor Markets of Supply and Demand Shocks," Upjohn Institute Staff Working Paper 99-57, July 1999, for effects on the local labor market of an increased supply of low-wage workers.

16. Jacob Mincer and Solomon Polachek, "Family Investments in Human Capital: Earnings of Women," *Journal of Political Economy* 82 (1974): S76–S108; S. Loeb and M. Corcoran, "Welfare, Work and Self-sufficiency," *Journal of Policy Analysis and Management* 20, no.1 (2001): 1–20; O'Neill and Hill, "Gaining Ground."

17. The Census Bureau imputes the value of the EITC based on a family's earnings and family composition. We use the value of the EITC as estimated by the Census and provided on CPS micro-data files.

18. In estimating the value of nonmedical benefits, the bureau bases its estimates on market value, which essentially is the net cost of providing the benefit. However, for medical benefits, the bureau estimates the fungible value, which is an amount set below market value, depending on the income level of the recipient. (Those with lower incomes are assumed to place a lower value on medical benefits.) The bureau estimates the value of housing subsidies by estimating the difference between the rent in the subsidized property and the property's market value. (Vouchers are more straightforward.) The value of the housing subsidy is reported on a monthly basis. Information was not provided on the number of months housing benefits were received during the year. We arbitrarily assumed nine months of receipt.

19. The State Children's Health Insurance Program (SCHIP) provides federal matching funds to states and has given them leeway to extend benefits to families with incomes above the poverty line. Initially states extended coverage only to children. More recently many states have begun to cover parents as well, but usually with stricter income eligibility requirements. See Matthew Broaddus et al. "Expanding Family Coverage: States' Medicaid Eligibility Policies for Working Families in the Year 2000," Center on Budget Policy and Priorities, February 2002.

20. The reporting of the presence of partners may not be accurate and may have been understated prior to welfare reform when a larger proportion of single mothers were on welfare. On marital status and cohabitation under AFDC, see R. A. Moffitt,

R. Reville, and A. E. Winkler, "Beyond Single Mothers: Cohabitation and Marriage in the AFDC program," *Demography* 35, no. 3 (1998): 259–78; on the effects of welfare reform on the living arrangements of teenagers, see Robert Kaestner, S. Korenman, and J. O'Neill, "Has Welfare Changed Teenage Behaviors?" *Journal of Policy Analysis and Management* 22, no. 2 (2003): 225–48.

21. Federal time limits are likely to provide smaller incentives to leave welfare in New York compared to other states because the state constitution requires the state to provide the needy with assistance.

22. Such a restriction might suggest the month of August 2001. However, we were initially interested in calculating the monthly rate of case closing, defined as the proportion of cases open in a given month that closed in the following month. Thus, we chose July 2001 so that the month used to determine whether a case had closed, the following month, would be in August 2001, which is as late as possible without being affected by the events of September 11, 2001. However, too few cases closed in a single month to calculate accurate closing rates by duration of benefits receipt for our sample.

23. As noted, the sample also includes a small number of women interviewed in America Works offices. For ease of exposition, we refer to the entire sample as the BEGIN sample.

24. This finding is consistent with earlier work on the effects of America Works on welfare use. See M. Anne Hill, R. Kaestner, and T. Main, "A Preliminary Evaluation of Welfare-to-Work Programs in New York City," manuscript, Baruch College, Center for the Study of Business and Government.

25. M. J. Bane and D. T. Ellwood, *Welfare Realities* (Cambridge: Harvard University Press, 1994); June O'Neill, Laurie J. Bassi, and Douglas A. Wolf, "The Duration of Welfare Spells," *Review of Economics and Statistics* 69, no. 2 (1987): 241–48.

12

Reflections of the Commissioner

Jason A. Turner

I remember distinctly where I was when Mayor Giuliani phoned me and offered me the chance to work for him during almost his entire second term, the four-year period from February 1998 through December 2001. Many ask me what the experience was like. One way to describe it is that it felt like I was carried off on a speeding bullet train, with my face pressed against the window. Events sped by like the blurring countryside with almost no time to make meaning of the larger picture. Yet inside the hurtling coach itself, my immediate environment was composed, deliberative, and purposeful. After the experience was over, the train having sped away, I stand on the platform puzzling through the series of events almost as a third-party observer.

The overall purpose of this book is to describe what the mayor and the city's welfare department attempted to accomplish during its administration. Here, however, I will reflect upon my own personal experiences.

AN UNANTICIPATED OPPORTUNITY

Although I had graduated from four years at Columbia University in the same city I was now to become welfare commissioner, as a bona fide Republican at no time had I allowed my aspirations to extend to America's largest metropolis. Moreover, most improbably, from my vantage point, the city was actually doing something exceptionally constructive with welfare, something I had always believed was the central answer to the conundrum of how to help nonworking, able-bodied adults. Mayor Giuliani had taken a work program for single adults that had existed for many years, puttering along at an insignificant size, and blown it up into a full-throttled initiative on a scale not replicated anywhere in the country (before or even since). At its peak the Work Experience Program, or WEP, occupied the days of over 40,000 adult welfare recipients. The program helped clean the streets, answer telephones in city offices, and beautify the parks (raising parks rated "clean" from a percentage in the low 80s to the high 90s). WEP helped close down city offices after work, provide hospitals with extra help, and remove graffiti from the streetscape. Its unprecedented size and reach had already helped move thousands to private employment. Now at the beginning of his second term the mayor wanted to make work a universal expectation for able-bodied adults.

I had been summoned to city hall for my interview the Saturday before Christmas in 1997. The mayor was conducting full-scale business that day, ushering staff in and out like a traffic cop. I was interviewed on the basis of work I had done in Wisconsin, whose welfare innovations had been featured in a cover story in the *New York Times* magazine a few months before. As I entered the mayor's office he closed the door behind, we exchanged pleasantries and got down to business. Nervously I handed the mayor a summary of next-step ideas I would propose to carry out as commissioner, in the form of eight initiatives. Some of the ideas, such as creating Job Centers where welfare applicants would go first, the mayor already favored. Other ideas, such as opening up the drug abuse treatment system to faith-based providers or utilizing private for-profit temporary employment agencies to help bridge the gap to full-time work, I thought could give the mayor pause. To my surprise he liked all the ideas, and he seemed more intent on getting started than on conducting any more planning or deliberations. His upbeat affirmation of my eight points caused me to feel confident that I knew where the mayor stood philosophically. It allowed me to accept risk and controversy in carrying out the agenda (especially in New York's hothouse environment), because I knew the mayor and I agreed on where we should be headed.

Little did I know how much would be riding on my initial first impressions, because we were in for four years of over-the-top initiatives, four years of strong opposition from the opponents of reform, four years of lawsuits and counter-lawsuits with the poverty interests, and four years of hounding from the *New York Times*. Through all those tough four years there were many opportunities for the mayor to distance himself from me and some of our less-popular reforms. He never took these opportunities, and in so doing he ended up with a subordinate who was fiercely loyal to him and his administration.

Once offered the commissioner's job, I pondered the next step. The mayor had offered me only one piece of advice. He said that in his experience his most effective commissioners were almost always those who brought in a significant team of their own people. I didn't need to be persuaded. You see, the first thing to understand about the prospect of temporarily inheriting a $15 billion welfare department with 17,000 employees, is this: You are never going to actually "run" the beast, but if you have enough lieutenants you can substantially influence it!

I began with the assumption that of my senior 13 aides reporting directly to me, I would retain incumbents only if I were sure they would add to our coming assertive agenda. After a few weeks on the job, I had made my decision, and I let go of nine incumbents and retained four. The action caused an immediate furor in the newspapers ("Social-services chief starts by axing nine top aides" said the *New York Post*). But there were no calls from city hall asking me to reconsider, and the mayor's press secretary said, "He's in there to straighten the agency out, and this is how it's done."

When I finished filling out my senior team, it was an impressive line-up, recruited from Wisconsin, Washington, and internal promotions. My number two man was Mark Hoover, a very smart and practical 30-year career veteran of Wisconsin state government who had held a job in almost every department. Andy Bush had worked as a Republican aide to the congressional committee responsible for AFDC and later had helped plan the Wisconsin reforms. Our new chief agency lawyer was the improbable Jack McKay, a seventy-year-old Georgian who had made his legal career in and out of the military. Half a dozen other recruits possessed of idealism and exceptional ability were just enough to subject the agency to my leadership.

OUR FIRST DAYS

Mark, Andy, and I had spent the night before our arrival at HRA in one room of a cheap hotel (at least by New York standards), with one of us on a mattress squeezed between the other two beds. We awoke with high anticipation and headed downtown for the start of our first day.

The main welfare building in lower Manhattan was once heralded as a modern marvel when it was built in the fifties ("acres of glass!" proclaimed the agency's newsletter). Now it was a run-down dowager with scaffolding to protect pedestrians from falling brick. (A posted notice said, "Please excuse the scaffolding, which will be up for the next six weeks for brick repairs." The date of the notice was a year and a half earlier.) The halls were dingy and the elevators were often out of order, but in this respect not unlike most city agencies.

When we arrived, however, we were not at all concerned about the central administration building. Rather, we intended to look outside our walled domain to what was happening through the "street transactions" between the local welfare office and its beneficiaries. This is where change, for better or worse, would be fought out. It is where the personal interactions occur between caseworkers and recipients, where the demands and responses from each take place. It is where jobs are accepted or declined, where cash benefits are properly paid or botched, where professionalism and enthusiasm can be infectious or where indifferent service is met with a shrug. To alter the dynamics of these "street transactions" is the whole game, and to even make incremental but lasting improvements requires dogged determination.

Most agency chief executives don't affect what is happening at the street level because they involve themselves almost exclusively with central office staff. (One of my predecessors, perhaps realizing this, thought of locating each of her weekly staff meetings at a local welfare office. But these meetings comically were conducted only with her central office staff, and no sooner was the meeting finished up than the entire cabal was whisked back to the downtown administration building.) Nor do most commissioners have an ongoing feedback system that tells them what transactions are occurring at the farther reaches of the agency empire. My colleague, Andy, was flabbergasted when he learned of the paucity of meaningful information driving an agency of this size. He later described his revelation to me metaphorically:

When we arrived from Wisconsin we saw the Human Resources Administration as an enormous aircraft carrier, plowing deliberately through the waves. The newly appointed commissioner stepped out of the helicopter onto the deck, having arrived with his deputy and a few others. As the commissioner called the thousands from below up onto the deck in turn for a review of operations, I decided to go up into the pilot house on the bridge to look at the agency guidance system and to see how it worked. Inside was an array of meters and dials, each plotting and indicating its measures. As the ship made its path through the waves, I took an interest in looking at the wiring system behind the dials to find the data's source. It was confusing at first, but with patience, following the wires in turn, I found one, then another, then followed them all through and along until I found they were attached to mostly . . . *nothing*. The wires went nowhere! Some were literally not hooked up to anything, and others just twisted back and forth, manipulating data into ever-more-unreliable internal loops. I opened the bridge portal and yelled to the commissioner and his deputy standing on the open deck down below, "Hey guys! This thing has no guidance system."

Andy was later to create our own guidance system called JobStat, the subject of another chapter. But at first we were confronted with the task of how to learn more about what was going on at the street level. I decided to start by visiting each of the 26 welfare offices that handed out the checks (there are about a hundred HRA offices in total throughout the city, so many that occasionally in my city walks at night I would stumble upon an office I was unaware of).

An old-style New York City welfare office is, for the uninitiated, a severely depressing place. Our worst (eventually closed by us) was in a dangerous part of Brooklyn in an old school building with bars on the windows, surrounded by chain-link fence topped by barbed wire. Staff members were afraid to walk to the subway in the dark. In most offices the wait to be seen by clerks at the application window could last half a day, and one would almost never see the same clerk twice. When tempers flared fights would break out, leaving hapless private security guards unequipped to do more than call the police for help. Arson was not unheard of.

But that was not all. As an indicator of bureaucratic breakdown, an average of 20 percent of the case files could not be located when requested. They were sitting on top of aging steel cases, on the floor, forgotten somewhere, whatever (can you imagine a doctor losing track of 20 percent of his patient files?). To compound the bureaucratic disorganization, the line staff at most local offices were motivated more by their pay and benefits than customer service. And when we started, few of the center directors, each with 80 to 100 employees, in my judgment could have obtained jobs in the private sector with comparable responsibility because, among other things, they lacked initiative. (We eventually turned over a number, promoted others, and brought in a few from the private sector.)

After returning from my sobering two-week tour of local offices, I realized that to change the system in a meaningful way the entire organization would have to be reformed from top to bottom. To form a baseline describing how far we had to go, I asked the staff how many adults on the caseload were able to work but were currently idle. In Wisconsin such a question could have been answered quickly and with some authority, but here in New York it set off an odyssey involving months of investigation.

At its core was the problem of the ubiquitous urban welfare computer, which sees all, runs all, and manages nothing. Letters to recipients are written and addressed by a computer program, people are summoned to the office and paid cash and given assignments and offered child-care subsidies all through reliance on the almighty computer. Caseworkers fill out paper forms, which are coded into the system, and every transaction supposedly resides somewhere in the wiring. But as we learned, except for hard information about how many cases were open and how much in benefits was being paid out, most of the information embedded in the wires was incomplete or outright wrong.

The computer showed a large pool of inactive recipients even though our work program manager for single adults said she had everyone engaged. What was the story? When we investigated, we learned that the programming had become overautomated. Certain transactions, for example, the assignment of an individual to a training activity, often resulted in the initiation of other automated parallel actions. Each of these parallel actions was designed to solve a problem (such as helping to find a child-care provider for the assigned adult), but over time they became layered in such a way as to hide recipients in what we called computer "cul de sacs." In the end, we delayered the program down to the individual case files and, Hal-like, recoded all into a fresh and accurate activity report to be used in our new JobStat system.

As we learned early on, even the most basic management questions and issues required a re-think, but over time our efforts can be summarized as follows:

- We invested in major interior physical renovations of each local office, with a new computer system on each desk.
- We changed over the HRA management system to achieve a data-driven outcome orientation, performance contracting with private vendors, the introduction of merit pay for city staff, and new quality hires and promotions into mid-level management.
- We completely revised the program to require looking for work beginning the first day of application, continuing in work through WEP for those on the rolls, and ending in a closed case due to private employment.

THE GOOD THINGS I INHERITED WHEN I CAME TO WORK IN THE CITY

Among the circumstances that made our HRA tenure successful, in my opinion, is that our agency did not house the program for abused and neglected children. The mayor had removed this program from HRA during his first term so as to report directly to him through a trusted, long-term colleague. Experience shows that running the program for abused children is dangerous for the longevity and health of a commissioner, and once saddled with it, he becomes its slave. Every day there are new reports of abuse and neglect, and weeding the urgent from the less serious inevitably produces mistakes and, in the extreme, the deaths of innocent children. The mayor was wise to carve it out of the welfare agency after a tragic death of a child in his first term, and I became the bureaucratic beneficiary, allowing me to focus intently on welfare and work. My second inheritance was the fully functioning WEP program. Before I became commissioner, Mayor Giuliani had solved the problem of creating a large alternative "practice" work system for those not in the private labor market by creating large numbers of work experience positions that remain, as of this writing, the only very large-scale project of its kind.

Along the way to creating such a large system, the mayor and his City

Hall aide, Richard Schwartz, solved the challenges that have bedeviled others setting out on this path. The greatest challenge was not mainly logistic, but rather that the commissioners from other agencies had to be persuaded to take on the task of creating and supervising an entirely new and inexperienced labor force. It was not a part of their core mission but was made a part of it through persuasion, example, and not-so-concealed threats from City Hall. On one occasion, Schwartz informed the mayor at a cabinet meeting that the commissioner for public housing had agreed to set up a large WEP operation, to the shock and dismay of the uninformed commissioner present. The mayor looked at the commissioner approvingly, and the cornered commissioner understood there was no way out.

But a few other commissioners, most notably Henry Stern of the Parks Department, could see early on that although the program would be costly in terms of management and supervisory attention, it could theoretically help the agency provide additional service to the public that was otherwise not within their budget. By the end of the mayor's second term, WEP had proven that for agencies that used it productively, service capacity could be measurably improved, and City Hall found itself acting as referee among commissioners who demanded their share of a shrinking pool of available WEP workers.

But another initial problem for the mayor was gaining acceptance from the public employee unions, which are especially powerful politically in New York. The mayor promised the head of the largest union that work experience participants would not substitute for regular public employees, but would instead supplement their work activities, and he kept his word. (The Parks commissioner went a step further and awarded park laborers supervising WEP participants a small wage supplement for those who chose this option, which proved to be a popular decision.) The mayor removed WEP workers from the public hospitals when opponents argued that they were too close to performing regular functions, and he constrained their use in the subway system. Over the years he skillfully balanced enough overall support to continue this effort central to his reforms.

To the basic WEP idea, we added complementary activities to create a simulated full-time workweek of 35 hours. To accomplish this we created a "three plus two" strategy, or three days of work and two of complementary activities such as education, training, substance abuse treatment, or job search. Both work activity and training were less effective than the two combined, and the resulting full-time schedule matched what was required in the private sector, allowing participants to organize their lives and schedule in a realistic way.

WORKING WITH THE BUREAUCRACY

One often reads that a government bureaucracy will work to defeat innovation and change, and will assert its own agenda through cunning, but strictly speaking this is rarely true. The bureaucracy favors expanding its own size and influence, and is often sluggish, to be sure, but it is not otherwise a self-conscious organism. Moreover, in my experience, career bureaucrats who have been successful like to work under conditions of clear and direct guidance from the chief executive. Too often political appointees do not communicate clearly and forcefully what they wish to achieve, or are insufficiently persistent when faced with obstacles.

Nevertheless, as we have remarked, a chief executive retains only so much ability to steer an organization the size of the New York welfare department. In fact, in comparison to businesses of comparable size, governments always are at a disadvantage in this regard. Let me explain:

In business, the overall objective of the enterprise is to maximize the excess of revenue over costs. Because of this, business operations are well suited to decentralization. Suppose we think of a large automobile manufacturer. Once a new design has been approved at the top, all parts of the organization can get on with their tasks without constantly checking back up the chain. The engineers must stay within budget, the factory floor has to push iron out the door, and the salesmen are on commission.

Compare that to government, where revenue maximization is not the goal and there is in fact no single objective, only that which derives ultimately from elected officials. Unlike the understood goals of a private enterprise, government objectives must be deduced from the pronouncements of elected officials and agency heads, then translated and transferred throughout the organization in the form of policies and programs right down to the line worker. (We were surprised to learn that HRA central office policy was being transmitted to local offices using . . . the U.S. Postal Service!)

For a local manager in a welfare bureaucracy there are no obvious right answers to his most pressing day-to-day issues. Should he help welfare applicants obtain the maximum level of benefits (for income security) or look for alternatives to welfare (to maximize self-reliance)? Should the manager favor training and education (for higher wages) or guide recipients into immediate employment (to get on the employment ladder)? Should the application window emphasize office efficiency or individualized service? No answers to these important questions can be deduced by a local manager except through reference to guidance from policymakers above him. For this reason, unlike the business executive, for the commissioner to change the direction of a large bureaucracy, he must find the means to send a torrent of signals reaching all levels of the organization. There are many vehicles for communication, and here are some I used:

- To emphasize greater professionalism, we instituted a dress code at central office (some were wearing bathroom slippers!) and required respectful behavior of welfare applicants at the local offices to reduce the abuse of our employees.

- To communicate the HRA primary goal of employment to all 17,000 employees, we rented a Broadway theater during the day for two consecutive weeks. As the staff from all over the city rotated through half-day sessions, I explained from the stage—as did all my top staff present—how each employee could help achieve our goals.
- To send a financial signal in line with our employment goals, we measured line workers' productivity by determining what portion of their caseload went to work. This figure, combined with recommendations from their superiors, allowed each to earn up to a 20 percent bonus on top of their regular pay. (This initiative was bitterly fought by the employees' union "representing" their interests, can you imagine?)
- To be explicit about the objectives of our facilities, we renamed the welfare offices Job Centers, performed major renovations, and instituted immediate work-search requirements at the time of application.
- To constantly measure our progress against goals we instituted the data-driven weekly JobStat sessions, in which all local offices and private vendors participated.

We needed all of these and more to send a constant stream of signals to our employees. At the close of the Giuliani tenure, our staff volunteered over and over that they always knew what our objectives were and in almost any given situation could determine the right course of action almost as though the commissioner were making the decision himself.

REPORTING TO THE MAYOR

The Giuliani City Hall was a highly competitive environment, and nowhere was this more evident than the fabled 8 a.m. morning meetings, through which all commissioners rotated periodically, or by request if they had something to bring to the attention of the mayor. Often the mayor or his deputies would express dissatisfaction with the slow pace of reforms proposed by the city's chief bureaucratic overseers, the commissioners.

At one 8 a.m. meeting I witnessed a commissioner whose responsibility included selling off unneeded city property announce in a morning staff meeting with the mayor that over 50 surplus properties were set for auction that week. His presentation included colorful charts and lots of fanfare, but the mayor inquired as to how many properties were in the total city inventory. When he learned that the auction would encompass only a small fraction of the overall number, the mayor remained polite but made short work of the commissioner's goals by setting new high benchmarks that would dog him for the rest of his tenure. No amount of protest from the hapless commissioner was persuasive.

In addition to questions from the mayor himself, a presentation at the morning meeting invited all sorts of advice and comments—welcome and unwelcome—from the four deputy mayors. One had to be totally prepared, and I would think of every possible angle before going in (though invariably I would forget that the mayor always asked for the most up-to-date exact caseload reduction figures). Thankfully, most deputy mayors were not familiar or as interested in welfare as in other city topics and for the most part I moved through these presentations without reversals.

All but three commissioners reported on a day-to-day basis through a deputy mayor. My deputy mayor was Tony Coles, who was a law partner of the mayor's before coming to City Hall, and then was promoted to be the mayor's chief policy advisor. Tony and I were appointed in short succession, and each needed the other to make his bones on welfare with the mayor. Fortunately, Tony already had worked closely with the mayor on several policy matters, and the mayor had confidence in his judgment. Tony was thoughtful and as oriented as I was around a philosophy, not just a program. Both of us liked to take the kinds of risks necessary to move the agenda forward, a temperament that was rewarded by the mayor who prized boldness, especially when confronting an agency's established constituencies and interests. Tony also served as our advocate when, as inevitably happened, the major scope of our reforms also required the cooperation of other city departments and commissioners, or the state.

Of all the business I conducted with the mayor, he most liked to get out of City Hall and visit the newly opened Job Centers. The genuine enthusiasm of the staff as they embraced their new role as employment counselors rather than check-writers at first took the mayor somewhat by surprise. When we opened our first test Job Center in the relatively safe borough of Staten Island, to my relief our preparations went off without a hitch, and even I was pleased at the response of the staff. As was true almost everywhere in the country, most welfare workers did not like the old benefit system. Most urban welfare workers come from the same neighborhoods and backgrounds as the recipients themselves, and they understood up-close and ugly that the checks were neither helping move recipients out of poverty nor toward work. They were also unhappy with the old program's accompanying fraud and abuse, but mostly were told to do nothing when confronted with their suspicions. (The mayor's administration set up a separate unit to improve program integrity, the subject of another chapter in this book.) In contradistinction to the so-called advocates for the poor, our own employees formed the largest informed base of support for the mayor's reforms (even if this did not translate into votes at election time!).

CONFRONTING THE OPPONENTS OF REFORM

At a city council hearing one day, I made reference to the "poverty industry." The howls of protest at this remark could be heard all the way from lower Manhattan to the Bronx! Those who purport to represent the best interests of the poor prefer to be referred to as "advocates," and they take ever so seriously any challenge to their morally superior self-perception. But apart from my disagreements with them over what constituted good policy for the poor, I found such advocates and their affiliated organizations highly self-interested. These advocates and their organizations represent a sizable part of New York's economy, funded by federal, state, and local government and foundations. They take public positions that have the effect of expanding their size and influence, and they form lobbying associations and back candidates for office. To argue that they operate, as is often implied, in the interest only of those they claim to represent in my view is very naive. With the exception of the *New York Post*, most print and broadcast reporters were hostile to the Giuliani reforms. Thankfully, the mayor told me and the other commissioners to ignore the press and to get on with our jobs. But I often wondered whether there was anything more I could do. One day the *New York Times* reporter assigned to the city welfare commented to my press secretary that dozens of faxed press releases from poverty organizations would cross her desk weekly, but virtually none from the other side, most conspicuously our own agency. I puzzled over this disparity, and if I had to point out the greatest shortcoming of our work at HRA, it was our lack of success in tackling this problem and communicating to the public through the existing media. In retrospect there were two reasons for our lack of success. One was the hostility of the established media to the Giuliani reforms root and branch. But the other was our own lack of time to attend to educating the media reporters who were looking for information.

In a common *New York Times* welfare story cycle, a poverty organization that opposed our reforms would find a sympathetic individual who had allegedly been harmed by department policy, whether it be work, child care, or access to benefits. The reporter would be informed of this transgression by the poverty organization and would interview the harmed individual, with background and quotes provided by the organization that organized the interview. Then and only then would the reporter call HRA for a "response." A thoughtful response would involve looking up the individual's case in the computer; tracking down the workers who had contact with the individual; determining whether the individual's complaints were merited; if not merited then determining what actually transpired; if the complaints were merited then determining whether the fault lay in policy or its failed execution; and finally weighing what is best for the individual in question against the good of the overall welfare population or even society in general (i.e., a given policy can be good for most but not for all). Do you think it would be possible for HRA to follow through in such a manner with each case brought forth by the media? Do you think it could do so by deadline at six o'clock? Do you think the *New York Times* metro reporter is looking for such analysis? Some reporters were so hostile, almost perpetually angry, that there was nothing we could do that would be persuasive. But there were others who I believe were honest and open enough to be subject to evidence, if we had brought them inside the agency and spent time with them. Reaching each one of these reporters, however, would have required days or weeks of time from me and my top staff, time we could not devote. Toward the end of my tenure at HRA, it became apparent that the nonprofit agencies we worked with to help participants were better spokesmen for us than we were. They understood what we were trying to accomplish, and they also could describe the practical difficulties because they worked the street, as we did. Unlike HRA, they were considered by the media to be the "good guys." Next time around I will bear this in mind.

Our most aggressive opponent was the independently elected city comptroller who was running for mayor in the 2001 election. We had recently completed an overhaul of our contracts with job training and placement agencies, winnowing down dozens of formerly contracted agencies of widely varying capabilities to about 15 or so excellent ones. Out of the blue the comptroller announced that he was refusing to register the new contracts, which was his responsibility, on the grounds that the process used to select them was flawed. I was shocked by this turn of events, as we had followed all the correct procedures and could not fathom the motives behind his announcement. No sooner had the comptroller made this announcement than he backtracked, saying he would register all of the contracts save one. Since all of the contracts had been awarded using the same allegedly flawed process, it was not clear what his logic was. His motivation became clearer when he announced that the one contract he would not register was that of a large, national, for-profit, welfare-to-work company, Maximus. The comptroller now asserted that he detected favoritism only in making this award.

City Hall staff and the city office of contracts checked with me and others to be sure that the contracts were awarded properly. Then the city fired back in the person of Mayor Giuliani himself. He opposed the comptroller in public pronouncements and, more importantly, lodged a suit against the comptroller's actions. Refusing to back down or distance himself from me or the agency, the mayor vowed to see this dispute through to the end. When the dust settled, the court found no evidence of favoritism and ordered the comptroller to register the disputed contract, which he did. But the affair was a tremendous distraction and time-sink for both the agency and the mayor, and later I learned it had demoralizing effect on some HRA staff who might have assumed that where there is smoke there must be fire. In retrospect, I should have called together the staff to explicitly refute the comptroller's false accusations and to reassure them that the mayor was completely behind HRA and its leadership.

MAINTAINING BALANCE: THE BIG PICTURE

Public managers usually arrive at their responsibilities at a disadvantage. Unlike their business counterparts who mostly rise through the ranks over time and are able to view their organization from many angles as they proceed up the ladder, public managers are thrust into top positions of tremendous bureaucratic responsibility as a result of an election. Often they take on their assignments without much prior management experience but with high hopes of making an important difference in the lives of those they touch. With their good intentions and lack of experience, during their all-to-brief tenure many of these public managers carry forth without realizing they have been "cocooned." It is easy to understand why many government chief executives think they are producing even as they become ever more isolated. The commissioner of the Human Resources Administration, like the commissioners of all city agencies and the mayor himself, occupies an alluring position. Each will be ministered to and flattered, and all his ideas will be deemed worthy and fashioned into speeches to be dispatched to the unenlightened. Moreover, there is much to occupy a well-meaning commissioner's time, which can make him or her believe that progress is being made, while in fact nothing of the sort is taking place. Many of the projects that a commissioner will find himself busied with are internal matters, not affecting in any material way the nature of the agency's interaction with those it is intended to serve. Reviewing the assorted piles from his in-box, the commissioner will perceive that his most important decisions revolve around the following:

(1) Working the budget process to obtain more resources for the agency;
(2) Allocating administrative resources inside the agency;
(3) Reviewing personnel decisions;
(4) Refereeing conflicts over turf; and
(5) Reacting to pressures of external groups and organizations with interests in agency matters.

Most of these activities well up as demands from the agency's internal constituencies, including its own employees. These issues, while not necessarily critical to the larger scheme of agency business, are pressing to those who have access to the commissioner, and they are difficult to delegate away. This is why they constitute the "in-box" of most urgent matters. Rather than characterize these matters as unimportant, it is more accurately said that they are for the most part parochial. In my judgment, as the successful commissioner carries out his responsibilities, he must constantly bear in mind two constituencies: first, his political superior, in my case the mayor, and second, the citizens of the electorate, not just the narrower group constituting the agency's direct beneficiaries. Keeping these two constituencies foremost, a commissioner will sometimes arrive at decisions that are the same as those favored by the narrower interests of the agency's direct constituency, but they will often diverge.

To take one example, the three constituencies—made up of the mayor, the general electorate, and welfare recipients themselves—all want the welfare agency to deliver superlative welfare-to-work services that result in more employment at higher earnings. The three constituencies agree on this agenda, and the commissioner's mission may seem straightforward, even if challenging to deliver in practice. It is not that simple, however. Many welfare recipients and the advocacy groups that claim to represent their interests indeed want superlative services, but they want these services provided only on a voluntary basis. In other words, they wish the agency to make services available only to those who choose to participate. The general electorate, however, has a different interest. For the most part it wishes welfare recipients to make every effort to help themselves and to obtain employment and become self-reliant regardless of their desire to participate in welfare-to-work activities. In this instance the commissioner who accepts the will of the general electorate, and of course his boss, the mayor, will arrive at overlapping but not congruent decisions in relation to the agency's narrower constituency of recipients and the advocacy groups. Political conflict will be inevitable.

The overarching, contrasting philosophical points of view on the issue of welfare might be best reduced to the question of "agency," or broadly, whether an individual largely creates and controls his environment, or vice versa. Those with a view from the left tend to believe that large forces outside the control of the poor are largely responsible for their circumstances, and only changes to the social and economic structure can be expected to yield major improvements. Those with a right-of-center view, including myself, tend to think that the poor are largely able to control their life circumstances, and the question for policymakers is how to best help them mobilize their internal resources so as to seize the opportunities that exist and improve upon them from there. In this view, work and self-reliance are not within the government's power to unilaterally bestow, but rather something individuals must achieve through their own efforts, with help and support from government to be sure. Welfare author Lawrence Mead says that the dependent poor accept the notion of the importance of work, but for many of them, work is an aspiration, not something that must be achieved at any cost. Many desire to work, but not with a force sufficient to bind actual behavior. The task of government is to help individuals develop and use their internal capacities. But if the conservative diagnosis is right, then how exactly should government be organized from this point forward to expand on the ability of the remaining dependent poor to improve their working lives?

Those of us who have always worked since we left school forget that adapting to the demands and rhythms of the workplace is at first unnatural. There is a workplace culture that we don't even think about, but it has rules that nevertheless must be learned, usually by example and acculturation. We don't like standing or sitting in one place all day long. There is the notion of chain of command, the idea that one must remain at his post for an entire eight-hour shift, that one must get along with coworkers that he might not wish to socialize with, and that one must sublimate his ego to that of his boss. Those who have never or only intermittently been employed at first find the workplace culture difficult to adapt to. This is why most long-term recipients get jobs easily but lose them again until they have remained in the labor market for some time.

The major contribution of Mayor Giuliani's administration to national welfare reform is that it produced the only system as of this writing with large-scale, alternative, practice work that has the potential to acculturate large numbers of the never-employed to the world of work. (The current Wisconsin system also aspires to this end but on a far-reduced scale.) The extraordinary success of the first round of 1996 national reforms reduced the country's caseload by more than 60 percent from its peak. It did so by changing the office culture and by encouraging applicants and recipients to move into private employment right away. But for the remaining welfare population still on the rolls and not employed in the private economy, not much has changed. As of early 2005, for the most part states had not taken on the challenge of large-scale engagement in work activity as was anticipated by the 1996 national legislation. We may find national policymakers looking back to Mayor Giuliani's eight-year experiment for their next practical idea.

Index

About the Contributors

E. S. Savas, the editor, is professor at the School of Public Affairs of Baruch College of the City University of New York. He served as First Deputy City Administrator of New York and as Assistant Secretary of the U.S. Department of Housing and Urban Development, the latter under President Reagan. Best known for his work on privatization, his 15 authored or edited books have been published in 21 foreign editions to date. He has degrees from the University of Chicago and Columbia University and an honorary doctorate from the University of Piraeus (Greece).

Burt S. Barnow is associate director for research at the Institute for Policy Studies at Johns Hopkins University. His research focuses on program evaluation and labor economics. Prior to coming to IPS, he worked at the Lewin Group and the U.S. Department of Labor.

Douglas J. Besharov is the Joseph J. and Violet Jacobs Scholar in Social Welfare Studies at the American Enterprise Institute and a professor at the University of Maryland School of Public Policy. He was the first director of the U.S. National Center on Child Abuse and Neglect. From 1991 to 1992, he served as the administrator of the AEI/White House Working Seminar on Integrated Services for Children and Families. Since 1996, he has directed the University of Maryland's Welfare Reform Academy.

James Clark was the welfare reform director in Florida for ten years and director of social services in South Carolina (1995–1999) under Governor David Beasley. In 2001–2001 he served as assistant secretary for Children and Family under Governor Jeb Bush in Florida, and most recently has been working with the Israeli government on a welfare reform initiative.

Peter Germanis was a senior policy analyst in the Office of Policy Development at the White House from 1984 to 1990. From 1991 to 1997, he held various positions within the Office of Family Assistance at the U.S. Department of Health and Human Services, including director of the Division for Program Evaluation. From 1997 to 2004, he was a research associate at the American Enterprise Institute and assistant director of the University of Maryland's Welfare Reform Academy. He is currently a "national policy expert" in the Office of Family Assistance of the U.S. Department of Health and Human Services.

Sanders Korenman is professor of public affairs, Baruch College, City University of New York; research associate of the NBER; and member of the Board on Children, Youth, and Families of NAS. He served on the full-time faculties of Princeton University and the University of Minnesota, and as senior economist for President Clinton's Council of Economic Advisers.

Arthur L. Levine is professor emeritus, School of Public Affairs, Baruch College, City University of New York. His publications include studies of government management and policy issues. He held administrative positions with NASA from 1958 to 1972, and has consulted with agencies at the national and local levels.

Thomas J. Main is assistant professor at the School of Public Affairs of Baruch College, where he teaches courses on American government, public policy, and urban affairs. His main research interests are homelessness, welfare reform, and urban politics. His articles have appeared in the *Journal of Urban Affairs* and *Public Affairs Quarterly*.

Demetra Smith Nightingale is principal research scientist at the Institute for Policy Studies at Johns Hopkins University. She directed the New York City study as director of the Welfare and Training Research Program at the Urban Institute. Her research focuses on employment, welfare, and social policy. Among her books is *The Government We Deserve: Responsive Democracy and Changing Expectations*, with Eugene Steuerle, Edward Gramlich, and Hugh Heclo (1998). She received her Ph.D. in public policy from the George Washington University.

June O'Neill is the Wollman Professor of Economics and director of the Center for the Study of Business and Government, Zicklin School of Business at Baruch College, City University of New York. From 1995 to 1999 Dr. O'Neill served as director of the Congressional Budget Office. Earlier she was director of policy and research at the U.S. Commission on Civil Rights, senior economist on the President's Council of Economic Advisors, senior research associate at the Urban Institute, and research associate at the Brookings Institution.

Sally Satel, a practicing psychiatrist, is lecturer at Yale University School of Medicine and a resident scholar at the American Enterprise Institute. Her articles have been published in the academic literature as well as in the *New Republic,* the *Wall Street Journal,* the *New York Times,* and other publications. Dr. Satel is a member of the federal Center for Mental Health Services Advisory Council. Her book, *PC, M.D.—How Political Correctness is Corrupting Medicine* appeared in 2001.

Kay E. Sherwood is a management consultant who has worked with foundations, nonprofit organizations, and state and federal government agencies to develop and assess programs in the human services and enhance organizational effectiveness. Before starting her own business, Ms. Sherwood worked for ten years at the Manpower Demonstration Research Corporation (MDRC) where she was director of Special Projects.

John Trutko, president of Capital Research Corporation, has worked for over 20 years as a policy analyst and program evaluation specialist. Mr. Trutko has a B.A. degree in political science from the University of Rochester and M.A. degree in economics from the University of Sussex (in England).

Jason A. Turner directed the former AFDC program at the U.S. Department of Health and Human Services between 1989 and 1993 and was responsible for the federal implementation of the newly enacted welfare-to-work program. From 1993 to 1997, under Governor Tommy Thompson of Wisconsin, he directed the planning for a work-based replacement of welfare, culminating in the well-known *Wisconsin Works* program. He was recruited by Mayor Giuliani to run New York City's welfare and Medicaid programs from 1998 through the end of 2001. He consults on work-based reforms in the U.S., in Eastern and Western Europe, and in Israel.